Viking Kings of Britain and Ireland

VIKING KINGS OF BRITAIN AND IRELAND
The Dynasty of Ívarr to A.D. 1014

Clare Downham
Lecturer in Celtic
School of Language and Literature
University of Aberdeen

DUNEDIN

Published by
Dunedin Academic Press Ltd
Hudson House
8 Albany Street
Edinburgh EH1 3QB
Scotland

ISBN 978-1-906716-06-6

British Library Cataloguing in Publication Data
A catalogue record for this book is available from the British Library

Typeset by Nancy R McGuire, Aberdeenshire
Cover design by Makar Publishing Production
Printed and bound by CPI Group (UK) Ltd., Croydon, CR0 4YY
Printed on paper from sustainable resources

For two women of great character

Contents

List of Illustrations

Credits

Figure 1: C. Downham, 'Ireland *c.* 1000', *Atlas of Medieval Europe*, edited by David Ditchburn *et al.*, second edition (Abingdon, 2007), p. 37, reproduced with kind permission from Routledge publishers.

Figure 2: C. Downham, 'England *c.* 1000', *Atlas of Medieval Europe*, edited by David Ditchburn *et al.*, second edition (Abingdon, 2007), p. 35, reproduced with kind permission from Routledge publishers.

Figure 11: Image prepared by Reginald Piggott and devised by S.D. Keynes; reproduced with kind permission from Professor S.D. Keynes,

Trinity College, Cambridge.

Figures 12 and 13: Images prepared by Helen Stirling of Helen Stirling Maps.

Figure 15: Image prepared by Don Williams of Bute Cartographics after a hand-drawn map by Clare Downham.

Abbreviations

AB	The Annals of Boyle; or, The Annals in MS. Cotton Titus A xxv
AClon	The Annals of Clonmacnoise
AFM	The Annals of the Four Masters; or, *Annála Ríoghachta Éireann*
AI	The Annals of Inisfallen
ALC	The Annals of Loch Cé
ALL	The Annals from the Book of Leinster; or, *Do Fhlaithesaib Hérend iar Creitim*
ARC	The Annals of Roscrea
ASC	The Anglo-Saxon Chronicle
AT	The Annals of Tigernach
AU	The Annals of Ulster
ByS	*Brenhinedd y Saesson*
ByT	*Brut y Tywysogyon*
CS	*Chronicum Scotorum*
FAI	The Fragmentary Annals of Ireland

Acknowledgements

This book is largely the product of my doctoral research. No person deserves greater thanks for their input into this project than David Dumville. It was his idea that I research this topic and he read sections of text as they emerged, providing many valuable corrections, comments, criticisms, and insights. Latterly I have been grateful for his support as my closest friend, and in the Easter vacation when the final chapter of this book was written, he assisted by looking after our baby daughter Jennifer so that I could spend uninterrupted hours typing on the computer.

The funding-bodies and institutions which made this work possible are the University of Cambridge, the Arts and Humanities Research Board, and the School of Celtic Studies, Dublin Institute for Advanced Studies. I am particularly grateful to Fergus Kelly, Director of the School of Celtic Studies, who oversaw the completion of my doctoral dissertation. I benefited greatly from the opportunity to study at both Dublin and Cambridge, and also the University of St Andrews where my interest in mediaeval history was cultivated as an undergraduate.

Others who provided valued assistance include my mother, Liz Ridout, who generously typed large numbers of translated chronicle-entries into the database which was developed alongside my doctoral dissertation. Lesley Abrams, Julia Barrow, Kristin Bornholdt-Collins, Nick Evans, Máire Ní Mhaonaigh, Ralph O'Connor, Donnchadh Ó Corráin and Oliver Padel have all helped by reading and commenting on work included in this book. There are also many others who have contributed in an indirect way. It is hard to list them all upfront, but credits to them may be found scattered in footnotes throughout the book. I should also like to thank my colleagues in Dublin and my colleagues and students in Aberdeen for generating pleasant work environments which have been conducive to research.

In practical matters I am extremely grateful to Nancy McGuire who set the pages and to Dunedin Academic Press who have worked with amazing speed to get the book published, and who have been very accommodating and pleasant to work with.

ACKNOWLEDGEMENTS

This work is dedicated to Granny (Elizabeth Christina Cook, née MacDougall) and Nan (Freda Annie Downham, née Inman). I feel such great love for these two women who provide, in their different ways, examples of everything I should aspire to be. I am unable to express my gratitude in more words; despite numerous attempts at this sentence, my mind gets overwhelmed with memories and emotions. *In your quiet way of understanding so many things, may it just suffice to say thank you for all the good things you represent for me and I do not require that you read this book.*

Prefatory Note: Ethnicity and Viking Age Politics

I need to clarify my use of the term 'viking'. The name has acquired many shades of meaning and been used in a variety of ways in both scholarly and popular literature.[1] It is widely known that the word is derived from Old Norse *víkingr* which is usually translated as 'sea-rover' or 'pirate'.[2] However, it is clear that not every pirate from the past can be called a 'viking'. In this book the word is used to describe people of Scandinavian culture who were active outside Scandinavia. I have used the term with reference to Danes, Norwegians, Swedes, Hiberno-Scandinavians, Anglo-Scandinavians or the inhabitants of any Scandinavian colony who affiliated themselves more strongly with the culture of the coloniser than with that of the indigenous population. Such an umbrella-term seems necessary to avoid the semantic difficulties posed by ethnic labels. For example, when did the families of Scandinavian settlers become English, and how Scandinavianised were the English? There are problems of being over-specific with ethnic terminology as identities are subjectively, not just objectively, created or assigned.[3] The historian risks using ethnic categories which may not have been universally recognised or rigidly applied, and who belonged to a particular group may have been a matter of debate in the past, and not just now.

The partial nature of ethnic designations is exemplified in the primary sources. In Ireland the inhabitants of viking settlements were called 'Foreigners' (*Gaill, echtrainn, allmuire*), until they were displaced by a different group of foreigners in 1171.[4] Nevertheless, from the tenth century, when inhabitants of the viking settlements in Ireland went abroad, they were sometimes identified with the land of their abode.[5] John Hines has concluded in a recent study that 'It is indeed quite clear that the

---

[1] Fell, 'Modern English *Viking*'.
[2] Byock, *Viking Age Iceland*, pp. 11-13; Mac Shamhráin, *The Vikings*, p. 9.
[3] Amory, 'The Meaning', p. 28; Hadley, 'Viking and Native', p. 46; Hadley, 'Cockle', p. 118.
[4] Other terms include: 'heathens' (*gentiles, pagani*), and 'Northmen' (*Nordmanni*).
[5] For debate over this issue in relation to Welsh chronicles see *ByS, s.a.* 940 [=941] (ed. and trans. Jones, pp. 30-31); Maund, *Ireland*, p. 157; Duffy, 'Ostmen', p. 382.

adjective *írskr* ('Irish') itself could apply in the Old-Norse sources to Scandinavians from Ireland as well as to the native Irish'.[6]

There has been controversy over the Irish terms *Finngaill* and *Dubgaill*, *Gall-goídil* and *Lochlannaig*, which were used in the Viking Age to distinguish rival groups of vikings. Some discussion of these terms is found within the body of this book.[7] However, it seems necessary to deal with *Finngaill* and *Dubgaill* at the outset. The interpretation of these terms is quite fundamental to the interpretation of the history of vikings in Ireland. These terms literally mean 'Fair Foreigners' and 'Dark Foreigners' respectively. The colour terms are found in Irish and Welsh chronicle-entries from the ninth and tenth centuries.[8] Historians have long speculated whether these distinctions referred to physical features (in particular hair-colour), weaponry, or dress-colour.[9] However, the prevalence of distinctions of this sort between two viking armies seems unconvincing.

Alfred Smyth has drawn attention to the fact that 'dark' was used in Irish genealogical literature to denote newer or later groups or individuals in contrast to 'fair' or earlier ones.[10] This link is made explicit in 'The Annals of Clonmacnoise', a seventeenth-century translation, which describes 'new and old Danes'.[11] Smyth's argument has provided the starting point for David Dumville's analysis of the meaning of 'Dark Foreigners' and 'Fair Foreigners'. Dumville has questioned the primary assumption made by most historians, that they represent separate cultural groups. He has noted that Smyth's argument shows that the colour-terms were not ethnic identifiers and has argued that the received racial interpretation is over-simplistic, anachronistic, and generally misleading.[12]

---

[6] Hines, *Old-Norse Sources*, p. 21.

[7] See below, pp. 13-15, 17.

[8] The colour-distinction can be expressed in a variety of languages, e.g. *gentiles nigri*, *kenedloed duon*.

[9] *Cogadh*, ed. and trans. Todd, pp. xxx-xxxi; Steffensen, 'A Fragment', p. 59; Hore, 'The Scandinavians', p. 432; Mac Mathúna, 'The Vikings in Ireland', p. 48.

[10] Smyth, 'The *Black* Foreigners'; cf. *Cogadh*, ed. and trans. Todd, pp. xxx-xxxi; Steffensen, 'A Fragment', p. 59; Hore, 'The Scandinavians', p. 432; Mac Mathúna, 'The Vikings in Ireland', p. 48

[11] *Annals of Clonmacnoise*, s.a. 922 (ed. Murphy, p. 148); cf. *Annals of Ulster*, s.a. 926 [=927].2 (ed. and trans. Mac Airt and Mac Niocaill, pp. 378-79).

[12] Dumville, 'Old Dubliners'; Mac Shamhráin, *The Vikings*, p. 48.

The earliest ethnic definitions of 'Dark Foreigner' as Dane and 'Fair Foreigner' as Norwegian emerge after the terms fell out of use.[13] They appear in the eleventh-century 'Osraige Chronicle', elements of which are embedded within 'The Fragmentary Annals of Ireland'.[14] It can be argued that, when this text was composed, political changes in Scandinavia made people in Ireland aware of a distinction between Norwegians and Danes.[15] Thus a new interpretation was imposed on the earlier terms 'Fair Foreigner' and 'Dark Foreigner' which were found in the Irish chronicles mined for the Osraige Chronicler's account of ninth-century viking affairs.[16]

Dumville has suggested, as an alternative to the conventional interpretations, that *Dubgaill* and *Finngaill* identified viking groups under different leadership. The 'Fair Foreigners' or 'old vikings' were labelled following the advent of 'Dark Foreigners' on Irish shores. The 'dark' or 'new' vikings may identify those under the leadership of the family of Ívarr. This association is supported by evidence from the Irish chronicles. The 'dark' vikings who are first mentioned in 851 were led by Ívarr and his associates Óláfr, Ásl and Hálfdan.[17] Their heirs, who were also recognised as leaders of 'Dark Foreigners', were members of the dynasty of Ívarr.[18] Thus Dumville's theory offers an alternative to some of the complications which historians have built around issues of ethnicity.[19]

---

[13] *Chronicum Scotorum*, s.a. [941].3 (ed. and trans. Hennessy, pp. 204-05), may provide the last contemporary witness to use of this terminology in the chronicles. *Annals of Loch Cé*, s.a. 1014.3 (ed. and trans. Hennessy, I, 4-5), appears to be a twelfth-century record. The apparent non-ethnic use of the terms 'dark' and 'fair' in this text may be seen in the examples of *Dubhlochlonnach*, *Fionnlochlonnach*, and *Dhubhdhanaroibh*. Use of the colour-terminology may be in emulation of earlier chronicle-records and therefore deliberately anachronistic.

[14] *Fragmentary Annals*, ed. and trans. Radner, p. xxvi.

[15] Mac Shamhráin, *The Vikings*, p. 29.

[16] Downham, 'The Good'.

[17] For example: *Annals of Ulster*, s.a. 851 [=852].3, 852 [=853].2, 855 [=856].6, 866 [=867].7, 874 [=875].3, 876 [=877].5 (ed. and trans. Mac Airt and Mac Niocaill, pp. 310-13, 322-23, 330-33). I am grateful to Stefan Brink and Henrik Williams for advising me on possible Old Norse forms of MI. Auisle / OE. Eowils.

[18] For example: *Annals of Ulster*, s.a. 916 [=917].3, 917 [=918].4, 926 [=927].2 (ed. and trans. Mac Airt and Mac Niocaill, pp. 366-69, 378-79).

[19] Cf. Smyth, *Scandinavian Kings*, pp. 114, 135. For general acceptance of Dumville's view, see Hall, *Exploring the World*, pp. 89-90. For the continuing use of the terms 'Fair' and 'Dark' foreigner in Ireland, see p. 36, n. 141 below, and Downham, '"Hiberno-Norwegians"'.

One can also challenge whether people were aware of ethnic divisions between 'Norwegians' and 'Danes' in a colonial context during the ninth and early tenth centuries. There is no evidence of a meaningful distinction between Norway and Denmark in a broad geo-political sense before *circa* 900. Furthermore it took at least half a century before these countries could be regarded as unified kingdoms with distinct national identities.[20] In the Norse language of the Viking Age a distinction was not drawn between 'Danish' and 'Norwegian'.[21] It is therefore necessary to question whether distinctions between Danes and Norwegians were made in other places.

The Latin terms *Danus* and *Normannus* are often translated as 'Dane' and 'Norwegian' but for the period in question this seems to be fundamentally misguided. For example in Frankish Latin sources both terms are used as general appellations for Scandinavians or vikings, and their application seems to be a matter of authorial preference.[22] The same argument may be put for the terms *Dene* and *Norðmann* in English sources. In 'The Anglo-Saxon Chronicle', up to the mid-tenth century *Denisc* is the most commonly used term for vikings. This has usually been translated as 'Danish' although as Paul Bibire has pointed out there was no equivalent adjectival form of *Norðmann*; so the term may apply to Scandinavians in general.[23] *Hæðen* which may be narrowly translated as 'heathen' briefly emerges as a more popular term in the 850s and 860s.[24] *Wicing* 'viking', and *Norðmann* are found less frequently.

---

[20] *The Old English Orosius*, I.i (ed. Bately, pp. 13-16); Christiansen, *The Norsemen*, pp. 118-23.

[21] Cleasby and Vigfusson, *An Icelandic-English Dictionary*, p. 96.

[22] Renaud, *Les Vikings*, p. 78; Christiansen, *The Norsemen*, pp. 116-18. Cf. Bouet, 'Les Chroniqueurs', p. 59, n. 6: '*Dani* est le terme le plus fréquemment employé par Abbon, les *Annales de Fontenelle*, Dudon (synonyme de *Daci*), Guillaume de Jumièges et Étienne de Rouen, *Les Annales de Jumièges*, Richer et Flodoard préfèrent le terme *Normanni*. Seul l'auteur des *Annales de Fontenelle* semble distinguer *Dani* de *Normanni* '. I would argue that the *Annales de Fontenelle* may be using these terms interchangeably.

[23] I am grateful to Paul Bibire for making this suggestion after my paper 'The Norwegian Kingdom of Dublin and the Danish Kingdom of York? Stereotyping Ethnicity in Viking Age Politics', Dark Age Studies Seminar, University of St Andrews, 5 March 2007.

[24] For the broader implications of this term, see Vos, 'The Other Side'. I am grateful to the author for sending a copy of this work.

In versions B, C, D and E of 'The Anglo-Saxon Chronicle' under the year 787 we find that *Norðmenn* are identified as being *Denisc*.[25] In the 'D' text under the year 943 a king Óláfr and his followers are identified as *Dene* but in the previous year they are taken to be *Norðmenn*. This challenges assumptions which have been made about the ethnic connotations of these labels. Even where there is a perceived contrast between 'Dane' and 'Norwegian' in the years 920 (A text) and 942, these distinctions result from the way these annals have been translated and they can be interpreted in another way. In both cases it can be argued that there is a repetition of terms with similar meanings to produce a particular effect. Under the year 920 when the subjection of various Insular peoples to the English king is recorded, this list is made to sound as impressive as possible: 'And then the king of the Scots and all the people of the Scots, and Ragnall, and the sons of Eadwulf and all who lived in Northumbria both English and "Danish", and also Northmen and others, and also the king of the Strathclyde Britons and all the Strathclyde Britons, 'chose him as father and lord'.[26] In 942 the poem which celebrates the conquest of an area of Mercia including the five boroughs, emphasises the previous subjection of Mercians to alien lordship 'they were formerly "Danes", oppressed in need under Northmen, in the fetter-chains of heathens'.[27]

It may be naïve to think in a colonial context that viking armies could consistently be characterised by being either 'Danish' or 'Norwegian', or,

---

[25] *ASC.B*, ed. Taylor, p. 28; *ASC.C*, ed. O' Keeffe, p. 50; *ASC.D*, ed. Cubbin, p.16; E in *Two of the Saxon Chronicles*, ed. Plummer, I, 55 (*s.a.* 787). Cf. Æthelweard, *Chronicon*, III.1 (ed. and trans. Campbell, p. 27). *The Anglo-Saxon Chronicle*, ed. Swanton, p. 54, n. 4.

[26] ASC.A, ed. Bately, p. 69 (*s.a.* 920): Scotta cyning 7 eall Scotta þeod 7 Rægnald 7 Eadulfes sunu ealle þa þe on Norþhymbrum bugeaþ ægðer ge Englisce ge Denisce ge Norþmen ge oþre 7 eac Stræcledweala cyning 7 ealle Stræcledwealas. For the pairing of Englisc/Ængle and Denisc/Dene as opposites, see *The Anglo-Saxon Chronicle*, trans. Whitelock *et al.*, pp. 61, 69 (*s.aa.* 900, 918).

[27] *ASC.A*, ed. Bately, p. 73; *ASC.B*, ed. Taylor, p. 53; *ASC.C*, ed. O'Keeffe, p. 79; *ASC.D*, ed. Cubbin, p. 43 (*s.a.* 942): *Dæne wæran æror under Norðmannum nyde gebegde on hæþenra hæfteclommum lange þrage* has been translated, 'the Danes were previously subjected by force under the Norsemen, for a long time in bonds of captivity to the heathens' (*The Anglo-Saxon Chronicle*, trans. Whitelock *et al.*, p. 71). I am grateful to Paul Bibire, Robert Millar and David Parsons for their advice on this alternative translation.

even if such differences existed, that they could be upheld over time.[28] The picture which emerges from our sources is that viking armies were often mixed, and they also recruited adherents in the countries where they operated.[29]

In other words, one can argue that historians have been responsible for generating a theory of ethnic division between Danes and Norwegians in Insular history during the ninth and early tenth centuries which may not have existed at the time. Nevertheless, it is hard to find a terminology for Scandinavian settlers which will satisfy everyone. I have preferred to use 'viking' as a multi-faceted term, for in each place where Scandinavians settled their culture interacted with that of the indigenous peoples. As a result new cultural identities emerged. Arguably one of the things which makes the study of vikings so fascinating is to see how these identities evolved, and how they are remembered today.[30]

[28] Anglo-Saxon law only recognised one Scandinavian group, namely 'Danes': Robertson, *The Laws*, ed. and trans. Robertson, pp. 29-39. Dawn Hadley (*The Vikings*, pp. 67-69) has made the case that this was a regional, not an ethnic, identity.
[29] Hadley, *The Vikings*, p. 306; Higham, 'Viking-Age Settlement', p. 303, Lund, 'Allies', p. 47. In the closing years of the tenth century and early years of the eleventh century, vikings from different parts of Scandinavia joined together to attack England. The recruitment of indigenous peoples into viking armies is attested from the ninth century. See below, p. 12. For attempts to control inter-cultural relations, see *Alfred*, trans. Keynes and Lapidge, pp. 171-72 and 312, n. 7.
[30] Hall, *Exploring the World*, pp. 218-29.

Figure 1: Ireland *c.* AD 1000

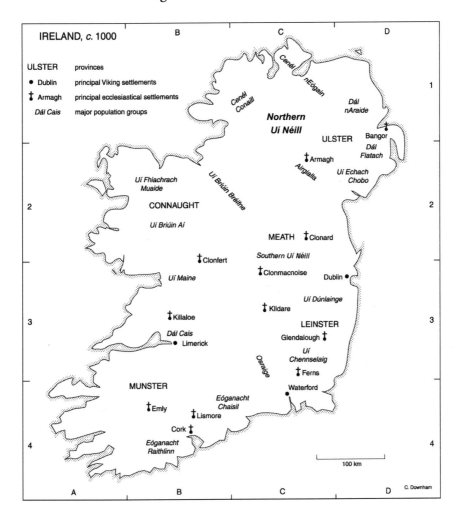

IRELAND, *c.* 1000

ULSTER   provinces
● Dublin   principal Viking settlements
† Armagh   principal ecclesiastical settlements
Dál Cais   major population groups

Cenél Conaill

Cenél nEógain

Dál nAraide

Northern Uí Néill

ULSTER

Bangor

Dál Fiatach

Uí Fhiachrach Muaide

† Armagh

Airgialla

Uí Echach Chobo

CONNAUGHT

Uí Briúin Bréifne

Uí Briúin Aí

MEATH   † Clonard

Southern Uí Néill

† Clonfert

† Clonmacnoise

Dublin ●

Uí Maine

Uí Dúnlainge

† Kildare

† Killaloe

LEINSTER

Glendalough †

Dál Cais
● Limerick

Uí Chennselaig

Osraige

† Ferns

MUNSTER

Waterford

Eóganacht Chaisil

† Emly

† Lismore

Cork †

Eóganacht Raithlinn

100 km

C. Downham

Figure 2: England *c.* AD 1000

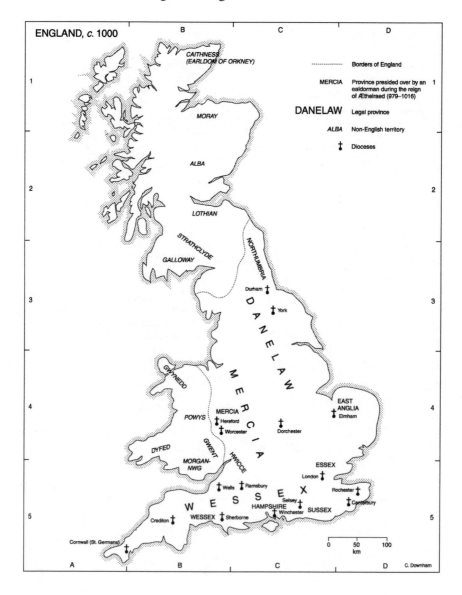

1

Ívarr and his Dynasty

VIKINGS plagued the coasts of Ireland and Britain in the 790s. Over time, their raids became more intense, and by the mid-ninth century vikings had established a number of settlements in Ireland and Britain and had become heavily involved with local politics. A particularly successful viking leader named Ívarr campaigned on both sides of the Irish Sea in the 860s. His descendants dominated the major seaports of Ireland and challenged the power of kings in Britain during the later ninth and tenth centuries. In 1014, the battle of Clontarf marked a famous stage in the decline of viking power in Ireland, and it coincided more or less with the conquest of England in 1013 by the Danish king Sveinn Forkbeard, which marked a watershed in the history of vikings in Britain. The descendants of Ívarr continued to play a significant role in the history of Dublin and the Hebrides until the twelfth century, but they did not threaten to overwhelm the major kingships of Britain or Ireland in this later period as they had done before.[1]

The aim of the present book is to provide a political analysis of the deeds of Ívarr's family from their first appearance in Insular records down to the year 1014. Such an account seems necessary as previous overviews of this subject are either outdated or highly controversial.[2] As a result, some arguments have recently been put forward which encourage a re-evaluation of our primary sources for the Viking Age: The existence of a so-called 'dynasty of Ívarr' in the kingdom of Man and the Isles has recently been challenged.[3] The existence of links between the kingdoms of York and Dublin in the late ninth and early tenth centuries has also been questioned.[4] In my opinion, neither revision is sustainable. I therefore present a case

---

[1] Downham, 'England'; Downham, 'Living on the Edge'.
[2] *Cogadh*, ed. and trans. Todd; Haliday, *The Scandinavian Kingdom*; Smyth, *Scandinavian Kings*; Smyth, *Scandinavian York*, I-II; Ó Corráin, 'High-Kings'; Page, 'A Tale'.
[3] Hudson, *Viking Pirates*, pp. 68-70.
[4] Abrams, 'The Conversion of the Scandinavians of Dublin', p. 22; Davidson, 'The (non) Submission', p. 208.

which is in some ways conservative, but I hope that within it the reader will find new ideas, some of which may be worthy of consideration.

This book is organised to facilitate navigation, so that readers can locate discussion on whichever area, period, or viking leader interests them most. Apart from the introduction and conclusion, each chapter is devoted to tackling a different part of the 'Insular Viking Zone'.[5] Within it, the dealings of Ívarr and his successors are laid out in chronological order. An appendix contains a prosopography of vikings who are named in Irish chronicle-records up to the battle of Clontarf. Despite the geographical division of chapters, attention is drawn to the interrelated nature of Insular politics in the Viking Age through discussion and through cross-referencing between different sections of the book.

In many ways, it is an exciting time to be engaged in Viking Studies. Recent theoretical approaches to the subject have raised many interesting questions regarding identity, material culture, and structures of authority. Archaeological finds and excavations have also offered potentially radical insights into vikings' settlement and society. This flurry of recent studies encourages a reconsideration of the fundamentals of viking history in Britain and Ireland. For that reason, a re-evaluation of historical events based on the primary sources can be useful, for these are nuts and bolts which help in constructing a more sophisticated understanding of vikings. I therefore hope that this book will be useful to a range of scholars who will draw on it to develop their own thoughts on the subject.

Identifying a Dynasty

Benjamin Hudson has suggested that 'ua Ímair', a label which appears in Irish chronicles from 896 to 948, may be 'a generic designation of Vikings whose ancestry is otherwise unknown'.[6] This suggestion challenges the validity of the concept that there was such a thing as a dynasty of Ívarr, although Hudson has not gone so far to reject it.[7] Is it unwise therefore to discuss the history of vikings using this paradigm?

---

[5] This term was coined by Colmán Etchingham, 'North Wales'. I use it in a broad sense to mean areas of Britain and Ireland where vikings were active.

[6] Hudson, *Viking Pirates*, p. 19.

[7] *Ibid.*, p. 20.

The medieval Gaelic word 'ua' (plural 'uí') meant grandson or, more generally, a descendant in the direct male line.[8] It is the origin of the element 'O' which is so common in anglicised forms of Irish surnames. The dual meaning of the word can sometimes lead to ambiguities. The transmission of names in Irish chronicles indicates that we are dealing with real and not imaginary descendants of Ívarr.[9] There is a chronological progression in that sons of Ivarr are named, then grandsons and great-grandsons (Figure 1).

Another factor which favours the deduction that these individuals share descent from one and the same Ívarr is the repetition of first names including Ímair (Ívarr), Ragnall (Rögnvaldr), Gofraid (Guðrøðr), Amlaíb (Óláfr), and Sitriuc (Sigtryggr). This recurrent pattern of names among those identified as sons or grandsons or great-grandsons of Ívarr indicates that we are dealing with members of the same family.[10] This element of conservatism in naming-practices among Ívarr's descendants was probably one way in which they expressed their identity and heritage and perhaps familial affection.

Furthermore, it is not in the character of Irish chronicles to be vague in stating biological links. The parentage of other viking and Irish leaders was recorded in a systematic way. Often these links can be compared with those stated in other sources, comparisons which demonstrate their general accuracy.[11] This suggests that annalists were seeking to be as precise as possible about the paternity and grand-paternity of the figures whom they mentioned. The reason for this concern with accuracy may be because a man's male ancestry said much about his status, or potential status, within Irish society.

The label 'ua Imair' is not found in Irish chronicles after 948 in describing descendants of the ninth-century king Ívarr.[12] In other words, this practice ended with the third generation of descendants of Ívarr. Therefore in Irish legal terms it was restricted to members of Ívarr's

---

[8] *Dictionary*, ed. Quin, p. 618, cols. 1–3.

[9] Surnames using 'ua' (conventionally 'Ua') to denote a distant ancestor do not emerge until the late tenth century: Byrne, *Irish Kings*, pp. xxxi, xxxiv.

[10] Dumville, 'Old Dubliners', p. 84; Christiansen, *The Norsemen*, p. 44.

[11] A number of examples has been provided by Jaski, 'Additional Notes'.

[12] References to 'ua Ímair' in 995 and 1035 relate to grandsons of later persons called Ívarr in this dynasty: *Annals of Inisfallen, s.a.* [995] (ed. and trans. Mac Airt, pp. 170-71); *Annals of Ulster, s.a.* 1035.5 (ed. and trans. Mac Airt and Mac Niocaill, pp. 472-73).

Figure 3: Direct references to male descendants of Ívarr in Irish Chronicles	

son of Ívarr (*mac Ímair*)

A.D. 881	Barid mac Imair (CS)
A.D. 888	Juffrie mc Iwer (AClon) Sichfrith m. Imair (AU) Sichfrith mac Imair (CS)
A.D. 893	m. Imair (AU)
A.D. 894	m. Imhair (AU)
A.D. 896	Sitriuc mac Iomhair (AFM) Sitriucc m. Imair (AU)

grandson of Ívarr (*[h]ua [h]Ímair*)

A.D. 896	Amhlaoibh ua h-Iomhair (AFM) Amlaim h. Imair (AU) Amlaibh .H. Imair (CS)
A.D. 904	Imhar ua hImhair (AU) da .H. Imair (CS)
A.D. 914	Ragnall h. Imair (AU)
A.D. 917	Sitrioc, ua hIomhair; Sitriucc ua hIomhair (AFM) Sitriuc h. Imair; Sitriuc hu Imair; Sitriuc h. Imair (AU) Ua Imair (CS)
A.D. 918	Sitriuc h. Imair (AU)
A.D. 919	Cháech hú Ímair (AI)
A.D. 920	Sitriuc ua hImair (AU)
A.D. 921	Godfrey o'Himar (AClon) Gofraith ua hIomhair (AFM) Gothbraith hua Ímair (AI) Goithbrith h. Imair; Gothbrith oa Imhair; Ragnall h. Imair (AU) Goffraicch .H. Imair (CS)
A.D. 924	Gothbraith hua Ímair (AI) Gothbrith h. n-Imair (AU)
A.D. 927	Sittrick o'Himer (AClon) Sitriuc ua hIomhair (AFM) Sitriuc h. Imair (AU) Sitriuc .H. Imair (CS)
A.D. 930	Gofraith ua hIomhair (AFM) Gothfrith h. Imhair (AU)
A.D. 931	Ua n-Iomhair (AFM)
A.D. 934	Gothfrith h. hImair (AU)

great-grandson of Ívarr (*[h]ua / mac [h]ua [h]Ímair*)

A.D. 935	Amlaibh h. n-Imair (AU) [see 938]
A.D. 938	Amlaim h. n-Imair (AU) [=Amhlaibh mac Gofradha (AFM) Amhlaiph m. Gothfrith (AU) hAmhlaibh mac Cothfrith (CS)]
A.D. 940	Harold o'Hymer (AClon) Aralt ua hIomhair .i. mac Sitrioca (AFM) Arailt huí Ímair (AI) Aralt mac .H. Imair .i. mac Sitric (CS)
A.D. 948	Blacaire mᶜ Imer (AClon) Blacaire ua n-Iomhair (AFM) Blacaire .H. Imair (CS) [=Blocair m. Gofrith (AU)]

derbfhine ('certain kindred'). This was a family-unit comprising the descendants in a male line from a common great-grandfather.[1] The significance of the *derbfhine* was that any male belonging to the *derbfhine* of a previous king was eligible to inherit part of his property. It was also more likely that a new king would arise from within this immediate kin-group.[2] Among the descendants of Ívarr's great-grandsons we can see a process of dynastic segmentation (the emergence of rival lineages as subsets within an expanding kin-group).[3] Something in common to both Irish and viking royal dynasties was that they 'began as families and developed into large cousinhoods of military competitors'.[4] In Ireland the sons of one great-grandson of Ívarr (Óláfr Guðrøðsson) rivalled the sons of another (Óláfr Sigtryggsson) for control of the kingship of Dublin. It was the line of Óláfr Sigtryggsson which succeeded. Óláfr Sigtryggsson (better known through his Irish nickname *Cuarán*) can be seen as the progenitor of a new dynasty, albeit one which descended in a direct male line from Ívarr.[5] We can be fairly secure in identifying the descendants of Ívarr's grandsons as far as 1014, as other historians have done, by linking individuals through the patronyms used in Irish chronicles and by cross-referencing the information in different sources. To make the method of these identifications as clear as possible, I have included a prosopography of all vikings named in Irish chronicles before 1014 as an appendix to this book.

In sum, I do not find that 'ua Ímair' occurs in Irish chronicles as a label for vikings of uncertain descent.[6] Close analysis of the chronicle-evidence shows how the label was applied to Ívarr's grandsons and great-grandsons. A sense of the correctness of these family-connections is reinforced by the recurrence of names among Ívarr's descendants, the general accuracy of Irish chronicles in relation to other families, as well as the use of dynastic names in Irish society to show eligibility for kingship. The tracing of Ívarr's descendants through the Irish chronicles highlights how his progeny came

---

[1] *Dictionary*, ed. Quin, p. 204, col. 32, lines 23–46; Kelly, *A Guide*, pp. 12-13

[2] Ó Corráin, *Ireland*, pp. 37-38.

[3] Ó Corráin, 'Irish Regnal Succession'.

[4] Christiansen, *The Norsemen*, p. 60.

[5] In the seventeenth century the merchant-families of Dublin claimed descent from this famous king: *Leabhar Mór*, ed. and trans. Ó Muraíle, III, 775.1. Earlier legends also developed around him: *Historia Gruffudd ap Cynan* (ed. and trans. Evans, *A Mediaeval Prince*, pp. 25, 56); *Havelock* (ed. Smithers).

[6] Hudson, *Viking Pirates*, p. 19.

to dominate the viking settlements of Ireland. Irish chronicles also refer to these descendants' activities in England, mainland Scotland, the Hebrides, and Wales; and this evidence can be compared with that of other Insular sources. This book is essentially the product of such research.

Modern historians talk of 'the dynasty of Ívarr' (Irish 'Uí Ímair') as a convenient label to identify those viking leaders who were descended from him. However, a collective term for all the descendants of Ívarr is lacking in medieval Irish chronicles. Contemporaries were more concerned to identify viking leaders in terms of their immediate kin-group (*derbfhine*). Therefore it is not clear whether all descendants of Ívarr would have identified themselves as such. Nevertheless, some late sources show that inhabitants of Ireland's viking towns did look back to Ívarr as a founding figure. According to Gerald of Wales, the viking towns of Dublin, Waterford, and Limerick were each created by one of three brothers: Óláfr, Sigtryggr, and Ívarr.[7] There are also references to Ívarr as an apical ancestor of viking kings in 'The Great Book of Genealogies' compiled by Dubhaltach Mac Fhir Bhisigh in the mid-seventeenth century. In that book his descendants are described as 'Clann Íomhair' and 'the seed of Ívarr'.[8] Ívarr is also found in the guise of Ívarr inn beinlausi, the legendary son of Ragnarr loðbrók.[9] The claim seems to have evolved under the influence of accounts which were circulating in Britain and Ireland in the eleventh century.[10] None of these tales can be regarded as historically accurate, but they do suggest a continuing interest in Ívarr as a founding-figure in the history of vikings in Ireland and Britain.[11]

The dynasty of Ívarr may be comparable with other viking dynasties, including the descendants of Rurik in Russia and the descendants of Rollo

---

[7] *Topographia Hiberniae* (ed. O'Meara, 'Giraldus Cambrensis', p. 175; trans. O'Meara, *Gerald*, p. 122).

[8] *Leabhar Mór*, ed. and trans. Ó Muraíle, III, 769.2, 775.1, 775.2, 776.2.

[9] McTurk, *Studies*, pp. 54-55; *Saxonis Gesta Danorum*, ed. Olrik and Raeder, pp. 250-68; *Saxo*, trans. Davidson and Fisher, I, 279-97; *Fornaldar sögur*, ed. Guðni Jónsson, I, 219-85; *The Saga*, trans. Schlauch, pp. 185-258.

[10] *Gesta Normannorum Ducum*, ed. and trans. van Houts, I, xxxvii; Whitelock, 'Fact', p. 266; Ó Corráin, 'Viking Ireland', p. 447.

[11] Other legends sought to link the vikings of Ireland with the Norwegian king Haraldr hárfagri or his associate Rögnvaldr of Møre: Downham, 'Eric', pp. 65-69.

in Normandy.[12] It was not unique to vikings that power should be organised by dynasties. Across medieval Europe the family was the main social and political unit. In terms of offering protection, status, and identity, no other institution was more dominant.[13] The foundation of viking dynasties in a colonial context mirrors this general state of affairs. It may also reflect the nature of raiding, trading, and migration from Scandinavia. The activities of Ívarr and his brothers in England highlight the fact that close relatives sometimes co-operated to fund ventures, to lead armies, and to consolidate their power in a colonial setting.[14] For men and women in the Viking Age to travel overseas and to try to establish a new life were aspirations which incurred a high level of risk. Their motives were various. Life abroad must have presented better (or more exciting) opportunities than were available at home.[15] By operating as a family in the new environment, people could mitigate some of these risks, and the chance of material advancement might be greater. No doubt stress and mistrust fractured some family-bonds in this situation, while others remained strong.

Among Ívarr's descendants, the forging of new alliances in Britain and Ireland was frequently accompanied by binding dynasties together through ritual or fictive kinship (marriage, fosterage, or god-parentage). In this way innovative relationships were construed in a way which could reinforce (rather than threaten) the integrity of the dynasty because they were mediated by the language of kinship. An impressive example of how such alliances could endure can be traced between one branch of the descendants of Ívarr and those of Aed Finnliath (overking of the Northern Uí Néill) over three generations (which is further discussed below).[16]

The identity of the descendants of Ívarr was also reinforced through use of emblems which may have had a dynastic significance. 'The ring of Þórir' and 'the sword of Carlus' served as royal insignia in Dublin.[17] Rings and swords frequently appear in medieval literature as signs of kingship. Who Þórir and Carlus were is a matter of debate. The name Þórir is a derivative

---

[12] Duczko, *Viking Rus*; Rukavishnikov, '*Tale*'; Searle, *Predatory Kinship*. This might be a fertile area for future research.

[13] Christiansen, *The Norsemen*, pp. 38-39.

[14] See below, pp. 64-71.

[15] Dumville, 'Old Dubliners', p. 79.

[16] See below pp. 19, 24, 40, 239, 247, 269 and p. 30, n. 30.

[17] *Annals of the Four Masters, s.aa.* 994 [=995], 1029 (ed. and trans. O'Donovan, II, 732-33, 818-19).

of the divine name Thor. Þórir of the ring may be linked with 'The Wood of Þórir' which was located to the north of Dublin.[18] A significant viking leader of this name fell in battle in Ireland in 848, and at least three later viking leaders in Ireland bore that name.[19] Carlus could refer to a son of Ívarr's brother or associate Óláfr who died in 868.[20] Alternatively it may refer to one of the famous Frankish kings of the Viking Age named Charles. As monograms of the name Charles appear on viking coins minted at York, this seems to be a distinct possibility.[21]

Symbols associated with kings of Dublin were incorporated into the designs of coins minted in areas of England ruled by descendants of Ívarr. Some of these designs may have had dynastic significance. There is a clear parallel for this theory in that Viking Rus can be shown to have etched dynastic symbols on coins.[22] Alfred Smyth has suggested that the sword emblem which appears on tenth-century Anglo-Scandinavian coins represents 'the sword of Carlus'.[23] It is possible (though unverifiable) that the Thor's hammers displayed on these coins refer to the ring of Þórir. Hammer-amulets were often suspended on rings, sometimes with the ring being the dominant feature.[24] Both symbols, the hammer and the sword, recur on coins issued by different kings of York in the early tenth century.

The concept of dynasty may have been important to the descendants of Ívarr. Successive viking kings no doubt used a variety of other methods to advertise their legitimacy to rule. Royal courts were centres of patronage and ceremonial display.[25] Thing-sites and monuments may also have served

[18] *Annals of Inisfallen, s.a.* [1000] (ed. and trans. Mac Airt, pp. 174-75); *Annals of Tigernach, s.a.* [974] [=975] (ed. and trans. Stokes, II, 230); cf. *Chronicum Scotorum, s.a.* [973] [=975] (ed. and trans. Hennessy, pp. 222-23); *Cogadh,* §113 (ed. and trans. Todd, pp. 198-99). Hogan's identification is based on a misinterpretation: *Onomasticon*, p. 139.

[19] *Annals of the Four Masters, s.a.* 846 [=848], cf. 923 [=925] (ed. and trans. O'Donovan, I, 474–77 and II, 612–13); *Annals of Inisfallen, s.aa.* [866], [922] (ed. and trans. Mac Airt, pp. 132-33, 146-47).

[20] *Annals of the Four Masters, s.a.* 866 [=868] (ed. and trans. O'Donovan, I, 504–05).

[21] Blackburn, 'The Coinage', p. 331.

[22] Duczko, *Viking Rus,* pp. 228-37

[23] Grierson and Blackburn, *Medieval European Coinage,* I, 323, 325; Smyth, *Scandinavian York,* I, 107. See below, pp. 119-20.

[24] Davidson, 'Thor's hammer', p. 7; e.g. Duczko, *Viking Rus,* Fig. 24b.

[25] For court-poetry, see *Gunnlaugs saga Ormstungu,* §8 (ed. and trans. Foote and Quirk, pp. 18-19); *The Metrical Dindsenchas,* ed. and trans. Gwynn, I, 52-53; Breathnach, 'The Documentary Evidence', pp. 37-41. Margo Griffin-Wilson has kindly drawn my attention

as symbols of royal authority.[26] After conversion, patronage of the Church was also a way in which descendants of Ívarr sought to legitimise their power.[27] Nevertheless, I would argue that biological descent and a sense of dynasty remained at the core of legitimising the power of these viking kings.[28]

In the following sections of this book the activities of Ívarr's descendants are analysed region by region, beginning with Ireland, then England, North Britain, the Hebrides, and Wales. This approach demonstrates how the dynasty had a lasting impact in each area.

to a stanza possibly dedicated to Óláfr Cuarán in an Irish metrical tract: Ó hAodha, 'The First', p. 235.

[26] Holm, 'Viking Dublin', p. 257.

[27] For example *Chronicum Scotorum, s.aa.* [978] [=980], [1026] [=1028] (ed. and trans. Hennessy, pp. 226-27, 266-67).

[28] Tolochko, 'Kievan Rus', p. 131: 'the Kievan state was a family owned company'. This comparison may be relevant when we explore the activities of the dynasty of Ívarr.

2

Ireland

THE wealth of chronicle-data relating to vikings in Ireland stands in contrast to other regions covered in this book. Ten principal Irish chronicles have survived which deal with some or all of the period under discussion ('The Annals of Boyle', 'The Annals of Clonmacnoise', 'The Annals of Inisfallen', 'The Annals from the Book of Leinster', 'The Annals of Roscrea', 'The Annals of the Four Masters', 'The Annals of Tigernach', 'The Annals of Ulster', *Chronicum Scotorum*, and 'The Fragmentary Annals of Ireland').[1] These are compilations ranging in date from the eleventh to the seventeenth century, though based for the most part on contemporary records.[2] In some chronicles pseudo-historical saga-narratives have been added, as in 'The Fragmentary Annals of Ireland', 'The Annals of Clonmacnoise', and 'The Annals of the Four Masters'.[3] These interpolations can often be identified on stylistic grounds. Apart from these additions, Irish chronicles are considered by scholars to be largely accurate records, albeit partisan in their presentation of events.[4] Only a streamlined account of the deeds of Ívarr's family in Ireland is presented in the following pages, to trace the origins and significance of the dynasty.[5]

Vikings were attacking Ireland for over half a century before Ívarr and his brothers appeared on the scene. By the 820s vikings had raided the points on the Irish coast which stood farthest from Scandinavia, and from the 830s Irish chroniclers recorded the founding of numerous camps at coastal points and deep into the interior of the island (Figure 2).[6] Not only

[1] 'The Annals of Loch Cé' commence in 1014 with an account of the battle of Clontarf. The principal surveys are: Mac Niocaill, *The Medieval Irish Annals*; Grabowski and Dumville, *Chronicles*.

[2] Ó Máille, *The Language*; Hughes, *Early Christian Ireland*, pp. 97-159; Dumville, 'A Millennium', p. 108.

[3] *Ibid.*, p. 104; Ó Corráin, 'Muirchertach'.

[4] Etchingham, *Viking Raids*; Downham, 'Irish Chronicles'.

[5] For some preparatory work see Downham, 'The Good'; Downham, 'Non-Urban Settlements'; Downham, 'The Historical Importance'. I plan to deal with the subject more thoroughly in a separate publication.

[6] *Annals of Inisfallen, s.a.* [824] (ed. and trans. Mac Airt, pp. 124-25); *Annals of Ulster, s.a.* 823 [=824].9 (ed. and trans. Mac Airt and Mac Niocaill, pp. 280-81).

did these serve as bases for attacking local settlements (and particularly churches) but they were also places for ransoming and trading booty, both human and otherwise, to those who were brave enough to approach them.[7] Vikings had also made common cause on occasion with their new neighbours. In 842, Comán, abbot of Linns (a site near Dundalk bay), was fatally wounded and then burnt by a raiding band of both 'heathens' and 'Irish'.[8] Such joint expeditions were to become common in future years as vikings' military skills became recognised as a valuable asset in the frequent wars that were fought between Irish kings.

Ireland at this time consisted of more than one hundred and fifty separate kingdoms, subject to six provincial overkings (Connaught, Leinster, Munster, Ulster, Northern Uí Néill and Southern Uí Néill).[9] The overkings of the Northern and Southern Uí Néill were the most powerful. Nevertheless there was plenty of scope within the political system for rivalries at different levels to erupt into small-scale wars.[10] The highly localised character of Irish political structures was one factor which limited the territorial acquisitions of vikings in Ireland.[11] Their main bases, including Dublin, were located on the coast, and each may have ruled a restricted hinterland.[12] Although vikings made strenuous efforts in the 840s to rule large swathes of Irish territory, these efforts came to nought in a series of battles won by Irish kings in 848.[13]

It is in the context of these major defeats in 848 that we get news of a new group of vikings arriving in Ireland, who can be linked with Ívarr and his brothers.[14] A viking leader called Þórir was slain in battle in Leinster in

[7] 'Vita Sancti Findani', ed. Holder-Egger, 502-06; Christiansen, 'The People', 148-64; Omand, 'The Life'; Downham, 'Non-urban Settlements' (forthcoming).

[8] *Annals of Clonmacnoise, s.a.* 839 [=842] (ed. Murphy, p. 139); *Annals of Ulster, s.a.* 841 [=842].10 (ed. and trans. Mac Airt and Mac Niocaill, pp. 300-01).

[9] Byrne, *Irish Kings*, p. 46; David Dumville has mentioned in conversation that the number needs to be upwardly revised, and this impression was reinforced during my minor study of one area of Leinster: Downham, 'The Loígis'. The medieval province of *Mide* (Meath) comprised the territories of Southern Uí Néill. It is not to be confused with modern Co. Meath.

[10] Ó Corráin, *Ireland*, pp. 28-32.

[11] Downham, 'The Vikings', p. 234.

[12] Downham, 'Non-urban Settlements' (forthcoming).

[13] Downham, 'The Vikings', pp. 235-36.

[14] Dumville, 'Old Dubliners'.

Figure 4: Ninth-century chronicle references to viking camps in Ireland

Arklow	(Co. Wicklow)	836
Carlingford Lough?	(Co. Down / Louth)	852
Clondalkin	(Co. Dublin)	867
Cluain Andobair	(Co. Offaly)	845
Cork	(Co. Cork)	848, 867
Dublin	(Co. Dublin)	837, 841, multiple references
Dún Mainne	(Co. Kerry)	867
Dunrally	(Co. Laois)	862
Limerick	(Co. Limerick)	845, 887
Rosnaree	(Co. Meath)	842
Linns, nr. Annagassan	(Co. Louth)	841, 842, 851, 852
Lough Foyle	(Co. Derry)	898
Lough Neagh	(Co. Antrim / Armagh / Derry / Tyrone)	839, 840, 841
Lough Ree	(Co. Longford / Roscommon / W'meath)	844, 845
Lough Swilly?	(Co. Donegal)	842
St Mullins	(Co. Carlow)	892
Strangford Lough	(Co. Down)	879
Waterford	(Co. Waterford)	860, 892
Wexford	(Co. Wexford)	892
Youghal	(Co. Cork)	866

Sites of uncertain location

Cael Uisce	842
Port Manann	866
sites between Cenél nEogain and Dál nAraide	866
site destroyed by king of Uí Bairrche thíre	868

---

848. He was identified as the deputy of the king of *Laithlind*.[15] This is the first mention of *Laithlind* in Irish chronicles, and its identification is disputed. The king of *Laithlind* may be the same as 'the king of the foreigners' who in the following year was reported to have sent an army to

---

[15] *Annals of the Four Masters*, s.a. 846 [=848] (ed. and trans. O'Donovan, I, 474-77); *Annals of Ulster*, s.a. 847 [=848].5 (ed. and trans. Mac Airt and Mac Niocaill, pp. 306-07); *Chronicum Scotorum*, s.a. [848] (ed. and trans. Hennessy, pp. 148-49).

contend with those vikings who had settled in Ireland before them.[16] Then in 851 a band called 'Dark Foreigners' arrived at Dublin and inflicted a great slaughter on the 'Fair Foreigners'; they then proceeded to the viking base at Linns with the same effect.[17] In 852, the 'Dark Foreigners' defeated the 'Fair Foreigners' in battle at Carlingford Lough.[18] Then in 853 Óláfr, son of the king of *Laithlind*, arrived in Ireland, and the vikings in Ireland submitted to him.[19] This Óláfr was a kinsman, and perhaps more specifically a brother, of Ívarr.[20]

To understand this sequence of events, we should take into account that the label 'dark' was used in Irish genealogical literature to denote newer or later groups or individuals in contrast to 'fair' or earlier ones.[21] David Dumville has identified the 'Dark' or 'New' foreigners' arriving in Ireland with Ívarr and his associates.[22] I should take a step further than Dumville and suggest that the term 'Dark' was applied to followers the king of *Laithlind* (who had become a recurrent phenomenon for the chroniclers) as a convenient way of distinguishing them from the vikings who were already in Ireland. The established vikings were dubbed 'Fair' foreigners in contrast. What we see in the years from 848 to 853 is the efforts of a new band of vikings to extend their sphere of activity into Ireland and to dominate the

---

[16] *Annals of the Four Masters*, s.a. 847 [=849] (ed. and trans. O'Donovan, I, 476-77); *Annals of Ulster*, s.a. 848 [=849].6 (ed. and trans. Mac Airt and Mac Niocaill, pp. 308-09); *Chronicum Scotorum*, s.a. [849] (ed. and trans. Hennessy, pp. 148-51).

[17] *Annals of the Four Masters*, s.a. 849 [=851] (ed. and trans. O'Donovan, I, 480-83); *Annals of Ulster*, s.a. 850 [=851].3 (ed. and trans. Mac Airt and Mac Niocaill, pp. 310-11); *Chronicum Scotorum*, s.a. [851] (ed. and trans. Hennessy, pp. 149-51). The much quoted poem *Is acher in gáith innocht* ('Bitter is the wind tonight') which refers to 'fierce warriors of *Lothlinn*' was written down at this time: Ó Néill, 'Irish Observance', pp. 178-80.

[18] *Annals of the Four Masters*, s.a. 850 [=852] (ed. and trans. O'Donovan, I, 484-85); *Annals of Ulster*, s.a. 851 [=852].3 (ed. and trans. Mac Airt and Mac Niocaill, pp. 310-11); *Chronicum Scotorum*, s.a. [852] (ed. and trans. Hennessy, pp. 152-53).

[19] *Annals of the Four Masters*, s.a. 851 [=853] (ed. and trans. O'Donovan, I, 486-87); *Annals of Ulster*, s.a. 852 [=853].2 (ed. and trans. Mac Airt and Mac Niocaill, pp. 312-13); *Chronicum Scotorum*, s.a. [853] (ed. and trans. Hennessy, pp. 152-53).

[20] Explicit in *Fragmentary Annals of Ireland* §239 (ed. and trans. Radner, pp. 94-97) but this is from an eleventh-century saga-element in the text. Cf. *Annals of Ulster*, s.a. 866 [=867].6 (ed. and trans. Mac Airt and Mac Niocaill, pp. 322-23). See below, p. 16.

[21] Smyth, 'The *Black* Foreigners'; *Annals of Clonmacnoise*, s.a. 922 (ed. Murphy, p. 148); cf. *Annals of Ulster*, s.a. 926 [=927].2 (ed. and trans. Mac Airt and Mac Niocaill, pp. 378-79).

[22] Dumville, 'Old Dubliners'; Hall, *Exploring the World*, pp. 89-90.

viking groups who were there before.[23] After the 'Dark Foreigners' achieved a level of success in 852, their leaders, Óláfr and his kinsmen, came to settle in Ireland.

This naturally raises the question of *Laithlind*'s location. Anders Ahlqvist has recently suggested that this term, which he has translated into English as 'mud-pool', was a derogatory name for Dublin.[24] Nevertheless, the description of the arrival in Ireland of warriors associated with *Laithlind* favours the interpretation that it was located overseas.[25] Donnchadh Ó Corráin has argued that *Laithlind* in the ninth and tenth centuries described the Northern Isles of Scotland and the Hebrides, but the evidence is not conclusive.[26] The name *Laithlind* was later replaced by the word *Lochlann*. It is not clear that these were necessarily the same place, or whether the two names were simply conflated.[27] From the eleventh century *Lochlann* meant Norway.[28]

Because of these ambiguities we cannot identify the origins of Óláfr and Ívarr. Much speculation based on non-contemporary sources has arisen concerning the background of these leaders. The temptation to use the abundant and colourful legends of a later age, when contemporary evidence is patchy and laconic, is perhaps understandable but nonetheless highly problematic. Thirteenth- and fourteenth-century Scandinavian sagas have been used to identify Ívarr as Ívarr inn beinlausi, son of the legendary Danish king Ragnarr loðbrók. These texts cannot be seen as reliable sources

---

[23] Mac Shamhráin, *The Vikings*, p. 48.

[24] Ahlqvist, '*Is acher*', p. 25. However, could it be that the scribe of Sankt Gallen, Stiftsbibliothek, MS 904 was making a pun linking the 'Dark Foreigners' of *Laithlind* with *indneime andracht*, 'dark poison', with which he glossed on the same page the Latin words *tetri … uiri* ('poisonous slime') given that *uiri* also means 'men'?

[25] For example, *Annals of Ulster, s.a.* 852 [=853].2 (ed. and trans. Mac Airt and Mac Niocaill, pp. 312-13): 'Amhlaim m. rígh Laithlinde do tuidhecht a n-Erenn'.

[26] Ó Corráin, 'The Vikings in Scotland'. Cf. Dolley, *The Hiberno-Norse Coins*, pp. 18-19; Sawyer, *The Age*, p. 211.

[27] Etchingham, 'The Location' (forthcoming). I am grateful to the author for sending a copy of this article prior to publication.

[28] *Dictionary*, ed. Quin, p. 442, col. 214, line 80. If *Lothlinn* and *Lochlann* were the same, its meaning may have narrowed over time, without changing its sense entirely. *Lochlann* might have originally described areas inhabited by vikings to the north of Ireland, including Norway and the Scottish Isles. By the mid-eleventh century the geographical scope of this name focused on Norway which had in the meantime developed as a distinct political unit, whose inhabitants distinguished themselves from viking settlers outside Scandinavia.

for ninth-century events.[29] Other attempts to trace Ívarr's ancestry lead us to the so-called 'Osraige chronicle', an eleventh-century saga embedded in 'The Fragmentary Annals of Ireland'. Here it is claimed that the father of Ívarr and Óláfr was a king of *Lochlann* (Norway) named Guðrøðr son of Rögnvaldr son of Guðrøðr.[30] It is possible that the author of the early thirteenth century *Orkneyinga saga* was seeking to allude to Ívarr's pedigree when he stated that Rögnvaldr of Møre (ancestor of the earls of Orkney) had a son by this name who was killed 'in the west' on expedition with Haraldr hárfagri (Harold Finehair).[31] None of these accounts is credible. While medieval writers seem to have been as interested as modern historians about Ívarr's origins, it is perhaps wiser to accept that we do not know what these really were.

From 853, Irish chronicles record the activities of 'three kings of the foreigners', Óláfr, Ívarr, and Ásl, in Ireland and Britain.[32] According to the eleventh-century saga-component of 'The Fragmentary Annals of Ireland', they were brothers.[33] This link is not made explicit in other chronicles. According to 'The Annals of Ulster', Ásl was killed in 867 *parricidio a fratribus* 'by kinsmen in parricide'.[34] In the saga-account of 'The Fragmentary Annals of Ireland' Ásl's brothers Ívarr and Óláfr are identified as the culprits. This supports the conclusion that the historical characters were indeed brothers.[35] The repetition of the names Óláfr and Ívarr among the descendants of Ívarr is strong evidence that they were kinsmen. A brother of Ívarr called Hálfdan was active in both England and Ireland, and 'The Anglo-Saxon Chronicle' mentions a 'brother of Ívarr and Hálfdan' who raided Devon in 878.[36] Thus it appears that some viking armies were led as family-enterprises. Óláfr, Ívarr, Ásl, and Hálfdan were to play a remarkable role in Insular politics for a quarter of a century.

[29] McTurk, 'Ragnarr'.
[30] *Fragmentary Annals*, §401 (ed. and trans. Radner, pp. 144-45); Steffensen, 'A Fragment'.
[31] *Orkneyinga Saga* §4 (trans. Pálsson and Edwards, pp. 26-27).
[32] e.g. *Annals of Ulster, s.aa.* 856 [=857].1, 858 [=859].2, 862 [=863].4, 863 [=864].2, 865 [=866].1, 866 [=867].6 (ed. and trans. Mac Airt and Mac Niocaill, pp. 314-23).
[33] *Fragmentary Annals*, §239 (ed. and trans. Radner, pp. 94-97).
[34] *Annals of Ulster, s.a.* 866 [=867].6 (ed. and trans. Mac Airt and Mac Niocaill, pp. 322-23).
[35] Although it is possible that the saga-author made up an inventive account of Ásl's demise based on earlier chronicle records.
[36] *ASC.A*, ed. Bately, p. 50; *ASC.B*, ed. Taylor, p. 37; *ASC.C*, ed. O'Keeffe, p. 61; *ASC.D*, ed. Cubbin, p. 27; E in *Two of the Saxon Chronicles*, ed. Plummer, I, 75.

The Careers of Óláfr and Ívarr

Óláfr was the dominant viking in Irish affairs during the 850s and 860s. In 853 the vikings of Ireland are said to have submitted to him and he took tribute from the Irish.[37] This record gives the impression that Óláfr and his men were regarded as fearsome enemies, as both Irish and vikings were initially prepared to meet his demands rather than fight.[38] Nevertheless, in the years that followed, Óláfr faced two main opponents in Ireland. One was a band of vikings called *Gallgoídil* (literally 'Foreigner-Gaels'). They have been identified as vikings of mixed Gaelic and Scandinavian culture.[39] This group is only recorded in Irish chronicles within the years 856, 857 and 858 (it may be that after that time vikings of mixed ethnicity were not sufficiently novel or distinct in the Irish political scene to warrant special appellation).[40] The 'Foreigner-Gaels' were allied with Mael Sechlainn, overking of the Southern Uí Néill, who was the other main opponent of Óláfr. Mael Sechlainn was the most powerful Irish king at this time and the lands which he controlled lay close to the viking base of Dublin in the fertile east midlands of Ireland.

Under the year 856 the 'Annals of Ulster' and *Chronicum Scotorum* report that a 'great war' broke out between the 'heathens' and Mael Sechlainn with his *Gall-goídil* allies. In the same year two prominent churches of Slane and Lusk in Southern Uí Néill territory were attacked. Lusk lay thirteen miles north of Dublin and Slane could be reached from Dublin by boat. It seems likely that these churches were raided from the

---

[37] *Annals of the Four Masters*, s.a. 851 [=853] (ed. and trans. O'Donovan, I, 486-87); *Annals of Ulster*, s.a. 852 [=853].2 (ed. and trans. Mac Airt and Mac Niocaill, pp. 312-13); *Chronicum Scotorum*, s.a. [853] (ed. and trans. Hennessy, pp. 152-53).

[38] Tribute had previously been taken in Ireland in 798 and 847: *Annals of Ulster*, s.a. 797 [=798].2 (ed. and trans. Mac Airt and Mac Niocaill, pp. 252-53); *Annales Bertiniani*, s.a. 847 (ed. Grat *et al.*, p. 54; *Annals of St Bertin*, trans. Nelson, p. 65).

[39] The saga-element in 'The Fragmentary Annals of Ireland': *Fragmentary Annals*, §§247, 260 (ed. and trans. Radner, pp. 98-99, 104-05) asserts that they were Irish people who adopted viking ways, or who were fostered by vikings. This has been rejected by Crawford, *Scandinavian Scotland*, p. 47; Ó Corráin, 'The Vikings in Scotland', p. 326; Ní Mhaonaigh, 'The Outward Look', pp. 391-92.

[40] Vikings who settled in Ireland by 841 could have fathered a new generation of warriors by the late 850s: Dumville, *The Churches*, pp. 27-28; Young, 'A Note', p. 24.

viking port which was under the control of 'Dark Foreigners'.[41] In 857 the sphere of war moved to Munster, where Mael Sechlainn had made several attempts to impose his authority over the province's kings. He took hostages from the province in 854, 856 and 858.[42] The weakness of the provincial overkings of Munster had been exacerbated in 856 by a viking attack on the royal centre at Loch Cend (Co. Limerick) with the killing of many people including Gormán son of Lonán, a member of the royal dynasty.[43] The fragile condition of Munster no doubt attracted rival parties to compete for resources there. In 857 Óláfr and Ívarr defeated an army of *Gallgoídil* in Munster.[44] Then in 858 a large force of *Gallgoídil* was defeated at Ara Tíre (Co. Tipperary) by Ívarr in alliance with an Irish king, Cerball of Osraige.[45] This battle was fought on the borders of Munster and Southern Uí Néill territory. The *Gallgoídil* seem to have received support from Cenél Fiachach, a population-group who dwelt within the borders of Southern Uí Néill. Cerball, who fought on the side of Ívarr, ruled a

---

[41] *Annals of the Four Masters*, s.a. 854 [=856] (ed. and trans. O'Donovan, I, 486-89); *Annals of Ulster*, s.a. 855 [=856].3, 855 [=856].8 (ed. and trans. Mac Airt and Mac Niocaill, pp. 314-15); *Chronicum Scotorum*, s.a. [856] (ed. and trans. Hennessy, pp. 154-55).

[42] *Annals of the Four Masters*, s.aa. 852 [=854], 854 [=856], 856 [=858] (ed. and trans. O'Donovan, I, 487-91); *Annals of Ulster*, s.aa. 853 [=854].2, 855 [=856].2, 857 [=858].4 (ed. and trans. Mac Airt and Mac Niocaill, pp. 312-17); *Chronicum Scotorum*, s.aa. [854], [856], [858] (ed. and trans. Hennessy, pp. 152-55).

[43] *Annals of the Four Masters*, s.a. 853 [=856] (ed. and trans. O'Donovan, I, 486-87); *Chronicum Scotorum*, s.a. [856] (ed. and trans. Hennessy, pp. 154-55); Hogan, *Onomasticon*, p. 496.

[44] *Annals of Ulster*, s.a. 856 [=857].1 (ed. and trans. Mac Airt and Mac Niocaill, pp. 314-15); *Chronicum Scotorum*, s.a. [857] (ed. and trans. Hennessy, pp. 154-55). The *Gallgoídil* were led by Caitill Find. Alfred Smyth has proposed that he was the same as a Hebridean chieftain, Ketill flatnefr, named in Icelandic sagas: *Scandinavian Kings*, pp. 117-19; cf. *Laxdœla saga*, §§1-4 (ed. Einar Ól Sveinsson, pp. 1-9; 'The Saga', trans. Kunz, pp. 276-78). This view has rightly been criticised by Donnchadh Ó Corráin, 'High-Kings', p. 301: there is no reason to assume that a Ketill named in thirteenth-century sagas was the same as a man of a similar name active in Southern Ireland in 857. It is just conceivable that Caitill Find may have been active in Wales before pursuing a career in Ireland: *Annales Cambriae* (ABC), ed. and trans. Dumville, pp. 10-11; *ByS*, ed. and trans. Jones, pp. 18-19; *ByT* (Pen. 20), ed. Jones, p. 4; *ByT* (Pen. 20), trans. Jones, p. 4; *ByT* (RBH) ed. and trans. Jones, pp. 6-7.

[45] *Annals of the Four Masters*, s.a. 856 [=858] (ed. and trans. O'Donovan, I, 490-91); *Chronicum Scotorum*, s.a. [858] (ed. and trans. Hennessy, pp. 156-57); *Fragmentary Annals*, §263 (ed. and trans. Radner, pp. 104-05). These *Gallgoídil* are identified as being from Leth Cuinn (the northern half of Ireland, which included Meath). This may reinforce the theory that *Gallgoídil* were acting as agents of, or in alliance with, Mael Sechlainn.

territory along the eastern border of Munster. He is one of the most famous kings of the Viking Age in Ireland because of a saga about his deeds which was preserved in 'The Fragmentary Annals of Ireland'.[46] Cerball had strengthened his position during the decline of the power of provincial overkings in Munster. In 859 he sought to challenge the supremacy of Mael Sechlainn by allying with Ívarr and Óláfr in an attack on Meath, the heartland of Southern Uí Néill territories.[47] As a consequence of this raid, a royal meeting was held at Rathugh, in the territory of Cenél Fiachach, in the same year. At this gathering Cerball submitted to Mael Sechlainn and shed his allegiance with Óláfr and Ívarr, who thereafter became his enemies.[48]

Following the royal conference at Rathugh, Óláfr and Ívarr aligned themselves with another enemy of Mael Sechlainn, the overking of the Northern Uí Néill, Aed Finnliath. In 860 Mael Sechlainn and Cerball led an army against the Northern Uí Néill to Moy, near Armagh, but failed to secure a decisive victory.[49] This prompted Aed and Óláfr to lead raiding expeditions against Meath in 861 and 862, although an effective defence was mounted in both years.[50]

According to 'The Fragmentary Annals of Ireland' Aed cemented his alliance with Óláfr by giving his daughter to him in marriage. This may have been the first in a series of alliances between the descendants of Aed Finnliath and the family of Ívarr.[51] These families were drawn together at

---

[46] Downham, 'The Career'; Downham, 'The Good'.

[47] In this period the territory of Meath (in Irish *Mide* which meant 'Middle') corresponded with modern Counties Westmeath, Meath and neighbouring areas. It should not be confused with the area of modern County Meath: Downham, 'The Vikings', p. 242.

[48] *Annals of the Four Masters, s.a.* 857 [=859] (ed. and trans. O'Donovan, I, 490-93); *Annals of Ulster, s.a.* 858 [=859].3 (ed. and trans. Mac Airt and Mac Niocaill, pp. 316-17) ; *Chronicum Scotorum, s.a.* [859] (ed. and trans. Hennessy, pp. 156-57). Perhaps in a related event the king of Munster was stoned to death by vikings in the same year.

[49] *Annals of the Four Masters, s.a.* 858 [=860] (ed. and trans. O'Donovan, I, 492-93); *Annals of Ulster, s.a.* 859 [=860].1 (ed. and trans. Mac Airt and Mac Niocaill, pp. 316-17); *Chronicum Scotorum, s.a.* [860] (ed. and trans. Hennessy, pp. 156-57); *Fragmentary Annals*, §279 (ed. and trans. Radner, pp. 110-11); Hogan, *Onomasticon*, p. 525.

[50] *Annals of the Four Masters, s.aa.* 859 [=861/862], 860 [=862] (ed. and trans. O'Donovan, I, 492-95); *Annals of Ulster, s.aa.* 860 [=861].1, 861 [=862].2 (ed. and trans. Mac Airt and Mac Niocaill, pp. 318-19); *Chronicum Scotorum, s.a.* [861] (ed. and trans. Hennessy, pp. 156-57).

[51] *Fragmentary Annals* §292 (ed. and trans. Radner, pp. 112-13). Information from the saga-element of this text cannot be relied upon as accurate.

times when both opposed the overkings of the Southern Uí Néill. The northern and southern branches of Uí Néill were rivals for supremacy in Ireland, and the Southern Uí Néill and the viking port of Dublin were uncomfortable neighbours. Nevertheless the Northern Uí Néill and the vikings of Dublin also struggled against each other many times. These clashes and alliances signify the prominence that was rapidly acquired by the 'Dark Foreigners' in Irish politics.

Mael Sechlainn died in 862.[52] During his reign he had subjected the overkings of Munster and Leinster to his authority, perhaps assisted by his *Gall-goídil* allies. After his death, Meath was divided between two rulers, Lorcán son of Cathal and Conchobar son of Donnchad. The viking kings Óláfr, Ívarr, and Ásl sought to exploit the political divisions within the ruling dynasty of Meath and to extend their control over Southern Uí Néill territories from their base in Dublin. In 863 they allied with Lorcán and plundered the lands of Brega.[53] In 864 Óláfr drowned Lorcán's rival Conchobar at the church of Clonard, which was one of the major ecclesiastical establishments that received patronage from the overkings of Meath.[54]

Óláfr and his allies may have also sought to extend their influence south of Dublin by campaigning in Leinster. In 863, Muirecán son of Diarmait, overking of Uí Dúnchada was slain by vikings. The chronicles which report Muirecán's death identify him as king of Naas and the eastern plain of the River Liffey – the geographical limitations of this label indicate the political decline of his dynasty: thirty years before, its leaders had claimed to be

---

[52] *Annals of Clonmacnoise, s.a.* 859 [=862] (ed. Murphy, p. 141); *Annals of the Four Masters, s.a.* 860 [=862] (ed. and trans. O'Donovan, I, 494-95); *Annals of Ulster, s.a.* 861 [=862].5 (ed. and trans. Mac Airt and Mac Niocaill, pp. 318-19); *Chronicum Scotorum, s.a.* [862] (ed. and trans. Hennessy, pp. 156-57).

[53] *Annals of the Four Masters, s.a.* 861 [=863] (ed. and trans. O'Donovan, I, 496-97); *Annals of Ulster, s.a.* 862 [=863].4 (ed. and trans. Mac Airt and Mac Niocaill, pp. 318-19). This territory was ruled by Flann son of Conaing who had been a former ally of Óláfr, in 861 and 862, against Maelsechlainn.

[54] *Annals of Clonmacnoise, s.a.* 862 [=864] (ed. Murphy, p. 141); *Annals of the Four Masters, s.a.* 862 [=864] (ed. and trans. O'Donovan, I, 498-99); *Annals of Ulster, s.a.* 863 [=864].2 (ed. and trans. Mac Airt and Mac Niocaill, pp. 320-21); *Chronicum Scotorum, s.a.* [864] (ed. and trans. Hennessy, pp. 158-59). Suairlech (*ob.* 870), abbot of Clonard, had led the clerics of Meath at the royal conferences at Rathugh: Byrne, 'The Community', p. 163.

overkings of all Leinster.[55] This loss of influence may be attributed both to the successful career of Mael Sechlainn, overking of the Southern Uí Néill, who had imposed his authority over the men of Leinster. The decline may also have resulted from successive viking raids from Dublin.

After the notable successes of Óláfr, Ívarr and Ásl in Ireland in the early 860s, the three kings decided to pursue ambitions in Britain. Ívarr seems to have been away from Ireland from 864 until 871, and his career can be traced in England and Strathclyde.[56] In 866 Óláfr and Ásl went to Pictland with an army of vikings from Ireland and Britain.[57] The absence of these kings from Ireland may have encouraged native kings to challenge viking power. In 865 or 866 Flann son of Conaing, overking of Brega, won a battle against vikings.[58] This engagement may have been initiated by Flann as an act of revenge because his territory had been raided by Óláfr, Ívarr, and Ásl in 863. A series of viking camps in the north-east of Ireland was destroyed by the overking of the Northern Uí Néill, Aed Finnliath, in 866, although it is not clear if these bases were linked with Óláfr and his associates or with a rival group of vikings.[59] Vikings also faced defeat in Munster with the destruction of viking camps at Cork and Youghal (Co. Cork) and the rout of a viking army in Kerry.[60] In Leinster, vikings were defeated in battle on at least two occasions in 866 and 867. During these campaigns Óláfr's fort at Clondalkin, close to Dublin, was destroyed and

---

[55] *Annals of the Four Masters*, s.a. 861 [=863] (ed. and trans. O'Donovan, I, 496-97); *Annals of Ulster*, s.a. 862 [=863].2 (ed. and trans. Mac Airt and Mac Niocaill, pp. 318-19); *Chronicum Scotorum*, s.a. [863] (ed. and trans. Hennessy, pp. 158-59); Byrne, *Irish Kings*, pp. 162-63.

[56] See pp. 64-67, 139-42 below.

[57] *Annals of Clonmacnoise*, s.a. 864 [=866] (ed. Murphy, p. 141); *Annals of Ulster*, s.a. 865 [=866].1 (ed. and trans. Mac Airt and Mac Niocaill, pp. 320-21).

[58] *Fragmentary Annals*, §326 (ed. and trans. Radner, pp. 118-19).

[59] *Annals of Clonmacnoise*, s.a. 864 [=866] (ed. Murphy, p. 141); *Annals of the Four Masters*, s.a. 864 [=866] (ed. and trans. O'Donovan, I, 500-01); *Annals of Ulster*, s.a. 865 [=866].4 (ed. and trans. Mac Airt and Mac Niocaill, pp. 320-21).

[60] *Annals of the Four Masters*, s.aa. 864 [=866], 865 [=867] (ed. and trans. O'Donovan, I, 502-05); *Annals of Inisfallen*, s.a. [866] (ed. and trans. Mac Airt, pp. 132-33); *Fragmentary Annals*, §§337-42 (ed. and trans. Radner, pp. 122-25); Hogan, *Onomasticon*, p. 398. The vikings in Kerry were identified as followers of a viking chieftain called Þórarr: Downham, 'Tomrar's death'.

one hundred heads of viking chieftains were said to have been gathered together as trophies by the victors.[61]

These setbacks may have brought Óláfr back to Ireland. In addition to the Irish attacks on viking bases, Óláfr's significance in Ireland may have been further compromised by the murder of Ásl in 867, as a result of internecine conflict.[62] 'The Annals of Inisfallen' attest to Óláfr's return to Ireland in 867 when he committed an unspecified act of treachery against the church of Lismore (Co. Waterford) in Munster.[63] The overking of the Northern Uí Néill, Aed Finnliath, appears to have relinquished his support for Óláfr at this time. Óláfr's son Carlus (Charles) fell in battle against Aed in 868. This battle, fought at Killineer (Co. Louth) by the River Boyne, was reported at length in a number of chronicles and it must have been regarded as a significant event.[64] Óláfr responded in the following year by attacking Armagh, the most important church under the patronage of the Northern Uí Néill overkings.[65]

In 870 the situation for the vikings in Dublin was improved by divisions among the ruling elite in Leinster and by the defeat of a king of southern Brega by a 'Dark foreigner' called Úlfr.[66] In the same year Óláfr went to North Britain where he campaigned with Ívarr. The two kings returned in 871, bringing many shiploads of slaves captured from England and

[61] *Annals of Clonmacnoise*, s.a. 865 [=867] (ed. Murphy, p. 142); *Annals of the Four Masters*, s.aa. 864 [=866], 865 [=867] (ed. and trans. O'Donovan, I, 502-05); *Annals of Ulster*, s.a. 866 [=867].8 (ed. and trans. Mac Airt and Mac Niocaill, pp. 322-23); *Fragmentary Annals*, §§329, 349 (ed. and trans. Radner, pp. 118-19, 128-29).

[62] *Annals of Clonmacnoise*, s.a. 865 [=867] (ed. Murphy, p. 142); *Annals of Ulster*, s.a. 866 [=867].6 (ed. and trans. Mac Airt and Mac Niocaill, pp. 322-23).

[63] *Annals of Inisfallen*, s.a. [867] (ed. and trans. Mac Airt, pp. 134-35).

[64] *Annals of Boyle*, §255 ('The Annals', ed. Freeman, p. 325); *Annals of Clonmacnoise*, s.a. 866 [=868] (ed. Murphy, p. 142); *Annals of the Four Masters*, s.aa. 866 [=868] (ed. and trans. O'Donovan, I, 504-09); *Annals of Inisfallen*, s.a. [868] (ed. and trans. Mac Airt, pp. 134-35); *Annals of Ulster*, s.a. 867 [=868].4 (ed. and trans. Mac Airt and Mac Niocaill, pp. 322-25); *Chronicum Scotorum*, s.a. [868] (ed. and trans. Hennessy, pp. 160-61); Hogan, *Onomasticon*, p. 214; O'Dononvan (ed. and trans., *Annals of the Four Masters*, I, 504, note a) suggested that the battle was located at Killaderry Co. Dublin.

[65] *Annals of Clonmacnoise*, s.a. 867 [=869] (ed. Murphy, p. 142); *Annals of Ulster*, s.a. 868 [=869].6 (ed. and trans. Mac Airt and Mac Niocaill, pp. 324-25).

[66] *Annals of Clonmacnoise*, s.a. 868 [=870] (ed. Murphy, p. 143); *Annals of Ulster*, s.a. 869 [=870].7 (ed. and trans. Mac Airt and Mac Niocaill, pp. 326-27); *Chronicum Scotorum*, s.a. [870] (ed. and trans. Hennessy, pp. 162-63).

Strathclyde to trade in the markets of Dublin.[67] Óláfr then went back to Britain where he was killed in an attempt to gather tribute from the Picts.[68] His associate Ívarr remained in Ireland. Recognition of Ívarr's importance in Irish and British affairs is shown by the title 'king of the Northmen of all Ireland and Britain' assigned to him in the 'Annals of Ulster' at his death in 873.[69] Nevertheless, it was the achievements of Ívarr's sons and grandsons that was to secure the fame of his dynasty, as much as the deeds which he performed in his own lifetime.

The Next Generation

In the next generation the economic and political significance of Dublin continued to grow. This is suggested by the evidence of silver-hoards deposited in the east and midlands of Ireland.[70] It is also evidenced by viking burials which have been recovered at a number of sites across a wide area in Dublin. The grave-finds provide a view of the lives of ninety or more the early settlement's elite, showing their celebration of military prowess through the prevalence of weaponry, and their beliefs in an afterlife. The graves also show the early settlers' economic activity and external contacts through the presence of weights, scales and prestige items from Scandinavia and continental Europe.[71] The evidence suggests that Dublin quickly became part of a long-distance viking trading network.[72] The success of Dublin may have helped to establish Ívarr's dynasty, which was to rule this port until the twelfth century. Nevertheless the early attempts of the sons of Ívarr to strengthen their position in Ireland were threatened by family-rivalries and external hostility during the final years of the ninth century.

---

[67] *Annals of Ulster*, *s.a.* 870 [=871].2 (ed. and trans. Mac Airt and Mac Niocaill, pp. 326-27); *Chronicum Scotorum*, *s.a.* [871] (ed. and trans. Hennessy, pp. 162-63).

[68] See below, p. 142.

[69] *Annals of Boyle*, §256 ('The Annals', ed. Freeman, p. 325); *Annals of the Four Masters*, *s.a.* 871[=873] (ed. and trans. O'Donovan, I, 518-19); *Annals of Ulster*, *s.a.* 872 [=873].3 (ed. and trans. Mac Airt and Mac Niocaill, pp. 328-29); *Chronicum Scotorum*, *s.a.* [873] (ed. and trans. Hennessy, pp. 164-65).

[70] Sheehan, 'Early Viking-Age Silver', pp. 171-72.

[71] Ó Floinn, 'The Archaeology', pp. 131-43.

[72] Valante, 'Urbanization', p. 98.

After Ívarr's death his son Bárðr took control of Dublin. One of Bárðr's first actions was to lead a raid against the south-west of Ireland, perhaps to demonstrate his newly won authority.[73] Nevertheless, divisions were beginning to emerge among the leaders of the 'Dark Foreigners'. A son of Óláfr, called Eysteinn, was killed in 875 by Hálfdan brother of Ívarr, who had recently arrived from Britain, perhaps in a bid to win power in Ireland.[74] After a brief sojourn in England, Hálfdan led a campaign against 'Fair Foreigners' based at Strangford Lough on the north-east coast of Ireland, where he was killed in 877.[75] This event highlights the continued existence of viking groups other than the 'Dark Foreigners' within Ireland.[76] The 'Fair Foreigners' followed up their success in 879, by raiding the church of Armagh and capturing the abbot who was later freed (perhaps after the payment of a ransom).[77] Such a raid would have been a deliberate insult to the incumbent overking of the Northern Uí Néill, Aed Finnliath.

Bárðr may have strengthened his position in Ireland by making an alliance with the Northern Uí Néill overking, who had previously been both an ally and an enemy of Óláfr. According to 'The Fragmentary Annals of Ireland', Bárðr fostered a son of Aed Finnliath.[78] It is impossible to verify this information, as the statement comes from an eleventh-century saga-element within the text. Nevertheless the author of this saga did draw a share of his information from earlier written accounts and there is evidence for further ties between the descendants of Ívarr and Aed.[79] Fosterage was an institution which could strengthen alliances. In particular it offered benefits to an outsider, or lower-status king, who could become integrated into the family of a stronger or more established ruler.[80] Bárðr may have also sought to associate himself with the Irish political elite by marriage, for

---

[73] *Annals of the Four Masters*, s.a. 871[=873] (ed. and trans. O'Donovan, I, 518-19); *Annals of Inisfallen*, s.a. [873] (ed. and trans. Mac Airt, pp. 134-35).

[74] *Annals of Ulster*, s.a. 874 [=875].4 (ed. and trans. Mac Airt and Mac Niocaill, pp. 330-31).

[75] *Annals of Ulster*, s.a. 876 [=877].5 (ed. and trans. Mac Airt and Mac Niocaill, pp. 332-33); *Chronicum Scotorum*, s.a. [877] (ed. and trans. Hennessy, pp. 166-67).

[76] Downham, 'Irish Chronicles'.

[77] *Annals of Ulster*, s.aa. 878 [=879].6, 887 [=888].1 (ed. and trans. Mac Airt and Mac Niocaill, pp. 334-35, 342-43); *Chronicum Scotorum*, s.aa. [879], [888] (ed. and trans. Hennessy, pp. 166-67, 170-71).

[78] *Fragmentary Annals*, §408 (ed. and trans. Radner, pp. 146-47).

[79] e.g. *Annals of Ulster*, s.aa. 913 [=914].3, 920 [=921].7 (ed. and trans. Mac Airt and Mac Niocaill, pp. 360-63, 372-73); See below, p. 40.

[80] Parkes, 'Celtic Fosterage'.

one of his sons, Uathmarán, bore an Irish name derived from the Irish word *uathmar*, meaning 'awesome'.[81]

Bárðr died in Dublin in 881 soon after a raid on the church of Duleek in Brega (Co. Meath).[82] He was succeeded by his brother Sigfrøðr son of Ívarr. There is evidence that during his reign 'Fair Foreigners' were acting in alliance with the Southern Uí Néill against the 'Dark Foreigners'. In 883 a viking leader caller Óttar son of Iarnkné was allied with Muirgel, a daughter of Mael Sechlainn (the king who had fought so vigorously against Ívarr and his associates). Together they are said to have caused the death of a son of Ásl, although the circumstances are unknown.[83] Three years later Óttar's brother Heløri was campaigning in Ulster, and his death in Connaught is reported in 891.[84] Óttar's family may have briefly come to the fore as rivals of the sons of Ívarr due to the weakness of Sigfrøðr who was killed by a kinsman in 888.[85]

Another son of Ívarr, Sigtryggr, succeeded to the kingship. Despite the evident political unease, vikings of Dublin fought effectively against both the Southern Uí Néill and Northern Leinster in the late 880s and early 890s.[86] Sigtryggr was challenged in 893 by a jarl (also called) Sigfrøðr who is mentioned in English sources.[87] It is possible that this jarl had some claim to the throne of Dublin by being a member of the same kin-group. Both leaders, Sigfrøðr and Sigtryggr, left Ireland in 893 (with separate fleets) to engage in warfare in Britain. Sigtryggr returned the following year, but it is

---

[81] Ó Cuív, 'Personal Names', p. 80.

[82] *Annals of the Four Masters*, s.a. 878 [=881] (ed. and trans. O'Donovan, I, 526-27); *Annals of Ulster*, s.a. 880 [=881].3 (ed. and trans. Mac Airt and Mac Niocaill, pp. 336-37); *Chronicum Scotorum*, s.a. [881] (ed. and trans. Hennessy, pp. 166-67).

[83] *Annals of Ulster*, s.a. 882 [=883].4 (ed. and trans. Mac Airt and Mac Niocaill, pp. 336-37); *Chronicum Scotorum*, s.a. [883] (ed. and trans. Hennessy, pp. 168-69).

[84] *Annals of the Four Masters*, s.aa. 885 [=886], 887 [=891] (ed. and trans. O'Donovan, I, 538-41); *Annals of Ulster*, s.a. 885 [=886].1 (ed. and trans. Mac Airt and Mac Niocaill, pp. 342-43); *Chronicum Scotorum*, s.aa. [886], [891] (ed. and trans. Hennessy, pp. 168-73).

[85] *Annals of Clonmacnoise*, s.a. 888 (ed. Murphy, p. 143); *Annals of Ulster*, s.a. 887 [=888].6 (ed. and trans. Mac Airt and Mac Niocaill, pp. 344-45); *Chronicum Scotorum*, s.a. [888] (ed. and trans. Hennessy, pp. 170-71).

[86] *Annals of the Four Masters*, s.aa. 885 [=888], 886 [=890], 887 [=891] (ed. and trans. O'Donovan, I, 536-41); *Annals of Ulster*, s.a. 887 [=888].5 (ed. and trans. Mac Airt and Mac Niocaill, pp. 344-45); *Chronicum Scotorum*, s.aa. [888], [891] (ed. and trans. Hennessy, pp. 170-73).

[87] *Annals of Ulster*, s.a. 892 [=893].4 (ed. and trans. Mac Airt and Mac Niocaill, pp. 346-47). See below, p. 73.

not clear whether he retained his position in Ireland.[88] He was killed by other vikings in 896.[89] He may have been succeeded by Glúniarann who led the vikings of Dublin in an attack on Armagh in 895.[90] No clue is given as to Glúniarann's origins, although the name appears later within the dynasty of Ívarr.[91] It is an Irish rendering of the Norse name Iarnkné 'Iron-knee'. No further deeds of Glúniarann are recorded in Irish chronicles. The troubled circumstances of the Dublin kingship are highlighted by the ambiguity as to who was leading the port at this time.

In 896 viking activity had focused on the area north of Dublin. Glúntradna son of Glúniarann and Óláfr, grandson of Ívarr, fell in battle against Aiteid, overking of Ulster, in Conaille, a territory north of Brega on Ireland's east coast. It may have been a result of their campaigns that Flannacán son of Cellach, overking of Brega (a region north of Dublin), was killed by vikings.[92] The death of three prominent viking leaders in 896 had a deleterious effect on the political stability of Dublin. [93]

In 902 two major enemies of Dublin joined forces to exploit these difficulties. Mael Finnia son of Flannacán, the overking of Brega (whose father had been killed by vikings in 896), and Cerball son of Muirecán, overking of Leinster, attacked the port. The result was dramatic and momentous. 'The Annals of Ulster' describe the expulsion of the 'heathens' from Dublin, who left many of their ships to escape 'half dead after they

---

[88] In 895 a son of Ívarr, perhaps Sigtryggr, was allied with the Southern Uí Néill: *Annals of the Four Masters*, s.a. 890 [=895] (ed. and trans. O'Donovan, I, 546-47).

[89] *Annals of the Four Masters*, s.a. 891 [=896] (ed. and trans. O'Donovan, I, 548-49); *Annals of Ulster*, s.a. 895 [=896].3 (ed. and trans. Mac Airt and Mac Niocaill, pp. 348-49).

[90] *Annals of the Four Masters*, s.a. 890 [=895] (ed. and trans. O'Donovan, I, 546-47); *Annals of Ulster*, s.a. 894 [=895].6 (ed. and trans. Mac Airt and Mac Niocaill, pp. 348-49).

[91] *Annals of Inisfallen*, s.a. [989] (ed. and trans. Mac Airt, pp. 168-69); *Annals of the Four Masters*, s.a. 1031 (ed. and trans. O'Donovan, II, 822-23).

[92] *Annals of the Four Masters*, s.a. 891 [=896] (ed. and trans. O'Donovan, I, 546-49); *Annals of Ulster*, s.a. 895 [=896].9 (ed. and trans. Mac Airt and Mac Niocaill, pp. 350-51); *Chronicum Scotorum*, s.a. [896] (ed. and trans. Hennessy, pp. 174-75).

[93] Nevertheless, Dubliners may have been involved in viking attacks on Leinster in 900: *Chronicum Scotorum*, s.a. [900] (ed. and trans. Hennessy, pp. 176-77). Other campaigns were led by vikings in the north-east of Ireland during these years, but the leaders of these armies are not named: *Annals of the Four Masters*, s.a. 895 [=900] (ed. and trans. O'Donovan, I, 552-55).

had been wounded and broken'.[94] One group took refuge on 'Ireland's Eye', a small island off the coast of Brega, where their enemies proceeded to besiege them.[95]

The family of Ívarr do not figure again in Irish chronicles for over a decade. Radiocarbon-data suggest that Dublin was still occupied during this period.[96] Perhaps the chronicle-records of the expulsion of the heathens or foreigners of Dublin in 902 refer only to the elite. Such was the stratified nature of medieval society that ordinary people were largely ignored in these accounts. It may be that a segment of the population remained, simply paying their dues to a new Irish overking. A huge silver-hoard deposited at Drogheda about 905 may represent money acquired by Flannacán of Brega as a result of his role in the attack.[97] The distribution of silver-hoards in the following decade suggests that overkings of the Southern Uí Néill later reaped the economic benefits of Dublin's subjection.[98] The capture of Dublin was a major blow to the power of Ívarr's descendants. It had no doubt been facilitated by rivalries among viking leaders, which had divided the people of Dublin into factions in the 890s. The expulsion was to have a knock-on effect in Britain, and in particular it may have impacted negatively on the fortunes of vikings in England.[99]

The Expulsion from Dublin and the Return of the Dynasty

The vikings who were expelled from Ireland divided into various groups. Some may have travelled to France.[100] Others went to Britain. 'The Fragmentary Annals of Ireland' and Welsh chronicles give an account of the arrival of a viking leader Ingimundr on Anglesey in 903 and his subsequent

---

[94] *Annals of the Four Masters*, s.a. 897 [=902] (ed. and trans. O'Donovan, I, 556-57); *Annals of Ulster*, s.a. 901 [=902].2 (ed. and trans. Mac Airt and Mac Niocaill, pp. 352-53); *Chronicum Scotorum*, s.a. [902] (ed. and trans. Hennessy, pp. 178-79).

[95] *Annals of the Four Masters*, s.a. 897 [=902] (ed. and trans. O'Donovan, I, 556-57).

[96] Simpson, 'Forty Years', p. 25.

[97] Graham-Campbell, 'The Viking-Age Silver', p. 48.

[98] Downham, 'The Vikings', p. 251.

[99] See below, pp. 83-86.

[100] Mac Shamhráin, *The Vikings*, pp. 75-79; Musset, *Nordica*, pp. 279-96; Picard, 'Early Contacts', p. 92; Mawer, *The Vikings*, p. 51.

Figure 5: The family of Ívarr

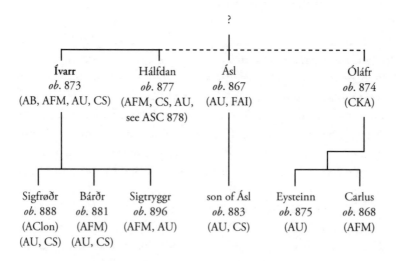

arrival in Cheshire.[101] The evidence of the impressive silver-hoard recovered at Cuerdale in Lancashire favours the view that a contingent allied with vikings from York in an abortive plan to re-conquer Dublin.[102] Two battles were also fought in Pictland by grandsons of Ívarr in 904.[103]

Alfred Smyth and Donnchadh Ó Corráin have argued that the Hebrides were a major sphere of activity of exiles from Dublin during the first decades of the tenth century.[104] This theory is supported by evidence of viking activity on the north coast of Ireland. The perception that vikings were entirely absent from Irish affairs in the years from 902 to 914

---

[101] *Fragmentary Annals*, §429 (ed. and trans. Radner, pp. 168-69); *Annales Cambriae*, *s.a.* [902] (ed. and trans. Dumville, pp. 14-15); *ByS*, *s.a.* 900 [=903] (ed. and trans. Jones, pp. 26-27); *ByT* (Pen. 20), *s.a.* 900 [=903] (ed. Jones, pp. 6-7; trans. Jones, p. 6); *ByT* (RBH), *s.a.* [903] (ed. and trans. Jones, pp. 10-11).

[102] See below, pp. 78-79, 83.

[103] *Annals of Ulster*, *s.a.* 903 [=904].4 (ed. and trans. Mac Airt and Mac Niocaill, pp. 354-55); *Chronicum Scotorum*, *s.a.* [904] (ed. and trans. Hennessy, pp. 180-81).

[104] Smyth, *Scandinavian York*, I, 61; Ó Corráin, 'The Vikings in Scotland', p. 336.

Figure 6: The Grandsons of Ívarr and Royal Succession at Dublin to 1014

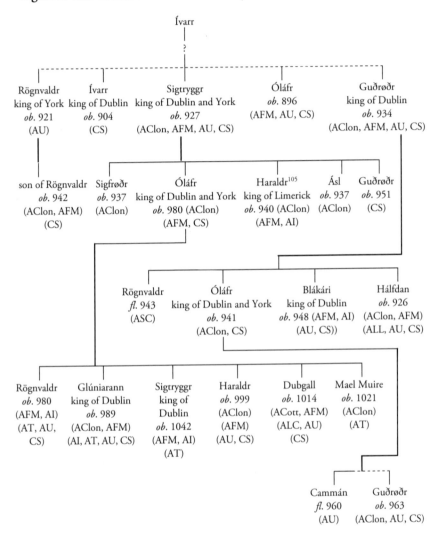

[105] Todd identified Haraldr as a son of Sigtryggr Ívarsson, who died in 896: *Annals of the Four Masters*, s.a. 891 [=896].14 (ed. and trans. O'Donovan, I, 548–49); *Annals of Ulster*, s.a. 895 [=896].3 (ed. and trans. Mac Airt and Mac Niocaill, pp. 348–49); *Cogadh*, ed. and trans. Todd, p. 271. However, *Chronicum Scotorum*, s.a. [939] [=940].2, identifies him as 'Haraldr, son of the grandson of Ívarr, namely the son of Sigtryggr, king of the foreigners of Limerick' (Aralt mac .H. Imair .i. mac Sitric, rí Gall Luimnigh), ed. and trans. Hennessy, pp. 202–3. This indicates that Sigtryggr, grandson of Ívarr, was his father.

is challenged by this northern evidence.[106] In 904 vikings plundered Ailech (Elagh, bar. Inishowen, Co. Donegal).[107] This was the royal seat of the Northern Uí Néill overkings of Cenél nEogain. This raid coincides with a war between two brothers of the leading dynasty: Domnall and Niall, sons of Aed Finnliath.[108] The timing of this raid could suggest that these vikings were well informed of events in the region. Viking leaders in the Hebrides would have been well placed to receive such intelligence.

Further viking operations are reported off the north-east coast of Ireland during the exile of Ívarr's family from Ireland. In 913 a sea-battle is reported between a fleet from Ulster and vikings off the English coast.[109] In the following year two viking fleets clashed near Man. In this engagement Rögnvaldr, grandson of Ívarr, defeated his rival, Bárðr son of Óttar.[110] In addition to historical evidence for viking fleets around the north coast of Ireland, three silver-hoards were deposited about 910 in the north-eastern counties of Down, Antrim, and Londonderry.[111] These suggest viking contact with north-eastern coasts of Ireland. The location of these finds has greater significance because most silver-hoards are found in the central and east midlands of Ireland.[112] These northern hoards are therefore rather unusual, and their closeness in date of deposition is striking. A link between Ívarr's family and the Hebrides in the early years of the tenth century could

[106] An overking of Ulster named *Dubgall*, 'Dark foreigner' (Modern English 'Dougal'), died in 925. His name may reflect an alliance between Ulster and 'Dark Foreigners' in the late ninth century or during their period of expulsion from Dublin: *Annals of Ulster, s.a.* 924 [=925].1 (ed. and trans. Mac Airt and Mac Niocaill, pp. 376-77).

[107] *Annals of the Four Masters, s.a.* 900 [=904] (ed. and trans. O'Donovan, I, 560-61); *Annals of Ulster, s.a.* 903 [=904].4 (ed. and trans. Mac Airt and Mac Niocaill, pp. 354-55); *Chronicum Scotorum, s.a.* [904] (ed. and trans. Hennessy, pp. 180-81); Hogan, *Onomasticon*, p. 17.

[108] *Annals of the Four Masters, s.a.* 900 [=904] (ed. and trans. O'Donovan, I, 560-61); *Annals of Ulster, s.a.* 904 [=905?].4 (ed. and trans. Mac Airt and Mac Niocaill, pp. 354-55; this entry is an interlinear addition by an unidentified hand).

[109] *Annals of Ulster, s.a.* 912 [=913].5 (ed. and trans. Mac Airt and Mac Niocaill, pp. 360-61).

[110] *Annals of Ulster, s.a.* 913 [=914].4 (ed. and trans. Mac Airt and Mac Niocaill, pp. 362-63).

[111] Graham-Campbell, 'Some Archaeological Reflections', p. 344; Graham-Campbell, 'A "Vital" Yorkshire Viking Hoard', p. 80. In addition a furnished burial has been discovered at Larne (Co. Antrim) which has been dated to the late ninth or early tenth century: Harrison, 'Viking Graves', p. 66.

[112] Sheehan, 'Early Viking-Age Silver', pp. 198-202.

also have laid the foundation for this dynasty's subsequent control of these islands.[113]

The re-establishment of viking power in Ireland can be dated to 914. In this year a 'great fleet of boats' arrived at Waterford Harbour.[114] This may be identified with the fleet led by a jarl Óttar which travelled from Brittany to Ireland via Wales in this year, which is recorded in 'The Anglo-Saxon Chronicle'.[115] Óttar may have been an enemy of the dynasty of Ívarr. He may have been the father of Bárðr who fought a naval battle against Rögnvaldr, grandson of Ívarr, in the same year.[116] In 915 more vikings settled at Waterford and they raided churches and other settlements throughout Munster. It is not clear if these were directed by the dynasty of Ívarr or whether they unwittingly set the scene for their return by establishing a foothold in the island which was then seized. In 917 Rögnvaldr and Sigtryggr, grandsons of Ívarr, led their fleets to Ireland.[117] Rögnvaldr took Waterford and Sigtryggr took his army to Glynn, a site near the River Barrow, on the border of Leinster.[118] Niall son of Aed waged war against vikings in Munster but was defeated by the forces of Rögnvaldr. At Glynn, Sigtryggr defeated an army of the Leinstermen with heavy losses

---

[113] See below, pp. 177-79.

[114] *Annals of the Four Masters*, *s.a.* 910 [=914] (ed. and trans. O'Donovan, II, 580-81); *Annals of Ulster*, *s.a.* 913 [=914].5 (ed. and trans. Mac Airt and Mac Niocaill, pp. 362-63); *Chronicum Scotorum*, *s.a.* [913] [=914] (ed. and trans. Hennessy, pp. 186-87); *Dictionary*, ed. Quin *et al.* p. 479, col. 51, ll. 20-69; Downham, 'The Historical Importance', p. 83.

[115] *ASC.A*, ed. Bately, p. 65; *ASC.B*, ed. Taylor, p. 48; *ASC C*, ed. O'Keeffe, p. 74; *ASC D*, ed. Cubbin, p. 39; *Annals of Ulster*, *s.a.* 917 [=918].4 (ed. and trans. Mac Airt and Mac Niocaill, pp. 368-69); Price, 'The Vikings', p. 360.

[116] *Annals of Ulster*, *s.a.* 913 [=914].4 (ed. and trans. Mac Airt and Mac Niocaill, pp. 362-63).

[117] *Annals of Clonmacnoise*, *s.a.* 910 [=915] (ed. Murphy, p. 145); *Annals of the Four Masters*, *s.aa.* 913 [=915], 915 [=917] (ed. and trans. O'Donovan, II, 584-91); *Annals of Ulster*, *s.aa.* 914 [=915].7, 916 [=917].2 (ed. and trans. Mac Airt and Mac Niocaill, pp. 364-67); *Chronicum Scotorum*, *s.a.* [914] [=915] (ed. and trans. Hennessy, pp. 186-87).

[118] Hogan, *Onomasticon*, p. 226. The identification of this site is supported by its location on the border of Leinster, its proximity to Waterford and the reference in the *Annals of the Four Masters*, *s.a.* 915 [=917] (ed. and trans. O'Donovan, I, 590-91) that the battle was fought by Tech Moling. For an alternative location in the barony of Salt, Co. Kildare, see: *ibid.* II, 589, note e, and II, 590, note h; Bhreathnach, 'Columban Churches', p. 12. This alternative location is favoured by the fact that vikings plundered Kildare after the conflict which is nearer to Salt. However I would argue that the attack was motivated by political reasons rather than it being a convenient distance away from the battle field.

on the Irish side. These victories enabled Sigtryggr triumphantly to enter Dublin in 917.[119]

Rögnvaldr departed with a fleet for England in the following year and was soon able to establish his authority over York.[120] This departure of viking troops may have encouraged Niall son of Aed to try once more to expel the dynasty of Ívarr from Ireland. He led a large coalition of troops from Northern and Southern Uí Néill to the south of Dublin. 'The Annals of Ulster' specify the day of the ensuing battle as 14 September 919. The Irish forces were slaughtered and Niall was killed along with one of his kinsmen. There also fell a member of the ruling dynasty of the Southern Uí Néill, the overking of Ulster, and four other kings.[121] The devastating failure of this Irish coalition secured the hold of the descendants of Ívarr over Dublin and Waterford. Nevertheless, warfare continued in the following year between the Southern Uí Néill overking Donnchad son of Flann and the forces of Dublin.[122]

The return of the dynasty of Ívarr to Ireland may have spurred a phase of renewal and re-orientation of the settlements at Dublin and Waterford. Certainly at Dublin there is evidence for a rapid expansion, with more emphasis on the Liffey-waterfront (north of the 'dark pool' which seems to represent the earliest core of settlement).[123] A more organised system of plot-divisions was introduced and by the mid to late tenth century a defensive bank encircled an area between the River Poddle and the Liffey.[124]

---

[119] *Annals of Clonmacnoise*, s.a. 917 (ed. Murphy, p. 146); *Annals of the Four Masters*, s.a. 915 [=917] (ed. and trans. O'Donovan, II, 588-89); *Annals of Ulster*, s.a. 916 [=917].4 (ed. and trans. Mac Airt and Mac Niocaill, pp. 366-67); *Chronicum Scotorum*, s.a. [916] [=917] (ed. and trans. Hennessy, pp. 188-89).

[120] *Annals of the Four Masters*, s.a. 916 [=918] (ed. and trans. O'Donovan, II, 592-93); *Annals of Ulster*, s.a. 917 [=918].4 (ed. and trans. Mac Airt and Mac Niocaill, pp. 368-69); See below, pp. 91-94.

[121] *Annals of Clonmacnoise*, s.a. 915 [=919] (ed. Murphy, p. 146); *Annals of the Four Masters*, s.a. 917 [=919] (ed. and trans. O'Donovan, II, 592-99); *Annals of Ulster*, s.a. 918 [=919].3 (ed. and trans. Mac Airt and Mac Niocaill, pp. 368-71); *Chronicum Scotorum*, s.a. [918] [=919] (ed. and trans. Hennessy, pp. 190-91).

[122] *Annals of Clonmacnoise*, s.a. 916 [=920] (ed. Murphy, pp. 146-47); *Annals of the Four Masters*, s.a. 918 [=920] (ed. and trans. O'Donovan, II, 598-99); *Annals of Ulster*, s.a. 919 [=920].6 (ed. and trans. Mac Airt and Mac Niocaill, pp. 369-71); *Chronicum Scotorum*, s.a. [919] [=920] (ed. and trans. Hennessy, pp. 190-93).

[123] Simpson, 'Viking Warrior Burials', pp. 18, 30, 54-60.

[124] Walsh, 'Dublin's Southern Town Defences'.

At Waterford there may have been a shift in settlement towards Waterford Harbour, which is hinted at in Irish chronicles.[125] There is debate whether Waterford's original settlement lay at Woodstown, three miles upstream on the River Suir. Hopefully future archaeological discoveries will shed light on this matter.[126] These changes in settlement-pattern in the early tenth century may reflect prosperity and the efforts of Ívarr's grandsons (or other prominent landholders) to improve access to major rivers for trade and to help protect the settlements against Irish attacks.

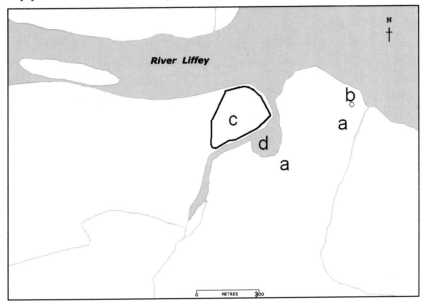

Figure 7: Dublin in the Tenth Century

a = early grave-clusters, **b** = thing-site, **c** = tenth-century embankments, **d** = the 'dark pool' (River Poddle).

For a map of sites farther to the north and west, see Ó Floinn, 'The Archaeology', p. 133.

---

[125] Downham, 'The Historical Importance', pp. 84, 95.

[126] It is possible that Woodstown was a satellite of Waterford, comparable with Óláfr's fort at Clondalkin, which lay six miles west of Dublin. However it would be more exciting if (and therefore I rather hope that) Woodstown represents the original site of Viking Waterford. It is possible that developments at Dublin and Waterford may be compared with those at Staraja Ladoga (the re-organisation and expansion of settlement with new defences) and Novgorod (the relocation of settlement) at a similar time: Duczko, *Viking Rus*, pp. 87, 101.

Sigtryggr moved to York in 920 and his place was taken in Dublin by Guðrøðr grandson of Ívarr.[127] It is not clear whether Sigtryggr, Rögnvaldr and Guðrøðr were brothers or cousins. One reason why patronyms are not given for these grandsons of Ívarr may be because they were children of a daughter (or daughters) of Ívarr.[128] Another possibility is that they were descended from a son (or sons) of Ívarr who pursued a career outside Ireland. Their legitimacy to rule in Ireland, in the eyes of contemporary chroniclers, would therefore be through their grandfather and not their parent, and this might dictate how their names were recorded. Guðrøðr had previously fought in England in a supporting role to Rögnvaldr grandson of Ívarr.[129] It seems that on Rögnvaldr's death in 921 Sigtryggr was next in line to rule York (which was a wealthier town than Dublin) and the lesser partner Guðrøðr was assigned control of Dublin. That this exchange of power occurred seemingly without a battle indicates that three leaders co-operated effectively to re-establish the power of their dynasty in Ireland and England. Nevertheless in the following generation internecine rivalries once more emerged.

Guðrøðr marked his arrival in Ireland by immediately plundering Armagh as a challenge to the power of the Northern Uí Néill. Guðrøðr's decision to spare the most sacred areas of the site may reflect either his religious principles or a desire not to alienate some of his followers who may have been Christian.[130] The heathenism of the Dublin-vikings has been rather overplayed in historians' accounts, and it can be argued that a significant number of vikings in Ireland had accepted Christianity by this time.[131] Guðrøðr's army proceeded to ravage the surrounding area but was

---

[127] *Annals of Clonmacnoise*, s.a. 917 [=921] (ed. Murphy, p. 146); *Annals of the Four Masters*, s.a. 919 [=921] (ed. and trans. O'Donovan, II, 604-05); *Annals of Ulster*, s.aa. 919 [=920].5, 920 [=921].5 (ed. and trans. Mac Airt and Mac Niocaill, pp. 369-73); *Chronicum Scotorum*, s.a. [920] [=921] (ed. and trans. Hennessy, pp. 192-93).

[128] Alex Woolf has put forward this idea in conversation.

[129] *Annals of Ulster*, s.a. 917 [=918].4 (ed. and trans. Mac Airt and Mac Niocaill, pp. 368-69).

[130] *Annals of Clonmacnoise*, s.a. 917 [=921] (ed. Murphy, p. 147); *Annals of the Four Masters*, s.a. 919 [=921] (ed. and trans. O'Donovan, II, 604-05); *Annals of Ulster*, s.a. 920 [=921].8 (ed. and trans. Mac Airt and Mac Niocaill, pp. 372-73); *Chronicum Scotorum*, s.a. [920] [=921] (ed. and trans. Hennessy, pp. 192-93).

[131] Downham, '"Hiberno-Norwegians"'. Johnson, 'An Archaeological and Art Historical Investigation', I, 73-76, 372, discussed ornaments from tenth-century Dublin bearing Christian symbols and other items which may be linked with heathen worship.

routed in a battle against Muirchertach son of Niall, overking of Cenél nEogain. Two fleets of vikings were also led against Northern Uí Néill territories but they failed to secure any victory.[132]

Rivalry with Limerick

During the early years of the tenth century the viking base at Limerick grew in significance and rivalled the settlements at Dublin and Waterford. It is not clear if the site had been settled continually by vikings since the first reference to a camp there in 845.[133] If so, it may have stayed in the hands of 'Fair Foreigners' who were subjected to the descendants of Ívarr.[134] In 921 the death of Rögnvaldr grandson of Ívarr (identified as 'king of Dark and Fair Foreigners') may have provided an opportunity for vikings in the west of Ireland to assert their independence from Dublin.[135] In 922 jarl Þórir Helgason of Limerick led an expedition up the River Shannon. He plundered a number of churches along the river and raided the islands of Lough Ree before turning inland against Meath. His men also raided

---

Thistle-brooches, which were produced and circulated in a Hiberno-Scandinavian milieu, often bear cross-motifs. More ambiguously, saltire-crosses are found on Hiberno-Scandinavian ring-money which circulated in the late ninth and early tenth centuries. Fiona Edmonds ('Hiberno-Saxon and Hiberno-Scandinavian Contact', pp. 167-205) has developed the theory that vikings from Ireland introduced cults of Irish saints into western England in the tenth century. A further point is that adult-baptism was not unknown in Ireland. Therefore, when kings from Dublin were recorded as baptised under the patronage of Anglo-Saxon kings, this does not necessitate that they were pagans beforehand. Spiritual kinship played a more dominant role in Anglo-Saxon society compared to the rest of Britain and Ireland and so royal baptisms are more likely to be recorded in England. Sponsored baptisms of vikings are not recorded in Irish chronicles (but fictive kinship-links of marriage and fosterage with Irish families are): Parkes, 'Celtic Fosterage', p. 374, n. 32; de Bhaldraithe, 'Adult Baptism'.

[132] *Annals of the Four Masters, s.a.* 919 [=921] (ed. and trans. O'Donovan, II, 604-07); *Annals of Ulster, s.a.* 920 [=921].7 (ed. and trans. Mac Airt and Mac Niocaill, pp. 372-73). Other viking raids against churches in Leinster in this year may or may not have been led from Dublin

[133] *Annals of Ulster, s.a.* 845.1 (ed. and trans. Mac Airt and Mac Niocaill, pp. 368-69); *Chronicum Scotorum, s.a.* [887] (ed. and trans. Hennessy, pp. 170-71).

[134] *Annals of Ulster, s.aa.* 916 [=917].2, 917 [=918].4 (ed. and trans. Mac Airt and Mac Niocaill, pp. 366-69). It is possible that Óttar was a leader of the Fair Foreigners of Ireland who was subjected to Rögnvaldr.

[135] *Annals of Ulster, s.a.* 920 [=921].4 (ed. and trans. Mac Airt and Mac Niocaill, pp. 372-73).

westwards into Connaught.[136] The campaign may have been timed to exploit the current conflict between these two provinces. In the following year vikings from Limerick waged war in Munster and succeeded in capturing the overking of the province, Flaithbertach son of Inmainén, although he was later released.[137]

These campaigns won negative attention from the vikings of Dublin. Guðrøðr, grandson of Ívarr, sought to assert his authority against the growing importance of Limerick by taking hostages from the south of Ireland and also by attacking the port in 924. His men were heavily defeated by Þórir.[138] In the same year the king of Limerick, Kolli (or Colla) son of Bárðr, led another campaign along the River Shannon to Lough Ree.[139] This king may have been a son of Bárðr son of Ívarr who died in 881, in which case Limerick hosted a branch of the dynasty of Ívarr which was a rival to Dublin. Alternatively (and I think it more likely in terms of chronology and the pattern of political alliances) Kolli may have been a son of the Bárðr Óttarsson who fought against a grandson of Ívarr in 914.[140] The struggle which was initiated between the vikings of Limerick and those of Dublin in 924 rumbled on until 937.[141]

---

[136] *Annals of Clonmacnoise, s.a.* 918 [=922] (ed. Murphy, p. 147); *Annals of the Four Masters, s.a.* 920 [=922] (ed. and trans. O'Donovan, II, 608-09); *Annals of Inisfallen, s.a.* [922] (ed. and trans. Mac Airt, pp. 146-47); *Annals of Ulster, s.a.* 921 [=922].3 (ed. and trans. Mac Airt and Mac Niocaill, pp. 374-75); *Chronicum Scotorum, s.a.* [921] [=922] (ed. and trans. Hennessy, pp. 192-93).

[137] *Annals of the Four Masters, s.a.* 921 [=923] (ed. and trans. O'Donovan, II, 610-11); *Annals of Ulster, s.a.* 943 [=944].1 (ed. and trans. Mac Airt and Mac Niocaill, pp. 390-91).

[138] *Annals of Ulster, s.a.* 923 [=924].3 (ed. and trans. Mac Airt and Mac Niocaill, pp. 376-77); *Annals of Inisfallen,* s.a. [924] (ed. and trans. Mac Airt, pp. 148-49).

[139] *Annals of the Four Masters, s.a.* 922 [=924] (ed. and trans. O'Donovan, II, 610-11); *Chronicum Scotorum, s.a.* [923] [=924] (ed. and trans. Hennessy, pp. 194-95). I had assumed that the spelling of this name 'Colla' in Irish records was a rendering of the Norse name Kolli; but Kevin Murray rightly pointed out when I gave a paper to the Department of Irish at University College Cork ('Vikings in Munster', 31 March 2004) that this could also be the Irish name Colla adopted by vikings.

[140] *Annals of Ulster, s.a.* 913 [=914].4 (ed. and trans. Mac Airt and Mac Niocaill, pp. 362-63).

[141] The title 'king of Dark and Fair foreigners' was assigned to three separate kings of the dynasty of Ívarr in Irish chronicles: Rögnvaldr (*ob.* 921), Sigtryggr (*ob.* 927) and Óláfr (*ob.* 941). I do not favour the received view that this title meant 'king of the Dark Foreigners of York and the Fair foreigners of Dublin', for this does not tally with the evidence. For example, Rögnvaldr was called 'king of Dark Foreigners' when he ruled Waterford and before he took York: *Annals of the Four Masters, s.a.* 915 [=918] (ed. and trans. O'Donovan,

While Limerick was flexing its muscles in the south-west and midlands of Ireland, Guðrøðr was seeking to extend his influence in Leinster. In 921 and 922 churches in the west of the province were raided by vikings. In 925 the Dubliners captured Faelán son of Muiredach, overking of Leinster, and his sons. They were later released. In the following year armies of Waterford and Dublin attacked Kildare, which was closely linked with Faelán's family.[142] These attacks may have been a bid by the dynasty of Ívarr who ruled both Waterford and Dublin to secure their position in south-east Ireland before battling against the vikings of Limerick.

As Mary Valante has noted in her doctoral dissertation, this rivalry was played out in the foundation of viking camps across Ireland, as each side sought to protect its sphere of influence against the enemy.[143] Although the territorial power of viking bases in Ireland was limited, these ports had widespread economic influence and their rulers cultivated a web of relations with Irish kings which made them major players in Irish politics. Limerick threatened the power of Dublin and Waterford both as a rival base of military and naval power and as a centre for commercial transactions.

In 926 an army from Waterford travelled westwards and founded a camp at Lough Gur, ten miles south of Limerick.[144] A battle was fought in

II, 588-89); *Annals of Ulster, s.aa.* 916 [=917].3, 917 [=918].4, ed. and trans. Mac Airt and Mac Niocaill, pp. 366-69). Óláfr *Cuarán* ruled both York and Dublin, but he is never assigned this title. I would argue that Irish chroniclers used these titles in a way which was meaningful in Ireland where both 'Fair' and 'Dark' Foreigners were recorded in previous years (see Duvmille, 'Old Dubliners', pp. 92-93 for the full list of references). The labels suggest that distinctions between Fair and Dark Foreigners continued in Ireland after the return of the dynasty of Ívarr in 917. The label 'Fair foreigners' falls out of use in Irish chronicles from 941 (until the eleventh century when it was reinterpreted in an anachronistic way). In other words it ceased to be relevant after the death of Óláfr Guðrøðsson who defeated the vikings of Limerick and established the hegemony of the dynasty of Ívarr over viking settlements in Ireland. Titles found in the obits of Irish chronicles recognised the status which individuals had achieved during their life (which did not always match the status which they held when they died).

[142] *Annals of Clonmacnoise, s.aa.* 920 [=925], 921 [=926] (ed. Murphy, p. 148); *Annals of the Four Masters, s.aa.* 923 [=925], 924 [=926] (ed. and trans. O'Donovan, II, 612-15); *Chronicum Scotorum, s.a.* [925] [=926] (ed. and trans. Hennessy, pp. 196-97); Byrne, 'Heads', pp. 261-62.

[143] Valante, 'Urbanization', p. 116.

[144] *Annals of Inisfallen, s.a.* [926] (ed. and trans. Mac Airt, pp. 148-49, and p. 548 *s.v.* Loch Gair); Hogan, *Onomasticon*, p. 499. Another possible location for 'Loch Gair' identified by Hogan was near Fermoy, Co. Cork. There is more evidence for the site near Limerick and this identification was preferred by Mac Airt.

the following year between the vikings of Waterford and Limerick at Kilmallock, roughly twenty-five miles south of Limerick on the River Maigue.[145] The army of Waterford was heavily defeated by its rivals who acted in alliance with other troops from Munster.

A fleet from Dublin led by Hálfdan son of Guðrøðr sailed north in 926 and established a camp at Strangford Lough. From there the fleet sacked Dunseverick (Co. Antrim), the capital of Dál Riata which overlooked the strategically significant North Channel into the Irish Sea.[146] Viking fleets had been active along the north-east coasts of Ireland in 923 and 924, but it is not clear whether Hálfdan's campaign was a continuation of these earlier raids or whether he was seeking to root out groups of vikings who were rivals to the dynasty of Ívarr.[147] Hálfdan then established a camp at Linns in Dundalk Bay in September 926, which was occupied until the following year.[148] This may have been founded as part of a supply chain down the east coast of Ireland to Dublin. At the end of 926 Hálfdan fell in battle against the forces of the overking of the Northern Uí Néill, Muirchertach son of Niall, in Ulster. This seems to have been the second defeat of Hálfdan's troops by Muirchertach in that year. The survivors were besieged near Carlingford Lough until a fleet came with Guðrøðr grandson of Ívarr to relieve them.[149]

In 927 fleets departed from both Dublin and Linns to support Guðrøðr's claim to the throne of York following the death of Sigtryggr

---

[145] Hogan, *Onomasticon*, p. 201.

[146] *Annals of Clonmacnoise, s.a.* 921 [=926] (ed. Murphy, p. 148); *Annals of the Four Masters, s.aa.* 924 [=926] (ed. and trans. O'Donovan, II, 612-15); *Annals of Ulster, s.a.* 925 [=926].1 (ed. and trans. Mac Airt and Mac Niocaill, pp. 376-77); *Chronicum Scotorum, s.a.* [925] [=926] (ed. and trans. Hennessy, pp. 196-97).

[147] *Annals of Clonmacnoise, s.a.* 920 [=924] (ed. Murphy, p. 147); *Annals of the Four Masters, s.aa.* 921 [=923], 922 [=924] (ed. and trans. O'Donovan, II, 608-11); *Annals of Ulster, s.aa.* 922 [=923].4, 923 [=924].2 (ed. and trans. Mac Airt and Mac Niocaill, pp. 374-77); *Chronicum Scotorum, s.a.* [922] [=923] (ed. and trans. Hennessy, pp. 194-95).

[148] *Annals of the Four Masters, s.a.* 924 [=926] (ed. and trans. O'Donovan, II, 614-15); *Annals of Ulster, s.a.* 925 [=926].5 (ed. and trans. Mac Airt and Mac Niocaill, pp. 378-79).

[149] *Annals of Clonmacnoise, s.a.* 921 [=926] (ed. Murphy, p. 148); *Annals of the Four Masters, s.a.* 924 [=926] (ed. and trans. O'Donovan, II, 614-15); *Annals of Ulster, s.a.* 925 [=926].6 (ed. and trans. Mac Airt and Mac Niocaill, pp. 378-79); *Chronicum Scotorum, s.a.* [925] [=926] (ed. and trans. Hennessy, pp. 196-97).

grandson of Ívarr.[150] Guðrøðr seems to have delegated power in Ireland to his sons during his absence. According to 'The Annals of Clonmacnoise' this prompted the enmity of the sons of Sigtryggr, who allied with a 'son of Helgi' and seized Dublin.[151] The 'son of Helgi' may be identified with Þórir Helgason of Limerick or one of his kin. Their success was only temporary, for Guðrøðr returned after six months and re-established himself in Dublin.[152] This rivalry does however mark an important division within the dynasty of Ívarr, which re-emerged at a later date as a feud between the descendants of Guðrøðr and Sigtryggr.

In 928 a 'son of Helgi' founded a base on Lough Neagh, perhaps to counter the recent operations of the Dublin-fleet along the north-eastern coasts of Ireland.[153] In the same year a fleet from Limerick arrived at Lough Corrib (Co. Galway) in Connaught and then sailed up the River Shannon to Lough Ree. This may have represented a two-pronged attack on the province of Connaught. The vikings of Lough Corrib were defeated by Connaughtmen in 930. After this defeat the troops of Limerick turned their attention eastwards and founded a camp at *Mag Raigne* in Osraige. Here they clashed with the forces of Uí Cheinnselaig (the dominant population-group of southern Leinster) and in a separate engagement with the forces of Dublin.[154] In 931 Guðrøðr came from Dublin to expel a grandson (or

---

[150] *Annals of Clonmacnoise, s.a.* 922 [=927] (ed. Murphy, p. 148); *Annals of the Four Masters, s.a.* 925 [=927] (ed. and trans. O'Donovan, II, 616-17); *Annals of Ulster, s.a.* 926 [=927].3 (ed. and trans. Mac Airt and Mac Niocaill, pp. 378-79); *Chronicum Scotorum, s.a.* [926] [=927] (ed. and trans. Hennessy, pp. 196-97). See below, p. 100.

[151] *Annals of Clonmacnoise, s.a.* 922 [=927] (ed. Murphy, p. 148).

[152] *Annals of Clonmacnoise, s.a.* 922 [=927] (ed. Murphy, p. 148); *Annals of the Four Masters, s.a.* 925 [=927] (ed. and trans. O'Donovan, II, 616-17); *Annals of Ulster, s.a.* 926 [=927].3 (ed. and trans. Mac Airt and Mac Niocaill, pp. 378-79).

[153] *Annals of the Four Masters, s.a.* 926 [=928] (ed. and trans. O'Donovan, II, 620-21); *Annals of Ulster, s.a.* 927 [=928].5 (ed. and trans. Mac Airt and Mac Niocaill, pp. 378-79). It may have been these vikings who were responsible for the death of Donnchad son of Domnall, a candidate for the overkingship of the Northern Uí Néill: *Chronicum Scotorum, s.a.* [926] [=927] (ed. and trans. Hennessy, pp. 196-99).

[154] *Annals of Clonmacnoise, s.a.* 925 [=930] (ed. Murphy, p. 149); *Annals of the Four Masters, s.a.* 928 [=930] (ed. and trans. O'Donovan, II, 624-25); *Annals of Inisfallen, s.a.* [930] (ed. and trans. Mac Airt, pp. 150-51); *Annals of Ulster, s.aa.* 929 [=930].1, 929 [=930].3-4 (ed. and trans. Mac Airt and Mac Niocaill, pp. 380-81); *Chronicum Scotorum, s.a.* [929] [=930] (ed. and trans. Hennessy, pp. 198-99).

great-grandson) of Ívarr from *Mag Raigne*.[155] This suggests that the vikings of Limerick had continued allying with sons of Sigtryggr, or other factions within the kin-group, who opposed Guðrøðr. The presence of an army from Limerick near the borders of Leinster was clearly meant to impede the operations of Guðrøðr and his son who were based at Dublin and Waterford respectively. The efforts of vikings from Waterford and Dublin to dominate Leinster are reflected in the raids made on Kildare in 928 and 929.[156]

It seems that the war between Limerick and Dublin impinged on all the provinces of Ireland. It also emerges from the chronicles that rivalries within the Northern Uí Néill became involved with this struggle. One branch, represented by Muirchertach son of Niall, opposed Dublin. In 926 Muirchertach had defeated Hálfdan son of Guðrøðr in battle. Hálfdan's brother, Óláfr, attacked Armagh in 932 and allied with Matudán overking of Ulster to plunder the lands of Muirchertach in 933.[157] Another branch of the Northern Uí Néill, represented by the sons of Domnall son of Aed Finnliath, appears to have supported Dublin. In 928 Donnchad son of Domnall was killed by vikings who seem to have hailed from Limerick. In 933, Fergal son of Domnall sided with his nephew Sigfrøðr son of Uathmarán, grandson of Ívarr and defeated Muirchertach son of Niall in battle in Meath, close to the River Shannon.[158]

---

[155] *Annals of Clonmacnoise, s.a.* 926 [=931] (ed. Murphy, p. 149); *Annals of the Four Masters, s.a.* 929 [=931] (ed. and trans. O'Donovan, II, 624-25).

[156] *Annals of Clonmacnoise, s.a.* 923 [=928] (ed. Murphy, p. 148); *Annals of the Four Masters, s.aa.* 926 [=928], 927 [=929] (ed. and trans. O'Donovan, II, 620-23); *Chronicum Scotorum, s.a.* [927] [=928] (ed. and trans. Hennessy, pp. 198-99).

[157] *Annals of Clonmacnoise, s.aa.* 922 [=926], 928 [=933] (ed. Murphy, pp. 148, 150); *Annals of the Four Masters, s.aa.* 924 [=926], 931 [=933] (ed. and trans. O'Donovan, II, 614-15, 628-29); *Annals of Ulster, s.aa.* 925 [=926].6, 932 [=933].3 (ed. and trans. Mac Airt and Mac Niocaill, pp. 378-79, 382-83); *Chronicum Scotorum, s.a.* [932] [=933] (ed. and trans. Hennessy, pp. 200-01).

[158] *Annals of Clonmacnoise, s.a.* 928 [=933] (ed. Murphy, pp. 149-50); *Annals of the Four Masters, s.a.* 931 [=933] (ed. and trans. O'Donovan, II, 628-29); *Annals of Ulster, s.aa.* 927 [=928].4, 932 [=933].1 (ed. and trans. Mac Airt and Mac Niocaill, pp. 378-79, 382-83); *Chronicum Scotorum, s.a.* [926] [=927] (ed. and trans. Hennessy, pp. 196-99). The record of a viking fleet moving from Lough Erne to Lough Gawna may be related to these events.

Guðrøðr died in 934, but this did not end the war.[159] It continued during the reign of his son Óláfr. The persistent presence of viking fleets on the River Shannon drew the Southern Uí Néill into the conflict, for this river defined the western boundary of their territories. In 936 the army of Dublin pillaged Clonmacnoise, the principal church of the Southern Uí Néill, which stood by the river. The overking Donnchad son of Flann waged war against Dublin in the same year and he succeeded in plundering and burning the port.[160] It was also on the River Shannon that the conflict between Limerick and Dublin was finally resolved. In 937 Guðrøðr won a decisive victory at Lough Ree where he captured the Limerick-king Óláfr 'Scabbyhead' and destroyed his ships.[161]

The rivalry between Limerick and Dublin marks an important chapter in the history of vikings in Ireland. The number of viking campaigns recorded in these years rivals any other period of Irish history. The influence of the vikings is reflected in the range of their campaigns across the island and in the involvement of Irish overkings in their war. This period has been regarded as the zenith of viking power in Ireland.[162] The victory of Óláfr Guðrøðsson freed him to turn his ambitions to England. After initial failure and defeat at the battle of *Brunanburh*, he returned but succeeded in winning control of viking Northumbria (and the southern and eastern Danelaw) in a second attempt in 939.[163]

Despite the quelling of Limerick, Dublin remained in conflict with the overkings of the Northern and Southern Uí Néill. In 938 a peace-agreement was made between these two kings and they joined forces to

---

[159] *Annals of Clonmacnoise, s.a.* 929 [=934] (ed. Murphy, p. 150); *Annals of the Four Masters, s.a.* 932 [=934] (ed. and trans. O'Donovan, II, 630-31); *Annals of Ulster, s.a.* 933 [=934].1 (ed. and trans. Mac Airt and Mac Niocaill, pp. 382-83); *Chronicum Scotorum, s.a.* [933] [=934] (ed. and trans. Hennessy, pp. 200-01).

[160] *Annals of Clonmacnoise, s.a.* 930 [=936] (ed. Murphy, p. 150); *Annals of the Four Masters, s.a.* 934 [=936] (ed. and trans. O'Donovan, II, 630-33); *Chronicum Scotorum, s.a.* [935] [=936] (ed. and trans. Hennessy, pp. 200-01).

[161] *Annals of Clonmacnoise, s.a.* 931 [=937] (ed. Murphy, p. 150); *Annals of the Four Masters, s.a.* 935 [=937] (ed. and trans. O'Donovan, II, 632-33).

[162] Charles-Edwards, 'Irish Warfare', pp. 44-45; Ryan, 'Pre-Norman Dublin', p. 72; Smyth, *Scandinavian York*, II, 18.

[163] *Annals of Clonmacnoise, s.a.* 931 [=937] (ed. Murphy, pp. 150-51); *Annals of the Four Masters, s.aa.* 935 [=937], 937 [=939] (ed. and trans. O'Donovan, II, 632-33, 638-39); *Annals of Ulster, s.aa.* 936 [=937].6, 937 [=938].5 (ed. and trans. Mac Airt and Mac Niocaill, pp. 384-87).

besiege Dublin. Although they failed to take the port, they ravaged the territories which lay under its influence from Dublin to Áth Truisten (a site near Mullaghmast, Co. Kildare).[164] The extent of the raid shows that Dublin had increased its territorial overlordship in preceding years across much of north Leinster.[165] The attack also demonstrated the dangers which the descendants of Ívarr still faced from coalitions of Irish kings. Nevertheless this joint attack by the dominant powers of Ireland did not overwhelm them.

Figure 8: Tenth-century chronicle-references to viking camps in Ireland		
Athcrathin	(Co. Down)	926
Carlingford Lough	(Co. Down/Louth)	923
Clonmacnoise	(Co. Offaly)	926
Dublin	(Co. Dublin)	917, & multiple references
Emly	(Co. Tipperary)	968
Glynn, nr St Mullins	(Co. Carlow)	917
Limerick	(Co. Limerick)	922, & multiple references
Linns, nr Annagassan	(Co. Louth)	926, 927
Lough Corrib	(Co. Galway)	929, 930
Lough Erne	(Co. Fermanagh)	924, 933, 936
Lough Foyle	(Co. Londonderry)	943
Lough Gur	(Co. Limerick)	926
Lough Neagh	(Co. Antrim/Armagh/Derry/Tyrone)	930, 933, 945
Lough Ree	(Co. Longford/Roscommon/W'meath)	931, 936, 937
Mag Raigne	(Co. Kilkenny)	930, 931
Strangford Lough	(Co. Down)	924, 926, 933, 943
Waterford	(Co. Waterford)	914, & multiple references
Wexford	(Co. Wexford)	935
Sites of uncertain location		
Loch Bethrach in Osraige (= *Mag Raigne?*)		930

[164] *Annals of the Four Masters, s.a.* 936 [=938] (ed. and trans. O'Donovan, II, 634-37).
[165] The neighbouring kings of Uí Dúnchada may have been brought temporarily under Dublin's subjection. In the same year vikings from Dublin attacked Kilcullen (Co. Kildare): *Annals of Clonmacnoise, s.a.* 932 [=938] (ed. Murphy, p. 151); *Annals of the Four Masters, s.a.* 936 [=938] (ed. and trans. O'Donovan, II, 634-35); *Annals of Ulster, s.a.* 937 [=938].6 (ed. and trans. Mac Airt and Mac Niocaill, pp. 386-87); *Chronicum Scotorum, s.a.* [937] [=938] (ed. and trans. Hennessy, pp. 202-03).

The Reign of Óláfr Sigtryggsson: Initial Power-Struggles

Following the departure of Óláfr Guðrøðsson his cousin, Óláfr Sigtryggsson, took power in Dublin. Óláfr Sigtrygsson is better known by his epithet *Cuarán*, which can be translated as 'sandal', perhaps a reference to the adoption of a Gaelic inauguration-rite among the vikings of Dublin which involved the wearing or throwing of a shoe (in essence a symbolic demonstration that the new king was able to 'fill the boots' of his predecessors).[166] Whatever the origin of the epithet, the bicultural ancestry of the name of Óláfr *Cuarán* accurately reflects the nature of his kingship and the character of viking settlements in Ireland. Vikings in tenth-century Ireland could no longer be deemed true 'Scandinavians'. A new identity had evolved combining elements of native and immigrant culture which was to continue, especially in Dublin, for centuries to come.[167]

Óláfr may have been one of the sons of Sigtryggr who opposed the rule of Guðrøðr grandson of Ívarr in 927. A brother of Óláfr, Haraldr Sigtryggsson, was in control of Limerick in 940.[168] It is possible that he was promoted to this post before Óláfr Guðrøðsson left for England and some temporary accommodation between the sons of Guðrøðr and the sons of Sigtryggr may have been reached. In 940, Óláfr Sigtryggsson left Ireland and went to York.[169] It is not clear whether he went in order to assist his cousin or whether he was seeking to take the throne for himself; however there is no evidence for a struggle between them. Óláfr Guðrøðsson died in the following year and Óláfr Sigtryggsson was chosen as his successor.[170] Leadership of Dublin passed into the hands of Blákári Guðrøðsson in 940 and he was to hold his position there for five years in the absence of his cousin.

---

[166] McCana, 'The *Topos*'. Cf. Breeze, 'The *Anglo-Saxon Chronicle*'; Breeze, 'The Irish Nickname'.

[167] Mytum, 'The Vikings and Ireland'; Downham, 'Living on the Edge'.

[168] *Annals of Clonmacnoise*, *s.a.* 933 [=940] (ed. Murphy, p. 151); *Annals of the Four Masters*, *s.a.* 938 [=940] (ed. and trans. O'Donovan, II, 639-41); *Annals of Inisfallen*, *s.a.* [940] (ed. and trans. Mac Airt, pp. 152-53); *Chronicum Scotorum*, *s.a.* [939] [=940] (ed. and trans. Hennessy, pp. 202-03).

[169] *Annals of Clonmacnoise*, *s.a.* 933 [=940] (ed. Murphy, p. 152); *Annals of the Four Masters*, *s.a.* 938 [=940] (ed. and trans. O'Donovan, II, 640-41).

[170] *Annals of Clonmacnoise*, *s.a.* 934 [=941] (ed. Murphy, p. 152); *Chronicum Scotorum*, *s.a.* [940] [=941] (ed. and trans. Hennessy, pp. 202-03).

Despite the changes in political leadership, Dublin's conflict continued with the Northern Uí Néill overking Muirchertach son of Niall. In 939 the fleet of Dublin attacked his capital at Ailech (Elagh, Co. Donegal). Muirchertach was taken prisoner but was later released by payment of ransom or 'by God', which may indicate that churches provided funds to secure his release.[171] In 941 Muirchertach attacked the Hebrides, which may have been in the hands of, or allied with, the dynasty of Ívarr. This raid may in part have inspired a twelfth-century poem which asserted that this overking made a circuit of Ireland and captured a king of Dublin. As Donnchadh Ó Corráin has shown, the story of this poem was incorporated into 'The Annals of the Four Masters', but the account cannot be trusted.[172] A fleet of vikings travelled to the north of Ireland in 942 when Downpatrick (Co. Down) was raided. In 943 ships from Dublin sheltered in Lough Foyle, bordering the heartlands of Muirchertach's territory, and here they made an alliance with a rival king, Ruaidrí ua Canannáin of Cenél Conaill.[173] The combined force defeated an army of Muirchertach's people, Cenél nEogain. Muirchertach was killed by Dubliners in the same year at Ardee (Co. Louth). The vikings celebrated his death by raiding Armagh (the burial place of several Cenél nEogain overkings) on the following day.[174] This victory by Blákári Guðrøðsson concluded many years of warfare between Muirchertach and the people of Dublin, which raged across two decades. The impact of these events is demonstrated in 944 when Cenél nEogain was unable to maintain its claim to overkingship over all Uí Néill. This position was seized by Congalach son of Maelmithig, overking of Brega.

---

[171] *Annals of Clonmacnoise, s.a.* 933 [=939/40] (ed. Murphy, p. 151); *Annals of the Four Masters, s.a.* 937 [=939] (ed. and trans. O'Donovan, II, 636-37); *Annals of Ulster, s.a.* 938 [=939].3 (ed. and trans. Mac Airt and Mac Niocaill, pp. 386-87); *Chronicum Scotorum, s.a.* [938] [=939] (ed. and trans. Hennessy, pp. 202-03).

[172] Ó Corráin, 'Muirchertach', pp. 240, 247; *Annals of the Four Masters, s.a.* 939 [=941] (ed. and trans. O'Donovan, II, 640-43); *Chronicum Scotorum, s.a.* [940] [=941] (ed. and trans. Hennessy, pp. 202-05).

[173] *Annals of the Four Masters, s.a.* 941 [=943] (ed. and trans. O'Donovan, II, 646-49); *Chronicum Scotorum, s.a.* [942] [=943] (ed. and trans. Hennessy, pp. 204-05).

[174] *Annals of Clonmacnoise, s.a.* 936 [=943] (ed. Murphy, pp. 152-53); *Annals of the Four Masters, s.a.* 941 [=943] (ed. and trans. O'Donovan, II, 646-49); *Annals of Inisfallen, s.a.* [943] (ed. and trans. Mac Airt, pp. 152-53); *Annals of Ulster, s.a.* 942 [=943].2 (ed. and trans. Mac Airt and Mac Niocaill, pp. 390-91); *Chronicum Scotorum, s.a.* [942] [=943] (ed. and trans. Hennessy, pp. 204-05).

Dublin and Waterford were also at war with Brega and Uí Fhailge (areas occupying the modern counties Meath and Offaly) from the late 930s to the 940s. In 939 the forces of Waterford plundered both territories in alliance with the overking of Munster, but they were heavily defeated by Aimergin, overking of Uí Fhailge.[175] The abbot of Killeigh (Co. Offaly), who was captured during this campaign, drowned in the following year, trying to escape from Dalkey Island, near Dublin, where he was imprisoned.[176] The record brings to mind the suicidal attempts of people to escape later slave-traders described by Olaudah Equiano.[177] We can only guess from the brief Irish chronicle-record the horrors of captivity. Another army from Dublin raided Uí Fhailge and Brega in 941, but they were also vanquished by Aimergin in alliance with Cenél Fiachach of Meath.[178]

The departure of Óláfr Guðrøðsson and Óláfr *Cuarán* from Dublin in 939 and 940 may have encouraged the overkings of northern Leinster to challenge Dublin's domination of the north-east of that province. Blákári had taken offensive action against Leinster and Meath in 942.[179] In the following year Lorcán son of Faelán, overking of Leinster, won a battle against the forces of Dublin but was killed while attacking the settlement. His successor, Braen son of Mael Mórda, strengthened his position by making common cause with Congalach overking of Brega (and the Southern Uí Néill). Together they sacked Dublin. Irish chronicle-accounts are emphatic about the destruction wrought by the Irish troops in 944. *Chronicum Scotorum* and 'The Annals of Clonmacnoise' report that 400

---

[175] *Annals of Clonmacnoise, s.a.* 934 [=939] (ed. Murphy, p. 152); *Annals of the Four Masters, s.a.* 937 [=939] (ed. and trans. O'Donovan, II, 638-39); *Chronicum Scotorum, s.a.* [938] [=939] (ed. and trans. Hennessy, pp. 202-03).

[176] *Annals of Clonmacnoise, s.a.* 934 [=940] (ed. Murphy, p. 152); *Annals of the Four Masters, s.a.* 938 [=940] (ed. and trans. O'Donovan, II, 644-45); *Chronicum Scotorum, s.a.* [939] [=940] (ed. and trans. Hennessy, pp. 202-03).

[177] Equiano, *Sold*, pp. 35, 38-39, 104-05.

[178] *Annals of Clonmacnoise, s.a.* 935 [=941] (ed. Murphy, p. 154); *Annals of the Four Masters, s.a.* 939 [=941] (ed. and trans. O'Donovan, II, 646-47); *Chronicum Scotorum, s.a.* [940] [=941] (ed. and trans. Hennessy, pp. 204-05). A related event is that the church of Inishmot (Co. Meath) was plundered by vikings in winter.

[179] *Annals of the Four Masters, s.a.* 940 [=942] (ed. and trans. O'Donovan, II, 646-47); *Annals of Ulster, s.a.* 941 [=942].7 (ed. and trans. Mac Airt and Mac Niocaill, pp. 388-89); *Chronicum Scotorum, s.a.* [941] [=942] (ed. and trans. Hennessy, pp. 204-05).

vikings were killed and the fortress was plundered and burnt.[180] 'The Annals of the Four Masters' paint a more graphic picture, asserting that the whole population was killed or taken into slavery, except a few who fled to Dalkey Island, while all the buildings of the town and its ships were burnt. Although the account in 'The Annals of the Four Masters' may be exaggerated, the attack could help to explain why Blákári was ousted from the kingship of Dublin soon after.[181] The weakened state of the settlement and its defences may have also encouraged the Southern Uí Néill overking, Congalach, to lead another attack on the town in 948.

The attack on Dublin coincided with King Óláfr's failure to maintain control of York. Both Óláfr and another king, Rögnvaldr Guðrøðsson, were expelled by the English king Edmund in 944. Rögnvaldr was presumably a brother of Blákári, and it may be that his rivalry with Óláfr aided the downfall of viking Northumbria.[182] Rögnvaldr tried his hand at regaining control of York but failed and was killed in England.[183] His cousin Óláfr returned to Ireland in 945 and seized Dublin from Blákári. In the same year we find Óláfr acting in concert with Congalach, overking of the Southern Uí Néill, to fight one of the Northern Uí Néill kings, Ruaidrí ua Canannáin of Cenél Conaill.[184] Óláfr may have become a client of Congalach following the devastation of Dublin. The two kings were allied against Ruaidrí ua Canannáin again in 947 when the Northern Uí Néill king attacked Brega. A battle ensued in which Ruaidrí was victorious and

---

[180] *Annals of Clonmacnoise*, s.a. 937 [=944] (ed. Murphy, p. 154); *Chronicum Scotorum*, s.a. [943] [=944] (ed. and trans. Hennessy, pp. 206-07).

[181] *Annals of Clonmacnoise*, s.a. 937 [=944] (ed. Murphy, p. 154); *Annals of the Four Masters*, s.a. 942 [=944] (ed. and trans. O'Donovan, II, 650-53).

[182] Woolf, 'Amlaíb', p. 37.

[183] *Annals of Clonmacnoise*, s.a. 937 [=944/5] (ed. Murphy, p. 154); See below, pp. 111-12.

[184] *Annals of Clonmacnoise*, s.a. 937 [=944/5] (ed. Murphy, p. 154); *Annals of the Four Masters*, s.a. 943 [=945] (ed. and trans. O'Donovan, II, 654-55); *Annals of Ulster*, s.a. 944 [=945].2, 944 [=945].7 (ed. and trans. Mac Airt and Mac Niocaill, pp. 392-93); *Chronicum Scotorum*, s.a. [944] [=945] (ed. and trans. Hennessy, pp. 206-07). Another fleet of vikings was active on Lough Neagh in the north of Ireland in 945. They were defeated by Domnall son of Muirchertach, overking of Cenél nEogain, and a 'king' of the vikings was killed. It is possible that this fleet was linked with Dublin, for the kings of Cenél nEogain were rivals of Congalach and during the early tenth century they were persistent enemies of Dublin.

the greatest losses seem to have been borne by the Dublin side. According to 'The Annals of Ulster', many of the vikings were killed or drowned.[185]

It was around this time that Blákári regained control of Dublin. These events left Óláfr powerless to intervene in English affairs at a time when York was back in viking control, though under the leadership of his rival, King Eiríkr.[186] A band of vikings raided Brega and other parts of the Southern Uí Néill in 948.[187] This led to a battle in which Blákári was killed by the forces of Congalach. Many of his followers were also captured or slain. With his rival dead, Óláfr left for England.[188] Leadership of Dublin then passed into the hands of Óláfr's brother Guðrøðr Sigtryggsson. Guðrøðr was heavily defeated in a battle in Meath in 950 against Congalach and Ruaidrí. According to 'Annals of the Four Masters', Ruaidrí had subjected Meath earlier in the year. However he was killed in the battle. Congalach was identified as the victor and Guðrøðr fled the scene.[189]

The vikings of Dublin led a campaign of retribution against Congalach in the following year by plundering major churches in Meath. According to 'The Annals of Ulster' three thousand people were taken captive during this campaign and a great booty of cattle and horses and gold and silver. Even if exaggerated, the record suggests that Guðrøðr and his followers enriched themselves in this event. The plague which raged in Dublin in the same year was interpreted as the wrath of God and Guðrøðr died soon after the attack.[190] Óláfr *Cuarán* returned from York in the following year, having failed to secure his position in England.[191] He remained king of Dublin

---

[185] *Annals of the Four Masters, s.a.* 945 [=947] (ed. and trans. O'Donovan, II, 656-59); *Annals of Ulster, s.a.* 946 [=947].1 (ed. and trans. Mac Airt and Mac Niocaill, pp. 392-93).

[186] See below, p. 113.

[187] *Annals of the Four Masters, s.a.* 946 [=948] (ed. and trans. O'Donovan, II, 658-59); *Annals of Ulster, s.a.* 947 [=948].1, 947 [=948].4 (ed. and trans. Mac Airt and Mac Niocaill, pp. 392-95); *Chronicum Scotorum, s.a.* [947] [=948] (ed. and trans. Hennessy, pp. 208-09).

[188] *Annals of Clonmacnoise, s.a.* 943 [=948] (ed. Murphy, p. 154).

[189] *Annals of Clonmacnoise, s.a.* 945 [=950] (ed. Murphy, p. 155); *Annals of the Four Masters, s.a.* 948 [=950] (ed. and trans. O'Donovan, II, 662-63); *Annals of Ulster, s.a.* 949 [=950].5 (ed. and trans. Mac Airt and Mac Niocaill, pp. 394-95); *Chronicum Scotorum, s.a.* [949] [=950] (ed. and trans. Hennessy, pp. 208-09).

[190] *Annals of Clonmacnoise, s.a.* 9[46] [=951] (ed. Murphy, p. 156); *Annals of the Four Masters, s.a.* 949 [=951] (ed. and trans. O'Donovan, II, 664-67); *Annals of Ulster, s.a.* 950 [=951].3 (ed. and trans. Mac Airt and Mac Niocaill, pp. 396-97); *Chronicum Scotorum, s.a.* [950] [=951] (ed. and trans. Hennessy, pp. 210-11).

[191] *Annals of Clonmacnoise, s.a.* 9[46] [=951] (ed. Murphy, p. 156). See below, pp. 113-15.

until 980 and may have restored some much needed stability to viking affairs in the port after the tumult of the preceding years.

The Reign of Óláfr Cuarán: Dynastic Segmentation

Óláfr Cuarán had clashed with Blákári son of Guðrøðr over control of Dublin in the 940s. Óláfr withstood this challenge and survived until 980. In the course of his long reign the descendants of Guðrøðr grandson of Ívarr were excluded from power. It was from Óláfr Sigtryggsson (alias Cuarán) that future kings of Dublin were descended. This segmentation of the royal dynasty may have been a corollary of the loss of Viking Northumbria. In the 940s the descendants of Guðrøðr and Sigtryggr, grandsons of Ívarr, had alternated control of Dublin and York. With York gone, resources were more limited and the weaker lineage of Guðrøðr was forced to the margins.

On his return to Dublin, Óláfr Cuarán set about consolidating his position. In 953 he allied with the overking of northern Leinster, Tuathal son of Ugaire. Together they attacked the south of the province.[192] In 956 Congalach son of Maelmithig, overking of the Southern Uí Néill, attacked Leinster and held an assembly on the banks of the Liffey, thereby challenging the power of both Tuathal and Óláfr. The forces of Leinster and Dublin co-operated to defeat Congalach. The Uí Néill overking was killed in the battle that followed, thus ridding Dublin of a major threat.[193] During the next few years Óláfr Cuarán was able to enjoy relatively peaceful relations with his Irish neighbours.

The greatest threat posed to Óláfr during the early 960s was from rivals within the dynasty of Ívarr. In 960 Cammán son of Óláfr Guðrøðsson was defeated at Dub. His opponent is not named and the location of the event

---

[192] Annals of the Four Masters, s.a. 951 [=953] (ed. and trans. O'Donovan, II, 668-69). Timolin (Co. Carlow) was plundered 'ó Laraic' which may mean from Port Lairge (Waterford), the first element of the name being missed out. I am grateful to Breandan Ó Ciobháin for this interpretation which makes more sense that my earlier reading of this record: Downham, 'Eric', p. 75, n.139. This would suggest that Dublin and Waterford were working in harmony at this date by combining their efforts against southern Leinster.

[193] Annals of Clonmacnoise, s.a. 951 [=956] (ed. Murphy, pp. 156-57); Annals of the Four Masters, s.a. 954 [=956] (ed. and trans. O'Donovan, II, 672-75); Annals of Ulster, s.a. 955 [=956].3 (ed. and trans. Mac Airt and Mac Niocaill, pp. 398-99); Chronicum Scotorum, s.a. [955] [=956] (ed. and trans. Hennessy, pp. 212-13); 'Do Fhlaithesaib Hérend iar Creitim', ed. Best and Bergin, I, 97.

is unclear. Many places in Ireland include the element *Dub* ('dark') and this name seems incomplete.[194] The name Cammán is Gaelic, a diminutive of *cam* meaning 'crooked'.[195] Cammán may therefore be identified with Sigtryggr *Cam* who raided an area north of Dublin in 962.[196] In that year a coalition of Leinstermen and the forces of Dublin vanquished Sigtryggr *Cam*. Óláfr *Cuarán* was wounded in his thigh by an arrow and the defeated Sigtryggr fled to his ships.[197] The sons of Óláfr (presumably sons of Óláfr Guðrøðsson) then proceeded to Munster where they raided sites in Waterford and Cork. Three hundred and sixty-five of the raiders are said to have fallen in a clash with a local Irish leader and the remainder escaped in three ships. According to 'The Annals of the Four Masters' this expedition to the south of Ireland was conducted by Óláfr's sons to avenge a brother of theirs.[198] The fleet was accompanied by *lagmainn* a borrowing from Norse *løgmenn* meaning 'Law-men'. This could suggest a legally sanctioned act of vengeance. Other references to *lagmainn* in Irish chronicles point to a connection with the Hebrides.[199] 'The Annals of the Four Masters' also inform us that the sons of Óláfr took their booty to Anglesey, which favours the conclusion that this branch of the dynasty of Ívarr had established a base in the Irish Sea.[200] These raids therefore present an insight into the efforts of the sons of Óláfr Guðrøðsson both to establish a new power-base in the Hebrides and to harry the coasts of Ireland adjoining the ports of Dublin and Waterford, perhaps in the hope that one day these towns would fall into their control. The death of Guðrøðr, one of the sons of Óláfr, is reported in the following year, but nothing more is said of his brothers in the Irish chronicles.[201] It appears that Óláfr *Cuarán* did not have to face significant trouble from this branch of the family again.

---

[194] *Cogadh*, ed. and trans. Todd, pp. 278, 288; Etchingham, 'North Wales', p. 171, n. 78; Ó Murchadha, 'Lagmainn', p. 136, n.1.

[195] *Dictionary*, ed. Quin *et al.*, p. 99, col. 62, lines 57-83.

[196] *Annals of the Four Masters*, s.a. 960 [=962] (ed. and trans. O'Donovan, II, 680-81).

[197] O'Donovan's translation of The Annals of the Four Masters missed out some of the text of this entry which rather changes its meaning.

[198] 'Oin', this is not clearly a Gaelic or a Norse name.

[199] Ó Murchadha, 'Lagmainn'.

[200] *Annals of the Four Masters*, s.a. 960 [=962] (ed. and trans. O'Donovan, II, 682-83).

[201] *Annals of Clonmacnoise*, s.a. 957 [=963] (ed. Murphy, p. 157); *Annals of Ulster*, s.a. 962 [=963].5 (ed. and trans. Mac Airt and Mac Niocaill, pp. 405-05); *Chronicum Scotorum*, s.a. 961 [=963] (ed. and trans. Hennessy, pp. 214-15).

For the remainder of the 960s Óláfr *Cuarán* involved himself in the politics of Leinster, attacking the province in 964 and involving himself in the family rivalries of Uí Dúnchada of northern Leinster in 967.[202] The men of Dublin assisted Cerball son of Lorcán of Uí Dúnchada in a raid on Brega in 967. This may have provoked Domnall ua Néill, the Cenél nEogain overking of the Northern and Southern Uí Néill, to check the power of Leinster and the people of Dublin. In 968 Domnall besieged his enemies for two months and succeeded in taking a great tribute (or booty) of cows.[203] This did not prevent Óláfr's operations in the Southern Uí Neill lands. An army of Dublin and the overking of Leinster, Murchad son of Finn, attacked the church of Kells (in the territory of the Southern Uí Néill) in 969.[204] Vikings plundered the church again in the following year and with the forces of Leinster they won a battle over Uí Néill at Ardmulchan (Co. Meath).[205]

Óláfr also sought to extend his influence among the Southern Uí Néill in alliance with Brega. According to *Banshenchas* (a list of famous married women in Irish history and literature compiled in the twelfth century), Óláfr's daughter was married to Domnall son of Congalach, overking of Brega.[206] In 970 the Northern Uí Néill overking Domnall ua Néill led a campaign against Brega and the neighbouring territory of the Conaille in the hinterland of Dundalk Bay. The churches of Monasterboice, Dunleer, Louth and Dromiskin (all in Co. Louth) were attacked against (rather than by) vikings and it appears that Óláfr's troops were posted at these locations on Brega's behalf. This campaign culminated in a battle fought at Kilmona (Co. Westmeath) with the Northern Uí Néill and their supporters being

---

[202] *Annals of the Four Masters, s.aa.* 962 [=964], 965 [=967] (ed. and trans. O'Donovan, II, 684-89)

[203] *Annals of the Four Masters, s.a.* 966 [=968] (ed. and trans. O'Donovan, II, 690-91); *Annals of Ulster, s.a.* 967 [=968].3 (ed. and trans. Mac Airt and Mac Niocaill, pp. 406-07); *Chronicum Scotorum, s.aa.* 965 [=967], [966] [=968] (ed. and trans. Hennessy, pp. 216-19).

[204] *Annals of the Four Masters, s.a.* 967 [=969] (ed. and trans. O'Donovan, II, 692-93); Murchadh was of the Uí Fáeláin in northern Leinster.

[205] *Annals of the Four Masters, s.a.* 968 [=970] (ed. and trans. O'Donovan, II, 692-93); *Annals of Ulster, s.a.* 969 [=970].1 (ed. and trans. Mac Airt and Mac Niocaill, pp. 408-09); *Chronicum Scotorum, s.a.* 968 [=970] (ed. and trans. Hennessy, pp. 218-19).

[206] 'The Ban-Shenchus', ed. Dobbs, pp. 188, 227. For commentary see Connon, 'The *Banshenchas*'.

pitched against Brega and Dublin. The Dublin side won.[207] The victory was significant, for in the following year Domnall ua Néill was driven from Meath. He later returned plundering 'the forts of the Irish and the foreigners' in the province, thus indicating the Dubliners' close involvement in the politics of this region.[208]

During the reign of the overking of the Southern Uí Néill, Mael Sechlainn son of Domnall, which began in 975, good relations between Meath and Dublin were sundered. Mael Sechlainn marked his accession to the overkingship by attacking Dublin.[209] Unwittingly, Óláfr may have strengthened Mael Sechlainn's status as Uí Néill overking two years later, for he oversaw the slaughter of two men eligible for the overkingship.[210] The continued strength of Dublin was demonstrated in 978 when the forces of Dublin defeated and killed the overking of Leinster, Ugaire son of Tuathal, with heavy losses on the Leinster side.[211] In the following year, the next overking of Leinster, Domnall Claen, was captured by an army from Dublin, and the church of Kildare was plundered by vikings.[212] His successor in the overkingship of Leinster, Braen son of Mael Mórda, chose to ally with Mael Sechlainn, overking of the Southern Uí Néill, against Dublin.

The power of Dublin was severely curtailed in battle at Tara (Co. Meath) in 980. The location of the event suggests that an army from Dublin attacked the Southern Uí Néill. Óláfr does not seem to have been

---

[207] *Annals of Clonmacnoise, s.a.* 951 [=956-78] (ed. Murphy, p. 157); *Annals of the Four Masters, s.a.* 968 [=970] (ed. and trans. O'Donovan, II, 692-93); *Annals of Inisfallen, s.a.* [969] [=970].4 (ed. and trans. Mac Airt, pp. 158-59); *Annals of Ulster, s.a.* 969 [=970].4 (ed. and trans. Mac Airt and Mac Niocaill, pp. 408-09); *Chronicum Scotorum, s.a.* [968] [=970] (ed. and trans. Hennessy, pp. 218-19).

[208] *Annals of the Four Masters, s.a.* 969 [=971] (ed. and trans. O'Donovan, II, 694-95); *Annals of Ulster, s.a.* 970 [=971].2, 970[=971].6 (ed. and trans. Mac Airt and Mac Niocaill, pp. 408-09); *Chronicum Scotorum, s.a.* [969] [=971] (ed. and trans. Hennessy, pp. 218-21).

[209] *Annals of Tigernach, s.a.* [975] (ed. and trans. Stokes, II, 230); *Chronicum Scotorum, s.a.* [973] [=975] (ed. and trans. Hennessy, pp. 222-23).

[210] *Annals of the Four Masters, s.a.* 975 [=977] (ed. and trans. O'Donovan, II, 704-05); *Annals of Ulster, s.a.* 976 [=977].1 (ed. and trans. Mac Airt and Mac Niocaill, pp. 412-13).

[211] *Annals of Clonmacnoise, s.a.* 971 [=978] (ed. Murphy, p. 158); *Annals of the Four Masters, s.a.* 976 [=978] (ed. and trans. O'Donovan, II, 704-07); *Annals of Ulster, s.a.* 977 [=978].3 (ed. and trans. Mac Airt and Mac Niocaill, pp. 412-13).

[212] *Annals of Clonmacnoise, s.a.* 972 [=979] (ed. Murphy, p. 158); *Annals of the Four Masters, s.a.* 977 [=979] (ed. and trans. O'Donovan, II, 708-09); *Chronicum Scotorum, s.a.* [977] [=979] (ed. and trans. Hennessy, pp. 224-25).

present at the event. He would have been old at the time of the battle, having ruled for forty years, and it was his sons who led the army. They were met by Mael Sechlainn with a gathering of forces from the Southern Uí Néill and Braen's men from Leinster. Rögnvaldr son of Óláfr fell in the engagement with many others. Mael Sechlainn followed up his victory with an attack on Dublin where Domnall Claen was released from captivity. A bombastic account of Mael Sechlainn's achievements was included in Irish chronicles. It asserts that he secured the release of all the Irish in bondage in Dublin, took a vast tribute and secured the release of Uí Néill lands from tribute to vikings.[213] Whatever the truth of this account, it is clear that he enjoyed a remarkable victory. Mael Sechlainn was to hound Dublin in future years and made a significant contribution to the political decline of the viking port. The loss of prestige and kin at the battle of Tara may have prompted Óláfr *Cuarán* to relinquish his kingship, for in 980 he went on pilgrimage to Iona where he died in the same year. The attributes that Óláfr may have cultivated as a leader in war – passion, discipline and self-sacrifice – were not altogether alien to the virtues espoused in medieval religious life. Pilgrimage was becoming increasingly popular among medieval rulers.[214] The aged king, perhaps aware of his declining health, vested his final efforts not in shoring up the troubled fortunes of Dublin, but in seeking salvation in the life that might follow.

The kingdom which Óláfr ruled seemed to be at the height of its influence when he acquired it in 939. The royal court at Dublin may have acted as a centre of patronage and display. Praise-poems about Óláfr *Cuarán* have survived in Middle Irish and he supported the Columban *familia* of churches.[215] Óláfr's reign witnessed notable successes including the territorial expansion of Dublin's hinterland. Nevertheless the power of Dublin may have been compromised by the cost of the preceding war with Limerick and by frequent changes in leadership while Óláfr campaigned in

---

[213] *Annals of Boyle*, §273 ('The Annals', ed. Freeman, p. 327); *Annals of the Four Masters, s.a.* 978 [=980] (ed. and trans. O'Donovan, II, 708-09); *Annals of Inisfallen, s.a.* [980] (ed. and trans. Mac Airt, pp. 162-63); *Annals of Tigernach, s.a.* [980] (ed. and trans. Stokes, II, 233-34); *Annals of Ulster, s.a.* 979 [=980].1 (ed. and trans. Mac Airt and Mac Niocaill, pp. 414-15); *Chronicum Scotorum, s.a.* [978] [=980] (ed. and trans. Hennessy, pp. 224-27); 'Do Fhlaithesaib Hérend iar Creitim', ed. Best and Bergin, I, 98.

[214] McGurk, 'Pilgrimage'.

[215] *The Metrical Dindsenchas*, ed. and trans. Gwynn, I, 52-53; Bhreathnach, 'Documentary Evidence', pp. 37-41; Ó hAodha, 'The First', p. 235.

England. He suffered serious setbacks including political failure in England and defeat at the hands of the Southern Uí Néill. Óláfr's reign therefore encompassed one of the high-points of viking power in Ireland and the start of a decline from which no full recovery was made.

The Dynasty of Ívarr at Limerick

During the second half of the reign of Óláfr *Cuarán*, Limerick begins to feature prominently in the chronicle-record. The port appears in the record with its own line of kings who came under increasing pressure during the rise of Dál Cais, a population-group in the north-west of Munster. Dál Cais usurped the power of the Eoganacht, who had historically supplied the overkings of that province. Eventually Limerick was taken under Dál Cais control and its resources were used to support the ambitions of the overking Brian Bóruma to dominate Ireland. Rulers of Dál Cais also created divisions between the vikings of Waterford and Dublin by allying with the former against the latter. Their policies can be seen as significant in eroding the political independence of the viking ports in Ireland.

In 967 Mathgamain, the Dál Cais overking, defeated the army of Limerick in a battle fought at Solloghed (Co. Tipperary), a few miles from the historic capital of Munster at Cashel.[216] To follow up his victory, Mathgamain travelled to Limerick the following day and plundered and burnt the settlement and its ships. In this orgy of destruction Mael Ruanaid, deputy-king of the Osraige, was killed in a viking counter-attack.[217] It may have been in response to Mathgamain's action that Emly was plundered in the following year.[218] This was one of the most celebrated churches of Munster. According to the twelfth-century saga *Cogad Gaedel re Gallaib* ('The War of the Irish with the Foreigners'), the army of Limerick was defeated here by Mathgamain in 969. *Cogad Gaedel re Gallaib* owes much of its information to earlier chronicles (but its author also reworked this material to suit the propagandist aims of its author); so the account may not be entirely reliable.[219]

---

[216] *Annals of Inisfallen, s.a.* [967] (ed. and trans. Mac Airt, pp. 158-59); Hogan, *Onomasticon*, p. 619.
[217] *Annals of the Four Masters, s.a.* 965 [=967] (ed. and trans. O'Donovan, II, 688-89).
[218] *Annals of Inisfallen, s.a.* [968] (ed. and trans. Mac Airt, pp. 158-59).
[219] *Cogad*, §51 (ed. and trans. Todd, pp. 82-84); Ó Corráin, *Ireland*, p. 117.

In 969 Mathgamain acted in alliance with vikings from Waterford to defend the eastern borders of Munster which had been invaded by the Leinster overking, Murchad son of Finn. Murchad may have timed his attack to coincide with Mathgamain's efforts to quell an area of southern Munster which seems to have resisted his authority. In the same year, it appears that Limerick-vikings were active in the vicinity of Dublin, for they killed Beolán Litil who may be identified as king of Southern Brega, an ally of Óláfr *Cuarán*.[220] These events suggest that Waterford and perhaps Limerick had recognised the overkingship of Mathgamain and that they were directed to fight against Murchad overking of Leinster and his Dublin collaborators.

If Limerick was subject to Mathgamain in 969, it did not remain so for long. In 972 the Munster overking led another attack on the port. Limerick was burnt on Mathgamain's orders and the 'foreigners' were expelled. This may be a reference to the exile of the ruling elite, rather than the population as a whole.[221] The motive for this attack is hinted at in 'The Annals of Inisfallen' for Mathgamain also banned mercenaries from Munster in 972. The word given for mercenary is *suaitrech*, a loan from Norse *svartleggja* ('black-leg'). Limerick may have been the origin of these mercenaries who supported Dubchrón ua Longacháin a local leader in Munster who opposed the supremacy of Dal Cáis. He was killed in the same year.[222]

In 974 Limerick gave hostages to an Eoganancht overking, 'the son of Bran', who opposed Mathgamain. The port was not only under pressure from neighbouring kings. In the same year vikings from the Hebrides attacked Ívarr, king of Limerick, on Scattery Island, an ecclesiastical site which appears to have had close links with the viking port.[223] Ívarr escaped,

[220] *Annals of the Four Masters*, s.a. 967 [=969] (ed. and trans. O'Donovan, II, 690-93); *Annals of Inisfallen*, s.a. [969] (ed. and trans. Mac Airt, pp. 158-59); *Annals of Ulster*, s.a. 968 [=969].3 (ed. and trans. Mac Airt and Mac Niocaill, pp. 408-09); *Chronicum Scotorum*, s.a. [967] [=969] (ed. and trans. Hennessy, pp. 218-19); Downham, 'The Vikings', p. 240, n. 52.

[221] *Annals of the Four Masters*, s.a. 969 [=971/972?] (ed. and trans. O'Donovan, II, 694-95); *Annals of Inisfallen*, s.a. [972] (ed. and trans. Mac Airt, pp. 158-59). This may be compared with the record of the expulsion of the foreigners of Dublin in 902, where it is evident that some of the population remained. See above, p. 27.

[222] *Annals of Inisfallen*, s.a. [972] (ed. and trans. Mac Airt, pp. 158-59).

[223] *Annals of the Four Masters*, s.a. 972 [=974] (ed. and trans. O'Donovan, II, 698-99); *Annals of Inisfallen*, s.a. [974] (ed. and trans. Mac Airt, pp. 160-61).

but in the following year King's Island in Limerick was captured again (presumably by Irish forces).[224] The final blow to Ívarr's reign was dealt in 977. Mathgamain's successor as overking of Dál Cais, Brian Bóruma, killed Ívarr and both of his sons at the ecclesiastical settlement on Scattery Island.[225] This seems to have ended the viking royal dynasty at Limerick. In the same year Brian also waged war against vikings in the territory of Uí Fhidgeinte which lay south of the Shannon-estuary. The war may have spilled over in 978 when Brian is said to have won a victory over the forces of Limerick and Uí Fhidgeinte.[226] From then on, the armies of Limerick appear to have been subservient to Brian. Brian also cultivated an alliance with Waterford and commanded the resources of the viking ports of the south-west of Ireland against Dublin.

Figure 9: The Royal Dynasty of Limerick

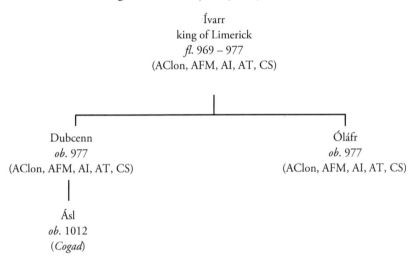

Ívarr
king of Limerick
fl. 969 – 977
(AClon, AFM, AI, AT, CS)

Dubcenn
ob. 977
(AClon, AFM, AI, AT, CS)

Óláfr
ob. 977
(AClon, AFM, AI, AT, CS)

Ásl
ob. 1012
(*Cogad*)

---

[224] *Annals of Inisfallen, s.a.* [975] (ed. and trans. Mac Airt, pp. 160-61).

[225] *Annals of Clonmacnoise, s.a.* 975 [=977] (ed. Murphy, p. 158); *Annals of the Four Masters, s.a.* 975 [=977] (ed. and trans. O'Donovan, II, 698-99); *Annals of Inisfallen, s.a.* [977] (ed. and trans. Mac Airt, pp. 162-63); *Annals of Tigernach, s.a.* [977] (ed. and trans. Stokes, II, 231); *Chronicum Scotorum, s.a.* [975] [=977] (ed. and trans. Hennessy, pp. 224-25).

[226] *Annals of the Four Masters, s.a.* 976 [=978] (ed. and trans. O'Donovan, II, 706-07). It is conceivable that this is a misplaced entry recording events of the previous year.

Figure 10: The Royal Dynasty of Waterford

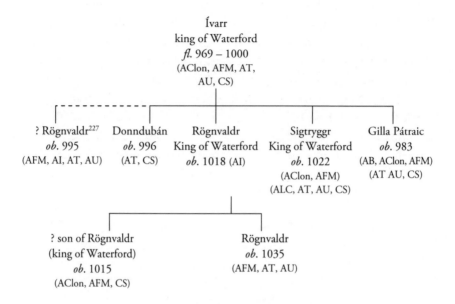

Ívarr
king of Waterford
fl. 969 – 1000
(AClon, AFM, AT,
AU, CS)

? Rögnvaldr[227]
ob. 995
(AFM, AI, AT, AU)

Donndubán
ob. 996
(AT, CS)

Rögnvaldr
King of Waterford
ob. 1018 (AI)

Sigtryggr
King of Waterford
ob. 1022
(AClon, AFM)
(ALC, AT, AU, CS)

Gilla Pátraic
ob. 983
(AB, AClon, AFM)
(AT AU, CS)

? son of Rögnvaldr
(king of Waterford)
ob. 1015
(AClon, AFM, CS)

Rögnvaldr
ob. 1035
(AFM, AT, AU)

From the Battle of Tara to the Battle of Clontarf

From the battle of Tara until the end of the tenth century there was a struggle between the royal dynasties of Waterford and Dublin. This rivalry was exploited by the leading Irish kings (Mael Sechlainn and Brian Bóruma) who sought to use viking forces to assist their own ambitions. In 983 Mael Sechlainn, overking of the Southern Uí Néill, allied with Glúniarainn son of Óláfr, king of Dublin, to defeat Ívarr, king of Waterford and Domnall Claen, overking of Leinster. Mael Sechlainn's alliance with Glúniarainn was encouraged by ties of blood as they had the same mother, Dúnliath, a princess of the Northern Uí Néill.[228] After this

---

[227] Rögnvaldr is named as a son of Ívarr in the *Annals of Ulster s.a.* 993 [=994].7 (ed. and trans. Mac Airt and Mac Niocaill, pp. 424-25), but as a grandson of Ívarr in the *Annals of Inisfallen, s.a.* [995] (ed. and trans. Mac Airt, pp. 170-71). He was killed by an enemy of Waterford, Murchad son of Finn. The existence of another Rögnvaldr Ívarsson, named as king of Waterford in 1018, begs an explanation. Perhaps a different relationship existed.

[228] *Annals of Clonmacnoise, s.a.* 977 [=983] (ed. Murphy, p. 159); *Annals of the Four Masters, s.a.* 982 [=983] (ed. and trans. O'Donovan, II, 714-15); *Annals of Ulster, s.a.* 982 [=983].2 (ed. and trans. Mac Airt and Mac Niocaill, pp. 418-19); *Chronicum Scotorum, s.a.* [981] [=983] (ed. and trans. Hennessy, pp. 228-29).

battle the Dál Cais overking, Brian Bóruma, allied with Ívarr of Waterford against Dublin. This drew Ívarr away from his former alliance with Leinster and in 984 a pact was made between vikings from Waterford and the Hebrides and Brian to attack Leinster and Dublin.[229] The combined armies ravaged through the province but appear not to have reached Dublin.

This rivalry between Waterford and Dublin intensified further after 989, when the death of Glúniarainn, king of Dublin, triggered a dispute over the royal succession between his brother Sigtryggr and Ívarr of Waterford. Mael Sechlainn took the opportunity to attack Dublin and he is said to have levied a heavy tax on the inhabitants of the port.[230] Ívarr of Waterford took control of the town on two occasions before 995 but he was expelled by Sigtryggr.[231] Although we do not know the parentage of Ívarr of Waterford, the names within his kin-group and the chain of events suggest that he was a member of the dynasty of Ívarr who could claim some right to rule Dublin. Sigtryggr son of Óláfr *Cuarán* regained power with the assistance of an army led by Mael Mórda, the overking of Leinster. Sigtryggr remained allied with Mael Mórda for the rest of his life.[232] This pact was aided by ties of blood, for Sigtryggr's mother Gormfhlaith was the sister of Maelmórda. Furthermore both kings faced determined efforts by Mael Sechlainn, overking of the Southern Uí Néill, and Brian, overking of Munster, to control them. In 995 Mael Sechlainn seized the regalia of Dublin, 'the Sword of Carlus' and 'the Ring of Þórir'.[233] In 997 and 998

---

[229] *Annals of Inisfallen, s.a.* [984] (ed. and trans. Mac Airt, pp. 164-65).

[230] *Annals of Clonmacnoise, s.a.* 982 [=989] (ed. Murphy, pp. 161-62); *Annals of the Four Masters, s.a.* 988 [=989] (ed. and trans. O'Donovan, II, 722-25); *Annals of Tigernach, s.a* [989] (ed. and trans. Stokes, II, 238); *Chronicum Scotorum, s.a.* [987] [=989] (ed. and trans. Hennessy, pp. 232-33). This reference to an ounce of silver or gold to be paid for each property is echoed in texts of the eleventh and twelfth centuries: e.g., *Aislinge Meic Conglinne*, ed. and trans. Meyer, p. 56; *Lebor na Cert*, ed. and trans. Dillon, p. 117.

[231] *Annals of Clonmacnoise, s.a.* 988 [=995] (ed. Murphy, p. 163); *Annals of the Four Masters, s.aa.* 992 [=993], 994 [=995] (ed. and trans. O'Donovan, II, 730-35); *Annals of Inisfallen, s.aa.* [990], [993] (ed. and trans. Mac Airt, pp. 168-71).

[232] Mac Shamhráin, 'The Battle', pp. 56-61.

[233] *Annals of Clonmacnoise, s.a.* 988 [=995] (ed. Murphy, p. 163); *Annals of the Four Masters, s.a.* 994 [=995] (ed. and trans. O'Donovan, II, 732-33); *Annals of Tigernach, s.a.* [995] (ed. and trans. Stokes, II, 242); *Chronicum Scotorum, s.a.* [993] [=995] (ed. and trans. Hennessy, pp. 234-35).

Mael Sechlainn and Brian took hostages from Dublin and Leinster.[234] Then in 999 a battle was fought at Glen Máma, west of Dublin, in which Brian and Mael Sechlainn won a victory over Sigtryggr.[235] Sigtryggr's brother Haraldr fell in the engagement and losses appear to have been heavy on both sides. The victory was followed by the sack of Dublin on New Year's Day A.D. 1000, when the settlement was burnt. Sigtryggr fled the port but was reinstated as king after submitting to Brian's authority later that year.[236] According to Ailbhe MacShamhráin, Brian's victory over Dublin gave him the confidence to challenge the power of the Uí Néill overking, Mael Sechlainn.[237] Brian organised a campaign to Tara in the same year in which the cavalry of Leinster and Dublin were sent as an advance-party to tackle the forces of Mael Sechlainn. They were heavily defeated (no doubt further weakening the forces of Dublin).[238] In 1002 Brian challenged Mael Sechlainn once more, bringing the armies of Munster, Connaught, Leinster and Dublin to Athlone on the River Shannon. Here Mael Sechlainn recognised Brian's authority and their combined forces travelled north in an attempt to exert power over the territories of the Northern Uí Néill.[239] Further expeditions were made in 1005, 1006 and 1007 when Brian led a

[234] *Annals of Boyle*, §277 ('The Annals', ed. Freeman, p. 327); *Annals of Clonmacnoise, s.a.* 991 [=998] (ed. Murphy, p. 164); *Annals of the Four Masters, s.a.* 997 [=998] (ed. and trans. O'Donovan, II, 736-37); *Annals of Inisfallen, s.a.* [997] (ed. and trans. Mac Airt, pp. 172-73); *Chronicum Scotorum, s.a.* [996] [=998] (ed. and trans. Hennessy, pp. 236-37).

[235] *Annals of Clonmacnoise, s.a.* 992 [=999] (ed. Murphy, p. 164); *Annals of the Four Masters, s.a.* 998 [=999] (ed. and trans. O'Donovan, II, 738-41); *Annals of Inisfallen, s.a.* [999] (ed. and trans. Mac Airt, pp. 172-73); *Annals of Ulster, s.a.* 998 [=999].8 (ed. and trans. Mac Airt and Mac Niocaill, pp. 428-29); *Chronicum Scotorum, s.a.* [997] [=999] (ed. and trans. Hennessy, pp. 236-37); Mac Shamhráin, 'The Battle', p. 61.

[236] *Annals of the Four Masters, s.a.* 999 [=1000] (ed. and trans. O'Donovan, II, 742-43); *Annals of Inisfallen, s.a.* [1000] (ed. and trans. Mac Airt, pp. 174-75); *Annals of Ulster, s.a.* 999 [=1000].4, 999 [=1000].7 (ed. and trans. Mac Airt and Mac Niocaill, pp. 428-29); *Chronicum Scotorum, s.aa.* [998] [=1000], [999] [=1001] (ed. and trans. Hennessy, pp. 238-39).

[237] Mac Shamhráin, 'The Battle', pp. 62-64.

[238] *Annals of the Four Masters, s.a.* 999 [=1000] (ed. and trans. O'Donovan, II, 742-43).

[239] *Annals of Clonmacnoise, s.a.* 993 [=1002] (ed. Murphy, pp. 164-65); *Annals of the Four Masters, s.a.* 1001 [=1002] (ed. and trans. O'Donovan, II, 744-47); *Annals of Ulster, s.a.* 1001 [=1002].1, 1001 [=1002].8 (ed. and trans. Mac Airt and Mac Niocaill, pp. 430-31); *Chronicum Scotorum, s.a.* [1000] [=1002] (ed. and trans. Hennessy, pp. 238-41).

coalition of forces, including the Dubliners, to impose his authority over the northernmost parts of Ireland.[240]

During these years it seems that Dublin still faced local difficulties through the animosity of Gilla Mochonna, overking of Southern Brega. His men burnt Dublin 'by stealth' in 1005, and 'The Annals of Ulster' record the torture that he liked to inflict on the 'foreigners'.[241] Gilla Mochonna's death in 1013 may have brought some relief to Sigtryggr. It was in the same year that Sigtryggr began a final attempt to limit the growing power of Brian Bóruma. He won a victory against the forces of the Southern Uí Néill, which had invaded the northern hinterland of Dublin. He then sent a naval expedition against Munster where his son Óláfr and one of his nephews were killed. Brian responded by plundering the north of Leinster in the autumn.[242]

In the opening months of 1014 Sigtryggr seems to have been busy negotiating for the support of viking fleets who were active in British waters, while Brian gathered support for an assault on Dublin and Leinster. The two sides met on Good Friday at Clontarf, a short distance north of Dublin. What followed has become one of the most famous battles in Irish history.[243] Sigtryggr's supporters at the battle of Clontarf included viking contingents from the Northern Isles, Hebrides and Scandinavia. The earl of Orkney, Sigurðr Hloðvisson, fell in the battle, along with Óláfr son of Lagmann of the Hebrides and Broðir, the leader of a fleet which may have

---

[240] *Annals of the Four Masters*, *s.aa.* 1004 [=1005], 1005 [=1006] (ed. and trans. O'Donovan, II, 752-57); *Annals of Ulster*, *s.aa.* 1004 [=1005].7, 1005 [=1006].4, 1006 [=1007].7 (ed. and trans. Mac Airt and Mac Niocaill, pp. 434-39); *Chronicum Scotorum*, *s.aa.* [1003] [=1005], [1004] [=1006] (ed. and trans. Hennessy, pp. 242-45).

[241] *Annals of the Four Masters*, *s.aa.* 1004 [=1005], 1012 [=1013] (ed. and trans. O'Donovan, II, 752-53, 768-71); *Chronicum Scotorum*, *s.a.* [1003] [=1005] (ed. and trans. Hennessy, pp. 242-43); 'By him foreigners were yoked to the plough, and two foreigners dragged the harrow after them by their scrotum'; *Annals of Ulster*, *s.a.* 1012 [=1013].4 (ed. and trans. Mac Airt and Mac Niocaill, pp. 444-45); Ó Súilleabháin, 'Nótaí' (I am grateful to Donnchadh Ó Corráin for this reference).

[242] *Annals of the Four Masters*, *s.a.* 1012 [=1013] (ed. and trans. O'Donovan, II, 768-71); *Annals of Ulster*, *s.a.* 1012 [=1013].5, 1012 [=1013].12 (ed. and trans. Mac Airt and Mac Niocaill, pp. 444-47); *Chronicum Scotorum*, *s.a.* [1011] [=1013] (ed. and trans. Hennessy, pp. 248-49).

[243] Downham, 'The Battle'.

included Danish warships.[244] Sigtryggr's long-time ally Mael Mórda, overking of Leinster, also fought (and died) in the engagement.

Brian's army consisted of the men of Munster, some troops from Connaught and a contingent led by the *mormaer* of Mar in Scotland. It is a matter of contention whether Mael Sechlainn and the men of Meath also participated in the conflict, but the accounts of 'The Annals of Ulster', 'The Annals of Boyle' and *Chronicum Scotorum* are among the sources that record them as present. Later propaganda issued in favour of Brian's descendants denied the Southern Uí Néill overking a place in the encounter.[245] Brian was killed at Clontarf but his forces were victorious over the army of Dublin.

The battle of Clontarf may not have had a decisive impact on Irish politics.[246] Mael Sechlainn succeeded Brian as the most powerful leader in Ireland. Nevertheless the hegemony of Uí Néill was soon ousted and Brian's grandson Muirchertach rose to be the dominant overking in Irish politics at the end of the century. Sigtryggr remained as king of Dublin and in the year after the battle he was once again fighting Mael Sechlainn.[247] Despite

[244] The presence of *Danair*, 'Danes', in Insular waters is recorded from the 980s, corresponding with renewed attacks on Britain from Scandinavia: *Annals of Ulster, s.aa.* 985 [=986].2, 986 [=987].1, 986 [=987].3, 989 [=990].1 (ed. and trans. Mac Airt and Mac Niocaill, pp. 418-23). Welsh chronicles indicate that Sigtryggr paid mercenaries to participate at Clontarf: *ByT* (Pen. 20), *s.a.* [1014] (ed. Jones, p. 14; trans. Jones, p. 11); *ByT* (RBH), *s.a.* [1014] (ed. and trans. Jones, pp. 20-21). The presence of a Scandinavian contingent at the battle could be explained by the employment of mariners who had participated in the conquest of England. Danes are identifed at the battle by the *Annals of Boyle,* §281 ('The Annals', ed. Freeman, p. 328); *Annals of the Four Masters, s.a.* 1013 [=1014] (ed. and trans. O'Donovan, II, 714-15). It is not entirely clear whether *Lochlainn,* the origin of troops mentioned in some Irish chronicles, refers to Norway or the Scottish islands.

[245] *Annals of Boyle,* §281 ('The Annals', ed. Freeman, pp. 327-29); *Annals of Clonmacnoise, s.a.* 996 [=1005-14] (ed. Murphy, pp. 166-67); *Annals of the Four Masters, s.a.* 1013 [=1014] (ed. and trans. O'Donovan, II, 772-81); *Annals of Inisfallen, s.a.* [1014] (ed. and trans. Mac Airt, pp. 184-85); *Annals of Ulster, s.a.* 1014.2 (ed. and trans. Mac Airt and Mac Niocaill, pp. 446-49); *Chronicum Scotorum, s.a.* [1012] [=1014] (ed. and trans. Hennessy, pp. 250-53); Downham, 'The Vikings', p. 243.

[246] Ryan, 'The Battle', pp. 47-49; Young, 'A Note', pp. 20-21; Ó Corráin, *Ireland*, p. 130; Ó Cróinín, *Early Medieval Ireland*, p. 266.

[247] *Annals of the Four Masters, s.aa.* 1014 [=1015], 1042 (ed. and trans. O'Donovan, II, 782-83, 842-43); *Annals of Inisfallen, s.a.* [1042] (ed. and trans. Mac Airt, pp. 206-07); *Annals of Tigernach, s.a.* [1042] (ed. and trans. Stokes, II, 273); *Chronicum Scotorum, s.a.* 1013 [=1015] (ed. and trans. Hennessy, pp. 254-55).

Sigtryggr's defeat at Clontarf, his long career (which lasted until 1036) was not entirely overshadowed by it. His reign witnessed successes both before and after the battle. In the 990s he introduced coin-minting to Dublin and towards the end of his reign he established a bishopric for the town.[248] He also cultivated links overseas, exemplified by his pilgrimage to Rome in 1028 and his alliance with English forces to attack Wales in 1030.[249] Clontarf's fame therefore lay not so much in its immediate political impact, but rather in the wide range of its participants and its scale. As a consequence the event was commemorated in Irish and Icelandic medieval literature.[250] It attracted grand interpretations as a great battle between Irish and foreigners or between Christianity and heathenism, although in truth it was neither.[251]

Nevertheless, within the broader scale of events, Clontarf can be seen to mark a significant stage in the decline of viking power in Ireland. The trio of battles fought and lost in 980, 999 and 1014 meant that the port became obliged to recognise the authority of powerful Irish overkings. The descendants of Ívarr continued to play a role in politics across the Irish Sea until the twelfth century and they commanded significant economic and military resources.[252] Nevertheless the times when the royal dynasty of the port could single-handedly threaten the power of the most powerful kings of Ireland became just a memory. These memories were preserved and re-formulated in the propaganda of eleventh- and twelfth-century Irish kings who celebrated in literature how their ancestors had prevented Ireland from being overrun by foreigners.[253]

Vikings' Political Impact

Overall it could be argued that vikings had a centrifugal effect on Irish politics. In the ninth century Uí Néill initially built up their influence during a period of viking wars in Ireland, but their power was eroded by successive wars against Dublin. At the end of the tenth century the Dál Cais overkings of Munster rose to a position of prominence, assisted by their

---

[248] Connon, 'Sitriuc', p. 429.
[249] *Annals of Tigernach*, s.aa. [1028], [1030] (ed. and trans. Stokes, II, 260, 262).
[250] Goedheer, *Irish and Norse Traditions*.
[251] Ó Corráin, *Ireland*, pp. 130-31.
[252] Duffy, 'Irishmen'; Downham, 'England'; Downham, 'Living on the Edge'.
[253] Ó Corráin, 'Nationality', pp. 31-32.

control of Limerick and Waterford. Following the breach of the historically sanctioned authority of Uí Néill, different provincial overkings contended for prominence within Ireland in the eleventh and twelfth centuries. At a provincial level in southern Ireland (where the influence of viking towns was greatest), power passed from historically prominent groups to those on the margins. The Eoganacht of Munster gave way to the rising power of Dál Cais in the west. In Leinster the power of Uí Dúnlainge in the north of the province gave way in the eleventh century to Uí Cheinnselaig in the south.[254]

Nevertheless, sweeping generalisations of this nature must also have their counter-arguments. Vikings played a significant role in the realignments of power in Ireland but they cannot be seen as wholly responsible. During the reign of Brian Bóruma the resources possessed by the viking towns helped in his bid to centralise authority in the island. Nevertheless, for various reasons Brian's family failed to secure lasting supremacy. In the eleventh and twelfth centuries, viking rulers became increasingly subject to powerful Irish kings. Even so, it can still be argued that the continuing efforts of Dublin to retain a measure of independence operated against the ambitions of those kings who wanted to bring all Ireland under their rule.[255]

In this chapter I have sought to provide an overview of the complex meanderings of viking politics in Ireland. The politics appear complex not so much because structures of power in Ireland were different from those of her neighbours, but because we have a rich body of written evidence which gives a detailed insight into events at a local level. It is in the Irish chronicles that we can trace the origins and endurance of the power of the dynasty of Ívarr: Ireland was the springboard for their considerable achievements overseas.

---

[254] The kingdom of the Osraige which lay on the borders of Munster and Leinster also grew in significance, for in the eleventh century, its overking Donnchad son of Gilla Phátraic temporarily held sway over Leinster.

[255] Downham, 'Living on the Edge'.

3

England: from the Conquest of York to the Battle of Brunanburh, 866-937

FROM the time of the first Scandinavian raids on England at the end of the eighth century, until the Danish conquest in 1013, the political geography and culture of the Anglo-Saxons were transformed through the influence of vikings. The dynasty of Ívarr played no small part in this transformation. 'Dark' vikings from Ireland had been active in Britain from the 850s and Ívarr can be identified as one of the leaders of 'a great army' which disembarked on the coast of East Anglia in 865/6.[1] Ívarr's arrival heralded one of the most intense periods of viking warfare in Britain. The city of York was captured by the army from East Anglia in 866/7 and this inaugurated a string of viking successes. In 869 East Anglia was conquered; then in 873 all Mercia was subjugated. Wessex also fell under viking control early in 878, and its king Alfred was forced into hiding in the marshes of Athelney (Somerset). It was not until Alfred's decisive victory at Edington (Wiltshire) in May 878 that the tide of viking conquests in England was effectively countered. The years from 878 to 937 were marked by a sustained struggle between the heirs of Ívarr based at York and the English kings based in Wessex.

The main primary sources for Anglo-Saxon England during the First Viking Age are 'The Anglo-Saxon Chronicle', Asser's 'Life of King Alfred'

---

[1] *Annales Cambriae* (ABC), ed. and trans. Dumville, pp. 12-13; *ByS*, ed. and trans. Jones, pp. 18-19; *ByT* (Pen. 20), ed. Jones, p. 5; *ByT* (Pen. 20), trans. Jones, p. 4; *ByT* (RBH), ed. and trans. Jones, pp. 8-9; Sawyer, *Anglo-Saxon Charters*, no. 206; *English Historical Documents*, trans. Whitelock, no. 90; *Annals of Ulster, s.a.* 855 [=856].6 (ed. and trans. Mac Airt and Mac Niocaill, pp. 314-15); *Chronicum Scotorum, s.a.* [856] (ed. and trans. Hennessy, pp. 154-55); *ASC A*, ed. Bately, p. 43; *ASC.B*, ed. Taylor, p. 30; *ASC.C*, ed. O'Keeffe, p. 54; *ASC.D*, ed. Cubbin, p. 21; E in *Two of the Saxon Chronicles*, ed. Plummer, I, 63.

and 'The Chronicle of Æthelweard' as well as royal diplomas.[2] All of these sources were connected with the households of English kings and for the most part they give a Wessex-based account which favours the ruling dynasty and gives patchy attention to other parts of the country. There are very few written sources which present a contemporary viking perspective on events and these mainly consist of coin-inscriptions and skaldic verse. The incomplete and partial nature of the surviving written sources for viking activity in England must be taken into account when one is constructing a historical narrative.

The Deeds of Ívarr

Mentions of Ívarr in Irish and British historical accounts enable us to piece together some of the stages in his career. Ívarr's absence from Irish records can be linked to his campaigns in England, and vice versa. Ívarr travelled to East Anglia in 865 as part of 'a great army'. The prior history of this force is obscure, although comments by Asser and (a century later) Æthelweard provide scope for speculation. Asser reported that the fleet came *de Danubia*, but modern historians have suggested that he had Denmark in mind (Asser may have confused *Dacia*, where the Danube was located, with *Dania*, 'Denmark').[3] 'The Chronicle of Æthelweard' records that 'the fleets of the tyrant Ívarr' arrived from the north, which could be a vague reference to Scandinavia or to a place where Scandinavians had settled.[4] Simon Keynes has concluded that the army which arrived in East Anglia consisted of several elements (including a contingent from Ireland).[5] The creation of composite armies for a particular campaign was a feature of viking warfare.[6]

---

[2] The core of 'The Anglo-Saxon Chronicle' was put together in 892 and was continued as a more or less contemporary record thereafter: Waterhouse, 'Stylistic Factors', pp. 3-8; Sawyer, *The Age*, pp. 14, 19. Asser composed his biography of Alfred in 893 and Æthelweard composed his chronicle, 978 × 988. Both authors drew information from 'The Anglo-Saxon Chronicle': *Asser's Life*, ed. Stevenson, pp. lxxi-lxxiv, lxxxii-lxxxiii; *Chronicon Æthelweardi*, ed. and trans. Campbell, p. xlii, n. 2. For the royal diplomas see Sawyer, *Anglo-Saxon Charters*.

[3] *Alfred*, trans. Keynes and Lapidge, p. 238, n. 44; Latham, *Revised Medieval Latin Word-List*, s.v. *Dacia*.

[4] Æthelweard, *Chronicon*, IV.1 (ed. and trans. Campbell, p. 35).

[5] Keynes, 'The Vikings in England', p. 54.

[6] Lund, 'The Armies'.

Ívarr may have joined up with vikings who had been active in England in the early 860s, or with another army from the Continent.[7]

'The Anglo-Saxon Chronicle' reports that the East Angles provided the vikings with horses and in the following year the army rode to Northumbria. This coincided with a civil war and vikings were able to seize control of York before the rival parties had come to terms. The rival kings Osberht and Ælle then joined forces but died in battle against the vikings, and their followers submitted to the viking army.[8] The viking army had travelled a long way from East Anglia, and they benefited greatly from the political disunity in Northumbria. It seems likely that the vikings had been tipped off concerning events in the north, whether from viking fleets travelling south or through English informants.[9]

In the winter of 867 the army travelled to Mercia and then returned to York for a year in 868. As York was a temporary base of operations, some measures may have been taken to secure the loyalty of this town in their absence, either by leaving some troops there or through the seizure of hostages. In Mercia, Nottingham served as a winter-base. The troops of the Mercian king, Burhred, and those of King Æthelred from Wessex failed in their siege of the town, and the Mercians were forced to make peace with the enemy. It was presumably as a result of this truce that the viking army left Nottingham and returned to York. In the following winter, we are told, vikings rode from York across Mercia to East Anglia, which was their next target.

In November 869 a decisive battle was fought and the East Anglian king Edmund was killed. After the battle, all of East Anglia was conquered.[10] Edmund was soon feted as a Christian martyr and his cult rapidly spread,

---

[7] *ASC.A*, ed. Bately, pp. 46-47; *ASC.B*, ed. Taylor, p. 33; *ASC.C*, ed. O'Keeffe, pp. 57-58; *ASC.D*, ed. Cubbin, pp. 23-24; E in *Two of the Saxon Chronicles*, ed. Plummer, I, 67, 69. Patrick Wormald suggested that vikings' increasing involvement in England in the mid-860s corresponded with declining opportunities for vikings in Francia: 'Viking Studies', p. 137.

[8] *ASC.A*, ed. Bately, p. 47: '7 þær was ungemetlic wel geslægen Norþanhymbra, sume binnan, sume butan, 7 þa cyningas begen ofslægene'. Cf. *ASC.B*, ed. Taylor, p. 34; *ASC.C*, ed. O'Keeffe, p. 58; *ASC.D*, ed. Cubbin, p. 24; E in *Two of the Saxon Chronicles*, ed. Plummer, I, 69. Alfred Smyth has argued that Ælle was in fact killed after the battle, but this opinion is derived from later sources: *Scandinavian Kings*, pp. 189-94.

[9] *Ibid.*, p. 182. Smyth has pointed out vikings' good nose for civil war or political disunity, and their ability to profit from it.

[10] *ASC.A*, ed. Bately, p. 47; *ASC.B*, ed. Taylor, p. 34; *ASC.C*, ed. O'Keeffe, p. 58; *ASC.D*, ed. Cubbin, p. 24; E in *Two of the Saxon Chronicles*, ed. Plummer, I, 71.

which led to extended descriptions of his death being recorded.[11] Æthelweard and Abbo of Fleury, who wrote at much the same time as one another, in the late tenth century, agree in identifying Ívarr as the viking leader responsible for killing the king.[12] According to 'The Chronicle of Æthelweard', Ívarr died in the same year as Edmund's martyrdom.[13] However, this record conflicts with Irish chronicles which report that Ívarr travelled to Strathclyde in 870 and then died in Ireland in 873.[14] This disparity has led some commentators to question whether the Ívarr named in Irish and English records is one and the same person.[15] However, Ívarr's disappearance from the English scene in 870 may have led later English chroniclers to conclude that he had died.[16] Furthermore, as Patrick Wormald has noted, the death of a saint-killer shortly after committing his crime was a hagiographic commonplace.[17] Ívarr's 'disappearance' might therefore have fitted with preconceived notions on the nature of divine vengeance.

Following the conquest of East Anglia, Ívarr seems to have been called north to aid his ally Óláfr. The two leaders undertook a four-month siege of Dumbarton Rock in Strathclyde. After the defenders eventually capitulated, a large haul of captives was taken to Ireland, which included slaves from

[11] This may account for various additions made in later versions of 'The Anglo-Saxon Chronicle' for this year: *ASC.F*, ed. Baker, p. 67 (*s.a.* 870); E in *Two of the Saxon Chronicles*, ed. Plummer, I, 71, *s.a.* 870. Both these versions belong to the first half of the twelfth century. The E-text comments on the destruction of churches around Peterborough, and the F-text names the leaders of the viking army as Ingware and Ubba.

[12] *Passio Sancti Eadmundi*, §10 (*Memorials*, ed. Arnold, I, 15; *Three Lives*, ed. Winterbottom, p. 79); Æthelweard, *Chronicon*, IV.2 (ed. and trans. Campbell, p. 36); Whitelock, 'Fact', p. 219.

[13] Æthelweard, *Chronicon*, IV.2 (ed. and trans. Campbell, pp. 36-37).

[14] *Annals of the Four Masters*, *s.a.* 871 [=873] (ed. and trans. O'Donovan, I, 518-19); *Annals of Ulster*, *s.aa.* 869 [=870].6, 870 [=871].2, 872 [=873].3 (ed. and trans. Mac Airt and Mac Niocaill, pp. 326-29); *Chronicum Scotorum*, *s.a.* [873] (ed. and trans. Hennessy, pp. 164-65); Wormald, 'Viking Studies', p. 143.

[15] Caution has been expressed by Stenton, *Anglo-Saxon England*, p. 250; Keynes, 'The Vikings in England', p. 54.

[16] 'The Anglo-Saxon Chronicle' shows no interest in Ívarr's activities following his departure from England. Instead it focuses on the activities of the viking army which menaced Wessex in the following year.

[17] Wormald, 'Viking Studies', p. 143.

England – perhaps brought by Ívarr.[18] Óláfr returned to North Britain and Ívarr died shortly afterwards, presumably in Ireland.[19]

Martin Biddle and Birthe Kjølbye-Biddle have suggested that remains of Ívarr represented the central burial in a mass-grave discovered at Repton (Derbyshire) where vikings over-wintered in 873.[20] They have sought to corroborate this by reference to account in the mid-thirteenth-century text *Ragnars saga loðbrókar* which states that Ívarr died (and was buried) somewhere in England.[21] The latter may be discounted, as it was written at a time and place far removed from the events. As to the burial at Repton, it is noteworthy that several kings and numerous jarls were associated with viking armies in England.[22] Jarls are mentioned often enough in 'The Anglo-Saxon Chronicle' to suggest that they were high-status military leaders who might have been buried with the same honour shown at the central burial in Repton. Furthermore the burial in question was opened in the eighteenth century, and we cannot be sure that the bones were those of a 'giant' viking.[23] Ívarr's bones cannot therefore be identified with those interred at Repton.

Ívarr's involvement in England was limited to the years 866×870. He is not given a great deal of attention in the near-contemporary English sources. Indeed he is not alluded to in 'The Anglo-Saxon Chronicle' until after his death.[24] Nevertheless Ívarr's role in the martyrdom of King Edmund, and the achievements of his descendants, secured his fame in later texts. He may be regarded as one of the most significant figures of ninth-century Irish and British history.

[18] *Annals of Ulster*, s.aa. 869 [=870].6, 870 [=871].2 (ed. and trans. Mac Airt and Mac Niocaill, pp. 326-27); *Annales Cambriae* (AB), s.a. [871] (ed. and trans. Dumville, pp. 12-13).

[19] *Annals of Ulster*, s.a. 872 [=873].3 (ed. and trans. Mac Airt and Mac Niocaill, pp. 328-29).

[20] Biddle and Kjølbye-Biddle, 'Repton', pp. 81-84.

[21] *Ragnars Saga Loðbrokar*, ed. Guðni Jónsson, *Fornaldar Sögur*, I, 280; *The Saga*, trans. Schlauch, pp. 251-52.

[22] Several of these are named among the fallen at Ashdown and later at the battle of Edington: *ASC.A*, ed. Bately, pp. 48-51; *ASC.B*, ed. Taylor, pp. 34-35, 37; *ASC.C*, ed. O'Keeffe, pp. 59, 61-62; *ASC.D*, ed. Cubbin, pp. 25, 27; E in *Two of the Saxon Chronicles*, ed. Plummer, I, 71, 77.

[23] Hall, *Exploring the World*, p. 84.

[24] *ASC.A*, ed. Bately, p. 50; *ASC.B*, ed. Taylor, p. 37; *ASC.C*, ed. O'Keeffe, p. 61; *ASC.D*, ed. Cubbin, p. 27; E in *Two of the Saxon Chronicles*, ed. Plummer, I, 75.

The Career of Hálfdan

Hálfdan was a brother of Ívarr.[25] He may have been promoted to royal status in England following the departure of Ívarr in 870. He first enters the historical record in 871, as a viking king who fought at the battle of Ashdown (Berkshire).[26] In this encounter the vikings were heavily defeated by a West Saxon army. Hálfdan's ally King Bagsecg and five jarls fell in combat. This may have left Hálfdan as sole king of the viking army for a brief period.[27] Later in 871 a new viking fleet arrived at Reading from overseas.[28] This fleet united with Hálfdan's men.[29] According to 'The Anglo-Saxon Chronicle', King Alfred fought 'all the army' (*alne þone here*) a little later in the year at Wilton (Wiltshire): this may mean the united forces of the armies from Ashdown and Reading (or possibly the full force of one army).[30] In this engagement, the vikings had the victory. The triumphant army did not follow up their success with an attempt to conquer Wessex. Instead they travelled east to establish winter-quarters at London where the Mercians made peace with them. Vikings may have seized control of London at this point, for the town was taken from them by Alfred in 883.[31] Towards the end of 872, vikings travelled from London and over-wintered at Torksey in Lindsey. Here the Mercians made peace again.

According to some, but not all, versions of 'The Anglo-Saxon Chronicle', the viking army went into Northumbria before arriving at

[25] The Anglo-Saxon Chronicle refers to a brother of Ívarr and Hálfdan. Geoffrey Gaimar, writing in the twelfth century, identified this brother as Ubba. However, he may have jumped to this conclusion from reading about Ubba's association with Ívarr in the legends of St Edmund's martyrdom. *L'Estoire*, ed. and trans. Hardy and Martin, I, 132, and II, 10, lines 3147-49; *L'Estoire*, ed. Bell, pp. 91-92, lines 2838-92; *ASC.A*, ed. Bately, p. 50; *ASC.B*, ed. Taylor, p. 37; *ASC.C*, ed. O'Keeffe, p. 61; *ASC.D*, ed. Cubbin, p. 27; E in *Two of the Saxon Chronicles*, ed. Plummer, I, 75; cf. *Alfred*, trans. Keynes and Lapidge, p. 248, n. 99.

[26] *ASC.A*, ed. Bately, pp. 48-49; *ASC.B*, ed. Taylor, pp. 34-35; *ASC.C*, ed. O'Keeffe, p. 59; *ASC.D*, ed. Cubbin, p. 25; E in *Two of the Saxon Chronicles*, ed. Plummer, I, 71, 73.

[27] Smyth, *Scandinavian York*, I, 18.

[28] *ASC.A*, ed. Bately, p. 48; *ASC.B*, ed. Taylor, p. 35; *ASC.C*, ed. O'Keeffe, p. 59; *ASC.D*, ed. Cubbin, p. 25; E in *Two of the Saxon Chronicles*, ed. Plummer, I, 73; Asser, *De Rebus Gestis Ælfredi*, §40 (*Asser's Life*, ed. Stevenson, p. 31; *Alfred*, trans. Keynes and Lapidge, p. 80).

[29] *Ibid.*

[30] *ASC.A*, ed. Bately, pp. 48-49; *ASC.B*, ed. Taylor, pp. 34-35; *ASC.C*, ed. O'Keeffe, p. 59; *ASC.D*, ed. Cubbin, p. 25; E in *Two of the Saxon Chronicles*, ed. Plummer, I, 71, 73; Smyth, *Scandinavian Kings*, p. 241.

[31] Dumville, *Wessex*, pp. 6-7; Keynes, 'King Alfred and the Mercians', pp. 12-23.

Torksey.[32] Dorothy Whitelock suggested that the incentive for vikings to campaign in Northumbria in late 872 was to suppress a revolt in Northumbria against an English leader who had been established by them.[33] This idea is based on the testimony of the second part of *Historia Regum Anglorum*, which was written in the twelfth century, as well as other twelfth-century writings emanating from Durham, and the early thirteenth-century *Flores Historiarum* of Roger of Wendover.[34] These sources assert that Northumbria (at least north of the Tyne) was ruled by English kings under viking suzerainty from 867 until the 890s. They state that the first of these kings, Ecgberht, was driven out by the Northumbrians in 872. This would provide a motive for the vikings' campaign. However, this information is late and its origins are uncertain.[35]

The motive for the vikings' Northern campaign may rather have been to subdue various parts of Mercia following the capture of London. If so, they achieved their goal the following year, when the army moved from Lindsey to Repton, and the Mercian king, Burhred, fled overseas (he died in Italy soon after).[36] The viking army then 'conquered all that land' ('þæt land eall geeodon')[37] and they established an English thegn Ceolwulf as a dependent ruler who swore to act under their direction.[38] This event fully secured the land-route between Northumbria and East Anglia; and it seems that the Mercian campaign may have been intended for that purpose. The campaigns of Hálfdan and his allies in 872 and 873 were highly successful.

---

[32] This is omitted from the D- and E-texts. It is interesting that this information should have been eliminated from a version ('The Northern Recension', the ultimate common source of DEF) written at York within a generation of A.D. 1000.

[33] *The Anglo-Saxon Chronicle*, trans. Whitelock *et al.*, p. 47, n. 14; Smyth, *Scandinavian York*, I, 18.

[34] *Symeonis Monachi Opera*, ed. Arnold, I, 55, 225, and II, 110; *The Church Historians*, trans. Stevenson, III, pt 2, p. 78; *Rogeri de Wendover Chronica*, ed. Coxe, I, 323-24; *Roger*, trans. Giles, I, 206; Rollason *et al.*, *Sources*, pp. 25-27, 32, 63; Sawyer, *Scandinavians*, pp. 9-10.

[35] Dumville, 'Textual Archaeology', p. 45.

[36] Keynes, 'Anglo-Saxon Entries', p. 110.

[37] For 874: *ASC.A*, ed. Bately, p. 49; *ASC.B*, ed. Taylor, p. 36; *ASC.C*, ed. O'Keeffe, p. 60; *ASC.D*, ed. Cubbin, p. 26; E in *Two of the Saxon Chronicles*, ed. Plummer, I, 73.

[38] Ceolwulf is not named in ASC (A). David Dumville has suggested that Ceolwulf's Mercians killed Rhodri Mawr of Gwynedd in 878 under the vikings' direction: 'Brittany', p. 157. Rhodri had previously killed Horm, chief of the *Dubgaill* in 856, according to the *Annals of Ulster*, *s.a.* 855 [=856].6, 876 [=877].3 (ed. and trans. Mac Airt and Mac Niocaill, pp. 314-15, 332-33).

The suffering which they brought to the native population is hinted at in various sources. In 872, Wærferth, bishop of Worcester rented out lands at Nuthurst in Warwickshire for twenty mancuses of gold, because of 'the pressing affliction and immense tribute of the barbarians' ('proxima afflictione et inmenso tributo barbarorum').[39]

After the conquest of Mercia was complete, Hálfdan led his troops independently to Northumbria. Three other kings present at Repton; Guthrum, Oscetel and Anwend, who may have arrived in England in 871, travelled south and established their rule over East Anglia.[40] Hálfdan soon drops from 'The Anglo-Saxon Chronicle'. As he no longer represented a great threat to Wessex, the chronicle-author(s) lost interest in him. 'The Anglo-Saxon Chronicle' reports that in the winter of 874/75, Hálfdan was based on the Tyne and thereafter made war on the Picts and Strathclyde Britons.[41] His battles in the north can be seen as the continuation of Ívarr's policies in Britain, as recorded in Irish chronicles. 'The Annals of Ulster' report a great battle between the Picts and the 'Dark heathens' (presumably led by Hálfdan) in 875.[42] According to 'The Annals of Ulster', Hálfdan also deceitfully killed a son of Óláfr in 875.[43] This suggests that rivalry existed among the associates of Óláfr and Ívarr, who had campaigned together in North Britain a decade before.[44]

In 876 Hálfdan shared out lands in Northumbria among his followers. This may have been intended to settle affairs before he went to campaign overseas. 'The Annals of Ulster' demonstrate that Hálfdan travelled to Ireland, perhaps seeking to win the position there which Ívarr had once held. However he was killed in 877 in a battle against 'Fair Foreigners' at

[39] Sawyer, *Anglo-Saxon Charters*, no. 1278; *English Historical Documents*, trans. Whitelock, no. 94; *Fragmentary Annals*, §410 (ed. and trans. Radner, pp. 148-49).

[40] *ASC.A*, ed. Bately, p. 49; *ASC.B*, ed. Taylor, p. 36; *ASC.C*, ed. O'Keeffe, p. 61; *ASC.D*, ed. Cubbin, p. 26; E in *Two of the Saxon Chronicles*, ed. Plummer, I, 75. An alternative possibility is that at least one of these rulers had been promoted to the status of king following the death of King *Bagsecg* at Ashdown in 871.

[41] *ASC.A*, ed. Bately, p. 50; *ASC.B*, ed. Taylor, p. 37; *ASC.C*, ed. O'Keeffe, p. 61; *ASC.D*, ed. Cubbin, p. 27; E in *Two of the Saxon Chronicles*, ed. Plummer, I, 75. This is the first mention of 'Strathclyde' in English sources. Numismatic evidence relating to the activities of Hálfdan's troops has been discussed by Graham-Campbell, 'The Northern Hoards', p. 226.

[42] *Annals of Ulster*, s.a. 874 [=875].3 (ed. and trans. Mac Airt and Mac Niocaill, pp. 330-31).

[43] *Annals of Ulster*, s.a. 874 [=875].4 (ed. and trans. Mac Airt and Mac Niocaill, pp. 330-31).

[44] Smyth, *Scandinavian York*, I, 19.

Strangford Lough on the north-east coast of Ireland.[45] Hálfdan's title in Irish records is consistently that of chieftain (*toísech*), not king, suggesting that he never received the same level of recognition among the vikings in Ireland as he had held in England, or that which had been achieved by his kinsman Ívarr.

Hálfdan's activity in England can be dated 871×876, although it is possible that he accompanied his brother Ívarr on campaign before that date. Hálfdan became in effect the first Scandinavian king of Northumbria. He oversaw the division of Northumbrian lands among the army which settled there, and he helped to secure the northern borders of his conquests. The pan-Insular careers of Ívarr and Hálfdan set a precedent for their successors' ambitions to unite at least Dublin and York under their rule.[46]

Northumbria after Hálfdan

After 876, there are nearly two decades in which very little can be said about events in Northumbria from the written evidence. The family of Ívarr nevertheless remained active in Britain. An unnamed brother of Ívarr and Hálfdan raided Dyfed in 878 and proceeded to Wessex with 23 ships where he was killed during an attack on a fort at Countisbury in north Devon along with a reported 840 men.[47] This attack may have been led from Ireland. Alfred's great victory at Edington (Wiltshire) which followed at Easter 878 seems to have successfully stemmed the tide of viking conquests in England.[48]

The 880s may have been a decade in which the energies of viking troops were devoted to consolidating their conquests – establishing control over native communities and accommodating new viking settlers. The number of viking immigrants arriving in the conquered areas has been greatly debated and I shall not attempt to solve that problem here.[49] It is sufficient in terms of political discussion to note that the settlers had a significant and

---

[45] *Annals of Ulster*, s.a. 876 [=877].5 (ed. and trans. Mac Airt and Mac Niocaill, pp. 332-33); *Chronicum Scotorum*, s.a. [877] (ed. and trans. Hennessy, pp. 166-67).
[46] Smyth, *Scandinavian York*, I, 20.
[47] *ASC.A*, ed. Bately, p. 50; *ASC.B*, ed. Taylor, p. 37; *ASC.C*, ed. O'Keeffe, p. 61; *ASC.D*, ed. Cubbin, p. 27; E in *Two of the Saxon Chronicles*, ed. Plummer, I, 75.
[48] Whitelock, 'The Importance'.
[49] For a list of articles, see Keynes, *Anglo-Saxon England*, p. 109.

long-term impact in the area which later came to be known as 'the Danelaw'.[50]

Numismatic evidence suggests that minting began in viking-held areas in England from in the mid-880s, and there are two coins from this time bearing the name of Hálfdan.[51] This is obviously too late for the Hálfdan whose career has just been discussed. It could however mark an early stage in the career of a king of that name who fell in battle in 910. No Scandinavian royal names have survived from Northumbria in the 880s, and coin-minting is not firmly attested there until the 890s.

Northumbrian vikings re-appear in the English record in 893 as they supported viking campaigns in the south and west of Britain.[52] These campaigns were instigated by two viking fleets which had arrived in Kent from the Continent in 892. These fleets were provided with reinforcements from East Anglia and Northumbria, and a large force travelled via the Thames and Severn to Buttington (Montgomeryshire).[53] At the same time the allied viking fleets raided the coast of Wessex and besieged Exeter. At Buttington the viking army was besieged by the English, and 'The Anglo-Saxon Chronicle' states that they were forced to eat their horses.[54] In their attempt to break this siege, the vikings were heavily defeated. The engagement at Buttington seems to be commemorated in 'The Annals of Ulster': 'The English won a battle against the Dark Foreigners in which countless multitudes fell'.[55] Reinforcements came from East Anglia and Northumbria to join the survivors. This new army then travelled north and sheltered within the old Roman walls of Chester, which, according to 'The Anglo-Saxon Chronicle', was deserted at this time.[56]

---

[50] Hadley, *The Vikings*, p. 69.

[51] Blackburn, 'The Coinage', pp. 327-28.

[52] *ASC.A*, ed. Bately, pp. 55-58; *ASC.B*, ed. Taylor, pp. 41-43; *ASC.C*, ed. O'Keeffe, pp. 66-68; *ASC.D*, ed. Cubbin, pp. 31-33; Shippey, 'A Missing Army'.

[53] *Alfred*, trans. Keynes and Lapidge, p. 287, n. 16.

[54] While eating horseflesh may have been a habit among Scandinavians at this time, this act may show a level of desperation for an army which might need horses for fighting and transport.

[55] *Annals of Ulster*, *s.a.* 892 [=893].3 (ed. and trans. Mac Airt and Mac Niocaill, pp. 346-47).

[56] David Griffiths has stated that there 'was arguably' an ecclesiastical presence in the city at this date. Archaeological evidence suggests that much of the city was deserted. Griffiths, 'The North-west Frontier', p. 169.

It may be that these two westward expeditions had a common motivation, and this may have been partly inspired by events in Ireland. As Stenton noted, the vikings at Chester were well located to gather reinforcements from Ireland.[57] A departure of vikings from Ireland is reported in 893 by 'The Annals of Inisfallen' and 'The Annals of Ulster'.[58] This was linked to a feud between rival viking factions in Dublin.[59] Two contingents left the port, one led by a son of Ívarr who returned to Ireland the following year.[60] The other group was led by jarl Sigfrøðr.

A person named Sigfrøðr, who may be the same jarl, led the Northumbrian fleet against Wessex in 893.[61] The identification of Sigfrøðr in England with Sigfrøðr in Ireland cannot be proved. It is however likely that there was contact of some kind between vikings in Ireland and England in this year. Alfred Smyth has suggested that jarl Sigfrøðr was a Northumbrian who sailed to Dublin, following his campaigns in Wessex: his attempt to seize control of the viking settlement failed and this caused the disruption noted in 'The Annals of Ulster'.[62] This seems more plausible than Angus's suggestion that Sigfrøðr was a native of Dublin who began his career in England after the fracas at Dublin.[63] Æthelweard implies that Northumbria was Sigfrøðr's homeland (*piraticus de Northimbriorum ... uertit ad proprias sedes*).[64] The power-struggle in Dublin followed from earlier disputes within the dynasty of Ívarr and these circumstances may have encouraged a viking leader from Northumbria to try his hand at winning control over Dublin.[65]

The viking campaigns in England in 893 were unsuccessful, but the marauders still posed a considerable threat to King Alfred in Wessex. In 894

---

[57] Stenton, *Anglo-Saxon England*, p. 267.

[58] *Annals of Ulster, s.a.* 892 [=893].4 (ed. and trans. Mac Airt and Mac Niocaill, pp. 346-47); *Annals of Inisfallen, s.a.* [893] (ed. and trans. Mac Airt, pp. 138-39).

[59] This could be linked to earlier struggles mentioned in Irish chronicles. See *Annals of Ulster, s.aa.* 874 [=875].4, 876 [=877].5, 882 [=883].4 (ed. and trans. Mac Airt and Mac Niocaill, pp. 331-33, 338-39).

[60] *Annals of Ulster, s.a.* 893 [=894].4 (ed. and trans. Mac Airt and Mac Niocaill, pp. 348-49).

[61] Æthelweard, *Chronicon*, IV.3 (ed. and trans. Campbell, p. 50); Smyth, *Scandinavian York*, I, 34; Angus, 'Christianity', p. 147.

[62] Smyth, *Scandinavian York*, I, 34.

[63] Angus, 'Christianity', p. 147.

[64] Æthelweard, *Chronicon*, IV.3 (ed. and trans. Campbell, p. 50).

[65] See above, p. 25.

they left Chester and raided Wales.[66] This departure seems to have been prompted by the English army's destruction of crops and seizure of livestock around Chester, which left the vikings desperately short of supplies. Furthermore, the Welsh king Anarawd of Gwynedd, who had once been an ally of the Northumbrians, had submitted to Alfred by 893. The vikings may have used these attacks to threaten him.[67] The vikings then withdrew across the friendly territories of Northumbria and East Anglia to reach Essex.[68] In this manner they were able to avoid further conflict with the English.

By 894, Alfred seems to have been eager to make peace with the vikings at York. He may have wished to prevent further alliances between viking groups. This made the marauders harder to defeat, and the alliance which had taken place between vikings from Kent, East Anglia, and Northumbria threatened war on a number of fronts. An English ealdorman, Æthelnoth, was sent to York to negotiate with the Northumbrian leadership.[69] Æthelnoth may be identified as the general who led English troops at Buttington in 893 and the ealdorman of Somerset who had a leading role in resisting the vikings when they conquered much of Wessex in 878.[70] If so, he was a crucial figure in English government at that time. This suggests that the Northumbrian threat was taken very seriously by Alfred. The peace-treaty which resulted is mentioned by Æthelweard and in *Historia Regum Anglorum*, Part II, although there is no clue as to the terms which were agreed.[71] This chain of events indicates the strength of the viking polity of Northumbria in the 890s.[72]

---

[66] *ASC.A*, ed. Bately, pp. 58-59; *ASC.B*, ed. Taylor, p. 43; *ASC.C*, ed. O'Keeffe, p. 69; *ASC.D*, ed. Cubbin, p. 33.

[67] Dumville, 'The "Six" Sons', p. 9.

[68] *ASC.A*, ed. Bately, pp. 58-59; *ASC.B*, ed. Taylor, p. 43; *ASC.C*, ed. O'Keeffe, p. 69; *ASC.D*, ed. Cubbin, p. 33; Dumville, *Wessex*, pp. 1-23.

[69] Æthelweard, *Chronicon*, IV.3 (ed. and trans. Campbell, p. 51).

[70] Æthelweard, *Chronicon*, IV.3 (ed. and trans. Campbell, pp. 42-43, 50).

[71] *Historia Regum Anglorum*, Part II (*Symeonis Monachi Opera*, ed. Arnold, II, 119; *The Church Historians*, trans. Stevenson, III, pt 2, p. 85).

[72] The rapid integration of viking settlers within Northumbria is suggested by the speed with which the appellation 'Northumbrian' came to be used in 'The Anglo-Saxon Chronicle' to refer to viking armies operating from that region. Comparison may be made with vikings in East Anglia. For the issue of integration, see Abrams, 'Edward', pp. 135-36; Dumville, *Wessex*, p. 23.

The Reign of Guðrøðr

At this time Northumbria was under the control of king called *Guthfrith* (ON. Guðrøðr) whose death was recorded by Æthelweard under the year 895.[73] This is almost certainly the same king as *Guthred* (a non-contemporary and English form of the same name), whose death is reported in *Historia Regum Anglorum*, Part I, erroneously under the year 894.[74] Guðrøðr's reign is marked by decisive changes in the history of viking Northumbria and he became a focus of later legends. These find fullest expression in texts emanating from the church of Durham in the later eleventh and twelfth centuries.

The most influential of these legends is found in *Historia de Sancto Cuthberto*. A mid-eleventh-century date for this compilation has recently been suggested by Ted Johnson-South.[75] The *Historia* asserts that Guðrøðr son of Harðaknútr was a slave purchased by Eadred, abbot of Carlisle, following a vision of St Cuthbert. Eadred brought him before the viking army of Northumbria, and, in obedience to Cuthbert, they elected him as their king.[76] Several historians have cast doubt on this record as historical evidence.[77] The story is rather implausible and has literary parallels.[78] Like much else in the *Historia*, it may have been invented or may represent an elaboration of real events to demonstrate the power of St Cuthbert and support claims to property made by the church of Durham which was said to have received grants from this king. Alex Woolf has raised the possibility in conversation that Guðrøðr may have been a claimant to the throne of York who had been captured by the English and enslaved. This could

---

[73] Æthelweard, *Chronicon*, IV.3 (ed. and trans. Campbell, p. 51).

[74] *Historia Regum Anglorum*, Part I (*Symeonis Monachi Opera*, ed. Arnold, II, 92; *The Church Historians*, trans. Stevenson, III, pt 2, p. 67); Smyth, *Scandinavian York*, I, 44. Part I, section 6 of *Historia Regum Anglorum* is a short chronicle covering late ninth- and early tenth-century events. Some of its information may have been drawn from a tenth century-source, although the text reached its final form in 1042×1164.

[75] Johnson-South, ed. and trans., 'The "Historia"', p. 186; *Historia de Sancto Cuthberto*, ed. and trans. Johnson-South, pp. 32-36.

[76] *Historia de Sancto Cuthberto*, §13 (ed. and trans. Johnson-South, pp. 52-53).

[77] For example, Dumville, 'Old Dubliners', p. 88; Smyth, *Scandinavian York*, I, 100; 'The "Historia"', ed. and trans. Johnson-South, pp. 5-6; *Historia de Sancto Cuthberto*, ed. and trans. Johnson-South, pp. 4-8.

[78] Mawer, 'The Scandinavian Kingdom', p. 47.

explain some elements of the story. Nevertheless I am unwilling to fully accept the *Historia*'s account.

Guðrøðr is also mentioned in 'The History of the Archbishops of Hamburg-Bremen', which was completed by Adam of Bremen about 1075. Adam reported that Guðrøðr's sons; Sigtryggr, Óláfr and Rögnvaldr, were kings of Northumbria.[79] Two of the names of these alleged sons correspond with two 'grandsons of Ivarr' who ruled York in 918 × 927, while the third name, Óláfr, is a common name in that dynasty. Adam cited an unknown *Gesta Anglorum* for this information. As the text is lost, its worth can not be evaluated.[80] Nevertheless, this source does raise the question whether the Guðrøðr who ruled York in the 890s could have been son-in-law (or son) of Ívarr, unnamed in Irish sources because he did not wield power in Ireland. Such an argument is highly speculative, but so is the received account of Guðrøðr's origins based on *Historia de Sancto Cuthberto*. David Dumville has noted that the name Guðrøðr appears frequently among the descendants of Ívarr and has suggested that there was a link between this Northumbrian king and the Dublin royal family.[81]

Guðrøðr became a figure of later legend, presumably as he had an illustrious reign and because he was regarded as a significant figure in the early history of vikings at York. He may have been the instigator of the Northumbrians' campaigns in 893 and the host of Æthelnoth's embassy in 894. Guðrøðr may also have initiated the use of coin in Northumbria, as a mint appears to have been operating at York from the mid-890s.[82] Only one coin, from a hoard at Ashdon in Essex deposited around 895, bears an inscription 'GUDEF...' which may be linked to this king.[83] Mark Blackburn has argued on stylistic grounds that it was produced at a Southumbrian mint.[84] Guðrøðr may have enjoyed some form of authority

---

[79] *Gesta Hammaburgensis ecclesiae pontificum*, II.25 (*Quellen*, ed. and trans. Trillmich and Buchner, pp. 258-59; *Adam of Bremen*, trans. Tschan, pp. 70-71).

[80] Hudson (*Viking Pirates*, p. 20) has noted that John of Fordun identified Rögnvaldr, king of York, as a son of Guðrøðr. He may have drawn this information from the lost *Gesta*.

[81] Dumville, 'Old Dubliners', p. 88.

[82] Blackburn, 'The Coinage', p. 329.

[83] Grierson and Blackburn, *Medieval European Coinage*, I, 319.

[84] Blackburn, 'The Coinage', p. 327.

south of the Humber, for Æthelweard reports that Northumbrians held lands west of Stamford in 894.[85]

Guðrøðr's attitude towards Christianity may be indicated by the cross-design found on the coin from Ashdon. According to Æthelweard, Guðrøðr was buried at the *basilica summa* ('superior church') at York.[86] If *Historia de Sancto Cuthberto* is to be believed, Guðrøðr's Christian orientation could be linked with the church of Saint Cuthbert. However it is also possible that Guðrøðr received baptism as a consequence of his dealings with Wessex, and perhaps more specifically as a result of Æthelnoth's embassy in 894. A possible parallel is that Guðrøðr's near contemporary, the viking king Guthrum of East Anglia, had received baptism under the sponsorship of King Alfred as the result of a peace-treaty. Pertinent to the issue of Guðrøðr's religious affiliation is a letter of Pope Formosus addressed to the bishops in England, dated 891×896. The letter only survives in post-Conquest copies, but both F.M. Stenton and Dorothy Whitelock convincingly argued that the early sections of the letter are authentic.[87] Formosus criticised the bishops' lack of missionary zeal towards vikings and the practice of allowing ecclesiastical posts to remain vacant. Nevertheless, Formosus withdrew his 'sword of anathema' because of some recent good news from Plegmund, the new archbishop of Canterbury. This could relate to Guðrøðr's conversion, or to the progress of conversion in areas under his control.

Some ink has been spilled on the issue of religion in viking-held areas. Significant features of the ecclesiastical hierarchy were swept away by the first viking onslaughts. The archbishopric of York survived, as did the community of St Cuthbert (though in exile), and occasional reference is made to other churches, for example, that at Ripon.[88] There is a general

---

[85] Æthelweard, *Chronicon*, IV.3 (ed. and trans. Campbell, p. 51); Blackburn, 'The Coinage', p. 327. The treaty which was drawn up between a viking king of East Anglia, Guthrum, and King Alfred indicates that Guthrum ruled as far north as Stoney Stratford in Buckinghamshire, thus it may be that viking-held Mercia was carved up between the two viking kingdoms. For commentary on this text, see Davis, 'Alfred and Guthrum's Frontier'; Dumville, *Wessex*, pp. 1-27.

[86] Æthelweard, *Chronicon*, IV.3 (ed. and trans. Campbell, p. 51).

[87] *English Historical Documents*, trans. Whitelock, no. 227; William of Malmesbury, *Gesta Regum Anglorum*, II.129 (ed. and trans. Mynors *et al.*, I, 204-05); Stenton, *Anglo-Saxon England*, pp. 435, 438-39; Dumville, *Wessex*, pp. 191-92.

[88] Hadley, 'Conquest', p. 125.

lack of evidence for ecclesiastical hierarchies in the areas where vikings settled, and this could be interpreted as a lack of Christianity.[89] Nevertheless, Dawn Hadley has drawn attention to evidence for religious enthusiasm in the Danelaw, such as the proliferation of Anglo-Scandinavian Christian sculpture, and the promotion of individuals from the Danelaw to high office in the English Church in the tenth century.[90] Furthermore Julia Barrow has argued that English kings deliberately allowed ecclesiastical structures to lapse in areas of viking settlement which were beyond their control, thus depriving these regions of important agents of government.[91] This may explain part of Pope Formosus's anger in the 890s. Hadley has argued that a more decentralised ecclesiastical structure evolved to replace what had gone before. The existence of small secular churches serving highly localised communities may be deduced from the location of Anglo-Scandinavian sculpture and medieval records of urban churches.[92]

It is thus possible that a process of conversion had begun during the reign of Guðrøðr, and that the non-viking population continued to practise their Christian beliefs, although this latter is not clearly witnessed in the written sources. Nevertheless this would help to explain Guðrøðr's Christian inclinations. Guðrøðr seems to have been a successful ruler. He may have adopted policies, such as the adoption of coin and the Christian faith, to promote his power in the eyes of his subjects and neighbouring kings.

Royal Succession and the Cuerdale-Hoard

For the years after Guðrøðr's death, coin-evidence provides the most reliable guide to political leadership in viking Northumbria. This is largely due to the major hoard found at Cuerdale in 1840, which contained around five thousand Anglo-Scandinavian coins.[93] It is perhaps the most renowned archaeological discovery relating to the vikings in the British Isles. The hoard – which contained English, Continental and Kufic coins, ingots, and hack-silver – was deposited in a lead-lined chest about 905 by

[89] Abrams, 'The Conversion of the Danelaw'.
[90] Hadley, 'Conquest', p. 117.
[91] Barrow, 'English Cathedral Communities', pp. 26-28.
[92] Hadley, 'Conquest', pp. 119-27.
[93] Grierson and Blackburn, *Medieval European Coinage*, I, 320-21; Graham-Campbell, 'Some Archaeological Reflections', pp. 329-30.

the River Ribble. The sequence of coin-issues in the Cuerdale hoard indicates that Guðrøðr was succeeded at York by a certain Sigfrøðr who ruled until about 900. His reign was followed by that of Knútr until about 905. There also seems to have been a brief period when these two kings ruled together.[94] A few coins of *Alualdus* (Æthelwold) may also be dated to the years 900-902 from historical records.[95]

It has been argued by Alfred Smyth (and others) that the king Sigfrøðr mentioned on York coins may be the same as both the Northumbrian Sigfrøðr who led a fleet against Wessex in 893 and the jarl Sigfrøðr who was involved in factional struggles in Dublin in 893.[96] It is possible that Sigfrøðr has some relation to affairs in Ireland, although Smyth's chain of identifications may be somewhat tenuous. Some coins of Sigfrøðr show the king's name preceded by the letter 'C'.[97] This cannot be satisfactorily explained, but, given that coins are the sole evidence of this king's reign, it is worth considering. It may be an abbreviation of a baptismal name. A similar hypothesis has been put forward by Blackburn for later coins of Sigtryggr of Northumbria, whose name is preceded by the letters 'LVDO' (perhaps an abbreviation for Ludouicus).[98] A precedent for baptismal names appearing on royal coinage is the case of Guthrum of East Anglia (*ob.* 889/90), whose coins bore his baptismal name, Æthelstan.[99] There is a strong ecclesiastical element in the designs and inscriptions of the coins of Sigfrøðr and his successor Knútr, which suggests a desire to be portrayed like Christian kings. That 'C' marks a reference to a baptismal name on the coins of Sigfrøðr is a distinct possibility, in the absence of more convincing evidence. Alternatively 'C' may mark a reference to Knútr at a time when both kings may have been ruling Northumbria together.

Knútr's identity is difficult to establish. No mention of him is made in contemporary sources. Smyth has drawn attention to thirteenth- and fourteenth-century Scandinavian sagas which state that a Danish king

---

[94] Grierson and Blackburn, *Medieval European Coinage*, I, 321; Blackburn, 'The Coinage', p. 329.

[95] *ASC.A*, ed. Bately, pp. 61-62; *ASC.B*, ed. Taylor, p. 46; *ASC.C*, ed. O'Keeffe, pp. 71-72; *ASC.D*, ed. Cubbin, pp. 36-37.

[96] *Annals of Ulster*, s.a. 892 [=893].4 (ed. and trans. Mac Airt and Mac Niocaill, pp. 346-47); Smyth, *Scandinavian York*, I, 33-37.

[97] Grierson and Blackburn, *Medieval European Coinage*, I, 321.

[98] Blackburn, 'The Coinage', p. 335.

[99] Grierson and Blackburn, *Medieval European Coinage*, I, 318.

Knútr was active in Northumbria.[100] These sagas may suggest the existence of legends concerning a king of this name in Northumbria but they cannot be regarded as a reliable guide to his origins. The word 'CVNNETTI' is found (with variants) on coins combined with dies reading 'CNVT REX', which poses another mystery.[101] Mark Blackburn has recently argued against the idea originally put forward by D. H. Haigh, that it is linked to the name Hundeus (the name of a leader active in England and Francia around this time).[102] *Cunnetti* does not look like an Old-Norse personal name or a mint-name.[103] I am inclined to think that it is an attempt to latinize Knútr and put the name in a genitive case. However, Knútr's near contemporaries, Sigfrøðr and Æthelwold, employed Latin nominatives on their coins; so this argument is by no means watertight.

The Reign of Æthelwold

The other ruler who is named on Northumbrian coins from the turn of the tenth century is Æthelwold. He is much better attested in the historical record. 'The Anglo-Saxon Chronicle' portrays him as a rebel against Edward the Elder, king of Wessex, and downplays his claim to the throne.[104] Æthelwold was the son of King Æthelred, the elder brother of King Alfred, who ruled from 865 to 871.[105] As a son of Alfred's senior, Æthelwold had a good claim to be the next king. However, as Barbara Yorke has shown, Alfred promoted the cause of his son, Edward, as his successor, during his lifetime and in his will, to the detriment of his nephew Æthelwold.[106]

Following Alfred's death, Æthelwold made a bid for power. He seized the royal estate of Wimborne (Dorset) where his father had been buried. He fled Wessex, travelled to Northumbria, and won the recognition of the

---

[100] Smyth, *Scandinavian York*, I, 47-52.
[101] Stewart, 'CVNNETTI reconsidered'; Grierson and Blackburn, *Medieval European Coinage*, I, 321.
[102] Blackburn, 'The Coinage', pp. 330-31.
[103] *Ibid.*
[104] *ASC.A*, ed. Bately, pp. 61-62; *ASC.B*, ed. Taylor, p. 46; *ASC.C*, ed. O'Keeffe, p. 71; *ASC.D*, ed. Cubbin, p. 36.
[105] Yorke, 'Edward as Ætheling', p. 30.
[106] *Ibid.*, pp. 30-37.

viking army there.[107] Two years later he arrived with a fleet in Essex and there the local people submitted to him. In addition, an army from East Anglia joined his cause and harried Mercia.[108] The campaign failed when Æthelwold was killed in battle against Edward's troops at the Holme, near Biggleswade (Bedfordshire).[109] The battle took place at the end of 902 according to 'The Mercian Register' and Æthelweard, although different versions of 'The Anglo-Saxon Chronicle' suggest a range of dates 902×905.[110] The names of those who fell show that Æthelwold had won considerable support.[111] The viking side was victorious at the Holme, though deprived of its leader. One might assume that effective resistance to Edward collapsed after the battle. However, peace does not seem to have been established between Edward and the vikings of Northumbria until 906.[112]

Æthelwold's political significance in viking Northumbria is hard to determine. Recognition may have been given to him as an English overlord who was preferable to Edward. Alternatively, support may have been given to promote political divisions among the English. It is also possible that Æthelwold appealed to the English population in viking Northumbria. As so little is revealed about this fascinating sequence of events, various hypotheses can be argued. Charles Plummer linked Æthelwold's acceptance in Northumbria with Æthelweard's report that there was a disturbance among the people in English (north) Northumbria in the year of Alfred's death.[113] A curious report in *Historia Regum Anglorum*, Part II, records that

[107] *ASC.A*, ed. Bately, pp. 61-62; *ASC.B*, ed. Taylor, p. 46; *ASC.C*, ed. O'Keeffe, p. 71; *ASC.D*, ed. Cubbin, p. 36.

[108] *ASC.A*, ed. Bately, p. 62; *ASC.B*, ed. Taylor, p. 46; *ASC.C*, ed. O'Keeffe, p. 72; *ASC.D*, ed. Cubbin, p. 36.

[109] *ASC.A*, ed. Bately, p. 62; *ASC.B*, ed. Taylor, pp. 46, 49; *ASC.C*, ed. O'Keeffe, pp. 72, 75; *ASC.D*, ed. Cubbin, p. 36; E in *Two of the Saxon Chronicles*, ed. Plummer, I, 93.

[110] Wainwright, 'The Chronology', pp. 390-91; *The Anglo-Saxon Chronicle*, trans. Whitelock *et al.*, p. 59, n. 11; Dumville, *Wessex*, p. 10.

[111] A prince Brihtsige, who may have been of the royal line of Mercia, is named: *The Anglo-Saxon Chronicle*, trans. Whitelock *et al.*, p. 60, n. 4.

[112] *ASC.A*, ed. Bately, p. 63; *ASC.B*, ed. Taylor, p. 47; *ASC.C*, ed. O'Keeffe, p. 72; *ASC.D*, ed. Cubbin, p. 37; E in *Two of the Saxon Chronicles*, ed. Plummer, I, 95.

[113] Æthelweard, *Chronicon*, IV.3 (ed. and trans. Campbell, p. 51); *Two of the Saxon Chronicles*, ed. Plummer, II, 115.

one Osbrith was expelled 'from the kingdom' in the same year.[114] In Part I of *Historia Regum Anglorum*, the event is dated to 901.[115] It has not been possible to identify Osbrith.[116] However, the name corresponds with that of the Northumbrian king killed by vikings in 867.[117] Either the entry is grossly misplaced or it could refer to a descendant of that Northumbrian king. Records in the north at this date are somewhat patchy and provide little assistance in this matter. Twelfth-century historians claimed to identify a succession of kings in English Northumbria after 867.[118] However, the first to be named in earlier records is Eadwulf who died in 913.[119] The circumstances of English dissension in Northumbria and the identification of Osbrith are therefore extremely elusive. However, the sources do appear to draw a distinction between troubles among the English in Northumbria and the vikings' support for Æthelwold. Thus the two events may not be linked.[120]

Another concurrence with the rebellion of Æthelwold is the consecration of Æthelbald as archbishop of York. The event took place in London in 900.[121] Little is known of the circumstances in which this occurred. The coincidence with Æthelwold's rebellion may be due to more than chance. It is possible that Æthelbald was promoted by Æthelwold's supporters, or perhaps Edward sought to promote him as a loyal representative in the north. Nothing more is heard of Æthelbald after the rebellion and it is not certain that he ever travelled to Northumbria.

---

[114] *Historia Regum Anglorum*, Part II (*Symeonis Monachi Opera*, ed. Arnold, II, 121; *The Church Historians*, trans. Stevenson, III, pt 2, p. 86).

[115] *Historia Regum Anglorum*, Part I (*Symeonis Monachi Opera*, ed. Arnold, II, 92; *The Church Historians*, trans. Stevenson, III, pt 2, p. 67).

[116] Searle, *Onomasticon*, p. 371.

[117] *ASC.A*, ed. Bately, p. 47; *ASC.B*, ed. Taylor, p. 34; *ASC.C*, ed. O'Keeffe, p. 58; *ASC.D*, ed. Cubbin, p. 24; E in *Two of the Saxon Chronicles*, ed. Plummer, I, 69.

[118] Rollason *et al.*, *Sources*, p. 63.

[119] *Annals of Clonmacnoise*, s.a. 904 [=913] (ed. Murphy, p. 145); *Annals of Ulster*, s.a. 912 [=913].1 (ed. and trans. Mac Airt and Mac Niocaill, pp. 360-61); *Fragmentary Annals*, §456 (ed. and trans. Radner, pp. 180-81); Æthelweard, *Chronicon*, IV.4 (ed. and trans. Campbell, p. 53).

[120] Æthelweard, *Chronicon*, IV.3 (ed. and trans. Campbell, p. 51).

[121] Æthelweard, *Chronicon*, IV.4 (ed. and trans. Campbell, p. 52).

The Expulsion from Dublin

The opening years of the tenth century seem to have been a tumultuous time in terms of English-viking relations. This was not only because of Æthelwold's rebellion in 899; the expulsion of the vikings of Dublin from Ireland in 902 also influenced English affairs.[122] The vikings who were expelled from Ireland seem to have divided into various groups and pursued different fortunes.[123]

Nick Higham and James Graham-Campbell have argued that the River Ribble may have been a temporary base for many of the Dubliners.[124] Their argument is based on the evidence of the silver-hoard found at Cuerdale. This was deposited by a ford of the River Ribble around 905. A large proportion of the non-numismatic content of this hoard seems to have come from Ireland (this comprised at least 30% of the silver-weight in the hoard).[125] The combination of Irish hack-silver and the large number of recently minted Northumbrian coins suggests co-operation between vikings leaving Dublin and those based at York.[126] Christopher Blunt and James Graham-Campbell have suggested that the hoard was assembled at York.[127] Graham-Campbell has concluded that it was probably being carried westwards at the time of its deposition, and it could represent the pay-chest for an army intending to re-conquer Dublin.[128]

Viking activity in the North-west is also recorded in relation to one Ingimundr. This viking leader led his troops from Ireland to Anglesey in 902/3.[129] His defeat in battle at *Ros Melion* is recorded in *Brut y Tywysogion*.[130] This has been identified as a site near the eastern tip of Anglesey.[131] According to the 'Fragmentary Annals of Ireland', after this

---

[122] *Annals of Ulster*, s.a. 901 [=902].2 (ed. and trans. Mac Airt and Mac Niocaill, pp. 352-53).

[123] Mac Shamhráin, *The Vikings*, pp. 75-79; Musset, *Nordica*, pp. 279-96; Picard, 'Early Contacts', p. 92.

[124] Higham, *The Kingdom*, pp. 185, 187; Graham-Campbell, 'Some Archaeological Reflections', p. 344.

[125] *Ibid.*, pp. 339-40.

[126] *Ibid.*, p. 344.

[127] *Ibid.*, p. 343.

[128] *Ibid.*, pp. 340, 342-44.

[129] *Fragmentary Annals*, §429 (ed. and trans. Radner, pp. 166-69).

[130] *ByT* (RBH), s.a. 903 (ed. and trans. Jones, pp. 10-11); cf. *Annales Cambriae* (A), s.a. [902] (ed. and trans. Dumville, p. 14).

[131] Griffiths, 'The North-West Frontier', p. 179.

defeat at the hands of Cadell ap Rhodri, king of Gwynedd, Ingimundr and his troops settled near Chester with the consent of Æthelflæd, co-ruler of Mercia.[132] Ingimundr is then reported to have attacked Chester, but he failed to take it. It is not certain how much credence should be given to the episode at Chester described in 'The Fragmentary Annals of Ireland', which seems highly dramatised. Nevertheless, Chester was restored by Æthelflaed in 907, presumably as a defensive measure against an influx of viking settlers.[133]

It has been suggested that Ingimundr may be linked with *Agmund*, a Scandinavian leader who fell in battle at Tettenhall in 910, and with an *Agmund* who gave his name to the territory of Amounderness (*Agemundernes*) in Lancashire some time before 934.[134] It is not certain that Ingimundr and *Agmund* (?ON Øgmundr) are the same name; such a link is thus tenuous.[135] Nonetheless, the record of Ingimundr's arrival in Britain sheds light on an important episode of viking activity.[136]

During the late ninth and early tenth centuries a significant number of people seem to have emigrated from the viking settlements in the Gaelic-speaking world and established themselves in a wide arc of territory including Cumberland, Westmorland, Lancashire, East Yorkshire, the Faeroes and the Cotentin Peninsula.[137] The significance of this population-movement is represented by the large number of place-names which suggest the mixed Gaelic and Scandinavian origins of the settlers. The distribution of the Old-Norse place-name element, -*erg* (meaning shieling) in these areas has been used to speculate about the origin of some immigrants. This word was adopted from Gaelic (OI *áirge*, Scottish Gaelic *airigh*). This borrowing was thought to have taken place in the Hebrides where the word is attested in place-names.[138] Nevertheless it should not be concluded that settlers

---

[132] *Fragmentary Annals*, §429 (ed. and trans. Radner, pp. 166-69). Æthelflæd is said to have granted them lands around Chester. The record is not reliable as a source. However, it is evocative of Continental grants to vikings of lands near river-estuaries, in order to defend them against other vikings: Roesdahl, *The Vikings*, p. 196.

[133] *ASC.B*, ed. Taylor, p. 49; *ASC.C*, ed. O'Keeffe, p. 75.

[134] Wainwright, *Scandinavian England*, p. 136; Higham, *The Kingdom*, p. 184; Sawyer, *Anglo-Saxon Charters*, no. 407.

[135] Wainwright, *Scandinavian England*, p. 136.

[136] Jesch, 'Scandinavian Wirral'.

[137] Dumville, *The Churches*, p. 29.

[138] Smyth, *Scandinavian York*, I, 80.

from the Gaelic world came exclusively from these islands.[139] Another indicator of migrations from the Gaelic world are the inversion-compounds (place-names using Norse terms in Celtic word-order), found in Westmorland, Cumberland and to a lesser extent in Lancashire.[140]

It may be unwise to see the migrations of Gaelicised vikings to England as a singular consequence of the expulsion of vikings from Dublin in 902. Onomastic and archaeological evidence allows that settlement could have occurred within a short time or across many decades.[141] Settlers may have come from different parts of the Hebrides or Ireland and patterns of migration would have varied over time.[142] Nevertheless these settlements doubtless had an impact on York-Dublin politics by bringing English and Gaelic culture into closer contact. The exiles from Dublin at the beginning of the tenth century can be seen as part of a much broader picture of population-movement in the British Isles (and beyond) during the Viking Age.

From the Peace of Tiddingford (906) to the Battle of Corbridge (918)

The defensive measures taken by Æthelflæd of Mercia and her brother, Edward of Wessex, to secure their borders in the early years of the tenth century may have been a response to an increasing influx of viking migrants. In 906, Edward made peace with the East Angles and Northumbrians at *Yttingaford* (Tiddingford, Bedfordshire).[143] Versions A, B, C, and D of 'The Anglo-Saxon Chronicle' state that this occurred 'just as King Edward decreed'; however, the E-text of 'The Anglo-Saxon Chronicle' and *Historia Regum Anglorum*, Part I, state that Edward felt compelled to

---

[139] Breandán Ó Ciobháin has indicated that this place-name element also occurs in south-western Ireland, as I gather from conversation. Mícheál Ó Mainnín has kindly addressed my enquiry whether this place-name occurs in the north of Ireland. No definite attestation of this element has been found there.

[140] Higham, 'Scandinavian Settlements', pp. 199-205; Grant, 'A New Approach', pp. 75-90. Grant has underestimated the level of contact between vikings and Gaels in Ireland.

[141] Fellows-Jensen, 'Scandinavian Settlement in the Isle of Man'; Graham-Campbell, 'The Irish Sea', pp. 73-74.

[142] Graham-Campbell, 'The Irish Sea', pp. 75-78. See Fellows-Jensen, 'The Mystery', p. 46, for the possibility of population-movements from eastern to western England and Man.

[143] *The Anglo-Saxon Chronicle*, trans. Whitelock *et al.*, p. 60, n. 8; Hill, *An Atlas*, p. 55; Dumville, *Wessex*, p. 10.

make this agreement.[144]   The treaty of Tiddingford may have been an attempt to prevent co-operation between the vikings of York and Dublin, of a sort witnessed by the Cuerdale hoard of about 905. Edward may also have feared a re-run of the events of 893 when vikings from Northumbria and East Anglia made common cause with other viking groups against the English.

In the decade after Tiddingford, viking Northumbria seems to have suffered from political and economic decline. Numismatic records indicate that around 905 the royal coinage was replaced by an anonymous issue which lasted for about fifteen years. These coins bore York's name on one side (EBORAICE / EBORAICE CIVITAS) and the inscription 'SCI PETRI MO' (St Peter's mint or money) on the other.[145] The absence of a royal name on these coins requires an explanation. Several kings are named as leading the Northumbrians to battle in 910.[146] Nevertheless, the anonymous coins might indicate an absence of clear leadership. These coins also show a significant decline in weight-standard to roughly half of their initial value.[147] In a recent re-evaluation of this coinage, Blackburn has suggested that this drop in coin-quality took place from 905, rather than after 910 as previously thought.[148] This may reflect an economic decline in consequence of the demise of viking Dublin as a major trading partner. This change could also reflect political circumstances after the peace of Tiddingford in 906.

Political troubles may be hinted at in these years by the record of the transfer of St Oswald's body from Bardney (ten miles east of Lincoln) to English Mercia in 909.[149] This may have been a political act of appropriation by Æthelred and Æthelflaed. Alternatively, the motive may have been to move the relics away from a political hotspot for their protection (this might be compared with examples from Francia, Ireland

---

[144] *ASC.A*, ed. Bately, p. 63; *ASC.B*, ed. Taylor, p. 47; *ASC.C*, ed. O'Keeffe, p. 72; *ASC.D*, ed. Cubbin, p. 37; E in *Two of the Saxon Chronicles*, ed. Plummer, I, 95.

[145] Grierson and Blackburn, *Medieval European Coinage*, I, 322-23.

[146] *ASC.A*, ed. Bately, p. 64; *ASC.B*, ed. Taylor, pp. 47, 49; *ASC.C*, ed. O'Keeffe, pp. 73, 75; *ASC.D*, ed. Cubbin, pp. 37-38; E in *Two of the Saxon Chronicles*, ed. Plummer, I, 95.

[147] Smyth, *Scandinavian York*, I, 103.

[148] Blackburn, 'The Coinage', pp. 333, 340.

[149] *ASC.B*, ed. Taylor, p. 49; *ASC.C*, ed. O'Keeffe, p. 75; *ASC.D*, ed. Cubbin, p. 37.

and England of the transfer of relics in the wake of viking raids or war).[150] In the same year, King Edward sent an army from Wessex and Mercia to plunder Northumbria. The campaign lasted for five weeks. A sense of the great destruction wrought by this attack is provided by 'The Anglo-Saxon Chronicle'. The army 'ravaged very severely the territory of the northern army, both men and all kinds of cattle, and they killed many men' ('gehergode swyðe mycel on þam norðhere, ægþær ge on mannum ge on <ge>hwylcum yrfe, 7 manege men ofslogon').[151] In the following year the Northumbrians sent an army to plunder across Mercia and Wessex in revenge.[152]

That army, while returning to Northumbria, was intercepted in the area of Tettenhall and Wednesfield in Staffordshire.[153] A battle ensued and the Northumbrian side was heavily defeated. In 'The Anglo-Saxon Chronicle' the list of dead includes two kings, Hálfdan and Ásl (or Auðgísl).[154] Another, Ívarr, was named by Æthelweard.[155] Several noblemen are also named. David Dumville has recently drawn attention to the fact that the names of the dead kings match a trio of viking leaders which were active in the British Isles in the 860s and 870s.[156] At least two of the earlier kings (Ívarr and Hálfdan) were related.[157] Dumville has suggested that the kings of 910 were also members of the same family (the descendants of Ívarr) who ruled Dublin before 902 and after 917. The coincidence is perhaps too striking to be ignored.

---

[150] This can be compared with the transfer of relics of St Columba to Ireland to protect them against viking attacks – *Annals of Ulster, s.a.* 877 [=878].9 (ed. and trans. Mac Airt and Mac Niocaill, pp. 334-35); the transfer of the relics of St Cuthbert from Lindisfarne – Higham, *The Kingdom*, p. 179; and those of St Philbert from Noirmoutier – Nelson, 'The Frankish Empire', p. 28.

[151] *ASC.D*, ed. Cubbin, p. 37.

[152] *ASC.A*, ed. Bately, p. 63; *ASC.B*, ed. Taylor, p. 47; *ASC.C*, ed. O'Keeffe, p. 73; *ASC.D*, ed. Cubbin, p. 38.

[153] Æthelweard, *Chronicon*, IV.4 (ed. and trans. Campbell, p. 53), reported that the battle took place at Wednesfield (near Tettenhall). 'The Anglo-Saxon Chronicle', D-text, appears mistakenly to record the same battle three times: *ASC. D.*, ed. Cubbin, pp. 37-38; Angus, 'The Chronology', p. 202.

[154] *ASC.A*, ed. Bately, p. 63; *ASC.B*, ed. Taylor, p. 47; *ASC.C*, ed. O'Keeffe, p. 73; *ASC.D*, ed. Cubbin, p. 38.

[155] Æthelweard, *Chronicon*, IV.4 (ed. and trans. Campbell, p. 53).

[156] Dumville, 'Old Dubliners', pp. 88-89.

[157] Æthelweard, *Chronicon*, IV.3 (ed. and trans. Campbell, pp. 42-43).

'The Anglo-Saxon Chronicle' states that in 910 the 'army in Northumbria broke the peace and scorned every privilege that King Edward and his counsellors offered them' ('Her bræc se here þone frið on Norðhymbrum, 7 forsawon ælc riht þe Eadweard cyning 7 his witan him budon').[158] This could suggest that peace-negotiations had taken place since the West-Saxon invasion in 909 or it could refer back to the agreement of 906. The stance of the chronicler is that of the victorious side. The Northumbrians are portrayed as ungrateful rebels, rather than fearsome enemies. The defeat at Tettenhall seems to have been a further blow to viking Northumbria at a time when that polity may already have been suffering an economic (if not political) decline.

Æthelweard stated that in 910 the Northumbrian vikings broke their peace not only with King Edward but also with Æthelred 'who then ruled the Northumbrian and Mercian areas' ('qui tum regebat Northanybrias partes Myrciasque').[159] This statement needs to be examined. At Æthelred's death in 911, Æthelweard commemorated him as 'lord of Mercians' (*Myrciorum superstes*) but not Northumbria.[160] The implication is that Æthelred ceased to rule Northumbrians following the viking attacks in 910. If so, it could suggest that Æthelred had made inroads into Northumbrian territory which were then lost in 910. Another possibility is that Æthelred was established as lord of English Northumbria before 910. However the death of Eadwulf of Bamburgh as leader (in some sources 'king') of 'Northern England' is so widely reported in 913 that it seems hard to envisage that his fame derived from a three-year reign.[161] The Northumbrian 'rebellion' may have been a response to English infringement, or to the imposition of Æthelred as an overlord.

Æthelred's status as ruler of 'Northumbrian areas' is not verified in Mercian charters, although no charters exist which mention him after 903.[162] If Æthelred was recognised as overlord of viking Northumbria, this status may have been conferred on him at Tiddingford or some other

---

[158] *ASC.D*, ed. Cubbin, p. 38.
[159] Æthelweard, *Chronicon*, IV.4 (ed. and trans. Campbell, p. 52).
[160] Æthelweard, *Chronicon*, IV.4 (ed. and trans. Campbell, p. 53).
[161] *Annals of Clonmacnoise*, s.a. 904 [=913] (ed. Murphy, p. 145); *Annals of Ulster*, s.a. 912 [=913].1 (ed. and trans. Mac Airt and Mac Niocaill, pp. 360-61); *Fragmentary Annals*, §456 (ed. and trans. Radner, pp. 180-81); Æthelweard, *Chronicon*, IV.4 (ed. and trans. Campbell, p. 53).
[162] Sawyer, *Anglo-Saxon Charters*, nos. 218-23, 367, 367a and 371.

occasion in 903×910. Æthelweard's statement is hard to interpret but it raises interesting questions regarding the extent of Æthelred's power in 910. It could indicate a precedent for some of the Northumbrian vikings' acceptance of Æthelflæd of Mercia (Æthelred's wife) as their overlord in 918, as described in 'The Mercian Register'.[163]

After the battle of Tettenhall, Æthelflæd and Edward took measures to prevent further viking attacks. Edward seems to have encouraged his subjects to buy lands from the vikings, to infiltrate areas under their control, while the policy of building fortified centres or burghs in the 910s was used to restrict the movement of hostile armies along rivers and in frontier-areas.[164] As David Griffiths has pointed out, this burghal policy also served to strengthen royal power in the areas where the burghs were built.[165] Similarly, Edward may have used concerns about the defence of English territory to justify his appropriation of London and Oxford on the River Thames from Mercia following the death of Æthelred in 911.[166] From 914 burghs were constructed and manned with troops in border-areas as a way of making inroads into vikings' territory and securing the submission of neighbouring peoples (Figure 11). Edward's fortification of Manchester in 919 marked the first recorded encroachment into viking Northumbria by a West-Saxon king.[167]

While Edward and Æthelflæd were consolidating their position in England, the descendants of Ívarr were re-establishing themselves in Ireland. This was to have important consequences for the Northumbrian polity. Several viking groups appear to have been active in the Irish Sea in 914. The best documented group is that led by jarl Óttar. This was active in Brittany before it sailed to the Severn-estuary.[168] Óttar's fleet then raided south Wales and travelled inland to Archenfield (Herefordshire). Local English levies came to meet them, and in the battle which ensued Óttar's

[163] *ASC.B*, ed. Taylor, p. 50; *ASC.C*, ed. O'Keeffe, p. 76; *ASC.D*, ed. Cubbin, p. 40.
[164] Fleming, 'Monastic Lands', p. 253; Hadley, 'Conquest', pp. 112, 124. This policy was continued by Æthelstan: Sawyer, *Anglo-Saxon Charters*, nos 396, 397.
[165] Griffiths, 'The North-West Frontier', pp. 180-82.
[166] *ASC.A*, ed. Bately, p. 64; *ASC.B*, ed. Taylor, p. 48; *ASC.C*, ed. O'Keeffe, p. 73; *ASC.D*, ed. Cubbin, p. 38.
[167] *ASC.A*, ed. Bately, p. 69. Cf. Griffiths, 'The North-West Frontier', p. 177.
[168] *ASC.A*, ed. Bately, p. 65; *ASC.B*, ed. Taylor, p. 48; *ASC.C*, ed. O'Keeffe, p. 74; *ASC.D*, ed. Cubbin, p. 39. Cf. Price, 'The Vikings', p. 360.

Figure 11: England during the reign of Edward the Elder, 899-924

brother and a jarl *Hroald* were killed. The vikings agreed to give hostages, although part of the fleet escaped to Ireland.[169] The arrival of a viking fleet at Waterford is recorded in Irish chronicles in this year. This may be the same group, as a jarl Óttar is named as one of the vikings of Waterford in 918.[170]

What may have been a separate fleet, under the command of Rögnvaldr, grandson of Ívarr, was active in the northern part of the Irish Sea in this year. He fought a naval battle against Bárðr Óttarsson, whose identity is uncertain. Bárðr and nearly all of his army were slain in this engagement.[171] In 915 more vikings settled at Waterford, and in 917 Sigtryggr, grandson of Ívarr, established himself at Dublin.[172] English royal policy from this time may have been influenced by concerns about the renewal of viking power in Ireland.

The Battle of Corbridge

The re-conquest of Dublin renewed the strength of Ívarr's dynasty and it was not long before they sought to demonstrate their authority in Northumbria. In 918 Rögnvaldr, grandson of Ívarr, led a campaign which culminated in the battle of Corbridge (Northumberland). The circumstances of this battle have long been debated as a major event in the history of the vikings in England.

'The Annals of Ulster' report that Rögnvaldr led forces from Waterford and faced Causantín, king of Alba, and the English of Northern Northumbria in battle on the banks of the River Tyne.[173] The battle was somewhat indecisive. A viking jarl Óttar was killed and the vikings seem to have suffered the greater losses. However, 'The Annals of Ulster' report that

---

[169] *ASC.A*, ed. Bately, p. 65; *ASC.B*, ed. Taylor, p. 48; *ASC.C*, ed. O'Keeffe, p. 74; *ASC.D*, ed. Cubbin, p. 39.

[170] *Annals of Ulster*, s.aa. 913 [=914].5917 [=918].4 (ed. and trans. Mac Airt and Mac Niocaill, pp. 362-63, 368-69).

[171] *Annals of Ulster*, s.a. 913 [=914].4 (ed. and trans. Mac Airt and Mac Niocaill, pp. 362-63).

[172] *Annals of Ulster*, s.a. 914 [=915].7 (ed. and trans. Mac Airt and Mac Niocaill, pp. 364-65); *Chronicum Scotorum*, s.a. [914].5 (ed. and trans. Hennessy, pp. 186-87).

[173] *Annals of Ulster*, s.a. 917 [=918].4 (ed. and trans. Mac Airt and Mac Niocaill, pp. 368-69). *Historia Regum Anglorum*, Part I (*Symeonis Monachi Opera*, ed. Arnold, II, 93; *The Church Historians*, trans. Stevenson, III, pt 2, p. 68), reports their attack on *Dunbline* (either Dublin in Ireland or Dunblane in Scotland).

Rögnvaldr made a successful counter-attack before nightfall and slaughtered his enemies, although none of their kings or earls was slain.[174] This engagement may be identified with both the battle of *Tinemore* described in 'The Chronicle of the Kings of Alba' for the year 918 and the battle of Corbridge described in English sources.[175] As W. S. Angus suggested, the ambiguous outcome of this battle recorded in 'The Annals of Ulster' could explain why some sources claim that Corbridge was a victory for the vikings (e.g. *Historia de Sancto Cuthberto*) and others report it to have been a defeat (e.g. 'The Chronicle of the Kings of Alba').[176]

The location of Corbridge can reveal something of the circumstances of and the motives behind this battle. Corbridge is located by a crossing point of the River Tyne. This site also had strategic significance as a fort near to Hadrian's Wall. It presided over the 'Stanegate' a Roman road which ran west to east across Britain, and the road which ran north to south from Inveresk on the Firth of Forth to York. Rögnvaldr and his troops may have travelled overland from the Solway Firth or used the Clyde-Forth route across Alba to reach Northumbria.[177] It may be supposed that they were planning to reach York but that they found themselves being intercepted and confronted by enemy-forces.

Historia de Sancto Cuthberto confusingly reports that there were two engagements at Corbridge.[178] This has been taken seriously by Alistair Campbell, F.T. Wainwright and Alfred Smyth, and has become established as one of the facts of Northumbrian history.[179] However, reliance on the *Historia* on this matter may be misguided. According to *Historia de Sancto Cuthberto*, Causantín of Alba and Ealdred son of Eadwulf of Bamburgh were defeated at the first battle of Corbridge.[180] Campbell dated the event between the years of 913 (when Eadwulf of Bamburgh died) and 915, when, according to twelfth-century Northumbrian records, Bishop

---

[174] *Ibid.*

[175] 'The Scottish Chronicle', ed. and trans. Hudson, pp. 150, 157; *Historia de Sancto Cuthberto*, §§22, 24 (ed. and trans. Johnson-South, pp. 60-63).

[176] Angus, 'The Annals', p. 219.

[177] See Edmonds, 'Hiberno-Saxon and Hiberno-Scandinavian Contact', pp. 66-101, for a discussion of major routeways used during this period.

[178] *Historia de Sancto Cuthberto*, §23 (ed. and trans. Johnson-South, pp. 60-63).

[179] Campbell, 'Two Notes', pp. 85-91; Wainwright, *Scandinavian England*, pp. 163-79; Smyth, *Scandinavian York*, I, 63-64, 68-69.

[180] *Historia de Sancto Cuthberto*, §22 (ed. and trans. Johnson-South, pp. 60-61).

Cuthheard died.[181] Cuthheard is said by the *Historia* to have witnessed a miracle after the first battle of Corbridge, whereby one of Rögnvaldr's followers, who had been given lands seized from the church of St Cuthbert, was struck dead after denouncing the saint.[182] The *Historia* relates that the alleged second battle of Corbridge was also a victory for Rögnvaldr and more lands were seized from the Church.[183]

I agree with Johnson-South's argument that in the *Historia* 'the reference to Ragnall's second victory is extremely cursory ... on the strength of the single word *iterum* the majority of scholars have supposed that there must have been two battles of Corbridge ... we must consider the possibility that a single battle is being recorded twice here'.[184] Campbell's dating of the 'first' battle can be put aside on the grounds that the record concerning Cuthheard in *Historia de Sancto Cuthberto*, and the sources which date his death, are late and unreliable.[185] Irish chronicles and 'The Chronicle of the Kings of Alba' testify to only one battle which took place in 918. These chronicles are more reliable witnesses to events.[186] It seems that over-reliance on such a late and clearly biased source as *Historia de Sancto Cuthberto* has caused a gross misunderstanding of Northumbrian history.

After the battle of Corbridge, Rögnvaldr won control of York.[187] Proponents of the theory that there were two battles of Corbridge have suggested that Rögnvaldr began to rule after the alleged first battle in

[181] Campbell, 'Two Notes', p. 87.

[182] *Historia de Sancto Cuthberto*, §23 (ed. and trans. Johnson-South, pp. 60-63).

[183] *Historia de Sancto Cuthberto*, §24 (ed. and trans. Johnson-South, pp. 62-63).

[184] Johnson-South, 'The "Historia"', p. 159.

[185] Dumville, 'Textual Archaeology', pp. 45-48; Angus, 'The Annals', p. 221.

[186] *Annals of Ulster, s.a.* 917 [=918].4 (ed. and trans. Mac Airt and Mac Niocaill, pp. 368-69); *Fragmentary Annals*, §459 (ed. and trans. Radner, pp. 180-81); 'The Scottish Chronicle', ed. and trans. Hudson, pp. 150, 157.

[187] This event is reported in *Historia Regum Anglorum*, Part I, under the year 919, and it is erroneously placed under 923 in versions D and E of 'The Anglo-Saxon Chronicle'. It is clear that there is some chronological dislocation in the Northern Recension of 'The Anglo-Saxon Chronicle' (versions D and E) at this date. *ASC.D*, ed. Cubbin, p. 41; E in *Two of the Saxon Chronicles*, ed. Plummer, I, 105; *Historia Regum Anglorum*, Part I (*Symeonis Monachi Opera*, ed. Arnold, II, 93; *The Church Historians*, trans. Stevenson, III, pt 2, p. 68). Angus ('The Annals', p. 224) suggested that the correct date is 918.

914.[188] However, Mark Blackburn has argued that the coins minted at York in Rögnvaldr's name 'point to a later date, fitting in with Ragnald's only well-attested period in York, *c*.919-20/1'.[189] These coins are dated from the evidence of hoards, and they provide independent corroboration of the textual evidence.

The date of the battle of Corbridge and the beginning of Rögnvaldr's rule at York have had broader ramifications in the interpretation of events. The theory that Rögnvaldr ruled at York from 914 has been used to cast doubt on his identification with Ragnall ua Ímair, mentioned in Irish chronicles. Alistair Campbell argued that, because Ragnall ua Ímair was active in the Irish Sea in 914 and 917, he is unlikely to be the same Rögnvaldr who ruled York from 914.[190] This line of reasoning has not been universally accepted, but it has remained influential.[191] If it is accepted that there was one battle of Corbridge, not two, any objection which has been advanced against Rögnvaldr's identification as the grandson of Ívarr is removed. 'The Annals of Ulster' are explicit in this matter.[192] They report that *Ragnall rí Dubgall* went from Waterford to North Britain where he fought a battle on the banks of the Tyne in 918.[193] He can be identified as the *Ragnall h. hÍmair* whose arrival at Waterford is reported by the same chronicle in 917.[194] 'The Annals of Ulster' report the death of *Ragnall h.Ímair rí Finngall 7 Dubgall* in 921.[195] There seems little scope for doubt

---

[188] Campbell, 'Two Notes', pp. 86-88; Wainwright, *Scandinavian England*, p. 178; Smyth, *Scandinavian York*, I, 101-02; Rollason *et al.*, *Sources*, p. 66.

[189] Blackburn, 'The Coinage', p. 333.

[190] Campbell, 'Two Notes', pp. 88-91.

[191] Wainwright, *Scandinavian England*, p. 166, and Smyth, *Scandinavian York*, I, 63-64, argued that Rögnvaldr of Waterford and Rögnvaldr of York were the same but maintained that there were two battles at Corbridge. Lesley Abrams has expressed uncertainty over the identification of Rögnvaldr of York with Rögnvaldr from Ireland: 'The Conversion of the Scandinavians of Dublin', p. 22. Abrams's views have been endorsed by Davidson, 'The (non) Submission', p. 208.

[192] For the language of this chronicle see, Ó Máille, *The Language*.

[193] *Annals of Ulster*, s.a. 917 [=918].4 (ed. and trans. Mac Airt and Mac Niocaill, pp. 368-69).

[194] *Annals of Ulster*, s.a. 916 [=917].2 (ed. and trans. Mac Airt and Mac Niocaill, pp. 366-67).

[195] *Annals of Ulster*, s.a. 920 [=921].4 (ed. and trans. Mac Airt and Mac Niocaill, pp. 372-73).

that this Rögnvaldr, who fought at Corbridge and who went on to rule York, was a descendant of Ívarr.[196]

The theory that Rögnvaldr ruled York from 914 has also influenced perceptions of his popularity in Northumbria. F. T. Wainwright drew attention to a statement in 'The Mercian Register' that the people of York promised obedience to Æthelflæd, leader of the Mercians, shortly before her death in 918.[197] This was interpreted as evidence of disaffection with Rögnvaldr's rule. However, it may be that Rögnvaldr had made no attempt to seize York before this agreement was made.[198] He may have been willingly accepted after Æthelflæd's death in 918 as a strong leader who could help to maintain Northumbrian independence in the face of Edward's determination to enlarge his kingdom. In 919 Edward took Æthelflæd's territories under his control and seized and fortified Manchester in Northumbria, thereby indicating his predatory intentions in the North.[199]

The Submission at Bakewell

In 920, Edward constructed a new burgh at Bakewell in the Peak District.[200] As the most north-eastern of the burghs of this period, it seems to have been intended to face York as an outpost of English rule. At this point, Edward appears to have demanded recognition of his power by the peoples of North Britain. 'The Anglo-Saxon Chronicle' states that 'the king of Scots and the people of the Scots, and Rögnvaldr, and the sons of Eadwulf and all who live in Northumbria, both English and Danish, Northmen and others, and also the king of the Strathclyde Britons and all the Strathclyde Britons, chose him as father and lord' ('geces þa to fæder 7 to hlaforde Scotta cyning 7 eall Scotta þeod, 7 Rægnald 7 Eadulfes suna 7

---

[196] Wainwright, *Scandinavian England*, p. 166.
[197] *ASC.B*, ed. Taylor, p. 50; *ASC.C*, ed. O'Keeffe, p. 75; *ASC.D*, ed. Cubbin, p. 40. Cf. Wainwright, *Scandinavian England*, p. 178; Smyth, *Scandinavian York*, I, 108-09.
[198] *Fragmentary Annals*, §459 (ed. and trans. Radner, pp. 180-81). This portrays Æthelflæd as the instigator of an anti-Scandinavian alliance between the Mercians, the men of Alba, and the Britons. The same source credits her with a role at the battle of Corbridge. This record seems to derive from a saga which can be dated to the eleventh century. It is not reliable evidence. Cf. Davidson, 'The (non) Submission', p. 203.
[199] *ASC.A*, ed. Bately, p. 69.
[200] *Ibid.*

ealle þa þe on Norþhymbrum bugeaþ, ægþer ge Englisce ge Denisce ge Norþmen ge oþre, 7 eac Stræcledweala cyning 7 ealle Stræcledwealas').[201] Smyth followed Campbell in arguing that this statement might sum up the achievements of Edward's reign rather than represent a single event.[202] If so, the entry would be deliberately misleading. In the context of Edward's policy up to that point, of planting a burgh and then receiving the submission of surrounding peoples, the record of 920 may be accepted at face-value.

Previous examples include the occupation of the burgh at Tamworth in 918. Here 'all the nation in the land of the Mercians ... submitted to him; and the kings in Wales, Hywel, Clydog, and Idwal, and all Welsh people sought to have him as lord' ('him cierde to eall se þeodscype on Myrcna lande ... 7 þa cyningas on Norþwealum, Howel 7 Cledauc 7 Ieoþwel, 7 eall Norþweallcyn hine sohton him to hlaforde').[203] After Edward restored the burgh of Colchester (Essex) in 917, 'many people submitted to him ... and all the army in East Anglia swore agreement with him ... and the army which belonged to Cambridge chose him especially as its lord and protector' ('him cirde micel folc ... 7 eal se here on Eastenglum him swor annesse ... 7 se here þe to Grantanbrycge hierde hine geces synderlice him to hlaforde 7 to mundboran').[204] Other examples are stated in 'The Anglo-Saxon Chronicle' – at Towcester in 917, which followed a military campaign in the region, and at Stamford and Nottingham in 918.[205] The wording and tone of these statements are similar (and there may be an interesting distinction between the peoples who 'submit' to Edward, such as the English and Scandinavians of Mercia, and those who 'choose him as lord', which includes foreign kings and their peoples. The former appear to be in a more direct form of subjection, whereas the latter have him as their overking). On each occasion, emphasis is placed on the consensus of the peoples placing themselves under Edward's authority. However it is notable that these acts are preceded by the occupation or construction of a fortified site and a gathering of English troops. Such willingness may have been encouraged through acts of aggression and the issuing of ultimatums.

[201] Ibid.
[202] Smyth, Scandinavian York, I, 110; Campbell, 'Two Notes', p. 86.
[203] ASC.A, ed. Bately, pp. 68-69.
[204] Ibid., p. 68.
[205] Ibid., pp. 66-69.

Michael Davidson has argued in his recent analysis of the annal for 918 that Edward was in no position to dictate terms to fellow-kings in that year and that the meeting was primarily intended to achieve a peace-agreement.[206] This seems to be part of a current trend to play down aspects of English aggression in the tenth century.[207] While Edward might have portrayed himself as initiator of a peace-agreement in some circles, the record that the people of the North 'chose him as father and lord' in 'The Anglo-Saxon Chronicle' suggests that Edward gave, or wished to give, the impression that the event established his supremacy. Even if the Northern rulers were merely paying lip-service to his ambitions, later campaigns by English kings in North Britain – in 934, 945, and 948 – brutally sought to enforce this idea.[208]

The Reign of Sigtryggr (921-27)

Rögnvaldr's submission to Edward occurred in the same year as the arrival of his kinsman Sigtryggr, grandson of Ívarr, from Dublin. Sigtryggr's journey may have been provoked by events at Bakewell. One of his first deeds in England seems to have been an attack on Davenport in Cheshire. This is recorded in *Historia Regum Anglorum*, Part I, under the year 920, a date which may be accurate (it follows record of Rögnvaldr's reception at York about 918 and precedes record of Edward's death in 924).[209] This attack seems to have been in flagrant breach of the agreement made at Bakewell. Smyth has interpreted it as an inaugural act of defiance.[210] It broke through the ring of burghal defences which Æthelflæd and Edward had carefully planned and which had been completed at Bakewell. As Sigtryggr had abandoned the kingship of Dublin to his brother or cousin Guðrøðr in 920, it seems likely that he assumed some authority in Northumbria on his arrival, perhaps deposing Rögnvaldr who died in

---

[206] Davidson, 'The (non) Submission', p. 209.

[207] This contrasts with Alfred Smyth's less generous interpretation of English ambitions, *Scandinavian York*, I, 111.

[208] *ASC.A*, ed. Bately, pp. 70, 74; *ASC.B*, ed. Taylor, pp. 51, 53; *ASC.C*, ed. O'Keeffe, pp. 77, 80; *ASC.D*, ed. Cubbin, pp. 41, 44.

[209] *Historia Regum Anglorum*, Part I (*Symeonis Monachi Opera*, ed. Arnold, II, 93; *The Church Historians*, trans. Stevenson, III, pt 2, p. 68).

[210] Smyth, *Scandinavian York*, II, 2.

921.[211] Sigtryggr is named as king of York thereafter until his death in 927.[212]

If Sigtryggr's reign was more defiant towards the English king than Rögnvaldr's, there is little evidence of it to comment upon. For the crucial years from 921 to 924 no reports are given in 'The Anglo-Saxon Chronicle' or the Chronicle of Æthelweard. There is only one surviving English royal charter for these years, dated to 921 (however, its witness-list fits with the years 931×934 and it may therefore be of dubious worth).[213] Nevertheless, there is numismatic evidence that Sigtryggr ruled a considerable area south of the Humber (coins were minted in his name at Lincoln).[214] Since this coin-evidence was discovered, it has been suggested that the area around Lincoln was never held by Edward. However, this appears to contradict the claim made by 'The Anglo-Saxon Chronicle' that all the 'Danes' in Mercia submitted to King Edward in 918. It is possible that Sigtryggr's coinage at York indicates territorial gains (or one might describe it in terms of vikings' re-conquest), in the years from 921 to 924, south of the Humber.

It is possible to argue that Edward's power was failing in the later years of his reign. 'The Anglo-Saxon Chronicle' and Æthelweard tend to record the successes of Edward's reign but not its failings. Their silence regarding the later years of his reign may be telling. Furthermore, Edward's death was surprisingly ill-recorded by contemporary chronicles. This has been noted by Nick Higham.[215] It is not mentioned by Frankish chronicles, the Welsh *Annales Cambriae* and *Brut y Tywysogion* or the majority of Irish chronicles. The records made at his death could reflect his importance in the minds of neighbouring peoples in 924. Had Edward died shortly after the zenith of his power in 920, the event might have been more widely recorded. It is true that later writers praised Edward in glowing terms. For example, in the early twelfth century, John of Worcester called him 'the most invincible king', but such writers had only the evidence of Edward's victories from

---

[211] *Annals of Ulster*, s.a. 919 [=920].5, 920 [=921].5 (ed. and trans. Mac Airt and Mac Niocaill, pp. 370-73).

[212] *Annals of Ulster*, s.a. 926 [=927].2 (ed. and trans. Mac Airt and Mac Niocaill, pp. 378-79).

[213] Sawyer, *Anglo-Saxon Charters*, no. 379.

[214] Smyth, *Scandinavian York*, II, 6-7; Grierson and Blackburn, *Medieval European Coinage*, I, 323.

[215] Higham, 'Edward', pp. 4-5.

contemporary chronicles and nothing to contradict it.[216] Æthelweard's statement on Edward's death, 'here ended his name and his perseverance' may be more indicative.[217]

It is unwise to make too much of negative evidence. However it is possible to suggest that Edward's seizure and direct control of Mercian territory may have caused ill feeling and over-stretched the resources of royal government. This could have enabled Sigtryggr to strengthen his position south of the Humber without effective opposition from Edward. William of Malmesbury asserted that Edward died after defeating a rebellion at Chester. It is the only clue of disaffection at the end of Edward's reign, but this evidence alone is not reliable.[218]

The Reign of Æthelstan (924-39)

As several commentators have pointed out, Edward's fame seems to have been overshadowed by that of Æthelstan who enjoyed greater success in extending his rule across the areas of England colonised by vikings.[219] Æthelstan may have benefited from the policies of his father, but he also took more effective measures to curtail the independence of the kingdom of York. The first event recorded in 'The Anglo-Saxon Chronicle' for Æthelstan's reign was a meeting with Sigtryggr at Tamworth. This is reported in the D-text in annal 926.[220] On this occasion, Æthelstan gave his sister in marriage to Sigtryggr.[221] Smyth has pointed out that the policy of donating a royal bride had been used to bring Mercia under the control of

---

[216] *Ibid.*, p. 3.

[217] Æthelweard, *Chronicon*, IV.4 (ed. and trans. Campbell, p. 54).

[218] William of Malmesbury, *Gesta Regum Anglorum*, II.133 (ed. and trans. Mynors *et al.*, II, 210-11); Thomson, *William*, p. 172; Ward, 'Edward', pp. 160-61; Griffiths, 'The North-West Frontier', pp. 182-84. No other source mentions the rebellion at Chester. Edward died at 'Farndon in Mercia', but this could have been Farndon in Nottinghamshire, not Cheshire: Stenton, *Preparatory*, pp. 3-4. The story of the rebellion needs to be treated with much caution. The portrayal of the men of Chester as a rebellious lot with Welsh sympathies is found elsewhere: William of Malmesbury, *Gesta Regum Anglorum*, I.47 (ed. and trans. Mynors *et al.*, I, 64-65).

[219] Higham, 'Edward', pp. 3-6.

[220] *ASC.D*, ed. Cubbin, p. 41.

[221] According to the thirteenth-century chronicler Roger of Wendover, Sigtryggr was also baptised on this occasion. Roger added that the royal bride was soon cast aside with her virginity preserved: *Flores Historiarum*, s.a. 925 (*Rogeri de Wendover Chronica*, ed. Coxe, I, 385; *Roger*, trans. Giles, I, 245).

Wessex by 918, and the location of this meeting at Tamworth, the ancient royal centre of Mercia, may reflect Æthelstan's intentions.[222]

In the following year Sigtryggr died and Guðrøðr, grandson of Ívarr, came from Dublin to claim the kingship.[223] This was an abortive attempt by Guðrøðr, as Æthelstan successfully took Northumbria under his rule. 'The Annals of Ulster' report Guðrøðr's return to Dublin after six months.[224] According to the *Gesta Regum Anglorum* of William of Malmesbury, one of Æthelstan's first actions was to raze the vikings' *castrum* at York.[225] William stated that he quarried a tenth-century poem for his account. However, Michael Lapidge has shown that none of the poetry which William included in his account dates from the tenth century.[226] Luisella Simpson and Michael Wood have regarded Lapidge's argument as excessively dismissive.[227] However, even if William did use a contemporary source, it is lost, and we cannot judge its reliability. There is therefore scope for debate on the circumstances in which Æthelstan seized York and drove out Guðrøðr in 927.

Following Æthelstan's takeover of Northumbria, he sought to win recognition of his new status at a royal meeting at Eamont (Cumberland). This is reported in version D of 'The Anglo-Saxon Chronicle'.[228] Those attending were King Hywel of West Wales, King Causantín of Alba and Ealdred son of Eadwulf of Bamburgh. Another king, Owain of Gwent, is mentioned in 'The Anglo-Saxon Chronicle', but this may be an error for Owain of Strathclyde.[229] The event was considered as a momentous

---

[222] Smyth, *Scandinavian York*, II, 9.

[223] *Annals of Ulster*, s.a. 926 [=927].2, 926 [=927].3 (ed. and trans. Mac Airt and Mac Niocaill, pp. 378-79).

[224] *Annals of Ulster*, s.a. 926 [=927].3 (ed. and trans. Mac Airt and Mac Niocaill, pp. 378-79).

[225] William of Malmesbury, *Gesta Regum Anglorum*, II.134 (ed. and trans. Mynors *et al.*, I, 214-15).

[226] Lapidge, 'Some Latin Poems'.

[227] Simpson, 'The King Alfred/St Cuthbert Episode', p. 403; Wood, 'The Making', pp. 265-66.

[228] *ASC.D*, ed. Cubbin, p. 41; Edmonds, 'Hiberno-Saxon and Hiberno-Scandinavian Contact', p. 123.

[229] William of Malmesbury, *Gesta Regum Anglorum*, II.134 (ed. and trans. Mynors *et al.*, I, 214-15).

occasion by one of the king's chaplains who composed a poem to commemorate it.[230]

The meeting seems to have been intended to secure peace among the rulers of Britain. It was no doubt also intended as a show of political strength by Æthelstan. 'The Anglo-Saxon Chronicle' reports that oaths were taken, the participants agreed to renounce *deofelgeld* and then departed in peace.[231] *Deofelgeld* can be translated as 'idolatry' or perhaps more literally as 'devil-tribute'.[232] The comment indicates that Æthelstan was claiming some form of moral superiority over his British neighbours. The inclusion of this pledge at the meeting may have been calculated to win ecclesiastical approval. The implication is that some of the leaders who assembled at Eamont had previously allied with heathen vikings. Although these rulers gave oaths as requested in 927, Æthelstan's position was not unchallenged. Ten years later, Causantín and Owain allied with the vikings, and the poem *Armes Prydein Vawr* suggests that there was an anti-English party in Dyfed by the mid-tenth century.[233] Æthelstan's seizure of Northumbria may have meant that he posed a greater threat to neighbouring kings. It may also have been unpopular within Northumbria itself. However, through a combination of statesmanship and military force, Æthelstan kept the area under his control until his death in 939.

Æthelstan's methods of statesmanship are hinted at in various records.[234] Prominent among these was regular contact with leaders in the border-areas of his kingdom. This is not only demonstrated by the meeting at Eamont. Whitelock drew attention to the range of visitors at Æthelstan's 'great courts' which he held in the early part of his reign. These included representatives from Bamburgh and various Scandinavian *duces*. Up to eight such leaders attended the king one year.[235] Æthelstan also visited

---

[230] Lapidge, 'Some Latin Poems', p. 89; Wood, 'The Making', p. 258.

[231] *ASC.D*, ed. Cubbin, p. 41.

[232] *The Anglo-Saxon Chronicle*, trans. Whitelock *et al.*, p. 69.

[233] *ASC.A*, ed. Bately, pp. 70-72; *ASC.B*, ed. Taylor, pp. 51-53; *ASC.C*, ed. O'Keeffe, pp. 77-79; *ASC.D*, ed. Cubbin, pp. 42-43; E in *Two of the Saxon Chronicles*, ed. Plummer, I, 107; *Armes Prydein*, ed. and trans. Williams and Bromwich, p. xx; Smyth, *Scandinavian York*, II, 65-72; Dumville, 'Brittany', pp. 150, 152; Breeze, '*Armes*', p. 216. For speculation that the text was written after 950, see Etchingham, 'North Wales', p. 186; Fulton, 'Tenth-Century Wales', p. 14.

[234] Dumville, *Wessex*, pp. 141-71.

[235] Whitelock, 'The Dealings', p. 77.

Northumbria in person and held court at York on a least one occasion. According to Richer of Rheims, Æthelstan received Frankish ambassadors at York, and this event can be dated to 936.[236] William of Malmesbury stated that Æthelstan also entertained Haraldr hárfagri of Norway at York, but the details of this account are dubious.[237] Æthelstan's links with Northumbria and its leaders may have been deliberately cultivated to help keep the area in his power.

Æthelstan also took care to bring minting at York under his control. Blackburn has stated that Æthelstan made 'a clean sweep' of the coinage at York.[238] New types of coin were introduced. They not only appeared different from Anglo-Scandinavian coin-issues, but they adopted the English rather then the Anglo-Scandinavian weight-standard. A further political dimension to these coins was that later issues employed the English form of the mint-name (*Eforwic*) rather than the Latin name (*Eborace*) which had been used before. The complex use of markings and symbols on these coins also seems to indicate an elaborate system of control for this coinage, as Blackburn has pointed out.[239] Æthelstan's minting policy indicates his desire to integrate Northumbria with the rest of the English kingdom. It was also intended to symbolise his newly won authority to the users of these coins.

Æthelstan acted as a patron to various churches in Northumbria in a bid to win their support. He appears to have recognised the Church's power and usefulness as an agent of religious and secular power. We find that Archbishop Hrothweard of York was a witness to royal charters from April 928 until his retirement in the summer of 931.[240] No mention of him has been found before this date. It is possible that Hrothweard was promoted to the archbishopric after Æthelstan took York. If so, his pontificate was rather short. In 931 he was succeeded by Wulfstan. Soon after, in 934, Æthelstan made a generous grant to the church of York – of land which he had bought from vikings at Amounderness (Lancashire).[241] This territory

---

[236] Rollason *et al.*, *Sources*, p. 73.
[237] William of Malmesbury, *Gesta Regum Anglorum*, II.135 (ed. and trans. Mynors *et al.*, I, 216-17).
[238] Blackburn, 'The Coinage', p. 335.
[239] *Ibid.*, p. 336.
[240] Sawyer, *Anglo-Saxon Charters*, nos 399, 400, 405.
[241] *Ibid.*, no. 407.

stretched from the River Hodder in the east to the sea, and from the River Cocker in the north to the River Ribble in the south.[242] No doubt the grant was intended to win favour from Wulfstan and his clergy. It may also have been intended to place a strategic area of land (stretching north of a main route from Ireland to Northumbria) in loyal hands and, if some of the population was heathen, to bring it into the Christian fold.

In 934 Æthelstan also visited the shrine of St Cuthbert at Chester-le-Street. He presented several precious gifts, including books and vestments, to this major church.[243] To commemorate the event, Æthelstan's name was written above the list of Northumbrian kings in that church's *Liber Vitae* in what appears to be a script of West Saxon court-style.[244] This seems to be a symbolic gesture, perhaps akin to Brian Bóruma's gift to Armagh in 1005, and its commemoration in 'The Book of Armagh'.[245] It may be no coincidence that these various gifts to St Cuthbert were made as Æthelstan travelled north leading a military expedition against Alba. As David Rollason has shown, Æthelstan may have been motivated by piety to favour the cult of Cuthbert, a saint who could either bring victory or ill luck to his ambitions to rule Northumbria and to his military campaign. His favour was perhaps also calculated to win the support of agents of the Church in the North.[246] It seems that Æthelstan's ecclesiastical policy was moderately successful. Wulfstan appears to have remained loyal during Æthelstan's lifetime, and the Church of Cuthbert maintained good relations with West-Saxon kings in the following decades.[247]

For the year 934, 'The Anglo-Saxon Chronicle' and *Historia Regum Anglorum*, Part I, state that Æthelstan's army wasted large areas of Alba by sea and land.[248] Despite Æthelstan's efforts to win support for this invasion from both nobles and churchmen there seems to be some falling away of northern leaders as witnesses to his charters after 934. The attack may have

---

[242] Hart, *The Early Charters*, p. 117.

[243] Robinson, *The Times*, pp. 51-80; Hunter Blair, *An Introduction*, p. 193.

[244] Wood, 'The Making', p. 255.

[245] *Liber Vitae*, ed. Dumville and Stokes, fol. 15r.; Byrne, *Irish Kings*, p. 251; Ó Corráin, *Ireland*, pp. 124, 127.

[246] Rollason, 'St Cuth[b]ert', pp. 414-23.

[247] *Ibid.*, p. 413. Wulfstan was not however loyal to Æthelstan's successors.

[248] *ASC.A*, ed. Bately, p. 70; *ASC.B*, ed. Taylor, p. 51; *ASC.C*, ed. O'Keeffe, p. 77; *ASC.D*, ed. Cubbin, p. 41; *Historia Regum Anglorum*, Part I (*Symeonis Monachi Opera*, ed. Arnold, II, 93; *The Church Historians*, trans. Stevenson, III, pt 2, p. 68).

been unpopular in Northumbria, as it threatened to provoke a war in which the northern borderlands of England would be placed at risk. Causantín, king of Alba, campaigned against the English in 937, allied with vikings from Dublin. Their campaign culminated in defeat at *Brunanburh*, one of the most celebrated battles of Anglo-Saxon history. Charles Haliday demonstrated that the timing of the *Brunanburh*-campaign was largely determined by events in Ireland.[249] Óláfr Guðrøðsson, king of Dublin, was engaged in warfare against the vikings of Limerick in the 930s. In 937 he successfully captured the king of Limerick, Óláfr *Cenncairech*.[250] This event seems to have allowed Óláfr Guðrøðsson to turn his attention to Northumbria.

Much debate has been generated concerning the location of *Brunanburh*. The main arguments were summed up by Alistair Campbell in 1938, and his is still a fairly accurate guide.[251] In recent discussions the identification of the battle-site with Bromborough in Cheshire seems to be winning widest support.[252] This is because it is the only place-name in Britain which can derive etymologically from *Brunanburh*. Variant or different names are found for the battle-site in other sources.[253] If Dingesmere, mentioned in 'The Anglo-Saxon Chronicle', or the plains of Othlyn, mentioned in 'The Annals of Clonmacnoise', could be satisfactorily identified with one of the proposed *Brunanburh*-sites, this would, I think, clinch any argument.[254]

Causantín and Óláfr seem to have been the main leaders of troops opposing the English, while Æthelstan and his brother Edmund led the English side. Reports of the battle indicate that losses were heavy on both sides, and according to the near contemporary poem in 'The Anglo-Saxon Chronicle' it lasted all day. The English victory was nevertheless unambiguous. Causantín and Óláfr evaded death and fled to their lands.

---

[249] Haliday, *The Scandinavian Kingdom*, p. 69.

[250] *Annals of the Four Masters, s.a.* 935 [=937] (ed. and trans. O'Donovan, II, 632-33).

[251] Campbell, *The Battle*, pp. 43-81; Smyth, *Scandinavian York*, II, 41-55; Wood, 'Brunanburh'.

[252] Dodgson, 'The Background'; Higham, *The Kingdom*, p. 193; Griffiths, 'Anglo-Saxon England', p. 30; Hudson, *Kings*, p. 80; Crawford, 'The Norse Background', p. 110, n. 2.

[253] Bremner, *The Norsemen*, pp. 127-29; Smyth, *Scandinavian York*, II, 60, n. 96.

[254] *ASC.A*, ed. Bately, pp. 70-72; *ASC.B*, ed. Taylor, pp. 51-53; *ASC.C*, ed. O'Keeffe, pp. 77-79; *ASC.D*, ed. Cubbin, pp. 42-43; E in *Two of the Saxon Chronicles*, ed. Plummer, I, 107; *Annals of Clonmacnoise, s.a.* 931 [=937] (ed. Murphy, pp. 150-51).

One of Causantín's sons was killed in the engagement. Óláfr seems to have waited for Æthelstan's death before making another attempt at the Northumbrian throne.[255]

Much has been written about the battle of *Brunanburh*.[256] The volume of secondary literature seems disproportionate to its historical significance. In essence the battle prevented Dublin-vikings from re-conquering Northumbria for only two years. Nevertheless, the event seemed important to contemporaries. It was reported in chronicles from Wales, Ireland, and Scotland as well as 'The Anglo-Saxon Chronicle'. This indicates the scale of the battle and the political tensions which were brewing in its wake across Britain and in Ireland.[257] The fine poem in 'The Anglo-Saxon Chronicle', composed to celebrate the event, may have captured the imagination of many contemporaries. It has certainly captured the imagination of scholars of the Viking Age.[258]

The dealings of the dynasty of Ívarr in Northumbria from 865 to 937 testify to their significance outside Ireland. They ruled York in defiance of the kings of Wessex until 927, and extended their power intermittently southwards across the Humber. The reign of Æthelstan marked a major stumbling block to the ambitions of viking kings in England. Although vikings re-took York soon after his death, there is evidence of political upheaval. There were frequent changes in the kingship and the power of rulers was compromised by enmities within the dynasty of Ívarr as well as the continued opposition of English kings. In the following chapter the struggle of Ívarr's descendants to keep York will be described, as will their subsequent efforts to dominate affairs around the Irish Sea.

---

[255] *Annals of the Four Masters*, *s.a.* 937 [=939] (ed. and trans. O'Donovan, II, 638-39).

[256] For example, *The Battle*, ed. Campbell; Cockburn, *The Battle*; Smyth, *Scandinavian York*, II, 62-106.

[257] *Annales Cambriae* (A), *s.a.* [937] (ed. and trans. Dumville, p. 16); *Annals of Ulster*, *s.a.* 936 [=937].6 (ed. and trans. Mac Airt and Mac Niocaill, pp. 384-87); 'The Scottish Chronicle', ed. and trans. Hudson, pp. 150, 157.

[258] *ASC.A*, ed. Bately, pp. 70-72; *ASC.B*, ed. Taylor, pp. 51-53; *ASC.C*, ed. O'Keeffe, pp. 77-79; *ASC.D*, ed. Cubbin, pp. 42-43; E in *Two of the Saxon Chronicles*, ed. Plummer, I, 107.

4

England: from the battle of Brunanburh to the Danish Conquest (937-1013)

D ESPITE the defeats of the early tenth century, the descendants of Ívarr remained a force to be reckoned with in English politics. Their rule at York continued intermittently until 954. Indeed, the last Scandinavian king of York, Eiríkr, may have been a member of this family, contrary to assertions made in later Icelandic sagas.[1] Even after 954 the dynasty of Ívarr influenced affairs along England's western seaboard from their bases in the Hebrides and Man, North Wales and Ireland. They may also have had a hand in the momentous events which led up to the conquest of England by Sveinn, king of Denmark, in 1013.

Events in Northumbria, 937-946

F.M. Stenton called Æthelstan's achievement in uniting England in 927, 'an artificial piece of statecraft, which still depended for its existence on the strength and political ability of the reigning king'.[2] Thus despite the reversal suffered by vikings at *Brunanburh*, kings from Dublin were able to gain control over Northumbria soon after Æthelstan's death. 'The Annals of the Four Masters' report the departure of Óláfr Guðrøðsson from Dublin in 939, perhaps immediately after hearing news of the English king's death in October.[3] Óláfr seems to have been rapidly accepted as king of Northumbria and his cousin Óláfr Sigtryggsson (alias *Cuarán*) joined him in York in 940.[4] Óláfr's brother Blákári Guðrøðsson was left holding the reins of government in Dublin during his absence.[5] When Óláfr

---

[1] Downham, 'Eric'.
[2] Stenton, *Anglo-Saxon England*, p. 356.
[3] *Annals of the Four Masters*, s.a. 937 [=939] (ed. and trans. O'Donovan, II, 638-39).
[4] *Annals of the Four Masters*, s.a. 938 [=940] (ed. and trans. O'Donovan, II, 640-41).
[5] *Chronicum Scotorum*, s.a. 941 [=942] (ed. and trans. Hennessy, pp. 204-05).

Guðrøðsson died in 941, it was Óláfr *Cuarán* who succeeded to the throne of Northumbria.[6]

The renewal of viking power in England represented a substantial threat to the new English king Edmund and an immediate decline in his own power and prestige. The war between Edmund and the descendants of Ívarr continued from 940 to 943, although the exact chronology of events has been debated. The view established by Murray Beaven was that vikings from Northumbria overran the 'Five Boroughs' (Derby, Leicester, Lincoln, Nottingham and Stamford) in 940, and Edmund won them back in 942.[7] Beaven obtained the date 940 from a set of annals which run from 888 to 957 in the twelfth-century compilation *Historia Regum Anglorum*.[8] However, the chronology of this section is often at fault.[9] The D-text of 'The Anglo-Saxon Chronicle' dates the Northumbrian attack on the Five Boroughs to 942×943, not 940. An analysis of the records from 934 to the 950s has suggested that the chronology of the D-text of 'The Anglo-Saxon Chronicle' is more accurate for these particular years than that of *Historia Regum Anglorum*.[10] It may be that the Northumbrian attack post-dated Edmund's campaign.

The D-text of 'The Anglo-Saxon Chronicle' reports that in 941 the Northumbrians were false to their oaths and chose Óláfr from Ireland as their king. This probably refers to the election of Óláfr Sigtryggsson in that year. The records suggest that after the death of Óláfr Guðrøðsson in 941, some Northumbrians had given oaths of loyalty to Edmund. In the following year, 942, all versions of 'The Anglo-Saxon Chronicle' agree that Edmund victoriously 'redeemed' five boroughs from viking control. Some of this land had been in the possession of viking rulers of York in the years before 927. It is possible that descendants of Ívarr regained some authority

[6] *Annals of Clonmacnoise*, s.a. 934 [=941] (ed. Murphy, p. 152); *Chronicum Scotorum*, s.a. [940] [=941] (ed. and trans. Hennessy, pp. 202-03); *ASC.D*, ed. Cubbin, p. 43.

[7] Beaven, 'King Edmund'.

[8] *Historia Regum Anglorum*, Part I, s.a. 939 (*Symeonis Monachi Opera*, ed. Arnold, II, 93; *Church Historians*, trans. Stevenson, III, pt. 2, p. 68). Beaven argued that the second part of this annal belonged to the year 940.

[9] Hunter Blair, 'Some Observations', p. 117; Rollason *et al.*, *Sources*, p. 27; Downham, 'The Chronology', pp. 36-38.

[10] Downham, 'The Chronology', pp. 32-35.

south of the Humber after the death of Æthelstan.[11] Nevertheless, the poem celebrating Edmund's victory in 'The Anglo-Saxon Chronicle' refers to the area having been 'for a long time' (*lange þrage*) in bonds of captivity to the heathens. It is possible that a group of Scandinavian landowners who were loyal to the interests of vikings at York had been established in the region for a longer period. This viking elite may have been subdued or disenfranchised by Edmund's takeover.

That property changed hands in 942 can be seen in some of the surviving royal diplomas. In that year Edmund granted a group of estates in the Middle Trent valley to a loyal thegn called Wulfsige the Black.[12] Peter Sawyer has pointed out that these lands controlled strategic routes from Derby and Nottingham to Tamworth and Lichfield. He has regarded the charters 'as one of the means whereby Edmund reasserted English royal authority in central Mercia'.[13] Sawyer has also suggested that Edmund may have gained control of the five boroughs through purchase rather than military conquest.[14] Perhaps both methods were used. The poem suggests a dramatic climax in Edmund's acquisition of territory, which (I think) favours the interpretation that a military expedition was made, although fighting may not have been necessary. Edmund may have used the technique of his father Edward in taking an army to individual burghs and demanding oaths from local leaders: those who promised obedience retained authority, but those who objected were liable to lose their property.[15] Edmund's campaign to bring this area under tighter control may have been prompted by growing fears that the rulers of York were extending their influence across large swathes of England.

[11] Smyth, *Scandinavian York*, II, 6-7; Blackburn, 'Expansion', p. 135. Cf. Mawer, 'The Redemption', pp. 552, 556.

[12] Sawyer, *Anglo-Saxon Charters*, nos. 479, 484, 1606; Sawyer, 'The Charters of Burton', p. 34.

[13] *Ibid.*, p. 38.

[14] Sawyer, *Anglo-Saxon Lincolnshire*, p. 123. Sawyer argued that the poem contains the verb *gebycan*, 'to buy/redeem'. However, I follow Bosworth and Toller (*An Anglo-Saxon Dictionary*, p. 371) in interpreting this verb as *gebēgan* meaning 'to bow down'. See p. xix above. The verb *alȳsan* meaning to 'redeem' perhaps through purchase, at the end of the poem, may support Sawyer's theory, although comparable use of this verb (*He alȳsde leoda bearn of locan deofla*, 'he released the sons of men from the prison of devils', cited by Bosworth and Toller, p. 35) may have meant that this word seemed appropriate for the author's assertion that the boroughs were liberated from 'heathen fetter-bonds'.

[15] See pp. 89, 95-96 above.

According to version D of 'The Anglo-Saxon Chronicle', Óláfr Sigtryggsson fought against Edmund to regain control of the Five Boroughs. There are two separate entries under the heading 943 which are linked by their subject-matter, and it can be argued that this annal in D covers the years 942 and 943.[16] In 942 Óláfr stormed Tamworth and there were heavy losses on both sides; however, the vikings were victorious. Wulfrun was taken captive in the raid. Peter Sawyer has argued that she was a kinswoman of Wulfsige the Black, who received large grants of land in the Five Boroughs from Edmund in 942.[17] In 943, Edmund took revenge and besieged Óláfr at Leicester. Wulfstan, archbishop of York, was with the viking leader. He seems to have defected from support of the English kings following the death of Æthelstan. In the following years, Wulfstan appears to support the viking kings of York whenever he felt safe to do so. The king and the archbishop escaped from the Leicester by night, and Edmund was unable to claim victory.

Rather than persist in war, the kings sought to settle their differences through diplomacy. According to *Historia Regum Anglorum*, Part I, section 6, and the (thirteenth-century) *Flores Historiarum* of Roger of Wendover, the main mediators in this agreement were Wulfstan, archbishop of York, and Oda, archbishop of Canterbury. A boundary was established between the two kingdoms, along Watling Street.[18] If these reports are correct, the treaty accepted Óláfr's control in the Five Boroughs, reflecting the success of his campaigns and Edmund's keenness to agree terms. According to 'The Anglo-Saxon Chronicle' the peace was confirmed through Óláfr's baptism in 943 at which the English king stood sponsor.[19] The affirmation of a treaty through the ceremony of baptism has a number of parallels both in England and on the Continent, particularly in relation to agreements

[16] *ASC.D*, ed. Cubbin, pp. 43-44; *The Anglo-Saxon Chronicle*, trans. Whitelock *et al.*, p. 71. In the translation, the section marked '940-943 D' contains the annal-division *her*. This appears to represent an interpolation of two consecutive annals from 'the Northern Recension'. There is no division in D between the end of this section and the account of events datable to 943 which are common to versions ABC.

[17] Sawyer. 'The Charters of Burton', p. 30.

[18] *Historia Regum Anglorum*, Part I, *s.a.* 939 (*Symeonis Monachi Opera*, ed. Arnold, II, 93; *Church Historians*, trans. Stevenson, III, pt. 2, p. 68); *Flores Historiarum*, *s.a.* 940 (*Rogeri de Wendover Chronica*, ed. Coxe, I, 395; *Roger*, trans. Giles, I, 251).

[19] *ASC.A*, ed. Bately, p. 73; *ASC.B*, ed. Taylor, p. 53; *ASC.C*, ed. O'Keeffe, pp. 79-80; *ASC.D*, ed. Cubbin, p. 44; Binns, 'The York Vikings', p. 185.

between vikings and non-vikings.[20] This ritual served to bind parties together in spiritual kinship and it offered benefits to both sides. On the one hand it gave recognition to the newly baptised ruler, while on the other hand the godfather was placed in a symbolic position of superiority over his godson.[21]

Later in 943, Edmund sponsored the confirmation another king, Rögnvaldr Guðrøðsson. Rögnvaldr does not appear in Irish records; he was presumably a brother of Óláfr Guðrøðsson and had a claim to the throne of York and Dublin. Rögnvaldr's name appears on coins minted in York around 943-44.[22] It is possible that he accompanied Óláfr Sigtryggsson in York as heir apparent, equivalent to the Irish *tánaise*.[23] Another ruler, Sigtryggr, is named on a single coin from York. This is linked stylistically to those produced for Óláfr Sigtryggsson and Rögnvaldr. Sigtryggr may have ruled jointly with Óláfr for a brief period before Rögnvaldr's arrival.[24] If Rögnvaldr appeared in York towards the end of 943, this could suggest why a separate ceremony of confirmation was arranged between him and Edmund.

The political situation in Northumbria in 943 looks rather complex. Alex Woolf has suggested that Edmund may have benefited from and indeed encouraged rivalries between Óláfr *Cuarán* and Rögnvaldr.[25] Both kings were expelled by Edmund in 944.[26] According to the Chronicle of Æthelweard, 'the ealdorman of the Mercians' and Archbishop Wulfstan facilitated this expulsion of the 'traitors' (*desertores*).[27] This could suggest

---

[20] Lynch, *Christianizing Kinship*, pp. 215-25; Abrams, 'The Conversion of the Scandinavians of Dublin', p. 24; ASC.C, *s.a.* 879 (ed. O'Keeffe, p. 61); ASC.D, *s.a.* 926 (ed. Cubbin, p. 41); Coupland, 'The Rod', p. 538.

[21] Lynch, *Christianizing Kinship*, pp. 226-28.

[22] Blunt *et al.*, *Coinage*, pp. 211, 213.

[23] Jaski, *Early Irish Kingship*, pp. 247-51. Óláfr Sigtryggsson may have held a similar position in relation to Óláfr Guðrøðsson from 940.

[24] Sigtryggr should not be identified with the king of Dublin mentioned in the *Annals of the Four Masters*, *s.a.* 939 [=941] (ed. and trans. O'Donovan, II, 642-43). The latter seems to be a later poetic invention rather than a historical king. Blunt *et al.*, *Coinage*, p. 211; Ó Corráin, 'Muirchertach', p. 243.

[25] Woolf, 'Amlaíb', p. 37; Lynch, *Christianizing Kinship*, p. 224.

[26] ASC.A, ed. Bately, p. 74; ASC.B, ed. Taylor, p. 53; ASC.C, ed. O'Keeffe, p. 80; ASC.D, ed. Cubbin, p. 44; E in *Two of the Saxon Chronicles*, ed. Plummer, I, 111.

[27] Æthelweard, *Chronicon*, IV.6 (ed. and trans. Campbell, p. 54). *Historia Regum Anglorum*, Part I, states that the Northumbrians drove out the two kings, perhaps indicating the

that both kings had broken the promises which they made to Edmund in the previous year. Wulfstan's own credibility may have depended on the success of this agreement as he had been a major force behind it.[28] Following this coup, Óláfr travelled back to Ireland, and in 945 he ousted Blákári Guðrøðsson from Dublin and took the kingship. In 944 or 945, 'The Annals of Clonmacnoise' report, a viking king was killed at York. This is likely to have been Rögnvaldr. He is not mentioned again in the chronicles of Britain and Ireland.

The years from 937 to 944 are characterised by competition between the dynasty of Ívarr and English rulers for control of Northumbria and the Five Boroughs. During these political upheavals, the chronology of events is sometimes unclear. Indeed, Murray Beaven called this period 'one of the obscurest in our national annals'.[29] Despite the victories of English kings in 937 and 944, the struggle for control of Northumbria persisted for another decade.

From Tanshelf to the End of Northumbrian Independence

Edmund was assassinated in 946 and his brother, Eadred, came to the throne.[30] The new king immediately turned his attention to affairs in Northumbria. According to 'The Anglo-Saxon Chronicle', he reduced 'all Northumbria' (*eal Norþhymbra*) under his rule and that he obtained oaths of obedience from the people of Alba (*Scottas*).[31] These measures suggest that there had been an attempt to overthrow West Saxon rule in Northumbria at the end of Edmund's reign, perhaps with support from Mael Colaim of Alba. This uprising may have coincided with the establishment of a viking king, Eiríkr, at York. According to the somewhat neglected Life of St Cathroe (which is thought to have been composed at

presence of a pro-Edmund party in Northumbria: *Symeonis Monachi Opera*, ed. Arnold, II, 94; *Church Historians*, trans. Stevenson, III, pt 2, p. 69.

[28] Williams, '*Princeps*', p. 144; Sawyer, 'The Charters of Burton', p. 30. The ealdorman of Mercia, Ealhhelm, had been appointed by Edmund in 940.

[29] Beaven, 'King Edmund', p. 1.

[30] *ASC.A*, ed. Bately, p. 74; *ASC.B*, ed. Taylor, p. 53; *ASC.C*, ed. O'Keeffe, p. 80; *ASC.D*, ed. Cubbin, p. 44; E in *Two of the Saxon Chronicles*, ed. Plummer, I, 113.

[31] *ASC.A*, ed. Bately, p. 74; *ASC.B*, ed. Taylor, p. 53; *ASC.C*, ed. O'Keeffe, p. 80; *ASC.D*, ed. Cubbin, p. 44; E in *Two of the Saxon Chronicles*, ed. Plummer, I, 113.

Metz in the 980s) Eiríkr was ruling before Edmund's death.[32] It is possible that Edmund's murder in 946 was the result of growing disaffection with his power. This may have been a cause or a consequence of his loss of control in Northumbria. Nevertheless, if Eiríkr did rule at York in 946, his first reign was short-lived.

Eadred's imposition of authority in Northumbria was followed in 947 by a meeting at Tanshelf (on the River Humber, Yorkshire) in which Archbishop Wulfstan and the *witan* of the Northumbrians submitted to him.[33] Despite their oaths, two viking kings held the throne of York from about 947 until 954. These were Óláfr Sigtryggsson (alias *Cuarán*) and Eiríkr. I argue that both were members of the dynasty of Ívarr. Their internecine rivalry compromised the strength of viking Northumbria and assisted in its decline.

During the years 944-48 Óláfr Sigtryggsson was engaged in a struggle for control of Dublin against his cousin Blákári Guðrøðsson.[34] This prevented Óláfr from engaging in Northumbrian politics. Eiríkr exploited this weakness and successfully wooed to his side Northumbrian leaders who sought independence from the English kings. Thus Eiríkr ruled York briefly in 947-48 until an invasion by King Eadred led to his downfall. When Óláfr Sigtryggsson had secured his power in Dublin after the death of Blákári in 948, he naturally turned his ambitions to York, leaving his brother in control of Dublin. This development caused a division in the supporters for Northumbrian independence. Óláfr reigned in York from 950 to 952 but he was ousted by Eiríkr who reigned until 953 or 954.[35] No doubt some Northumbrian leaders backed one king against the other.

---

[32] *Vita sancti Cathroe*, § 17 (*Acta*, ed. Colgan, p. 497); *Early Sources*, trans. Anderson, I, 441; Dumville, 'St Cathróe', p. 173. Woolf ('Erik', p. 190) has dated the encounter to the years 939 and 943, but a later date, prior to the end of Edmund's reign is credible; Downham, 'The Chronology', p. 27.

[33] *ASC.D*, ed. Cubbin, p. 44.

[34] *Annals of the Four Masters*, s.aa. 943 [=945], 946 [=948] (ed. and trans. O'Donovan, II, 654-55); *Annals of Ulster*, s.a. 944 [=945].6, 947 [=948].1 (ed. and trans. Mac Airt and Mac Niocaill, pp. 392-93).

[35] Óláfr's power may have been compromised by continuing problems at Dublin including military defeat at the hands of Ruadrí ua Canannáin and a plague. He may have been forced to return to Ireland briefly in 951: *Annals of Clonmacnoise*, ed. Murphy, pp. 155-56; *Annals of the Four Masters*, ed. and trans. O'Donovan, II, 662-65; *Annals of Ulster*, ed. and trans. Mac Airt and Mac Niocaill, pp. 396-97; *Chronicum Scotorum*, ed. and trans. Hennessy, pp. 208-11.

However some leading men, including Archbishop Wulfstan, may have given their allegiance to whichever candidate seemed stronger at any given time.

Wulfstan was a crucial figure in Northumbrian politics. He had been promoted as a supporter of King Æthelstan in the early 930s. During the rest of his career he swapped his allegiance between various kings. This gives the impression that he was fickle and even that he exploited the rivalries of those who sought to control Northumbria, serving as 'king-maker' in northern affairs. Nevertheless Wulfstan may not have been as much in control as some historians have thought. He may have been guided by a consistent desire for self-preservation and to defend the interests of the Church in Northumbria, which made it necessary to adapt to the rapidly changing tide of events. It is also possible to argue that Wulfstan favoured Northumbrian independence when he thought it safe to do so. In 947, Wulfstan pledged himself to Eadred at Tanshelf. However he broke his pledge soon afterwards.[36] When the irate King Eadred brutally ravaged Northumbria in 948, the *witan* of the Northumbrians (probably including Wulfstan) deserted King Eiríkr and paid compensation to Eadred.[37] According to Simon Keynes, 'Wulfstan was apparently absent from meetings of King Eadred's councillors for what may have been an extended period in 947-8', although he did witness charters in both years.[38] This extended period probably corresponds with time when Eiríkr ruled at York.[39]

In 949, Wulfstan witnessed more royal diplomas.[40] His name also appears on a charter of 950, but the witness-list of this document may not be authentic.[41] According to the received chronology of events, Óláfr Sigtryggsson was king of York 949/50-952. Sawyer has seen no conflict in Wulfstan's attendance at the English court during Óláfr's reign as 'Wulfstan had similarly attended Edmund's court during Oláfr Sigtryggsson's first

---

[36] *ASC.D*, s.a. 947 (ed. Cubbin, p. 44).

[37] *ASC.D*, s.a. 948 (ed. Cubbin, p. 44). Cf. *Historia Regum Anglorum*, Part I, *s.aa.* 949-50 (*Symeonis Monachi Opera*, ed. Arnold, II, 94) where Eiríkr is called *quendam Danum Eiricum*.

[38] Keynes, 'Wulfstan', p. 493.

[39] See above, p. 113.

[40] Sawyer, *Anglo-Saxon Charters*, nos 544, 545?, 546, 549, 550, and 552.

[41] *Ibid.*, no. 552a; Abrams, *Anglo-Saxon Glastonbury*, pp. 211-14.

reign in York'.[42] It is possible, as Sawyer has suggested, that Óláfr and Eadred had reached a *modus uiuendi*, which made Óláfr more acceptable to Eadred as king of Northumbria than was Eiríkr. During Óláfr's reign, Wulfstan may have been acting as an ambassador for Northumbrian affairs at Eadred's court.

Wulfstan evidently began to support Eiríkr's claim to the kingdom of York over that of Óláfr. In 951 he ceased to witness charters at the English court. In 952, Óláfr was driven out by Northumbrians in favour of Eiríkr and Wulfstan was imprisoned on Eadred's orders. Historians have tended to link these two events, seeing Wulfstan as a supporter of Eiríkr's coup, which in turn caused the rift with Eadred.[43] Under these circumstances, it is hard to account for Wulfstan's presence at the English court in 953, attested in a royal charter.[44] The received dating suggests that Eiríkr was still on the Northumbrian throne at this time. However, Wulfstan may, as on previous occasions, have backed away from supporting Eiríkr under English royal pressure.[45] Wulfstan continued to witness Eadred's charters as archbishop in 955 but he may have been regarded as too dangerous to be let loose in Northumbria again. He was compensated with the bishopric of Dorchester, whose incumbent Oscytel exercised authority over the archdiocese of York at the end of Eadred's reign.[46] There are various uncertainties about the chronology of events during the final phase of viking rule at York. These difficulties highlight the complex and incomplete character of the textual sources during this tumultuous era of Northumbrian history.

Who was Eiríkr?[47]

The career of Eiríkr has attracted a lot of attention from historians. W.G. Collingwood established in 1902 the conventional identification of Eiríkr

---

[42] Sawyer, 'The Last Scandinavian Kings', p. 42.

[43] Campbell, 'Two Notes', p. 94; Smyth, *Scandinavian York*, II, 173; Keynes, 'Wulfstan', p. 493.

[44] Sawyer, *Anglo-Saxon Charters*, no. 560.

[45] Alternatively, as Sawyer has suggested, the D-text of 'The Anglo-Saxon Chronicle' may be mistaken in placing the end of Eiríkr's reign in 954. If so, I suggest that it would be one year rather than two years too late as Sawyer argued. The D-text annals 956 and 957 are also one year out of sequence, but the Chronicle is correct at 955.

[46] ASC. B, *s.a.* 971; ASC. C, *s.a.* 971.

[47] For the full argument, see Downham, 'Eric'.

of Northumbria with Eiríkr blóðøx (Eric Bloodaxe).[48] His case was based
on Icelandic sagas, which were analysed in his time as detailed and accurate
historical evidence. Nevertheless, attitudes towards the sources have
changed (albeit not uniformly) and there is scope for revision of the original
arguments. None of the English sources for Eiríkr's reign identifies him as
Eiríkr blóðøx. Nor do later sources from England acknowledge such a
connexion. For example, Eiríkr was portrayed as a Scottish king who
obeyed English royal authority, in a letter from King Edward I to Pope
Boniface VIII.[49] Thus the absence from English sources of any mention of
Eiríkr's previous rule over Norway is surprising, if it had been historical.

The most reliable clue to Eiríkr's identification in English sources is that
he was a son of Haraldr. This is stated in the E-text of 'The Anglo-Saxon
Chronicle'.[50] The early thirteenth-century author Roger of Wendover
supplied further details of family-connexions. He stated that Eiríkr died
with his son Henry (*filio suo Henrico*) and with his brother Reginald (*fratre
Reginaldo*).[51] It is possible that these details are a later invention
incorporated into the text and are not historically accurate. It is enough to
note that they do not match Scandinavian accounts of Eiríkr blóðøx.[52]

---

[48] Collingwood, 'King Eirík'. Previously the subject had been debated: Lappenberg,
Plummer, and Todd regarded Eiríkr as a son of Haraldr blátönn (Harold Bluetooth), while
Haliday and Stevenson argued that he was Eiríkr blóðøx. Lappenberg, *A History*, II, 124;
Two of the Saxon Chronicles, ed. Plummer, II, 148; *Cogadh*, ed. and trans. Todd, p. 267;
Haliday, *The Scandinavian Kingdom*, pp. 68, 96; *The Church Historians*, trans. Stevenson,
III, pt 1, p. 128, n. 1. The view that Eiríkr was a son of Haraldr Blátönn is unsustainable.

[49] *Ibid.*, p. 325; *Anglo-Scottish Relations*, ed. and trans. Stones, pp. 198-99 (no. 30): 'quodam
Yricio rege super ipsos Scotos statuto' ('a certain Eric installed as king over the Scots').

[50] E in *Two of the Saxon Chronicles*, ed. Plummer, I, 113 (*s.a.* 952); Henry of Huntingdon,
Historia Anglorum, V.22 (*Henry Archdeacon*, ed. and trans. Greenway, pp. 316-17); *Libellus
de Primo Saxonum uel Normannorum Aduentu* (*Symeonis Monachi Opera*, ed. Arnold, II,
378), *quendam Ericum filium Haroldi*.

[51] *Rogeri de Wendover Chronica*, ed. Coxe, I, 402; *Roger*, trans. Giles, I, 256.

[52] Nowhere in Norse literature is Eiríkr assigned a son called Henry or an equivalent.
Collingwood attempted to identify him as Hárekr son of Guthorm who is named among the
dead in Eiríkr's final battle in the thirteenth-century saga-compendium *Heimskringla*: see
Hákonar saga góða, §4 (*Snorri*, ed. Finnur Jónsson, pp. 72-73; *Heimskringla* trans.
Hollander, p. 99); Collingwood, 'King Eirík', p. 314. An unidentified King Rögnvaldr is
also named among the dead in *Heimskringla*. This is a tenuous similarity which could be
coincidental. Furthermore, Axel Seeberg and others have, in any case, suggested that
Heimskringla drew these names from an English source; so it may not be an independent
report. Seeberg, 'Five Kings', p. 107, n. 4.

Our knowledge of Eiríkr blóðøx derives from Scandinavian sources dating from the late twelfth century onwards. The earliest accounts of Eiríkr's life contain many contradictions, and it is clear that there were various stories circulating about his fate once he left Norway. According to the *Historia* of Theodoric the Monk, written in 1177×1188, Eiríkr reached England and died immediately.[53] *Ágrip*, composed in 1188×1200, states that Eiríkr was granted the earldom of Northumbria by Æthelstan, but that he soon lost control and died while living a pirate's life in Spain.[54] These accounts diverge in detail. They also contradict English sources about Eiríkr. For example, Roger's *Flores Historiarum* states that Eiríkr of York died in battle in England.[55] Because of their contradictory nature and late date, the Scandinavian histories and later sagas cannot be regarded as reliable sources for events in England during the mid-tenth century.

There survives a substantial body of skaldic poetry about Eiríkr in Icelandic sagas, which might provide assistance, as such poems are usually (but not always) assigned an earlier date of composition. However, once the poems are isolated from their prose surroundings, there is no evidence within them to prove a connexion between Eiríkr blóðøx and Eiríkr of York.[56] It could be that separate poems about the two men were drawn together into the saga-narratives. Furthermore, there are chronological difficulties in associating Eiríkr of York with Eiríkr blóðøx: the career of the two men does not exactly coincide.[57] All these factors compromise the plausibility of the assertion that Eiríkr of York and Eiríkr blóðøx are the same.

This leads on to a bigger question, why Eiríkr of York and Eiríkr son of Haraldr hárfagri were regarded as synonymous at the end of the twelfth century if it was not a historical reality in the tenth century. This may

---

[53] *Theodoricus Monachus*, ed. and trans. McDougall and McDougall, p. xii, and p. 1.

[54] *Ágrip*, ed. and trans. Driscoll, p. xii and p. 17. *Historia Norwegiae*, whose exact date is disputed, agrees that Eiríkr died in Spain (*Monumenta*, ed. Storm, p. 106).

[55] *Flores Historiarum*, *s.a.* 950 (*Rogeri de Wendover Chronica*, ed. Coxe, I, 401; *Roger*, trans. Giles, I, 256).

[56] Downham, 'Eric', pp. 59–63. To this should be added recent discussion by John McKinnell ('Eddic Poetry', p. 327) of *Eiríksmál* – the death-ode of Eiríkr blóðøx. McKinnell has noted the lack of Old English linguistic influence and that the poem's conventions suggest a Swedish or east Norwegian origin. This contradicts the later assertions that it was composed in Orkney at the behest of Eiríkr's widow Gunnhildr.

[57] Downham, 'Eric', pp. 57–58.

simply be the result of confusion of sources describing two kings of the same name. Alternatively, such a conflation could have been motivated by a narrative desire to fill the gap in the story of the life of Eiríkr blóðøx once he had left Scandinavia. The story of Eiríkr may belong to a genre of survival legends of mediaeval kings.[58]

The association of Eiríkr of York with Eiríkr blóðøx can also be judged in the light of other legends concerning Scandinavian colonies. By the late twelfth and thirteenth centuries stories linked Haraldr hárfagri, father of Eiríkr blóðøx, with viking settlements in Iceland, Normandy, the Northern Isles, the Hebrides and Ireland. As Haraldr hárfagri was credited with uniting Norway, these links became somehow emblematic of Scandinavian identity. This may be represented by an early ruler of the colony being descended from Haraldr, or being his close associate.[59] In other cases (most famously that of Iceland) the colony is said to have been populated by people fleeing Haraldr's tyranny in Norway.[60] Whichever way, the figure of Haraldr hárfagri looms large in these stories. It is not possible that all the stories are correct. Some may be regarded as myths.[61] Thus the association of Eiríkr son of Haraldr hárfagri with Northumbria may be a comparable legendary development.

The supposed muddle between Eiríkr of York and Eiríkr blóðøx would also not be the only case of confused identities in medieval Icelandic saga.[62] Matthew Townend has recently discussed the conscious or accidental re-contextualisation of memories of viking kings of York into a setting which was more meaningful to Icelandic saga-writers. One example is Óláfr Guðrøðsson, a descendant of Ívarr who ruled Dublin and York in the tenth century.[63] Óláfr Guðrøðsson, leader of the viking troops at *Brunanburh*, was reinvented as Óláfr the Red, king of Scotland, by later saga-writers. Alistair

---

[58] Cohen, 'From Throndheim'; Thacker, 'The Cult'.

[59] *Historia Gruffud*, §§4, 5 (*A Mediaeval Prince*, ed. and trans. Evans, pp. 24-26, 54-56); *Heimskringla, Haralds saga hárfagri*, §24 (*Snorri*, ed. Finnur Jónsson, pp. 78-79; *Heimskringla*, trans. Hollander, pp. 78-79); *Orkneyinga saga*, §8 (ed. Finnbogi Guðmundsson, pp. 12-20; trans. Pálsson and Edwards, pp. 29-33); *Fragmentary Annals*, §401 (ed. and trans. Radner, pp. 144-45); Steffensen, 'A Fragment'.

[60] *Egils saga*, §4 (ed. Nordal, p. 12; trans. Scudder, p. 12).

[61] For example, Sawyer, 'Harald Fairhair'; Thornton, 'The Genealogy', p. 103; Jesch, 'Norse Historical Traditions', pp. 146-47; *Dudo*, trans. Christiansen, p. 187, n. 114.

[62] Campbell, *Skaldic Verse*, p. 3.

[63] Townend, 'Whatever happened to York Viking Poetry?', pp. 75-76.

Campbell suggested that this was because at the time when the sagas were written 'the likeliest nation to invade England were the Scots'.[64] It is therefore possible that oral memories from Northumbria regarding Eiríkr of York were re-contextualised to fit with legends of the Norwegian king Eiríkr blóðøx. This could have been because Eiríkr of Norway was more famous than Eiríkr of York, due to the importance of the sons of Eiríkr blóðøx, who ruled Norway, and the fame of his father, Haraldr hárfagri.[65]

If Eiríkr of York was not Eiríkr blóðøx, the question needs to be asked who he was. Some light may be cast on this matter by the tenth-century *Life of St Cathroe*.[66] Cathroe belonged to an aristocratic or royal dynasty in Alba. He was also a kinsman of King Domnaldus of Strathclyde. In the *Life* it is stated that Eiríkr was married to a kinswoman of the saint.[67] This contradicts accounts of Eiríkr blóðøx, which assert that the Scandinavian Gunnhildr was his sole wife. However, the alliances represented in this marriage could favour the view that Eiríkr was a descendant of Ívarr.[68]

Numismatic evidence may also support this argument.[69] Two issues of King Eiríkr at York have been identified. The first imitated the coins of his predecessor Óláfr Sigtryggsson.[70] This could merely indicate administrative continuity. However, Eiríkr's second coin-issue imitated those of Óláfr's father Sigtryggr.[71] These coins bore a sword-emblem on the reverse. This has been regarded as a symbol which 'evoked the Hiberno-Norse conquest of 919',[72] and it has been identified more specifically as portraying the 'sword of Carlus', part of the royal insignia of the dynasty of Ívarr in the

---

[64] Campbell, *Skaldic Verse*, p. 6.

[65] Hines, 'Egill's *Höfuðlausn*', p. 88. Hines has added that 'the personal history of this temporary king [Eiríkr] of Northumbria did not provide an obviously well-suited character for historically false adoption as the father of kings of Norway'. However, Eiríkr blóðøx was deliberately portrayed as evil in Icelandic prose, perhaps as a foil to his good brother Hákon and to provide a moral tale regarding Eiríkr's loss of power in Norway.

[66] Woolf, 'Amlaíb', p. 39.

[67] *Vita Sancti Cathroe*, §17 (*Acta*, ed. Colgan, p. 497; *Early Sources*, trans. Anderson, I, 441).

[68] Woolf, 'Amlaíb', p. 39.

[69] Blackburn, 'Expansion', p. 125.

[70] Blunt *et al.*, *Coinage*, pp. 223-25; Grierson and Blackburn, *Medieval European Coinage*, I, 323-25; Smyth, *Scandinavian York*, II, 159.

[71] Blunt *et al.*, *Coinage*, pp. 228-29; Grierson and Blackburn, *Medieval European Coinage*, I, 323-25; Smyth, *Scandinavian York*, II, 160. Smyth's portrayal of Eiríkr as a puppet of Wulfstan may be exaggerated.

[72] Dolley, *The Hiberno-Norse Coins*, p. 26; Smyth, *Scandinavian York*, II, 160.

late tenth century.[73] It seems strange that an outsider-king would use images which could provoke memories of a rival dynasty's claim to his position. It may be that this harking back to an earlier coin-design was intended to legitimise Eiríkr's rule in Northumbria, as a kinsman of Sigtryggr.[74]

Mark Blackburn has recently argued that coin-emblems in Viking-Age Northumbria were carefully chosen to transmit political messages and that kings exercised a high degree of control over their selection.[75] This theory is supported by the similarity of the designs found on coins from York and the graffiti added to coins circulating among the Viking Rus. Symbols which appear on the coins of the Rus include crosses, Thor's hammers, weapons and dynastic emblems.[76] This points to a visual language of power promoted by viking kings in different countries to advertise their strength and legitimacy. For these reasons, I think that the imitation of earlier coin designs during the reign of Eiríkr is an important clue to his origins and identity.

From the collapse of Viking Northumbria to the meeting on the Dee

In 954, 'The Anglo-Saxon Chronicle' reports the Northumbrians drove out Eiríkr and accepted Eadred, king of Wessex and Mercia, as their king. No contemporary accounts survive concerning the fate of Eiríkr. Roger of Wendover stated that Eiríkr was killed in battle at Stainmoor (Westmorland).[77] This 'desolate spot' lay on a main route following the old Roman road from York across to the Irish-Sea coast.[78] If these assertions

---

[73] Grierson and Blackburn, *Medieval European Coinage*, I, 323, 325; Smyth, *Scandinavian York*, I, 107. This is, of course, speculative.

[74] One possibility is that Eiríkr was a brother of Maccus and Guðrøðr, kings of Man and the Isles. Cf. *Caithréim Chellacháin Chaisil*, §44 (ed. and trans. Bugge, pp. 25, 83, 148); Smyth, *Scandinavian York*, II, 177; Ó Corráin, '*Caithréim*', p. 57.

[75] Blackburn, 'Expansion', pp. 135-36; Blackburn, 'The Coinage', p. 346.

[76] Duczko, *Viking Rus*, pp. 133-36, 228-36.

[77] *Flores Historiarum*, s.a. 950 (*Rogeri de Wendover Chronica*, ed. Coxe, I, 401; *Roger*, trans. Giles, I, 256); cf. *Historia Regum Anglorum*, Part II, s.a. 1072 (*Symeonis Monachi Opera*, ed. Arnold, II, 197; *The Church Historians*, trans. Stevenson, III, pt. 2, pp. 142-43); *Chronica Magistri Rogeri*, s.a. 953 (ed. Stubbs, I, 57; *The Annals*, trans. Riley, I, 67).

[78] Collingwood, 'King Eirík', p. 322; Smyth, *Scandinavian York*, II, 174.

have any substance, they could imply that Eiríkr was trying to reach a base near the Irish Sea when he died.[79]

As Dorothy Whitelock pointed out, 'contemporaries naturally could not know that Eric was the last Scandinavian king to establish himself at York'.[80] The policy of the kings of England in the following decades would be influenced by the desire to bring the areas of Anglo-Scandinavian character firmly within their control. Immediately after Eiríkr's expulsion, Osulf, reeve of Bamburgh, was given control over York.[81] He may have been selected because of knowledge of affairs in southern Northumbria and because he had an established power-base in the north. As for ecclesiastical power, the see of York was held from 956 by Oscytel, who came from the eastern Danelaw.[82] Dorothy Whitelock suggested that English kings deliberately promoted men from the eastern counties to high rank in Northumbria as they would be 'familiar with the Anglo-Danish language and customs ... while there would be little danger of them working for Northumbrian independence'.[83] Both Oslac, earl of southern Northumbria, appointed in 963, and Oswald, archbishop of York, appointed in 971, had links with the eastern counties.[84]

Peter Sawyer has suggested that the unification of England in the tenth century was further secured through the granting of estates in frontier-regions to loyal supporters.[85] English kings used this technique before 954; therefore efforts may have been made to displace local landowners in strategic locations who had supported the cause of Northumbrian independence.

Eadred's takeover of Northumbria brought with it a degree of political and territorial appropriation which may have prompted the departure of some leading figures from the region. Some may have sought fortunes in other viking colonies. Kristin Bornholdt-Collins has linked the initiation of hoarding on Man with the arrival of political exiles from Northumbria in

---

[79] *Historia Regum Anglorum*, Part II, *s.a.* 1072 (*Symeonis Monachi Opera*, ed. Arnold, II, 197), and Roger of Wendover state that Eiríkr was killed by Maccus Ólafsson. Maccus is a name which can be linked to viking colonies around the Irish Sea: Thornton, 'Hey Macc!'.
[80] Whitelock, 'The Dealings', p. 72.
[81] *Ibid.*, p. 77.
[82] *Ibid.*, p. 75.
[83] *Ibid.*, p. 76.
[84] *Ibid.*, pp. 75, 78-79.
[85] Sawyer, 'The Charters of Burton', p. 39.

954.[86] Other emigrants may have travelled to Normandy. In the early twelfth century, Hugo of Fleury reported that Deirans (*Deiros*) were among the auxiliary troops of Richard I, duke of Normandy, in 962.[87] However, use of the name Deirans is unusual at this date and needs to be questioned. Place-names offer better evidence for migration to the Bessin and Cotentin in the early to mid-tenth century. Lucien Musset argued that the variety of names, from high-status settlements to fields, reflects the wide social range of the immigrants from the Danelaw.[88] A smaller and perhaps more socially exclusive group of Gaelic-Scandinavian settlers in the early to mid-tenth century is witnessed by place-names in the northern Cotentin.[89]

These population-movements from the Danelaw during the early to mid-tenth century can be linked to upheavals in Northumbria. They may have served to foster closer links between different areas of viking settlement. Numismatic and trading links between Ireland, the Danelaw and Normandy have been analysed by Peter Sawyer and others, and literary connections between these colonies have been explored by Elisabeth van Houts.[90] There is also the early eleventh-century tale of Moriuht, a (real or invented) poet enslaved in Ireland and sold first in Northumbria and then Normandy, described by Warner of Rouen.[91] The political dimension of this network of contacts may be observed in the years leading up to the Danish conquest of England in 1013, discussed below.[92]

The collapse of viking power in Northumbria marked a major blow to the dynasty of Ívarr. From 952 Óláfr Sigtryggsson focused his attention on winning back control of Dublin. Within Britain, members of the dynasty sought to develop power-bases in the west in compensation for the loss of York. This could also be interpreted as a policy of retrenchment with a view to reasserting their claims in Northumbria at a later date. The Isle of Man becomes more prominent in the archaeological and historical record from 954 until the end of the century.[93] An increase in viking activity is also seen

---

[86] Bornholdt-Collins, 'Viking Age Coin Finds', pp. 334-37.

[87] Hugo, *Liber* (*Hugonis Liber*, ed. Waitz, p. 384); Musset, *Nordica*, p. 146.

[88] *Ibid.*, pp. 155-56, 165-67.

[89] *Ibid.*, p. 155, n. 33, and pp. 165-66.

[90] Sawyer, 'Anglo-Scandinavian Trade'; Musset, *Nordica*, pp. 297-306; van Houts, 'Scandinavian Influence'; Ó Corráin, 'Viking Ireland', p. 447.

[91] Warner of Rouen, *Moriuht*, ed. and trans. McDonough; Dumville, 'Images', p. 259.

[92] See below, pp. 131-34.

[93] See below, pp. 182-96.

in Wales.[94] The dynasty of Ívarr continued to figure in English politics, as a threat to the western coasts and seaways and to the political stability of Wales.

In response to these dangers, English rulers sought to bring those viking leaders active in Wales and Man within their control. In 955, the year after the loss of York, a leader named *Syferth* (ON. Sigfrøðr) witnessed a charter at the court of Eadred.[95] He is named alongside the Welsh kings and it seems reasonable to link him with western Britain. Seven years later, perhaps the same King Sigfrøðr is mentioned in 'The Anglo-Saxon Chronicle'. He committed suicide in 962 and was buried at Wimborne (Dorset).[96] The record is unusual. As Alexander Murray has demonstrated, there was a deliberate reticence in recording suicides in chronicles of the central Middle Ages.[97] Furthermore, 'the occasion for a chronicler's mentioning suicide was very often the sanctions which followed it',[98] that is, the 'punishment' of the dead body through the means of its disposal. In this context the record of Sigfrøðr's burial at a royal church at a royal estate-centre seems all the more remarkable.[99] The circumstances and motive of his death can only be guessed at. However, the location could imply that Sigfrøðr was subjected to or allied with the English king.

Two years after the death of Eadred in 955, the English kingdom was divided between his nephews. Eadwig, who succeeded Eadred, remained king south of the Thames and continued to be identified as *Rex Anglorum* in his charters. The inhabitants of Mercia and Northumbria chose Edgar, younger brother of Eadwig, as their king. The partition indicates that regional identities in the Midlands and North remained strong. This was perhaps reinforced by the influence of viking settlers on cultural and political identity.[100] Edgar succeeded to the rest of England two years later and ruled successfully until 975. Edgar seems to have cultivated diplomatic links with Scandinavia and the descendants of Ívarr, and no viking attacks

---

[94] See below, pp. 218-21.
[95] Sawyer, *Anglo-Saxon Charters*, no. 566; Thornton, 'Edgar', p. 71.
[96] *ASC.A*, ed. Bately, p. 75.
[97] Murray, *Suicide*, I, 44-45.
[98] *Ibid.*, p. 101.
[99] Blair, 'Wimborne'.
[100] Northumbrian resistance to southern English rule was a recurrent theme in English politics during the tenth and eleventh centuries.

are recorded for his reign.[101] In addition, Edgar recognised the distinct legal practices and identity of the inhabitants of the Danelaw 'in gratitude for their loyalty'.[102] In the eulogy of Edgar written after his death in 'The Anglo-Saxon Chronicle' the king is criticised on one point alone, that he loved foreign customs too much and that he attracted too many people from abroad to his kingdom.[103] Nevertheless, Edgar's tolerance towards the diverse population within his kingdom, and his network of foreign contacts, seem to have stood him in good stead as a ruler.

Edgar's later reputation as *pacificus* ('peacemaker') was partly based on the meeting of Insular kings which took place at Chester in 973.[104] This event provides details of his relations with the dynasty of Ívarr. The earliest records of this event are found in the D- and E-texts of 'The Anglo-Saxon Chronicle' (which suggests that they were written before about 1030) and Ælfric's Life of St Swithin (composed in 992×1005).[105] After his coronation in 973, Edgar travelled to Chester with his fleet, and a number of Insular kings swore oaths of allegiance. The Chronicle states that six kings attended the meeting, whereas Ælfric mentioned eight, including the kings of *Cumera and Scotta*.

John of Worcester and William of Malmesbury listed the names of eight kings. Their accuracy is debatable. However, David Thornton has emphasised that most of the rulers named in twelfth-century sources can be identified as contemporaries of Edgar; so at least some of the names are likely to be accurate.[106] Mael Colaim of Strathclyde and Cinaed of Alba were almost certainly present. Two Welsh kings, Hywel ab Ieuaf and Iago ab Idwal are named in the lists, along with Dyfnwal, father of Mael Colaim of Strathclyde who died in 975.[107] Maccus Haraldsson, 'king of many islands', is also named, and Welsh chronicles confirm that he was ruling

---

[101] For his involvement in missions to Scandinavia, see Sawyer, 'Ethelred', p. 222.

[102] *English Historical Documents*, trans. Whitelock, no. 41; Wormald, *The Making*, 317-20; Hadley, 'Cockle', pp. 115-16.

[103] *ASC.D*, ed. Cubbin, p. 45; E in *Two of the Saxon Chronicles*, ed. Plummer, I, 114-15. This statement was elaborated by William of Malmesbury: *Gesta Regum Anglorum*, II.148 (ed. and trans. Mynors *et al.*, I, 240-41).

[104] See pp. 156, 192-94, 233 below. See also Dumville, *Wessex*, pp. 141-42, 144-45.

[105] *Ælfric*, ed. Needham, p. 80; *English Historical Documents*, trans. Whitelock, no. 239(G).

[106] Thornton, 'Edgar', p. 74.

[107] *Ibid.*, pp. 66-70; Sawyer, *Anglo-Saxon Charters*, no. 566; Loyn, 'Wales and England', p. 298; Maund, *Ireland*, pp. 55-56. For Bretons present, see Breeze, 'Edgar at Chester'.

Man and the Hebrides at this date.[108] The last king is *Siferth* (according to William of Malmesbury) or *Giferth* (according to John of Worcester). It is unlikely that he was the *Siferth* named at the English court in 955, who is thought to have died in 962.[109] He may have been another viking ruler or he was perhaps spuriously added to the list at a later date.[110] Thus it can be argued that at least one descendant of Ívarr attended this convention.

According to F.M. Stenton, the meeting on the Dee was an occasion when Edgar established his supremacy over neighbouring kings.[111] However, David Thornton and Julia Barrow have recently argued that it was more of a peace-summit.[112] 'The Anglo-Saxon Chronicle' portrays the rulers as 'equal workers', making oaths of co-operation with Edgar on land and sea. Ælfric is more explicit in mentioning the kings' subjection. However, Barrow and Thornton have argued that Ælfric and subsequent authors were biased in favour of Edgar and developed this idea to exalt his status.[113] Furthermore, both have denied the statements of John of Worcester and William of Malmesbury that the Insular kings' act of rowing their helmsman Edgar along the Dee is evidence of their submission. Thornton has suggested that the rowing incident did not happen but it was a later embellishment to the story.[114] Alternatively, Julia Barrow has argued that it symbolised equality as the event took place in neutral space (the river representing a border rather than royal territory).[115] Thornton and Barrow have convincingly demonstrated that the received view of this meeting is

---

[108] *Annales Cambriae* (B), ed. Williams, p. 19; *ByS*, *s.a.* 969 [971] (ed. and Jones, pp. 38-39); *ByT* (Pen. 20), *s.a.* 969 [971] (ed. Jones, p. 10; trans. Jones, p. 8); *ByT* (RBH), *s.a.* [971] (ed. and trans. Jones, pp. 14-15).

[109] Sawyer, *Anglo-Saxon Charters*, no. 566; Loyn, 'Wales and England', p. 298; Thornton, 'Edgar', p. 71. It is possible that this name was created from the witness-list of this charter. See above, p. 123.

[110] Thornton ('Edgar', p. 73) has suggested that this may be Maccus's brother. Williams ('An Outing', pp. 237-39) is more sceptical.

[111] Stenton, *Anglo-Saxon England*, pp. 369-70; Barrow, 'Chester's Earliest Regatta?', p. 83. Benjamin Hudson has argued that this meeting did not occur, but I find the combination of English and Welsh evidence compelling: Hudson, *Kings*, pp. 97-98; *ByS*, *s.a.* [973] (ed. and Jones, pp. 40-41); *ByT* (Pen. 20), *s.a.* [973] (ed. Jones, p. 10; trans. Jones, p. 8); *ByT* (RBH), *s.a.* [973] (ed. and trans. Jones, pp. 14-15).

[112] Barrow, 'Chester's Earliest Regatta?', pp. 92-93; Thornton, 'Edgar', pp. 78-79.

[113] Barrow, 'Chester's Earliest Regatta?', pp. 89-92; Thornton, 'Edgar', p. 77.

[114] *Ibid.*, pp. 63-64.

[115] Barrow, 'Chester's Earliest Regatta?', pp. 84-87.

too jingoistic. However, they may have over-emphasised the even-handed character of the meeting. Edgar was (metaphorically and perhaps physically) steering the course of action.

The circumstances which led to the convention at Chester may help to put events in context. Edgar did not enjoy ideal relations with his neighbours. Maccus and Guðrøðr had been campaigning in Wales, and their power there threatened English control over the sea-routes to and from Chester (England's second wealthiest port at this date). It was around 973 that Edgar introduced reforms to enhance his profits and authority in coin-minting.[116] His reforms perhaps responded to the large increase in silver circulating in Britain after 970 as a result of new mines opening in the Harz mountains of Germany.[117] This supply of silver boosted trade in the Irish Sea region (as can be seen in the number of hoards deposited in Ireland around this date).[118] It may therefore have seemed important to Edgar that he should secure royal control over Chester and relations with her trading partners. This increase in silver flow may also have encouraged neighbouring kings to meet with Edgar, as stable political relations would stimulate mercantile activity and boost their income.

Edgar may have also sought to insure against conspiracy between his neighbours. While his relations with the dynasty of Ívarr were at best ambiguous, Cinaed of Alba was more openly hostile and had campaigned against England since 971.[119] The English king may have decided to resolve these issues most effectively by bringing all parties together and through a show of strength. The meeting at Chester was co-ordinated to follow immediately after Edgar's coronation at Bath. Bath, with its ancient Roman remains, was perhaps an appropriate location in which to portray Edgar as a new Christian emperor.[120] As he had ruled for some years, this was largely a ceremonial gesture intended to boost his authority.[121] Edgar was keen to employ imperial imagery in his charter-styles and in his patronage of the

---

[116] Etchingham, 'North Wales', p. 180; Griffiths, 'Anglo-Saxon England', pp. 136-40; Thornton, 'Edgar', pp. 74-75. *Flores Historiarum, s.a.* 975 (*Rogeri de Wendover Chronica*, ed. Coxe, I, 416; *Roger*, trans. Giles, I, 264); Dolley and Metcalf, 'The Reform', pp. 147-52.

[117] Sawyer, *Anglo-Saxon Lincolnshire*, p. 180.

[118] Blackburn and Pagan, 'A Revised Checklist', nos 135-49.

[119] 'The Scottish Chronicle', ed. and trans. Hudson, pp. 151, 161.

[120] Miller, 'Edgar', p. 158.

[121] Nelson, 'Inauguration', pp. 62-63, 67.

arts.[122] It may be that imperial aspirations were also consciously expressed at Chester.[123]

For the remaining two years of his life, it seems, the agreement at Chester succeeded in preventing further attacks on Wales by the dynasty of Ívarr. Nevertheless, after Edgar's death, the sons of Haraldr resumed hostilities against Wales, and in the conflict-ridden years of Æthelred's reign the kings of the Isles appear to have initiated a series of raids on England.

The reign of Æthelred the Unready

The death of Edgar was followed by a sequence of political upheavals. Edgar's son Edward came to the throne, but he was too young to bring discordant elements within the kingdom to heel. Ælfhere of Mercia pillaged several monastic houses and the Northumbrian ealdorman Oslac was driven into exile. Disagreements came to a head in March 978 or 979, when Edward was murdered in a royal coup and his younger brother Æthelred succeeded to power. He was then only twelve years old. In the year after Æthelred's accession, Edward's remains were discovered and transferred to Shaftesbury Abbey where he was immediately venerated as a martyr.[124] The growth of Edward's cult stands in an uncertain relationship to his brother's reign.[125]

It was only a year after the transfer of Edward's relics that viking raids were renewed against England. The disasters which followed, with increasingly large armies invading England, and greater amounts of tribute being exacted, all leading to the Danish conquest in 1013, are well known.[126] The author who described events from 983 to 1016×1022, found in versions C, D and E of 'The Anglo-Saxon Chronicle', is our main authority for these years. He wrote with the benefit of hindsight (in the

---

[122] *Ibid.*, p. 68; Thornton, 'Edgar', pp. 76-77.

[123] Successive layers of gloss were added to descriptions of this event in the Middle Ages. The claim that the English fleet sailed around Scotland before reaching the Dee may be a story added in imitation of Emperor Agricola: Keppie, *Scotland's Roman Remains*, p. 11.

[124] *ASC.D*, ed. Cubbin, p. 47; E in *Two of the Saxon Chronicles*, ed. Plummer, I, 123-25.

[125] Fell, 'Edward', p. 10. Fell pointed out that hagiographies of English saints were also growing in popularity at this date and that this may have helped to stimulate his cult.

[126] For the debate over the level of tribute which was exacted, see Gillingham, '"The Most Precious"'; Gillingham, 'Chronicles'; Lawson, 'The Collection'; Lawson, '"Those Stories"'; Lawson, 'Danegeld'.

years after 1016).[127] Thus it is with an exaggerated sense of impending doom that events were recounted, as Simon Keynes has pointed out.[128]

Simon Keynes has compared the records of viking activity in England in the 980s with records of attacks on Wales and has concluded that some of the raids 'make better sense if associated with the Norsemen who were established in Ireland, the Isle of Man, and the Western Isles of Scotland'.[129] It seems worth exploring this statement. During the 980s most attacks focused on western Britain. In 980, seven ships raided Southampton, where many of the inhabitants were captured or slain. In the same year, Cheshire was ravaged by a 'northern' naval force and Thanet was attacked.[130] Guðrøðr Haraldsson, king of the Isles, was campaigning in North Wales at the same time. He may have been responsible for the attack on Cheshire, particularly as Guðrøðr's ally in Wales, Custennin ab Iago, was battling against Hywel ab Ieuaf who was allied with Ælfhere of Mercia.[131] In short, the Manx fleet may have attacked England in consequence of a dispute which began in Wales.

Guðrøðr raided Dyfed in 982, and this campaign could be linked with attacks across the Severn-estuary, against Devon and Cornwall in 981 and against Dorset in 982. There is then a gap in recorded attacks until 988. 'The Annals of Ulster' report the new arrival of *Danair* ('Scandinavians' or 'Danes') in the Irish Sea in 986.[132] Various theories have been advanced to explain why Scandinavian fleets came to plunder Britain at this time. Their arrival could be linked with an array of economic or political circumstances in the Scandinavian homelands.[133] One of their first reported attacks was on Iona.[134] They took the bishop to Dublin, perhaps intending to ransom him. Payments may not have been forthcoming, for they soon killed him. In the

---

[127] Keynes, 'The Historical Context', p. 84.

[128] Keynes, 'The Declining Reputation', pp. 230-36.

[129] Keynes, 'The Historical Context', p. 85.

[130] *ASC.C*, ed. O'Keeffe, p. 84; *ASC.D*, ed. Cubbin, p. 48; E in *Two of the Saxon Chronicles*, ed. Plummer, I, 125.

[131] See below, p. 223.

[132] *Annals of Ulster, s.a.* 985 [=986].2 (ed. and trans. Mac Airt and Mac Niocaill, pp. 418-19); *Cogadh*, ed. and trans. Todd, p. xxxi. The term *Danair* was later used to 'signify pirate, robber, ... barbarian, without distinction of nation': *Dictionary*, ed. Quin, p. 182, cols 82-84.

[133] Syrett, *The Vikings in England*, pp. 3-6.

[134] *Annals of Ulster, s.a.* 985 [=986].3 (ed. and trans. Mac Airt and Mac Niocaill, pp. 420-21); *Chronicum Scotorum, s.a.* [984] [=986] (ed. and trans. Hennessy, pp. 230-31).

following year, three ships of Scandinavians arrived on the shore of Dál Riata (N.E. Ireland) where a large number of them were killed.[135] The focus of initial activity, around the North Channel of the Irish Sea, could suggest that the invading force came from Norway or the Northern Isles. In 987, some of the new arrivals were allied with Guðrøðr Haraldsson in a battle at Man against an unnamed enemy.[136] The two sides may have allied to campaign against Wales in 988. Churches on the west and south coast of Wales were raided in this year and Watchet on the north coast of Devon was also ravaged. The activity of vikings from Ireland in the south-west of England during the 980s and 990s is suggested by numismatic evidence. Coin-dies were transferred or stolen from mints at Bath, Watchet and Lydford and used to produce coins at Dublin from about 995.[137] In 990 *Danair* also allied with the vikings of Dublin in their campaigns in Ireland.[138]

The striking fact is that after 990 there are no further attacks of *Danair* reported in Ireland or the Isles, while the number of attacks on England dramatically increased. England perhaps offered richer pickings, and the more centralised system of government there may have enabled greater tributes to be raised; but this cannot be the whole story. The pattern of attacks is very different from those of the First Viking Age when Ireland suffered in no lesser measure than England. It is almost as if the Scandinavian fleets had agreed with descendants of Ívarr not to mount further attacks within their sphere of influence.

During the early 990s a new field of viking activity developed in the east of England. The leader of the largest Scandinavian fleets against England from 991 to 994 was Óláfr. He has been identified as Óláfr Tryggvason, who ruled Norway from 995 to 1000.[139] The deeds of this king in Britain are celebrated in the poem *Óláfsdrápa* attributed to his contemporary,

---

[135] *Annals of Ulster*, s.a. 985 [=986].2 (ed. and trans. Mac Airt and Mac Niocaill, pp. 418-19).

[136] *Annals of Ulster*, s.a. 986 [=987].1 (ed. and trans. Mac Airt and Mac Niocaill, pp. 420-21).

[137] Bornholdt, 'Myth or Mint?', p. 204; Wallace, 'The English Presence', p. 212.

[138] *Annals of the Four Masters*, s.a. 989 [=990] (ed. and trans. O'Donovan, II, 726-27); *Annals of Ulster*, s.a. 989 [=990].1 (ed. and trans. Mac Airt and Mac Niocaill, pp. 422-23).

[139] Keynes, 'The Historical Context', p. 89; Andersson, 'The Viking Policy', pp. 1-2.

Hallfrøðr vandræðaskáld.[140] Sveinn Haraldsson, future king of Denmark and England, also campaigned in England as an ally of Óláfr. We know from Scandinavian rune-stones that the two kings drew their supporters from a wide geographical area.[141] It is possible that vikings from Ireland or the Isles also joined in their campaigns.

In 991, 'The Anglo-Saxon Chronicle' reports, Óláfr led ninety-three ships to Folkestone (Kent) and after pillaging the surrounding area he proceeded to Sandwich, Ipswich and Maldon.[142] There he won a significant victory against Byrhtnoth, ealdorman of Essex.[143] In the following year, Æthelred planned to defeat the Scandinavians at sea. However, Ælfric, ealdorman of Hampshire, is said to have warned the enemy of the attack. In consequence, the Scandinavians were able to defeat the English fleets which came to entrap them.[144] In 993 the north-east coasts of England became the hub of campaigns, and much booty was captured; it is not certain whether these raids were led by Óláfr or were the work of another force.[145] In 994 Óláfr and Sveinn attacked London but failed to take the city. They then harried the surrounding districts until a large tribute was offered to them.[146] As Keynes has noted, the invasions from 991 were on a bigger scale and more sustained that the hit-and-run raids of the 980s. They marked a severe threat to England.[147]

---

[140] Hines, *Old-Norse Sources*, pp. 13, 27; cf. *Orkneyinga Saga*, §12 (ed. Finnbogi Guðmundsson, p. 27; trans. Pálsson and Edwards, p. 37); *Heimskringla*, *Óláfs saga helga* (ed. Finnur Jónsson, p. 266; trans. Hollander, pp. 351-52).

[141] Syrett, *The Vikings in England*, pp. 25-81.

[142] *ASC.C*, ed. O'Keeffe, p. 87; *ASC.D*, ed. Cubbin, p. 49; E in *Two of the Saxon Chronicles*, ed. Plummer, I, 127.

[143] *ASC.A*, ed. Bately, p. 79; *ASC.C*, ed. O'Keeffe, p. 86; *ASC.D*, ed. Cubbin, p. 48; E in *Two of the Saxon Chronicles*, ed. Plummer, I, 127. The event is commemorated in a heroic Old English poem: 'The Battle of Maldon', ed. and trans. Scragg.

[144] *ASC.C*, ed. O'Keeffe, p. 86; *ASC.D*, ed. Cubbin, p. 48; E in *Two of the Saxon Chronicles*, ed. Plummer, I, 127. Thored, ealdorman of Northumbria, was captured in this battle.

[145] *ASC.C*, ed. O'Keeffe, pp. 86-87; *ASC.D*, ed. Cubbin, p. 49; E in *Two of the Saxon Chronicles*, ed. Plummer, I, 127.

[146] *ASC.C*, ed. O'Keeffe, p. 87; *ASC.D*, ed. Cubbin, p. 49; E in *Two of the Saxon Chronicles*, ed. Plummer, I, 127-29. Both Lawson and Gillingham have suggested that the amounts recorded in 'The Anglo-Saxon Chronicle' may not be accurate: see above, p. 127, n. 126.

[147] Keynes, 'The Historical Context', p. 88. Further viking attacks on Cornwall are reported in the 990s as part of the broader campaigns against England: *ASC.C*, ed. O'Keeffe, p. 88; *ASC.D*, ed. Cubbin, pp. 49-50; E in *Two of the Saxon Chronicles*, ed. Plummer, I, 131. *Orkneyinga saga*, §12 (ed. Finnbogi Guðmundsson, p. 27; trans. Pálsson and Edwards, p.

These invasions seem to have been encouraged by the hatred which several English nobles bore against Æthelred. In addition to Ælfric's collusion with Danes in 992, mentioned above, a charter of the 990s mentions that a thegn Æthelric in Essex was accused of conspiracy to receive Sveinn when he first came to attack Essex. This could refer back to events of 991.[148]

In 994, Æthelred was able to arrange a peace-agreement with Óláfr, who thereafter did not return to England.[149] Nevertheless, Sveinn was still at large. In 995 he attacked Man.[150] This assault may have been deliberately intended to challenge the dynasty of Ívarr, whose fortunes had been in decline since the 980s.[151] Devon, Cornwall and Wales were attacked from the south in 997 (perhaps indicating the existence of a base in Normandy). The same army raided eastwards along the coast to Sussex in 998 and attacked Kent in 999.[152] In the following year, Æthelred led an attack on Strathclyde and Man, while the enemy departed to Normandy.[153] The location of the English attack may point to co-operation between people in the Isles and Strathclyde and Scandinavian fleets. Sveinn had campaigned against Man five years before. The English and Danes may have been

37), states that Óláfr Tryggvason was baptised in Scilly before 994. However, Charles Thomas (*Exploration*, pp. 232-33) has argued that it seems to be a literary embellishment based on other conversion-stories.

[148] Æthelred was not reluctant to punish nobles whom he considered disloyal. He had the son of Ealdorman Ælfric blinded in 993, and Æthelric, a treacherous thegn from Essex, had his lands confiscated. Numerous other confiscations and punishments are mentioned during his reign: Keynes, 'Crime'.

[149] *ASC.C*, ed. O'Keeffe, p. 87; *ASC.D*, ed. Cubbin, p. 49; E in *Two of the Saxon Chronicles*, ed. Plummer, I, 129; Keynes, 'The Historical Context', pp. 103-07; Wormald, *The Making*, I, 321; Andersson, 'The Viking Policy', p. 8.

[150] *Annales Cambriae*, ed. Williams, p. 21; *ByS*, ed. and trans. Jones, pp. 48-49; *ByT* (Pen. 20), trans. Jones, p. 10; *ByT* (RBH), ed. and trans. Jones, pp. 18-19.

[151] That most able king of the Isles, Guðrøðr Haraldsson, had died in 989, and his son and successor Rögnvaldr does not seem to have equalled him in political stature. In 995 a civil war was raging in Dublin between Ívarr and Sigtryggr Óláfsson, and Mael Sechlainn, overking of Mide, was able to seize the royal insignia from the town. *Annals of Inisfallen, s.a.* [993] (ed. and trans. Mac Airt, pp. 170-71); *Annals of Tigernach, s.aa.* [989], [995] (ed. and trans. Stokes, II, 238, 241-42).

[152] *ASC.C*, ed. O'Keeffe, p. 88; *ASC.D*, ed. Cubbin, pp. 49-50; E in *Two of the Saxon Chronicles*, ed. Plummer, I, 131-33.

[153] For Anglo-Norman relations see Stenton, *Anglo-Saxon England*, pp. 375-76, 379; Andersson, 'The Viking Policy', pp. 4, 9; Breese, 'The Persistence', pp. 57-58; Keynes, 'The Historical Context', pp. 86, 94; Abrams, 'England'.

competing to bring the Isle of Man under their control, because of its strategic significance in terms of location and naval power.

During the early years of the eleventh century, the south and east of England were relentlessly assaulted. Eventually, Sveinn conquered England. In August 1013 he arrived with an invasion-force at Gainsborough (Lincolnshire), and quickly won support in the Danelaw. Niels Lund has pointed out that Æthelred's heavy handed approach towards the Danelaw, which included an attempt to curb its legal freedoms, may have encouraged the inhabitants to support a rival king.[154] Sveinn then ravaged south of Watling Street, obtaining the submission of each region as he went. London submitted last of all, and at Christmas 1013 Æthelred went into exile. Sveinn only held the kingdom for a matter of weeks before his own death in February 1014.[155]

In the events leading up to the conquest, it is not known whether any viking traders or mercenaries from Ireland were caught up either in the massacre of St Brice's Day in 1002 when Æthelred ordered the Danes in his kingdom to be killed, or in the battles which followed.[156] Nevertheless, it is a curious coincidence that from 1001 until 1013 very little viking activity in Ireland and in Wales is attested, by comparison with records of the preceding and following years. It could be that vikings from the west joined the other troops who were active in England under the command of either Sveinn or Æthelred. Such activity may have been encouraged by the efforts of Brian Bóruma in Ireland. His subjection of the viking towns limited the scope of viking leaders to obtain wealth or glory through war in Ireland. The new field of opportunity in England may have tempted some to raid across the Irish Sea.

Some rather significant (but ambiguous) evidence is provided by the work of William of Jumièges. He wrote his history of Normandy during the period 1050×1070, within living memory of the events in question.[157] He reported that, following Sveinn's death, his son Knútr (Cnut) sent messengers to two kings, Lagmann of the Swedes and Óláfr of the

---

[154] Lund, 'King Edgar', pp. 189, 193-94.
[155] *ASC.C*, ed. O'Keeffe, pp. 97-98; *ASC.D*, ed. Cubbin, pp. 58-59; E in *Two of the Saxon Chronicles*, ed. Plummer, I, 143-45.
[156] Stenton, *Anglo-Saxon England*, pp. 380-81.
[157] *Gesta Normannorum Ducum*, ed. and trans. van Houts, I, xx.

Northmen, to ask for armed support.[158] This second leader has been identified as Óláfr Haraldsson, future king and patron-saint of Norway, although there is some confusion in the sources on this issue.[159] As for Óláfr's companion, Lagmann, there was no king of Sweden with this name. Adigard des Gautries has recommended the emendation *Sudrorum* for *Suauorum*, identifying Lagmann as a king of the Hebrides.[160] This interpretation has been espoused by Elisabeth van Houts who has noted that William of Jumièges was prone to make 'ingenious identifications of peoples'.[161]

Support for this theory comes from the name. Lagmann is derived from Old Norse *lögmaðr* ('lawman'). This name was used in the Northern Isles and Hebrides from the tenth century, but it is not attested in Scandinavia.[162] According to 'The Annals of Ulster' and *Cogad Gaedel re Gallaib*, Óláfr son of Lagmann fought at Clontarf in 1014, alongside a contingent of warriors from the Hebrides.[163] James Henthorn Todd identified Lagmann as a son of Guðrøðr, a descendant of Ívarr and king of the Isles who died in 989.[164] This argument supports the theory that Lagmann ruled the Hebrides and Man in the early eleventh century.

---

[158] *Gesta Normannorum Ducum*, V.8 (ed. and trans. van Houts, II, 18-21).

[159] *Gesta Normannorum Ducum*, V.11-12 (ed. and trans. van Houts, II, 24-29); *Encomium*, ed. and trans. Campbell, pp. 76-82; Abrams, 'England', pp. 46-47 and p. 47, n. 20. It could be that William of Jumièges misidentified this character. Skaldic poems relate that Óláfr Haraldsson aided Æthelred rather than Cnut after the death of Sveinn: *Heimskringla: Óláfs saga helga*, §13 (*Snorri*, ed. Jónsson, pp. 187-88; *Heimskringla*, trans. Hollander, pp. 252-54); *English Historical Documents*, trans. Whitelock, no. 12; cf. Poole, *Viking Poems*, pp. 86-115. Theodoric the Monk read *Gesta Normannorum Ducum* and accepted William's assertion that the Óláfr who helped Cnut and was later baptised in Normandy was Óláfr Haraldsson. This is despite there being contrary stories circulating about the baptism of St Óláfr: *Theodoricus Monachus*, §13 (trans. McDougall and McDougall, pp. 16-17). Adam of Bremen identified the Óláfr who assisted Cnut as a son of Óláfr Tryggvason: *Gesta Hammaburgensis Ecclesiae*, II.51 (ed. Schmeidler, p. 112; *Adam*, trans. Tschan, p. 90); *Encomium*, ed. and trans. Campbell, p. 79, n. 4. Indeed, it is surprising that, if Óláfr Haraldsson was the Óláfr baptised in Rouen, there is so little evidence for his cult in Normandy: Abrams, 'England', p. 57.

[160] des Gautries, *Les Noms*, p. 69, n. 12.

[161] *Gesta Normannorum*, ed. and trans. van Houts, I, xxxv, li and II, 20, n. 1.

[162] Marstrander, *Bidrag*, p. 74; Ó Corráin, 'The Vikings in Scotland', p. 308.

[163] See below, pp. 197-98.

[164] *Cogadh*, ed. and trans. Todd, p. 271.

William of Jumièges reports that, after Lagmann and Óláfr assisted Cnut, Richard, duke of Normandy, sought their help against his enemy Odo, count of Chartres. Nevertheless, the Capetian ruler Robert II intervened to arrange a peace between the two sides. Lagmann and Óláfr were presented with gifts and persuaded to return to their own countries.[165] Lucien Musset and others have suggested that a contingent from Normandy fought at Clontarf on the side of Sigtryggr of Dublin and Óláfr son of Lagmann.[166] Lesley Abrams has recently demonstrated the tenuous nature of this assertion.[167] The presence of Normans is not substantiated in contemporary accounts; rather, it relies on late and fanciful reports of the battle.[168] The contemporary chronicle of Ademar of Chabannes reports the presence of *Nortmanni supradicti* at Clontarf, but these were *Normannorum ex Danamarcha et Iresca regione*.[169] Perhaps these records can provide a different perspective on events at Clontarf.

Lagmann was rubbing shoulders with the leading powers of north-western Europe in his day. Sigurðr of Orkney who also fought at Clontarf was likewise a prominent leader in North European politics. These factors may help explain why the battle drew so much interest from contemporaries in Britain, Ireland, Scandinavia and the Continent. Sigtryggr of Dublin may have been able to recruit mercenaries to fight at Clontarf, as so many mercenary fleets were active around Britain at this time. The participation of Ívarr's descendants in English events during the late tenth and early eleventh centuries drew his dynasty into a broader network of European relations. Some of these links continued in the eleventh century.

In conclusion, it can be argued that the dynasty of Ívarr continued to play a role in English affairs even after their major defeat at the battle of *Brunanburh*. Their acquisition of Northumbria after twelve years of English

---

[165] *Gesta Normannorum*, V.11-12 (ed. and trans. van Houts, II, 24-27). William reported that Óláfr was baptised in Normandy: *ibid.*, II, 28, n.1.

[166] Musset, *Nordica*, p. 305; Breese, 'The Persistence', p. 60; Bates, *Normandy*, p. 7.

[167] Abrams, 'England', p. 53.

[168] *Annals of Loch Cé, s.a.* 1014 (ed. and trans. Hennessy, I, 4-5). For an analysis of some of the names of those who fought at Clontarf, see Ó Corráin, 'The Vikings in Scotland', pp. 306-10.

[169] This fleet had been active in Aquitaine before it travelled to Ireland. *Ademari Cabannensis Chronicon*, III.54-55 (ed. Bourgain *et al.* pp. 172-73). Ademar was a native of Limoges who died in 1034.

rule in 939 suggests a significant level of residual support for Northumbrian independence. The contest for control of 'Five Boroughs' south of the Humber in 942 and 943 suggests that support for viking kings of York may have been widespread. The twin factors of English opposition and dynastic infighting also seem to have led to numerous changes in leadership in Northumbria until the collapse of viking rule at York. This infighting no doubt compromised the strength of the kingdom whose independence was quelled in 954.

After 954, there may have been an exodus of viking leaders from Northumbria. The main sphere of viking activity shifted westwards. The Isle of Man rose in significance as a base through which the dynasty of Ívarr sought to control the Irish Sea. The Manx appear to have allied with the Scandinavian fleets which were attacking England and Wales during the reign of Æthelred. Viking involvement in England had a long-term impact on the culture and identity of northern and eastern regions of the country. This is reflected in the term 'Danelaw' applied to these regions from at least the early eleventh century.[170] In the following chapters, the involvement of the dynasty of Ívarr in the rest of Britain will be analysed.

---

[170] Hadley, *The Vikings*, p. 69.

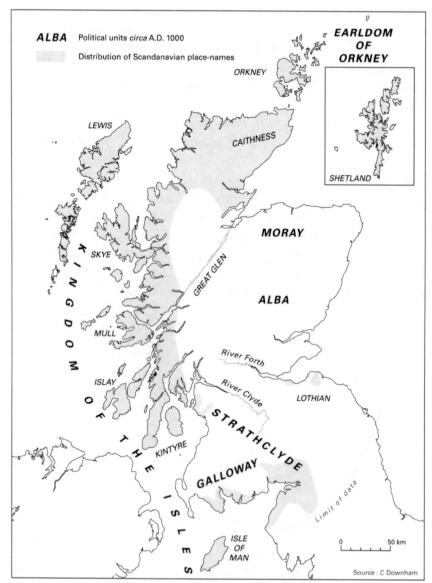

Figure 12: North Britain in the Viking Age

5

North Britain

DURING the period in question, vikings controlled the northern and western fringes of North Britain. The earldom of Orkney brought under its sway the Northern Isles, Caithness and Sutherland. In the west, the kings of Man and the Isles held the Hebrides and intermittently controlled parts of modern Argyll and Galloway. Within the territories which now comprise mainland Scotland, the dynasty of Ívarr can be seen to have played a part in the political history of three main areas, namely Alba, Strathclyde and Galloway.

Alba: 865-917

Alba is in origin the Gaelic word for the island of Britain. However, from about 900 its usage in the Gaelic world was narrowed down to describe the area of North Britain ruled by the descendants of Cinaed mac Ailpín.[1] It may have been self-consciously adapted as a suitable non-ethnic, yet ancient, name to reconcile the complicated inheritances of this polity. An essential but problematic source for this period is 'The Chronicle of the Kings of Alba'. This may be datable to the late tenth century but with a *terminus ante quem* of 1214. It shows that Alba came to be regarded as the child of Dál Riata in terms of royal genealogy and use of the Gaelic language.[2] However, as the heartlands of ancient Dál Riata (which had been dominated by the Picts since 741) fell into viking hands there was significant shift in the power-base of Cinaed's descendants towards the south and east of the area which once comprised Greater Pictland.[3]

The southern frontier of Alba abutted English Northumbria and Brittonic Strathclyde. The northern borders are unclear. Ross seems to have been a buffer-zone between areas of Scandinavian and Gaelic political

---

[1] Dumville, 'Ireland and Britain', pp. 176-83.
[2] Dumville, 'The Chronicle', p. 75.
[3] Graham-Campbell and Batey, *Vikings in Scotland*, pp. 84-98.

suzerainty.[4] The relationship of the territories of northern Pictland, such as Mar and Moray, to the kingdom of Alba, has been debated.[5] These may have been independent or semi-independent polities governed by mormaers (great stewards) who owed allegiance to the king of Alba. By 1014 kings of Alba were extending the limits of their power in Lothian and Strathclyde. However, the creation of a kingdom of Scotland, within the boundaries that we recognise today, took several more centuries to accomplish.[6]

Initially the interests of vikings in Alba appear similar in character to those displayed in Ireland. A series of hit-and-run raids was led against the Scottish and Irish coasts from the 790s.[7] A period of more intense warfare is also attested in both countries in the late 830s.[8] However, from that time the history of vikings' involvement in the two regions is dissimilar. No trading settlements in Pictland grew to the size of the viking towns in Ireland. A few *longphort*-names have been found, but these need not be indicators of viking settlement as the term evolved to describe a wide range of settlement-forms.[9] Silver hoards also indicate that there was less economic contact between vikings and non-vikings in Alba compared to Ireland.[10] These differences must reflect differing political circumstances as well as economic opportunities for vikings in these two areas.

Alfred Smyth has argued that the primary significance of Alba for vikings from Ireland was as a routeway across Britain to Northumbria.[11] Nevertheless, recent work by Nicholas Higham and Fiona Edmonds has

---

[4] The assemblage of recently discovered Viking-Age finds from Tarbat, Easter Ross, demonstrates that the Scandinavian settlers on the rich farmlands around the Cromarty Firth traded with other viking colonies. The assembly-site at Dingwall and the character of local Scandinavian place-names could suggest that the vikings of Easter Ross enjoyed a degree of political independence from the earldom of Orkney. Crawford, *Earl and Mormaer*; Graham-Campbell and Batey, *Vikings in Scotland*, p. 68.

[5] Dumville, *The Churches*, pp. 35-36; Woolf, 'The "Moray Question"'.

[6] Crawford, 'The Pawning of Orkney'; Barrow, *The Kingdom*, pp. 139-61.

[7] See for example: *Annals of Ulster, s.aa.* 793 [=794].7, 797 [=798].2, 801 [=802].9, 805 [=806].8, 824 [=825].17 (ed. and trans. Mac Airt and Mac Niocaill, pp. 250-53, 258-59, 262-63, 282-83).

[8] *Annals of Ulster, s.a.* 838 [=839].9 (ed. and trans. Mac Airt and Mac Niocaill, pp. 298-99).

[9] Meyer, 'Gäl. Long-phort'; Watson, *The History*, pp. 139, 145, 493. These sites may postdate the period of this study. The name Maccus, found in *Longformacus* (Berwickshire) has strong Scando-Gaelic associations: Fellows-Jensen, 'Scandinavians in Southern Scotland?', pp. 46-47; Thornton, 'Hey Macc!'.

[10] Sheehan, 'Viking-Age Hoards'; Graham-Campbell, *The Viking Age Gold*.

[11] Smyth, *Scandinavian York*, I, 35-36, 94-96.

shown that other routes across north-west England may have been equally significant in linking the vikings' power-bases of Dublin and York.[12] The main value of the Forth-Clyde route would have been for military or trading ventures where it was desirable for the entire journey between Dublin and York to be accomplished by ship, rather than disembarking on the west coast and travelling overland. It was possible, though arduous work, for viking ships to be loaded onto rollers and dragged by their crews between the Forth and the Clyde. Certainly archaeological evidence favours the view that such journeys took place, although they may not have been as crucial for York-Dublin relations as Smyth and others have suggested.

The overarching importance of the Forth-Clyde as the main route across Scotland is also challenged by the recent re-identification of *Fortriu* by Alex Woolf. This province of the Picts was a focus of viking activity in 866 and 904. Fortriu was formerly linked with a territory north of the Forth, but Woolf has argued that it was located in the area of Moray and Ross. If his argument is correct, this suggests that the dynasty of Ívarr was as interested in dominating routes across the Great Glen of Scotland in the late ninth century as they were in controlling the central lowlands.[13]

The best documented era of warfare between the associates of Ívarr and the kings of Alba commenced in the mid-860s. This can be associated with contemporary events in Britain and Ireland. In 866 Óláfr and Ásl, two of 'the three kings of the Northmen', led a combined force of vikings from Ireland and Britain to *Fortriu*.[14] According to 'The Annals of Ulster' they raided all the land of the Picts and took hostages, indicating a highly successful campaign. In 867, the year in which Ívarr and the viking army in England secured their control of York, Óláfr seems to have returned to Ireland. 'The Annals of Inisfallen' record that he committed an act of

---

[12] Higham, 'Viking Age Settlement'; Edmonds, 'Hiberno-Saxon and Hiberno-Scandinavian Contact', pp. 66-102.

[13] Woolf, 'Dún Nechtain'. Against this argument, other records of viking activity in North Britain relate to places in southern Scotland in the area which has been traditionally linked with Fortriu, for example Clunie, Dollar and Dunkeld. This inclines me to some uncertainty regarding Woolf's view, but a geographical bias of 'The Chronicle of the Kings of Alba' could be invoked to explain this as an anomaly.

[14] *Annals of Ulster*, s.a. 865 [=866].1 (ed. and trans. Mac Airt and Mac Niocaill, pp. 320-21); *Annals of Clonmacnoise*, s.a. 864 [=866].1 (ed. Murphy, p. 141); *Fragmentary Annals*, §328 (ed. and trans. Radner, pp. 118-19).

treachery against the church of Lismore.[15] The reference to the abbot Martán in this chronicle-entry makes it clear that the Lismore referred to is the one in Munster, rather than Lismore in northern Argyll. Yet one must ask why Óláfr left North Britain at a time when his campaigns there were going so well.

Óláfr's departure from Pictland may have been precipitated by a raid on his followers at Clondalkin (near Dublin) by Mael Ciaráin mac Rónáin (a leader of the Leinstermen).[16] A large number of viking chieftains is said to have fallen in this encounter. This could have undermined Óláfr's power in Ireland and provoked him to return there to secure his position. Óláfr's main ally, Ívarr, was preoccupied with affairs in York and the viking settlements in Ireland seem to have been more vulnerable to attacks at a time when they lacked royal leadership.[17] Óláfr's departure may also be linked to the death of his colleague Ásl. The Irish chronicle-accounts report that he was deceitfully killed in 867 by kinsmen.[18] 'The Fragmentary Annals of Ireland' provide a lengthy account of the deed, written in the early eleventh century, which perhaps has been woven imaginatively around information given in earlier chronicle-reports.[19] According to this chronicle, Óláfr killed his brother Ásl in a fit of jealousy, after Ásl had declared an amorous interest in his wife. The *femme fatale* is there identified as 'the daughter of Cinaed'. Historians' opinions are divided as to whether she should be identified as a daughter of Cinaed mac Ailpín who died in 858, or as a daughter of Cinaed mac Conaing, king of Brega, an ally of Óláfr who was killed in 851 (or indeed yet another Cinaed).[20] Either identification is possible, if the lady is not a figure of fiction. It seems probable that Ásl's death resulted from a power-struggle between the viking

---

[15] *Annals of Inisfallen, s.a.* [867].1 (ed. and trans. Mac Airt, pp. 134-35).

[16] *Annals of Clonmacnoise, s.a.* 865 [=867] (ed. Murphy, p. 142); *Annals of the Four Masters, s.a.* 865 [=867] (ed. and trans. O'Donovan, I, 502-03); *Annals of Ulster, s.a.* 866 [=867].8 (ed. and trans. Mac Airt and Mac Niocaill, pp. 322-23); *Fragmentary Annals,* §349 (ed. and trans. Radner, pp. 128-29).

[17] See p. 21 above.

[18] *Annals of Clonmacnoise, s.a.* 865 [=867] (ed. Murphy, p. 142); *Annals of Ulster, s.a.* 866 [=867].6 (ed. and trans. Mac Airt and Mac Niocaill, pp. 322-23); *Fragmentary Annals,* §347 (ed. and trans. Radner, pp. 126-27).

[19] *Ibid.,* p. xxvi.

[20] *Fragmentary Annals,* §234 (ed. and trans. Radner, pp. 126-27); Hudson, *Kings,* p. 45; Smyth, *Warlords,* p. 192.

kings. Under these circumstances Óláfr may have decided to return to Ireland to settle the difficulties that had arisen there, before campaigning anew in North Britain.

While the identity of Óláfr's alleged wife is uncertain, the *Banshenchas* reports the marriage of Mael Muire, daughter of Cinaed son of Alpín, to Aed Finnliath and then later to Flann Sinna.[21] These were two successive overkings of Uí Néill and possibly the most powerful men in the Ireland of their day. Mael Muire's death is recorded in the year 913.[22] These alliances were perhaps brokered by Cinaed or his sons with the desire to make common cause against vikings. Aed Finnliath's destruction of *longphuirt* in his territories in 866 may have been intended to curb the level of viking activity across the North Channel between Ireland and North Britain.[23] It is not certain whether this served to hinder viking activity in Pictland in 866 or whether it drove vikings from Ireland to seek their fortunes there.[24]

According to 'The Chronicle of the Kings of Alba' Óláfr had remained in Pictland from 1 January to 17 March.[25] This has been interpreted in different ways, in order to make sense of the chronology of this chronicle. Molly Miller suggested that this viking king was in Pictland from January 867 to March 869 and Alfred Smyth has suggested that he was there from 866 to 869.[26] However, Óláfr's action against Lismore in 867 counts against both theories.[27] It seems more likely that Óláfr stayed in Pictland for three months in the year 866.[28]

---

[21] 'The Ban-Shenchas', ed. Dobbs, pp. 186, 225, 311, 335. This text was compiled in the twelfth century, drawing information from biblical texts, sagas, dinnshenchas, and genealogies. Connon, 'The *Banshenchas*'.

[22] *Annals of Ulster*, s.a. 912 [=913].1 (ed. and trans. Mac Airt and Mac Niocaill, pp. 360-61).

[23] *Annals of Clonmacnoise*, s.a. 864 [=866] (ed. Murphy, p. 141); *Annals of the Four Masters*, s.a. 864 [=866] (ed. and trans. O'Donovan, I, 500-01); *Annals of Ulster*, s.a. 865 [=866].4 (ed. and trans. Mac Airt and Mac Niocaill, pp. 320-21).

[24] Miller, 'Amlaíb', p. 243.

[25] 'The Scottish Chronicle', ed. and trans. Hudson, pp. 148, 154.

[26] Miller, 'Amlaíb', p. 244; Smyth, *Warlords*, p. 158.

[27] *Annals of Inisfallen*, s.a. [867] (ed. and trans. Mac Airt, pp. 134-35).

[28] *Early Sources*, trans. Anderson, I, 352, n. 6; 'The Scottish Chronicle', ed. and trans. Hudson, p. 148. I suggest that the amendment to the Chronicle-text suggested by A.O. Anderson makes better sense of the chronology at this point. The word *tercio*, which appears later in the account should read *tercio decimo*, in reference to the thirteenth year of Causantín's reign, rather than describing a gap of three years after the last event described.

The next viking campaign recorded in North Britain can be dated to 870. In this year Ívarr and Óláfr joined forces to besiege Dumbarton Rock, capital of Strathclyde.[29] The kings travelled to Ireland the following year with their booty from this attack.[30] Óláfr soon returned to North Britain.[31] This suggests that his ambition was not merely the acquisition of wealth, but a campaign of conquest, and perhaps the desire to control the Forth-Clyde line as a route of communication. Óláfr is not mentioned in Ireland again and he was killed in Pictland by King Causantín son of Cinaed.[32] The event may be dated to 874.[33] According to 'The Chronicle of the Kings of Alba' Óláfr was killed *trahens centum*, which, as it stands, makes no sense. The text is clearly corrupt at this point. Anderson suggested that he was drawing a hundred [ships] and David Howlett has proposed that Óláfr was drawing a knife (*celtum*).[34] Another theory, put forward independently by Molly Miller and Benjamin Hudson, is that Óláfr was drawing tribute (*censum*).[35] If this last interpretation is correct, the description of hostage-taking in 866 followed by the mention of tribute-gathering in the 870s suggests that parts of Pictland were subjected to Óláfr and his associates. This situation was ended by Causantín's defeat of Óláfr. According to the twelfth-century 'Prophecy of Berchán', Causantín won two more battles against vikings.[36] However, contemporary sources only record Causantín's defeat at the hands of the vikings at Dollar, in southern Pictland.

---

[29] *Annals of Ulster, s.a.* 869 [=870].6 (ed. and trans. Mac Airt and Mac Niocaill, pp. 326-27); *Fragmentary Annals*, §388 (ed. and trans. Radner, pp. 142-43).

[30] *Annals of Ulster, s.a.* 870 [=871].2 (ed. and trans. Mac Airt and Mac Niocaill, pp. 326-27); *Chronicum Scotorum, s.a.* [871] (ed. and trans. Hennessy, pp. 1162-63); *Fragmentary Annals*, §393 (ed. and trans. Radner, pp. 144-45).

[31] *Fragmentary Annals*, §400 (ed. and trans. Radner, pp. 144-45); Ó Corráin, 'The Vikings in Scotland', pp. 297, 304-05.

[32] 'The Scottish Chronicle', ed. and trans. Hudson, pp. 148, 154.

[33] Following the interpretation of *tertio* mentioned above. See footnote 28. Miller ('Amlaíb', p. 244) suggested that his killing could be placed in 872.

[34] *Early Sources*, trans. Anderson, I, 352; Howlett, *Caledonian Craftsmanship*, p. 55.

[35] Miller, 'Amlaíb', p. 242; Hudson, *Kings*, p. 51.

[36] Hudson has argued that the first fourteen stanzas of the Prophecy were composed in the mid-ninth century, and that the compilation was completed in the late eleventh century: *Prophecy of Berchán*, ed. and trans. Hudson, pp. 14-16. Stanzas 7 to 9 are found in *Cogad Gáedel re Gallaib* which indicates that early sections of the text were composed by the early twelfth century: Ní Mhaonaigh, '*Cogad Gáedel re Gallaib*: Some Dating Considerations'. In contrast to Hudson, I should date the completion of this compilation around 1175. The text is divided into two parts, dealing first with Irish kings and then with Scottish ones. The end

The battle at Dollar is datable to 875 in 'The Annals of Ulster'.[37] 'The Chronicle of the Kings of Alba' states that this was soon after the death of Óláfr, which supports 874 as the date for his demise.[38] The battle may have been part of a campaign of revenge against Causantín and an attempt by the associates of Ívarr to regain control of the region. The date of the event also coincides with Hálfdan's attacks on Pictland and Strathclyde reported in 'The Anglo-Saxon Chronicle'.[39] Hálfdan was Ívarr's brother, and it may have been his troops who were responsible for the victory at Dollar.[40] According to 'The Chronicle of the Kings of Alba', the North Britons were slaughtered as far as Atholl ('occisi sunt Scoti co Achcochlam').[41] This slaughter could refer to the pursuit of those who fled from the battle or the plunder and destruction of the region by victorious vikings. 'The Chronicle of the Kings of Alba' reports that these vikings remained in Pictland for a year after the battle of Dollar. They may have been responsible for the death of King Causantín in 876.[42] This record of events allows the

of the Irish section mentions that Doomsday will come 140 years after the reign of a king identified as Flaithbertach Ua Néill, who died in 1036: *Prophecy*, ed. and trans. Hudson, p. 81. This suggests 1176 as a *terminus ante quem*. The end of the Scottish section refers to four kings after the reign of Donnchad mac Maíl Cholaim: *ibid.*, p. 92. This could suggest that the completion of the Prophecy took place during the reign of the fifth king, William the Lion (1165-1214). Thus both parts of the text may indicate a late twelfth-century date. I suggest that the text was compiled in reaction to Anglo-Norman intervention in the Gaelic world, spurred on by the treaties of Falaise and Windsor in 1174 and 1175. Some references to *Gaill* in the text may allude to Anglo-Normans while Henry II may be the figure of antichrist. Gerald of Wales mentioned prophecies of Berchán, written in Irish, which stated that a king from Downpatrick would expel the English from Ireland: *Expugnatio*, II.34 (ed. and trans. Scott and Martin, pp. 232-33). This may fit with references to Downpatrick in *Prophecy of Berchán*, §§10, 102, 103 (ed. and trans. Hudson, pp. 23, 38-39, 72, 82). I agree with A.O. Anderson's argument that errors in the Prophecy concerning late eleventh-century events in Scotland are unlikely to have been made by contemporaries, and this too favours a later date for its composition: *Early Sources*, trans. Anderson, I, xxxv. More work is needed on the context of the Prophecy and on the identification of kings mentioned within it. I am not persuaded by Hudson's identification of references to Óláfr and Ívarr within the Prophecy: *ibid.*, p. 74.

[37] *Annals of Ulster, s.a.* 874 [=875].3 (ed. and trans. Mac Airt and Mac Niocaill, pp. 330-31).

[38] 'The Scottish Chronicle', ed. and trans. Hudson, pp. 148-49, 154.

[39] ASC.A, ed. Bately, p. 50; ASC.B, ed. Taylor, p. 37; ASC.C, ed. O'Keeffe, p. 61; ASC.D, ed. Cubbin, p. 27; E in *Two of the Saxon Chronicles*, ed. Plummer, I, 75.

[40] 'The Scottish Chronicle', ed. and trans. Hudson, pp. 149, 154.

[41] *Ibid.*

[42] Dumville, 'The Chronicle', p. 81.

suggestion that Causantín was hunted and killed by the family of Ívarr in their attempt to bring his kingdom under their control.

Later Scottish king-lists report that Causantín was killed by vikings at Inverdovat in Fife, but this claim is not reliable.[43] The early twelfth-century saga *Cogad Gaedel re Gallaib* provides an alternative account of Causantín's demise. It states that he was killed in 877 by Hálfdan's followers who returned through Pictland following their failed expedition in Ireland in which Hálfdan was killed.[44] Because of the late date of composition of the *Cogad* and its pseudo-historical nature, this account should also be questioned. The reliability of the *Cogad* may be compromised by its assertion that the earth swallowed the men of Alba as they came to attack Hálfdan's troops. Hudson has shown that the earthquake-motif was used in hagiography and it derives ultimately from the bible.[45] A similar story is found in *Historia de Sancto Cuthberto* concerning a victory by Guðrøðr of York over the Scots.[46] Allen Mawer regarded these as the same event, arguing that Guðrøðr was fighting in support of the contingent from Ireland (that might suggest that Guðrøðr's reign began earlier than it has been conventionally dated).[47] Nevertheless the account in *Cogad* is evidently garbled, for contemporary records demonstrate that Causantín had died a year before Hálfdan.[48]

Causantín's reign was cursed by the most intense period of viking warfare known in North Britain. The attacks on Pictland correspond with the great viking campaigns against the English: large parts of Britain had fallen under viking control by 876. Instability continued in North Britain, as witnessed by the departure of Columba's relics to Ireland in 878 'in flight from the foreigners', which is an indication of viking activity in the region

---

[43] Anderson, *Kings*, pp. 267, 274. A. O. Anderson dated Version D (whose last-named ruler is Lulach, who died in 1058) to the reign of Mael Colaim III (1058-93): *Early Sources*, trans. Anderson, I, xlvi. Dauvit Broun has suggested a late thirteenth- or early fourteenth-century date for this text: *The Irish Identity*, pp. 112, 134-36. I am not entirely convinced by the argument that this list was deliberately truncated.

[44] *Cogad*, §25 (ed. and trans. Todd, p. 232).

[45] Hudson, *Kings*, p. 53 (Psalm 106.17).

[46] *Historia de Sancto Cuthberto*, §33 (ed. and trans. Johnson South, pp. 68-71).

[47] Mawer, 'The Scandinavian Kingdom', p. 44.

[48] *Annals of Ulster*, s.a. 875 [=876].1 (ed. and trans. Mac Airt and Mac Niocaill, pp. 330-31); *Chronicum Scotorum*, s.a. [876] (ed. and trans. Hennessy, pp. 164-65).

of Dunkeld.[49] Curiously, this is followed by a period of ten years in which no viking attacks are known to have occurred in North Britain. The contrast could hardly be greater. The silence corresponds with the reversal of vikings' fortunes in England following the battle of Edington in 878 and the departure of an army to the Continent in the following year.[50] Although vikings settled in East Anglia and Northumbria in the later 870s, they seem to have focused their attention on consolidating local power rather than leading ambitious campaigns in other parts of the island. To some extent, the intensity of warfare in Pictland reflected conditions in Britain as a whole.

When Domnall son of Causantín came to power in 889, viking hostilities were renewed. A battle was won by the people of Alba over vikings at *Innisibsolian*, identified by Hudson as the island of Seil in Argyll.[51] If the location is correctly identified, the event may suggest that Domnall campaigned beyond the borders of his kingdom against vikings from the Hebrides or Ireland. These events may mark the renewal of a feud between the decendants of Ívarr and Causantín. However, the evidence of *Cogad Gaedel re Gallaib* raises the possibility that these campaigns were linked with affairs in Dublin. According to the *Cogad*, Sigtryggr son of Ívarr travelled with an army to Alba around 892.[52] This corresponds with the record in 'The Annals of Ulster' for the year 893, which states that two viking leaders, a son of Ívarr and a jarl named Sigfrøðr, left Dublin because of political infighting.[53] Sigfrøðr may have joined the viking army which was at Chester in this year, while the son of Ívarr was in Alba.[54] The return of the son of Ívarr to Ireland is reported in 'The Annals of Ulster' for 894.[55] His return may be linked to the failure of the viking army against the people of Alba at *Innisibsolian*.

---

[49] *Annals of the Four Masters, s.a.* 875 [=878] (ed. and trans. O'Donovan, I, 522-23); *Annals of Ulster, s.a.* 877 [=878].9 (ed. and trans. Mac Airt and Mac Niocaill, pp. 334-35); *Chronicum Scotorum, s.a.* [878] (ed. and trans. Hennessy, pp. 166-67); Bannerman, 'Comarba', p. 43.

[50] *ASC.A*, ed. Bately, p. 51; *ASC.B*, ed. Taylor, p. 37; *ASC.C*, ed. O'Keeffe, p. 62; *ASC.D*, ed. Cubbin, p. 27; E in *Two of the Saxon Chronicles*, ed. Plummer, I, 77.

[51] 'The Scottish Chronicle', ed. and trans. Hudson, pp. 139, and 155, n. 29.

[52] *Cogadh*, §27 (ed. and trans. Todd, pp. 28-29).

[53] *Annals of Ulster, s.a.* 892 [=893].4 (ed. and trans. Mac Airt and Mac Niocaill, pp. 346-47).

[54] *Annals of Ulster, s.a.* 892 [=893].3 (ed. and trans. Mac Airt and Mac Niocaill, pp. 346-47).

[55] *Annals of Ulster, s.a.* 893 [=894].4 (ed. and trans. Mac Airt and Mac Niocaill, pp. 348-49).

King Domnall was killed by vikings in 900 at Dunottar (Kincardineshire).[56] This is an impressive natural fortress, which in the tenth century seems to have been a focus of royal power in the north of Alba.[57] As Barbara Crawford has suggested, the attack on Dunottar is likely to have been carefully planned and large-scale, and she has linked the event with vikings from Orkney.[58] This seems plausible, given that no departures of vikings from Ireland are reported in this year.

There is clearer evidence for the activities of Ívarr's family in North Britain during the reign of Domnall's successor, Causantín II. In 902 the viking elite of Dublin was expelled.[59] Their period of exile from Ireland lasted for over a decade and this posed a threat to political stability in North Britain as different members of the dynasty of Ívarr sought alternative bases of power. In 903, vikings plundered the royal church of Dunkeld and all Alba.[60] 'The Chronicle of the Kings of Alba' reports for the following year that these vikings were defeated by the men of Alba at *Sraith Herenn*. This may be identified with Strathearn in Perthshire (which could indicate continued activity in the area of Dunkeld) or with Strathdearn in Inverness-shire.[61] This event (or another defeat in the same year) is recorded in 'The Annals of Ulster' which reports that Ívarr grandson of Ívarr was killed in battle with many of his followers.[62]

Chronicum Scotorum reports another battle in 904 in which two grandsons of Ívarr and their ally *Catol*, defeated and killed Aed, *rí Cruithentuaithe*. The identification of Aed is problematic. It seems unlikely that he ruled peoples identified as *Cruithin* in Ireland (the term seems to

---

[56] 'The Scottish Chronicle', ed. and trans. Hudson, pp. 149, 155; Dumville, 'The Chronicle', p. 81. Cf. Anderson, *Kings*, pp. 267, 274.

[57] *Historia Regum Anglorum*, Part I, *s.a.* 934 (*Symeonis Monachi Opera*, ed. Arnold, II, 93; *The Church Historians*, trans. Stevenson, III, pt 2, p. 68); Hudson, *Kings*, p. 88.

[58] Crawford, *Scandinavian Scotland*, p. 56.

[59] *Annals of the Four Masters*, s.a. 897 [=902] (ed. and trans. O'Donovan, I, 556-57); *Annals of Ulster*, s.a. 901 [=902].2 (ed. and trans. Mac Airt and Mac Niocaill, pp. 352-53); *Chronicum Scotorum*, s.a. [902] (ed. and trans. Hennessy, pp. 178-79).

[60] 'The Scottish Chronicle', ed. and trans. Hudson, pp. 150, 155.

[61] Woolf, 'Dún Nechtain', p. 192. Woolf has identified *Sraith Herenn* with Strathdearn as part of his argument to locate Fortriu in northern Scotland. This is because 'The Annals of Ulster' report that Ívarr grandson of Ívarr was killed by the men of Fortriu. See the following note.

[62] *Annals of Ulster*, s.a. 903 [=904].4 (ed. and trans. Mac Airt and Mac Niocaill, pp. 354-55).

have fallen out of use for Dál nAraide by the early ninth century).[63] Thus Aed's association with British *Cruithin* (Picts) seems more likely. The long reign of king Causantín mac Aeda of Alba is conventionally dated from 900, and it lasted until 940×943. A. O. Anderson suggested that Aed may have been a relative of Causantín or a provincial ruler in Pictland.[64] William Hennessy identified him as a king of Pictland, whose obit may have been misplaced.[65] The late and unreliable 'Prophecy of Berchán' lists the brief rule of an unnamed king between the reigns of Domnall and Causantín II. If he was a historical king (rather than an error in the Prophecy) he may have been either too insignificant to be mentioned in other king-lists or unknown to their authors.[66]

The identity of *Catol* who is mentioned in this battle in 904 is also problematic. Commentators have recognised the name as Old Norse Ketill. There has been some speculation that he may be identified with the Ketill flatnefr who is named in Icelandic sagas, although the chronology does not fit.[67] As the forms for Old Norse Ketill and Welsh Cadell in Irish chronicles are indistinguishable, it may be that *Catol* was Cadell ap Rhodri, one of the kings of Greater Gwynedd, a possibility which is explored more fully below.[68] Despite the victory against Aed, the death of Ívarr grandson of Ívarr seems to have curbed these vikings' ambitions in Alba. No further viking attacks are reported until the dynasty of Ívarr had re-established itself in Dublin in 917.

The years from 865 to 918 mark a formative period in the history of North Britain. It was within this timeframe that Alba was coined as a new name for the territory ruled by the successors of Cinaed mac Ailpín. Dauvit Broun has argued convincingly that this new name took hold in the wake of the viking depredations in the late ninth century. He has suggested that the attacks had a negative impact on Pictish culture, leading to the name 'Pictland' being replaced.[69] The pressures of war against these raiders from across the sea may have also prompted leaders to promote a unified identity

[63] O'Rahilly, *Early Irish History*, p. 344.
[64] *Early Sources*, trans. Anderson, I, 398, n. 8.
[65] *Chronicum Scotorum*, ed. and trans. Hennessy, p. 180, n. 1.
[66] Prophecy of Berchán, §§ 148-49 (ed. and trans. Hudson, pp. 46-47, 86 and p. 86, n. 89); Dumville, 'Kingship', pp. 97-101.
[67] *Early Sources*, trans, Anderson, I, 398, n. 9.
[68] See below, pp. 207-08.
[69] Broun, 'Dunkeld', p. 123.

across the different cultures of North Britain. It may be possible to compare the situation in England where the court of King Alfred promoted a concept of 'English kin' (*Angelcynn*) to unite subjects in contrast to the vikings (*Dene*).[70] The evolution of common identity seemed intended to rally support against vikings and to help consolidate royal power over a diverse people. The long reign of Causantín mac Aeda during the early tenth century, may have witnessed such a process of consolidation in the politics of North Britain.

Alba: 918-1014

Causantín's reign began at a time when vigorous campaigns were being led by vikings against Alba. These enmities came to a head when the dynasty of Ívarr was restored to power in Ireland. In 918 Rögnvaldr grandson of Ívarr and two of his earls, Óttar and Krákubeinn, set off from Ireland to attack England. According to *Historia Regum Anglorum*, Part 1, whose record may (or may not) be based on a contemporary account, they plundered *Dunbline*, which might (with emendation) be identified with Dublin or Dunblane.[71] There are some difficulties in accepting either identification. Smyth has argued that the vikings travelled via the Forth-Clyde route, attacking Dunblane, located on a tributary of the River Forth, as they journeyed through North Britain.[72] If this is so, one must explain why the viking army took the northerly detour to Dunblane. Yet it seems unlikely that Rögnvaldr would attack Dublin in 918 as it had been seized by his ally Sigtryggr in the previous year.[73] Perhaps we might deduce from the written accounts that the army of Waterford assisted the capture of Dublin in 917 and over-wintered there before proceeding to England.

The army of Waterford travelled to Corbridge in Northumberland where the men of Alba, under Causantín son of Aed, inflicted significant losses on the viking troops. 'The Annals of Ulster' gives a relatively lengthy account of the action, describing the battle-formation of the viking army.

---

[70] Foot, 'The Making'.
[71] *Historia Regum Anglorum*, Part I, *s.a.* 912 (*Symeonis Monachi Opera*, ed. Arnold, II, 93; *The Church Historians*, trans. Stevenson, III, pt 2, p. 68). Part I, section 6, of the *Historia* contains some tenth-century material, but it was completed in 1042×1164: Downham, 'The Chronology', p. 36.
[72] Smyth, *Warlords*, p. 197.
[73] See above, p. 32.

The Jarls Óttar and Krákubeinn fell in the engagement, but a successful counter-attack was made on the rear of Causantín's army before nightfall.[74] Rögnvaldr's troops were then able to continue their journey to York.

'The Fragmentary Annals of Ireland' state that Causantín's hostility towards Rögnvaldr resulted from a pact organised by Æthelflæd of Mercia and the ruling powers in North Britain.[75] It is noteworthy that 'The Mercian Register' reports that the men of York were willing to accept Æthelflæd's overlordship in 918.[76] Nevertheless, the description of this agreement in a saga-element of 'The Fragmentary Annals of Ireland' contains errors which confirm its unreliability. The saga states that that 'the king of the pagans' died in the battle, which does not fit with contemporary records of Rögnvaldr's death in 921.[77] 'The Fragmentary Annals of Ireland' also report that Rögnvaldr fought Æthelflæd rather than Causantín. This contradicts earlier accounts given in 'The Annals of Ulster' and 'The Chronicle of the Kings of Alba'.[78]

The existence of divergent stories about the battle at Corbridge has prompted some historians to conclude that there were two engagements.[79] However, the primary sources can only be reconciled if we posit the existence of two Rögnvaldrs and two Óttars. It seems wiser to conclude that these accounts relate to one event. The number of contradictory reports of the battle may demonstrate the significance attached to it. Great events tend to attract different interpretations and inaccurate gossip. The uncertain outcome of the battle at Corbridge may have fuelled speculation among medieval writers.

The year 918 marks a watershed in Northumbrian and Mercian history with the death of Æthelflæd and Rögnvaldr's capture of York. After this date the relationship between Causantín II of Alba and the dynasty of Ívarr also underwent a dramatic change. By the 930s the two sides had clearly become allies. This may be, as Alfred Smyth has suggested, the consequence of Causantín's spirited defence of the North, indicating that he was more

---

[74] *Annals of Ulster*, *s.a.* 917 [=918].4 (ed. and trans. Mac Airt and Mac Niocaill, pp. 368-69).

[75] *Fragmentary Annals*, §459 (ed. and trans. Radner, pp. 180-81).

[76] *ASC.B*, ed. Taylor, p. 50; *ASC.C*, ed. O'Keeffe, p. 76; *ASC.D*, ed. Cubbin, p. 40.

[77] The same error is found in *Cogadh*, §29 (ed. and trans. Todd, pp. 34-35); *Annals of Ulster*, *s.a.* 920 [=921].4 (ed. and trans. Mac Airt and Mac Niocaill, pp. 372-73).

[78] *Annals of Ulster*, *s.a.* 917 [=918].4 (ed. and trans. Mac Airt and Mac Niocaill, pp. 368-69); 'The Scottish Chronicle', ed. and trans. Hudson, pp. 150, 157.

[79] See above, pp. 91-95.

desirable as an ally than a foe.[80] The two sides also shared a common interest after 918 to curb the growing threat of English domination.

In 920, after the English king Edward had fortified the burgh of Bakewell (Derbyshire), he called a meeting of Northern rulers, which included Causantín and Rögnvaldr.[81] Historians have long debated whether or not the participants in the meeting accepted Edward as 'father and lord', as stated in 'The Anglo-Saxon Chronicle'.[82] However, we may perceive from 920 the imperial ambitions of kings of Wessex. In 927, following the death of Rögnvaldr's successor Sigtryggr, Northumbria was taken under the control of Edward's son, King Æthelstan. Another meeting was called on the northern borders of the English kingdom, at Eamont (Cumberland) to which both Northern and Welsh rulers were called.[83] This time, the English king was in a stronger position to dictate terms. The participants agreed to renounce any alliance with vikings and peace was sworn. A contemporary poem, *Carta dirige gressus*, celebrates the subjection of Causantín of Alba to Æthelstan, and the unification of England.[84] This setback to the political aspirations of both Causantín and Óláfr Guðrøðsson may have encouraged them to cultivate better relations with each other.

After 927, the prospect of a descendant of Ívarr ruling York may have seemed less threatening to the king of Alba than the rule of Æthelstan. Therefore the alliance between Causantín II and Óláfr Guðrøðsson may have begun before Æthelstan's invasion of Alba in 934.[85] It is often assumed that the invasion was prompted by a 'rebellion' by Causantín to shake off English domination.[86] However, the invasion could also have been provoked by mistrust or greed. According to the twelfth-century chronicler John of Worcester, Óláfr Guðrøðsson married a daughter of Causantín before 937.[87] This evidence cannot be relied on. One of Óláfr's sons bore the Gaelic by-name Cammán, but Gaelic names were not uncommon

---

[80] Smyth, *Warlords*, p. 198.

[81] *ASC. A*, ed. Bately, p. 69.

[82] Davidson, 'The (non) Submission', p. 209.

[83] *ASC.D*, ed. Cubbin, p. 41.

[84] Lapidge, 'Some Latin Poems', p. 98.

[85] *ASC.A*, ed. Bately, p. 70; *ASC.B*, ed. Taylor, p. 51; *ASC.C*, ed. O'Keeffe, p. 77; *ASC.D*, ed. Cubbin, p. 41; *Historia Regum Anglorum*, Part I (*Symeonis Monachi Opera*, ed. Arnold, II, 93; *The Church Historians*, trans. Stevenson, III, pt 2, p. 68).

[86] Cf. Sawyer, *Anglo-Saxon Lincolnshire*, pp. 121-2.

[87] John of Worcester, *Chronicle, s.a.* 937 (ed. and trans. Darlington *et al.*, II, 392-93).

among viking leaders in Ireland.[88] More notably, Causantín's grandson Óláfr, bore a Scandinavian name.[89] This is a strikingly Norse name appearing within the royal line of Alba. It therefore seems probable that there was a marriage-alliance between the families of Causantín and Óláfr in the earlier tenth century. A sign of closer cooperation between the two dynasties may have provoked Æthelstan into military action. His attack on Alba took place in the year when Óláfr Guðrøðsson succeeded to the kingship of Dublin: Æthelstan may have feared that an invasion of northern England by the combined forces of Alba and Dublin was imminent.[90]

The evidence of contemporary English royal diplomas and *Historia Regum Anglorum* (Part I) suggests the sequence of events which led to Æthelstan's invasion of Alba in 934.[91] In May of that year the king convened a great court at Winchester. It was attended by four Welsh kings, twelve earls, and a large number of nobles.[92] As Hudson has argued, the event seems to have been orchestrated to drum up and secure support for the Northern campaign.[93] Æthelstan then set about wooing the support of the Northumbrians. Their acquiescence would be essential for an effective campaign. In June the king held court in Nottingham where he granted a large tract of land to the archbishopric of York.[94] The king then travelled north, and presented 'money and diverse gifts' to ingratiate himself with the church of St Cuthbert at Chester-le-Street. According to *Historia Regum Anglorum* (Part I) Æthelstan's army also took hostages from Northumbria, to ensure co-operation, before he crossed the border into Alba.

According to *Historia Regum Anglorum*, Part I, Æthelstan's land-army travelled as far north as *Wertermorum* (which may be translated as 'the moor

[88] *Chronicum Scotorum, s.a.* [857] (ed. and trans. Hennessy, pp. 154-55).

[89] Smyth, *Warlords*, p. 210; Dumville, 'The Chronicle', p. 81. See 'The Scottish Chronicle', ed. and trans. Hudson, p. 151, n. 34, and p. 159, n. 56.

[90] *Annals of Clonmacnoise, s.a.* 929 [=934] (ed. Murphy, p. 150); *Annals of Ulster, s.a.* 933 [=934].1 (ed. and trans. Mac Airt and Mac Niocaill, pp. 382-83); *Chronicum Scotorum, s.a.* [933] [=934] (ed. and trans. Hennessy, pp. 200-01). See p. 103, above.

[91] *ASC.A*, ed. Bately, p. 70; *ASC.B*, ed. Taylor, p. 51; *ASC.C*, ed. O'Keeffe, p. 77; *ASC.D*, ed. Cubbin, p. 41.

[92] Sawyer, *Anglo-Saxon Charters*, no. 425.

[93] Hudson, *Kings*, p. 76.

[94] Sawyer, *Anglo-Saxon Charters*, no. 407.

of Fortriu') and Dunfoeder (Dunottar, Kincardineshire).[95] Dunnottar was an important fortress in north-east Scotland.[96] The corresponding claim in 'The Annals of Clonmacnoise', that the army ravaged as far as Edinburgh, looks like an error.[97] *Historia Regum Anglorum*, Part I, also reports that the English fleet sailed to Caithness.[98] Such a northerly expedition highlights Æthelstan's determination to subdue Alba and perhaps even to scare the inhabitants of the Orkney-earldom away from an alliance with the dynasty of Ívarr and Causantín.

It is evident that Æthelstan's expedition took place on a grand scale and with careful forethought. It is uncertain how much he achieved by the attack. In the early twelfth century John of Worcester stated that Æthelstan took a son of Causantín as a hostage for good behaviour, but this event is not recorded in earlier accounts which have survived.[99] There are two royal charters in which Causantín is named as a witness, one in 934 and one in 935 (the earlier one may be a forgery).[100] 'The Annals of Clonmacnoise' state that Æthelstan won no great victory.[101] No doubt the campaign brought much destruction to homes and livelihoods, but, unless Æthelstan had a puppet-king in mind, it may have been intended to terrorise rather than conquer. Causantín managed to evade any major defeat on the battlefield. With hindsight it is possible to say that the raid of 934 failed to subdue Causantín for any great time. Nor did it obstruct his alliance with Óláfr, as was demonstrated by the battle of *Brunanburh*, three years later.

Retaliation for the attack on Alba seems to have been delayed, partly because Causantín may have needed to buy time to recuperate from the invasion. Óláfr also seems to have been preoccupied by affairs in Ireland until 937. Nevertheless, in that year a large invasion-fleet set out from Dublin. The defeat of the men of Alba and of Dublin at *Brunanburh* is

---

[95] *Historia Regum Anglorum*, Part I, *s.a.* 934 (*Symeonis Monachi Opera*, ed. Arnold, II, 93; *The Church Historians*, trans. Stevenson, III, pt 2, p. 68); Watson, *The History*, pp. 68-69.

[96] Woolf, 'Dún Nechtain', p. 197.

[97] *Annals of Clonmacnoise*, *s.a.* 928 [=934] (ed. Murphy, p. 149).

[98] *Historia Regum Anglorum*, Part I, *s.a.* 934 (*Symeonis Monachi Opera*, ed. Arnold, II, 93; *The Church Historians*, trans. Stevenson, III, pt 2, p. 68).

[99] John of Worcester, *Chronicle*, *s.a.* 937 (ed. and trans. Darlington *et al.*, II, 390-91).

[100] Sawyer, *Anglo-Saxon Charters*, nos 426, 1792.

[101] *Annals of Clonmacnoise*, *s.a.* 929 [=934] (ed. Murphy, p. 150).

famous.[102] Causantín lost a son and many of his followers, and he was forced to flee from the battle. The viking survivors fled to safety in Dublin. Æthelstan's success at *Brunanburh* secured his power in Northumbria for the remainder of his reign. However, Causantín is not found as a witness to any more English royal diplomas, and friendship seems to have continued between Alba and Dublin. The poem *Armes Prydein Vawr* mentions this alliance and calls the people of Wales to arms against the English. Most recent commentators have dated the prophecy to the years immediately after *Brunanburh*.[103]

York was to be held by the dynasty of Ívarr from late 939 or 940 to 944. King Edmund's strategy to keep Northumbria in English hands after 944 was different from that of Æthelstan. Instead of trying to break the alliance between Alba and Dublin by attacking Alba, he tried to isolate the dynasty of Ívarr by waging war on Strathclyde.[104] It appears that Edmund intended to win the support of King Mael Coilaim I of Alba (Causantín's successor) by granting the kingdom of Strathclyde to him in return for his obeisance.

Mael Coilaim seems to have been initially bought off, or at least he was not prepared to risk war with England. It is uncertain how consistently this king of Alba remained on England's side. Perhaps while Causantín lived in retirement at St Andrews (until his death in 952), there was pressure to continue the old king's policies. Causantín's continued loyalty to viking Northumbria and Strathclyde after *Brunanburh* is suggested by his hospitality to St Cathroe, a kinsman of Dyfnwal of Strathclyde and of the wife of Eiríkr of York whose courts the holy traveller visited.[105]

The ambiguous nature of relations between Alba and England after 945 is highlighted by events. The new English king, Eadred (946-55), found it necessary to subdue Northumbria on his accession, and he sought oaths of cooperation from the men of Alba. This suggests that there was resistance to Eadred's rule in the North. In 947 Northumbria revolted, and in 948 the

---

[102] *ASC.A*, ed. Bately, pp. 70-72; *ASC.B*, ed. Taylor, pp. 51-53; *ASC.C*, ed. O'Keeffe, pp. 77-79; *ASC.D*, ed. Cubbin, pp. 42-43; E in *Two of the Saxon Chronicles*, I, 107.

[103] Smyth, *Scandinavian York*, II, 66; Dumville, 'Brittany', p. 150; Breeze, 'Armes', p. 216; Fulton, 'Tenth-century Wales', p. 14. See below, p. 215.

[104] See for example *ASC.A*, ed. Bately, p. 74; *Annales Cambriae* (A), *s.a.* [945] (ed. and trans. Dumville, p. 16).

[105] See above, p. 119.

region was subjugated by Eadred. Then, in 949, Óláfr Sigtryggsson seized power in Northumbria.[106] In the following year, Mael Colaim led a raid on Northumbria as far as the River Tees; according to 'The Chronicle of the Kings of Alba' he was encouraged to do so by the retired Causantín (although the text shows that there seem to have been different opinions about how active Causantín's involvement was).[107] Mael Colaim's motive for this attack is an issue of debate.

Hudson has argued that the attack on Northumbria was aimed against Óláfr, in loyalty to England.[108] However, Smyth has regarded it as a raid intended to help Óláfr, by intimidating those who might oppose him.[109] In favour of Smyth's argument it is worth noting that Mael Colaim raided only as far as the Tees. It was therefore the English population of northern Northumbria (dominated by the rulers of Bamburgh) which bore the brunt of the attack, rather than the people around York. Above all, the raid may have been guided by Mael Colaim's immediate self-interest rather than an alliance with another power. It was after all a profitable raid. 'The Chronicle of the Kings of Alba' states that many goods, people, and livestock were seized in the attack.

In 'The Chronicle of the Kings of Alba', the raid on Northumbria is described as 'predam albidosorum idem nannindisi'. Hudson has translated this as 'the raid of the white ridges, the same as to the River Tees', that is as a geographical description of the attack, repeating the text's earlier statement that the army went as far as the Tees.[110] Smyth has (with simple emendation of *idem* to *id est*) translated it as 'the raid of the men from beyond the spine of Britain, that is, of the islands'. Smyth's translation of *nannindisi* as 'of the islands' seems more plausible than Hudson's, as it requires less amendment.[111] This could suggest that viking forces from the Isles were supporting Mael Colaim's raid or were targeted in the attack. An alternative and credible interpretation of this problematic record has also been advanced by Dauvit Broun. He has suggested that *Nainndisi* might

---

[106] *ASC.E*, in *Two of the Saxon Chronicles*, ed. Plummer, I, 113.

[107] 'The Scottish Chronicle', ed. and trans. Hudson, pp. 150, 157.

[108] Hudson, *Kings*, pp. 85-87.

[109] Smyth, *Warlords*, pp. 206-07.

[110] 'The Scottish Chronicle', ed. and trans. Hudson, pp. 151, 158.

[111] *Early Sources*, trans. Anderson, I, 452, n. 3; Smyth, *Warlords*, p. 206.

stand for *na aindeisi*, i.e. 'the miseries', 'referring to the unnatural dreadfulness of the raid'.[112]

From 949 until 954, a struggle took place between various factions for control of York. In 952 a victory was won by vikings over the men of Alba, the English, and the Britons.[113] This suggests that relations between Alba and England had improved. The event may be interpreted as a coalition against the forces of Eiríkr of York. If Eiríkr held power in the Scottish islands as a member of the dynasty of Ívarr (suggested above), Mael Colaim may have been sufficiently concerned by the prospect of his western neighbour ruling at York that he was prepared to throw in his lot with the English.[114] This could also explain the possible reference to *nannindisi* (islanders?) in the events of 949. However this may be stretching rather doubtful evidence too far.

After Mael Colaim's death in 954, Illulb (Hildulfr) son of Causantín succeeded to the throne of Alba. He was perhaps an opponent of the previous king who had been killed by political enemies. The beginning of Hildulfr's reign coincided with the collapse of viking rule in Northumbria. He may have benefited from resulting instability in the north of England by successfully incorporating Edinburgh (or Dunedin) into his kingdom.[115] It is possible that Hildulfr also maintained friendly relations with the dynasty of Ívarr. One of his sons bore the name Óláfr which was common among Ívarr's progeny. Nevertheless Hildulfr was killed by a viking fleet at Buchan in 962.[116] The location specified by later king-lists (of arguable date and reliability) is Inverculan – perhaps the estuary of the Cullen River (Banff) in the extreme north of Alba.[117] Barbara Crawford has argued that Orcadians were responsible for the attack. As the earldom was becoming more powerful under the sons of Einar in the late tenth century, they may have wanted to extend their influence on the Scottish mainland.[118] After the

---

[112] This interpretation is taken from Dauvit Broun's class handout 'Analysing the Chronicle of the Kings of Alba' for the Senior Honours course 'The Picts and the Formation of Alba' taught at the University of Glasgow in 2005/6. I am grateful to the author for a copy.

[113] *Annals of the Four Masters, s.a.* 950 [=952] (ed. and trans. O'Donovan, II, 668-69); *Annals of Ulster, s.a.* 951 [=952].2 (ed. and trans. Mac Airt and Mac Niocaill, pp. 396-97).

[114] See p. 120, n. 74 above.

[115] 'The Scottish Chronicle', ed. and trans. Hudson, pp. 151, 159.

[116] *Ibid.*; Dumville, 'The Chronicle', p. 81.

[117] Anderson, *Kings*, pp. 267, 275, 283; Watson, *The History*, p. 49, n. 1.

[118] Crawford, *Scandinavian Scotland*, p. 63.

death of Hildulfr, there was a decade of strife within Alba as rivals contested the throne.[119] Some semblance of stability was restored with the accession of Cinaed son of Mael Colaim in 971.[120] As it became clear that the dynasty of Ívarr could not reassert its authority in Northumbria, Cinaed may have cultivated better relations with England. He attended the royal meeting at Chester in 973 summoned by King Edgar, and he may have attended the royal court on other occasions.[121]

Links between Alba and the dynasty of Ívarr took a lower profile from the late tenth century. The dynasty of Ívarr may have cared less about access to routes across North Britain to Northumbria but rather more about dominating coastal areas around the Irish Sea. Similarly, kings of Alba may have been more concerned about the dangers posed by other leaders in North Britain and even within their own court. 'The Annals of Ulster' report that Cinaed was killed through treachery in 995.[122] Political strife within Alba continued after 995 with a sequence of short reigns and political killings until Mael Colaim II came to power in 1005: he ruled successfully until 1034.

The closing years of the tenth century witnessed the renewal of viking raids against England. This may have had indirect consequences for Alba as warships from Norway and Denmark travelled around the British seaways. These raids continued and intensified until the conquest of England by Sveinn Forkbeard in 1013. Mael Colaim II initially opposed the rule of Knútr. He attacked northern England and fought victoriously at Carham.[123] At the same time, Mael Colaim appears to have lost his grip over Moray; so his ambitions may have been channelled into strengthening his authority in Lothian and Strathclyde by way of compensation.[124] He also cultivated a wider range of external links than his predecessors, and increased Alba's political significance through his involvement with the broader power-

---

[119] *Annals of Ulster*, s.a. 964 [=965].4 (ed. and trans. Mac Airt and Mac Niocaill, pp. 404-05); 'The Scottish Chronicle', ed. and trans. Hudson, pp. 159-60.

[120] *Annals of Ulster*, s.a. 976 [=977].4 (ed. and trans. Mac Airt and Mac Niocaill, pp. 412-13); Hudson, *Kings*, p. 215.

[121] *ASC.D*, p. 46; Sawyer, *Anglo-Saxon Charters*, no. 783; Dumville, 'A Pictish or Gaelic Ecclesiastic', pp. 2-4. See p. 124 above.

[122] *Annals of Ulster*, s.a. 994 [=995].1 (ed. and trans. Mac Airt and Mac Niocaill, pp. 424-25).

[123] See below, p. 168.

[124] Duncan, *Scotland*, p. 100.

struggles which were taking place across north-west Europe. For this reason Mael Coluim caught the attention of eleventh-century Continental chroniclers and historians including Dudo of Saint-Quentin, Rudolf Glaber and Adam of Bremen.[125]

There is no evidence that Mael Colaim II fought in the battle of Clontarf. The mormaer of Mar, who fought on Brian's side, may have been pursuing a private grievance against the Orcadian vikings, rather than acting under Mael Colaim's direction.[126] According to 'The Prophecy of Berchán' (an unreliable twelfth-century source), Mael Colaim's mother came from Leinster, and the thirteenth-century *Orkneyinga saga* asserts that Sigurðr of Orkney had married Mael Colaim's daughter. If either of these statements were true, one would expect Mael Colaim to favour the side of Sigtryggr of Dublin.[127] However Mael Colaim may not have been bound by ties of kinship and he had good reason to be wary of the ambitions of Orcadian earls and kings of Dublin in North Britain.[128] Mael Coluim may have opted to await the outcome of events with minimal risk.

This survey of the involvements of the dynasty of Ívarr in Alba has focused on the written sources. However, archaeology and place-names also shed light on relations between vikings in Ireland and the people of Alba. Silver was a commodity much prized by vikings. The wealth of those who travelled east to west via the Forth-Clyde line seems to be witnessed in hoards found along the coastal route south of the Firth of Forth at

---

[125] Dudo of Saint-Quentin, *De Moribus*, §103 (ed. Lair, p. 265; *Dudo*, trans. Christiansen, p. 140); Radulphus Glaber, *Historiarum Libri*, II.3 (ed. and trans. France, pp. 54-57); Adam of Bremen, *Gesta Hammaburgensis Ecclesiae*, II.34 (ed. Schmeidler, p. 95; trans. Tschan, p. 78); Hudson, 'Cnut'.

[126] *Annals of Clonmacnoise*, *s.a.* 1007 [=1014] (ed. Murphy, pp. 166-67); *Annals of the Four Masters*, *s.a.* 1013 [=1014] (ed. and trans. O'Donovan, I, 774-75); *Annals of Inisfallen*, *s.a.* [1014] (ed. and trans. Mac Airt, pp. 184-85); *Annals of Ulster*, *s.a.* 1014.2 (ed. and trans. Mac Airt and Mac Niocaill, pp. 446-49); *Chronicum Scotorum*, *s.a.* [1012] [=1014] (ed. and trans. Hennessy, pp. 250-55). For a late account of his ancestry see *Leabhar Mór*, ed. and trans. Ó Muraile, III, 50-51 (§ 775.2).

[127] *Prophecy of Berchán*, §183 (ed. and trans. Hudson, pp. 52, 90); *Orkneyinga saga*, §12 (ed. Guðmundsson, p. 82; trans. Pálsson and Edwards, p. 38). It is noteworthy that a son of Mael Sechlainn, overking of Mide, bore the epithet 'Albanach': *Annals of Inisfallen*, *s.a.* [1013] (ed. and trans. Mac Airt, pp. 182-83).

[128] The dynasty of Ívarr may have established a foothold in Galloway at this date: Marianus Scottus, *Chronicon*, *s.a.* 1065 (ed. Waitz, p. 559); Hill, 'Whithorn', pp. 34-35, 39; Hudson, 'Cnut'.

Cockburnspath (Berwickshire) deposited about 940, and at Gordon (Berwickshire), deposited in the late ninth or early tenth century. Fine Scandinavian-style antler-combs have also been discovered along this route, at North Berwick and Dunbar, which have been assigned a ninth- or tenth-century date.[129]

On either side of the Forth-Clyde route there are late tenth-century hogback-memorials – at Inchcolm and Govan.[130] These recumbent sculptures are so named from their form, which is long and narrow with steep sides and an arched back. James Lang argued that hogbacks are viking 'colonial monuments' which evolved in Northern England.[131] Their location suggests the continued significance of the Forth-Clyde route after the fall of York in 954. The passage of trade across North Britain was one of the motives for the alliance which developed between the descendants of Ívarr and kings of Alba in the tenth century.

Nevertheless, evidence for viking settlement along the Forth-Clyde route before 1014 is ambiguous. Two possible non-Christian graves have been found.[132] Hogback-monuments are relatively common in the central lowlands.[133] However, many of these could have been carved as late as the twelfth century. Their general distribution cannot therefore be used as a guide to viking settlement before 1014.[134] Scandinavian place-name elements such as -bý appear in southern Scotland, but, like the hogbacks, these range in date as late as the twelfth century.[135] Thus, while there is strong evidence for Scandinavian influence on settlements in the central lowlands, it is uncertain when migration took place. It seems likely that some settlers came to the region in consequence of the trade-links which developed between Dublin and York. The bulk of Anglo-Scandinavian

---

[129] Graham-Campbell and Batey, *Vikings in Scotland*, p. 105.

[130] Crawford, *Scandinavian Scotland*, p. 172; Forte *et al.*, *Viking Empires*, p. 110.

[131] Lang, 'The Hogback'.

[132] Fellows-Jensen, 'Scandinavians in Southern Scotland?', p. 53.

[133] Crawford, 'The "Norse Background"', p. 111. The stones at Inchcolm Island, St Vigeans and Meigle have been dated to the mid- to late tenth century.

[134] Graham-Campbell and Batey, *Vikings in Scotland*, pp. 100-01.

[135] Fellows-Jensen, 'Scandinavians in Southern Scotland?', pp. 46, 54, for an additional twenty-eight place-names in southern Scotland which have a Scandinavian personal name combined with the English generic *-tūn*. One of the names cited, *Maccus*, could have been associated with vikings from the Gaelic world.

immigrants may have arrived subsequently.[136] This later evidence may have skewed historians' impressions of the significance of the Forth-Clyde route for the dynasty of Ívarr. It was no doubt significant, but perhaps not as essential as Smyth and others have made out.

Viking raiders, traders and the dynasty of Ívarr all played a part in the political affairs of Alba before 1014. After a long period of antagonism the kings of Alba made common cause with the vikings of Dublin against the English from the 930s.[137] Nevertheless, after the collapse of viking Northumbria this alliance declined. English kings sought to inhibit any renewal of this friendship between kings of Alba and vikings. Oaths of allegiance were sought from kings of Alba in 945, 946 and 973. In the meantime the interests of the dynasty of Ívarr became more focused on the Irish Sea and their impact was more keenly felt in the westerly regions of North Britain.

Strathclyde

The significance of Strathclyde to vikings travelling between York and Dublin in the later ninth and tenth centuries might be deduced from its geographical position alone: the Clyde Valley was part of a route across Britain.[138] The southern reaches of Strathclyde incorporated parts of the Roman road-network which crossed from the west coast of Britain to the

---

[136] Smyth, *Scandinavian York*, II, 278-82; Crawford, 'The "Norse Background"', pp. 110-12. South-eastern Scotland has less evidence for viking settlement than the central lowlands. No non-Christian graves have been identified here. Graham-Campbell and Batey (*Vikings in Scotland*, pp. 103-04) have noted that there is confusion as to whether two oval brooches linked with Errol (Perthshire) and another brooch possibly of Baltic origin, linked with the Bridge of Earn (Perthshire), were discovered locally or brought to the region by collectors. They have also questioned Simon Taylor's theory that a small cluster of *-bý* place-names in Fife may be dated to the tenth century. They may be linked to the better-attested influx of settlers from eastern England in the twelfth century (*ibid.*, pp. 102-03). The six Gaelic *-gall* names in Fife, discussed by Taylor, may also be questioned as evidence for viking settlement. The earliest attestation of this name-element in Fife is about 1290. In Ireland, the name *gall* (literally 'foreigner') changed in meaning from the end of the twelfth century to describe French-speakers and, by extension, the English. Thus *-gall* names in Fife could therefore postdate the period under discussion. Taylor, 'The Scandinavians', pp. 142-43, 148-49, 158-59.

[137] Smyth, *Scandinavian York*, I, 35-36, 94-96.

[138] Smyth, *Scandinavian York*, II, 278-82.

east.[139] Even after the fall of viking Northumbria, Strathclyde retained its importance for the dynasty of Ívarr, for its coasts adjoined the Irish Sea.

Our written sources for the history of Strathclyde before 1014 are limited, but these confirm that the kingdom played a role in Dublin-York relations. Onomastic and archaeological evidence also points to the large-scale influence of Gaelic-Scandinavian peoples on this Brittonic kingdom within the period under discussion. A number of these settlers may have come from Ireland, and the pattern of migration around the Irish Sea during the tenth century may have been influenced by the political activities of the dynasty of Ívarr.

The extent of Strathclyde during the Viking Age is a matter of debate. The kingdom of Dumbarton suffered a political low-point in the mid-eighth century, when wars are reported with Picts and Northumbrians.[140] By the 750s Northumbrian power had intruded into the kingdom's territory as far north as Kyle.[141] This left kings of Dumbarton in control of the Clyde Valley and surrounding districts.[142] Our next view is after vikings sacked its capital in 870. By the second quarter of the tenth century the kingdom of Strathclyde ran southwards to include north Cumbria or 'Cumberland'.[143] The south-eastern limits of Strathclyde's expansion are unclear. According to the tenth-century Life of Cathroe, the border of Strathclyde and viking Northumbria was located at Leeds (*usque Loidam ciuitatem*).[144] Alfred Smyth has contested this, arguing that Carlisle, not

[139] Collingwood, 'King Eirík', p. 322; Smyth, *Scandinavian York*, II, 174.

[140] *Annals of Ulster*, s.a. 749 [=750].4 (ed. and trans. Mac Airt and Mac Niocaill, pp. 204-05); *Historia Regum Anglorum*, Part I, s.a. 756 (*Symeonis Monachi Opera*, ed. Arnold, II, 40; *The Church Historians*, trans. Stevenson, IV, pt. 2, p. 34).

[141] *Continuatio Bedae*, s.a. 750 (*Bede's Ecclesiastical History*, ed. and trans. Colgrave and Mynors, pp. 574-75).

[142] Duncan, *Scotland*, pp. 65-66; Smyth, *Warlords*, p. 28.

[143] Kirby, 'Strathclyde', pp. 86-88; Jackson, 'Angles', p. 72; Stenton, *Anglo-Saxon England*, p. 332; 'The Scottish Chronicle', ed. and trans. Hudson, pp. 151, and 161, n. 74. I do not accept the argument that Cumbria and Strathclyde were separate entities, see Wilson, 'On the Use'. For the boundaries of Galloway, see below, p. 171.

[144] *Vita Sancti Cathroe*, §17 (*Acta*, ed. Colgan, p. 497; *Early Sources*, trans. Anderson, I, 441); Dumville, 'St Cathróe', p. 177, n. 35. Kapelle argued that Strathclyde included modern Lancashire: *The Noman Conquest*, p. 10.

Leeds, was the border, and that the author of the text confused the two places.[145]

Taking an interdisciplinary approach Kenneth Jackson argued that the border of Strathclyde ran along the Eden Valley and then south to Stainmore.[146] His theory was in part based on the distribution of Cumbric names and Scandinavian -*bý* names which focus in north Cumberland. However, this evidence has recently been criticised. Many -*bý* names could post-date the tenth century, and the Cumbric names may pre-date the period in question.[147] Furthermore the Cumbric names do not fit tidily within the boundaries posited by Jackson. The idea that Strathclyde once stretched south to Stainmore has a long textual history. Nevertheless, Dauvit Broun has made that case that this was a claim invented after the kingdom of Strathclyde ceased to exist, resulting from an amendment made by a redactor of a Scottish king-list.[148] While the southern limits of Strathclyde are ambiguous, one can argue that its kings made territorial gains between the later eighth and the early tenth century.[149] As this expansion took place at the expense of Northumbrian power, these changes probably occurred after English rule collapsed in 866/67, when vikings seized control of York.[150]

---

[145] Smyth, *Scandinavian York*, II, 181; cf. Woolf, 'Erik Bloodaxe', p. 193, n. 18. This has been rejected by Dumville, 'St Cathróe', p. 177, n. 35.

[146] Jackson ('Angles', pp. 72-79, 82-83) suggested that Cumbric speech (a Brittonic dialect) was re-introduced into parts of Cumberland after English occupation, representing conquests made by the kings of Strathclyde in the ninth and tenth centuries. This he argued, is indicated by Cumbric prefixes to English names and by the alteration of English place-names according to the stress-patterns of Cumbric speech, cf. Ekwall, *Scandinavians*, p. 117.

[147] Phythian-Adams (*Land*, pp. 77-87) and John Todd ('British [Cumbric] Place-Names') have argued that there was no such linguistic re-conquest (see previous note) but that Brittonic speech persisted in this area before and after the period under discussion. This view has not won universal acceptance: Price, *Languages*, pp. 121, 123. For debates concerning the date of -*bý* names, see Watts, 'North-Western Place-Names'; Fellows-Jensen, 'Place-names and Settlements'; Roberts, 'Late -*bý* Names'.

[148] Broun, 'The Welsh Identity', pp. 173-80.

[149] Jackson ('Angles', pp. 72-78, 83) noted a cultural division between northern and southern Cumbria, with hybrid Gaelic-Norse names predominating in the south, and -*bý* names having greater density in the north. Richard Bailey ('Aspects', p. 57) has shown that sculpturally these two regions were also distinct during the Viking Age, and this may have some bearing on where the south-western boundaries of Strathclyde were located.

[150] Collingwood, 'The Giant's Thumb', p. 58; Jackson, 'Angles', pp. 71-72; Wilson, 'On the Use', pp. 73-74; Smyth, *Warlords*, p. 227; Brooke, *Wild Men*, p. 70; Macquarrie, 'The

Until fairly recently, the prevailing idea was that Strathclyde flourished under the domination of, or in alliance with, its northern neighbour Alba.[151] However, this theory has lately come under attack.[152] Alongside this new trend in the scholarship there has been a growing interest in Scandinavian cultural links with Strathclyde (most noticeably in studies of the stone-sculpture at Govan).[153] This raises the question of the extent of viking influence on Strathclyde's development. From the mid-ninth century there is evidence of hostility between Strathclyde and Pictland. Britons of Strathclyde burned Dunblane, an ecclesiastical centre in southern Pictland, during the reign of Cinaed mac Ailpín (842-58).[154] This could indicate that kings of Strathclyde were seeking to extend their influence northwards and eastwards, perhaps taking advantage of the chaos wrought by contemporaneous viking attacks on Pictland.[155] If the attack on Dunblane indicates the growing political and military strength of Strathclyde, that seems to have been severely curtailed in 870. In this year, Óláfr and Ívarr destroyed Dumbarton, capital of Strathclyde, after a four-month siege.[156] The transfer of two hundred ships of slaves, including Britons from Strathclyde, is reported in 'The Annals of Ulster' for the following year when Óláfr and Ívarr travelled back to Ireland.[157]

From this time *Ail Cluaithe* (the Gaelic name for Dumbarton) disappears from historical record. This could imply, as P.A. Wilson suggested, that the political centre of the kingdom moved to another site.[158] Nevertheless, the region does not seem to have been permanently subjected.

Kings', p. 19; Dumville, *The Churches*, pp. 29-34. Place-name evidence has been used to trace these conquests.

[151] Collingwood, 'The Giant's Thumb', p. 58; Duncan, 'The Kingdom', p. 137; Smyth, *Warlords*, pp. 216-17, 222-28.

[152] Hudson, '*Elech*'; Sellar, 'Warlords', pp. 34-35; Macquarrie, 'The Kings', p. 15; Driscoll, 'Church Archaeology', p. 111; Broun, 'The Welsh Identity', pp. 125-30.

[153] *Govan*, ed. Ritchie; Driscoll, 'Church Archaeology'.

[154] 'The Scottish Chronicle', ed. Hudson, pp. 148, 153.

[155] See above, pp. 138-39.

[156] *Annals of Ulster*, s.a. 869 [=870].6 (ed. and trans. Mac Airt and Mac Niocaill, pp. 326-27).

[157] *Annals of Ulster*, s.a. 870 [=871].2 (ed. and trans. Mac Airt and Mac Niocaill, pp. 326-27).

[158] Wilson, 'On the Use of the Terms', p. 74. After 870 the geographical name 'Strathclyde' emerges for this kingdom.

The annal for 875/76 in 'The Anglo-Saxon Chronicle' reports that Hálfdan, brother of Ívarr, led further attacks against Strathclyde.[159]

The weakening of Strathclyde through viking attacks may have prompted Causantín son of Cinaed, king of Picts (862-77), to intervene. According to 'The Annals of Ulster' he instigated the assassination of Arthal, king of Strathclyde, in 872.[160] The families of Arthal and Causantín were linked by marriage and in consequence of further royal intrigue Causantín's brother, Aed, was killed by his associates in 878 and Eochaid son of Rhun (grandson of Arthal and of Cinaed mac Ailpín) succeeded to the Pictish throne.[161] It has been suggested that Eochaid also ruled Strathclyde at this time, but this is not certain. Further political turmoil ensued, and Eochaid was expelled from Pictland in 889.[162] The reign of Eochaid as a Strathclyde dynast in Alba shows an important link between these two polities in the late ninth century. W.G. Collingwood suggested that Strathclyde's boundaries were pushed south in campaigns during the reign of Eochaid which united the resources of both kingdoms under Eochaid's leadership.[163] This is one of several possibilities allowed by the rather meagre evidence.

The next event to be reported in Strathclyde's history is the notice in 'The Chronicle of the Kings of Alba' of the death of a King Dyfnwal.[164] No precise date is given, but the context suggests that it occurred in 908×915. A long-standing misinterpretation of this chronicle-entry has been noted by Benjamin Hudson.[165] Prior to his article, published in 1988, it was considered that the statement 'Doneualdus rex Britanniorum et Donenaldus filius Ede elig₇', indicated that Dyfnwal was succeeded by Domnall son of Aed, an otherwise unidentified brother of Causantín son of

---

[159] *ASC.A*, ed. Bately, p. 49; *ASC.B*, ed. Taylor, p. 36; *ASC.C*, ed. O'Keeffe, p. 61; *ASC.D*, ed. Cubbin, p. 26; E in *Two of the Saxon Chronicles*, ed. Plummer, I, 75. It is worth keeping in mind that in annals 865-92 the chronicle-year begins and ends in September.

[160] *Annals of Ulster, s.a.* 871 [=872].5 (ed. and trans. Mac Airt and Mac Niocaill, pp. 328-29); Ó Corráin, 'The Vikings in Scotland', p. 331.

[161] 'The Scottish Chronicle', ed. and trans. Hudson, pp. 149, 154.

[162] 'The Scottish Chronicle', ed. and trans. Hudson, pp. 149, 155; Duncan, *Scotland*, p. 116, note.

[163] Collingwood, 'The Giant's Thumb', p. 58.

[164] 'The Scottish Chronicle', ed. and trans. Hudson, pp. 150, 157.

[165] Hudson, '*Elech*'.

Aed.[166] This was because 'elig₇' was interpreted as an abbreviated form of *eligitur* ('is chosen'). This has long fuelled speculation that Strathclyde was under the control of Alba (the name adopted about 900 for Pictland). However, Hudson has pointed out that '₇' is not an abbreviation for *-itur*, and it could be interpreted as a downward stroke on the 'g' similar to those found elsewhere in the manuscript of 'The Chronicle of the Kings of Alba'.[167] *Elig* could be a genitive form of Ailech (Inishowen Peninsula, Co. Tyrone). Hudson has pointed out that the entry is more likely to refer to Domnall mac Aeda, king of Ailech, who died in 915. He was connected with the royal dynasty of Alba as his father had married Mael Muire, daughter of Cinaed mac Ailpín.[168] Hudson's argument convincingly undermined the received view that Strathclyde was held under the domination of Alba.

Uncertainty surrounds the mention of Strathclyde in 'The Fragmentary Annals of Ireland' in 918. This reports that, after the battle of Corbridge, Rögnvaldr grandson of Ívarr attacked Strathclyde but failed to take it under his control.[169] This follows details of an alliance pioneered by Æthelflæd, leader of the Mercians, between the people of Mercia, Alba and Strathclyde in the face of viking aggression. Sadly, 'The Fragmentary Annals of Ireland' are an untrustworthy guide because of their late date of compilation and imaginative admixture of saga-material.[170] Nevertheless, the record does raise the question whether viking kings of York sought to conquer lands which the rulers of Strathclyde had taken from the former English kingdom of Northumbria.

The Strathclyders not only had to deal with vikings and rulers of Alba, but English kings also sought to bring this area within their sphere of influence. This level of competition highlights the strategic importance of Strathclyde at this time. In 920, Edward the Elder, 'king of the Anglo-Saxons', presided over a meeting of Northern rulers which included the king of Strathclyde. A larger meeting was held shortly after Æthelstan seized control of Northumbria in 927. The leaders who gave oaths to Æthelstan at

---

[166] Macquarrie, 'The Kings', p. 14.

[167] Hudson, '*Elech*', p. 146.

[168] *Annals of Ulster*, s.a. 912 [=913].1 (ed. and trans. Mac Airt and Mac Niocaill, pp. 360-61); 'The Ban-Shenchus', ed. Dobbs, p. 186; Hudson, '*Elech*', p. 146.

[169] *Fragmentary Annals*, §459 (ed. and trans. Radner, pp. 180-83).

[170] *Fragmentary Annals*, ed. and trans. Radner, pp. xxvi, xxxiv.

that event are named by version D of 'The Anglo-Saxon Chronicle' as Hywel of Wales, Causantín of Alba, Ealdred of Bamburgh and Owain of Gwent.[171] In a later account of the event, written by William of Malmesbury in 1125, Owain is named as king of Strathclyde.[172] There was no contemporary king of Gwent by this name, but there was an Owain of Strathclyde; so William's identification may be seriously considered.[173] The gathering took place at Eamont (Cumberland) probably near the southern border of Strathclyde.[174] The implication of this meeting is that Æthelstan feared that neighbouring kings (particularly the king of Strathclyde) might make common cause with vikings. Further evidence of English involvement in the politics of Strathclyde is suggested by the presence of *Eugenius subregulus* at the court of Æthelstan in 931 and 935.[175] He witnessed royal charters along with other Welsh rulers, and he can be identified with the contemporary Owain, king of Strathclyde.

The role of the people of Strathclyde in the *Brunanburh* campaign in 937 is uncertain. They are not mentioned in contemporary Irish accounts or 'The Anglo-Saxon Chronicle'. However, Part I, section six, of *Historia Regum Anglorum* reports the flight of *rex Cumbrorum* with other defeated troops from the battle.[176] This short chronicle seems partly dependent on a tenth-century source, although it did not reach its final form until the late eleventh or twelfth century.[177] If the men of Strathclyde were present at

---

[171] *ASC.D*, *s.a.* 926, ed. Cubbin, p. 41.

[172] William of Malmesbury, *Gesta Regum Anglorum*, II.134 (ed. and trans. Mynors *et al.*, I, 214-15).

[173] Stenton, *Anglo-Saxon England*, p. 332.

[174] See above, p. 100.

[175] Sawyer, *Anglo-Saxon Charters*, nos 413, 434, 435, 436; Loyn, 'Wales and England', p. 294.

[176] The Britons are mentioned in what appears to be an account of the battle of *Brunanburh* in 'The Annals of the Four Masters'. In this chronicle the event can be dated by context to the year 940. The use of the name *Anlaf* for Óláfr in this record suggests that it was based on an English source. Both the chronological displacement and the derivative nature of this entry suggest that it was incorporated late into this seventeenth-century compilation: *Annals of the Four Masters*, *s.a.* 938 [=939/40] (ed. and trans. O'Donovan, II, 640-41); Etchingham, 'North Wales', p. 165.

[177] *Historia Regum Anglorum*, Part I, *s.a.* 937 (*Symeonis Monachi Opera*, ed. Arnold, II, 93; *The Church Historians*, trans. Stevenson, IV, pt. 2, p. 68); Downham, 'The Chronology', p. 36.

Brunanburh, it seems that their significance was overshadowed by other contingents in the battle.

Strathclyde's involvement in an anti-English alliance is more clearly witnessed in the prophetic poem *Armes Prydein Vawr*. This calls on the various Brittonic peoples to ally with the vikings of Dublin against the English. Strathclyde is given a prominent place as a polity which had already pledged its support in this endeavour.[178] This text seems to have been written in South Wales in the tenth century, shortly after the battle of *Brunanburh*.[179]

Æthelstan's successors strove to break the alliance between Strathclyde and the dynasty of Ívarr. In 944 his brother, Edmund I (939-46), ousted the viking leaders from York. In the following year he ravaged Strathclyde and granted it to Mael Coluim I, king of Alba.[180] This also ensured that Strathclyde would be too weak to support a viking campaign against Northumbria. This demonstration of English power sought to undermine Scandinavian influence in North Britain.[181] It was at this time (941×946) that St Cathroe, a noble or royal pilgrim from Alba, travelled across Britain to reach the Continent.[182] The journey is significant as it could be seen as a diplomatic mission as well as an act of piety. Cathroe passed from the court of Causantín of Alba to that of his kinsman Dyfnwal, king of Strathclyde. He then visited the court of Eiríkr of Northumbria. The Life of Cathroe states that Eiríkr's wife was also a relative of the saint. Cathroe's visits thus represent the network of alliances which existed at the time of *Brunanburh* or its aftermath, namely Alba, Strathclyde and vikings of Northumbria (I argue elsewhere that Eiríkr was a member of the dynasty of Ívarr).[183] The Life suggests that Cathroe did not originally intend to visit the court of Edmund, king of England, on his way south, but that he was called to meet

---

[178] *Armes Prydein*, ed. and trans. Williams and Bromwich, pp. xx, xxv-xxvi.

[179] *Ibid.*, pp. 2-3, lines 11, 15; Dumville, 'Brittany', p. 148.

[180] *ASC.A*, ed. Bately, p. 74; *ASC.B*, ed. Taylor, p. 53; *ASC.C*, ed. O'Keeffe, p. 80; *ASC.D*, ed. Cubbin, p. 44; E in *Two of the Saxon Chronicles*, ed. Plummer, I, 111; *Flores Historiarum*, *s.a.* 945 (*Rogeri de Wendover Chronica*, ed. Coxe, I, 398; *Roger*, trans. Giles, I, 252-53). The Welsh King Leolin (Llywelyn) of Dyfed, who according to Roger accompanied Edmund in the attack, may be an invention.

[181] Fulton, 'Tenth Century Wales', p. 13; Woolf, 'Amlaíb', p. 38.

[182] *Vita Sancti Cathroe* (*Acta*, ed. Colgan, pp. 494-507); partial translation by Anderson, *Early Sources*, I, 431-43.

[183] Downham, 'Eric'; Woolf, 'Amlaíb', p. 39.

him.[184] Edmund was probably aware of Cathroe's political connections. The alliance between Strathclyde and the vikings of York seems to have terminated by 952, as 'The Annals of Ulster' report that the men of Strathclyde, Alba and England lost a battle against vikings.[185] This took place in the year when Eiríkr began his second, short-lived, reign at York. West Saxon royal authority was re-imposed in Northumbria in 954.[186]

One might expect that, after the collapse of viking rule at York in 954, Strathclyde would lose some of its strategic and political significance. However, in 971 Britons were responsible for the death of Culén, king of Alba, and of his brother Eochaid, following their defeat in battle.[187] Culén's successor Cinaed raided Strathclyde in retaliation but was defeated in battle. 'The Chronicle of the Kings of Alba' reports that Cinaed then raided England to Stainmore 'et ad Cluaim et ad stangna Deranni'. This problematic passage has been translated by Hudson as 'as far as the Clough, and as far as the pools of Derwent'.[188] This raid may represent an attempt by Cinaed to regain territory granted to Mael Colaim I by the English king Edmund in 945.

English intervention in the affairs of Strathclyde in the late tenth century may have aimed at preventing further associations with vikings in the Irish Sea. In 973, Mael Colaim, king of Strathclyde, and possibly his father Dyfnwal appear to have been among those who swore obedience to King Edgar at Chester.[189] Maccus Haraldsson, a descendant of Ívarr, also attended this event.[190] The meeting may have been a response to viking activity in the Irish Sea in the 960s and 970s.[191]

---

[184] *Vita Sancti Cathroe*, §§17-18 (*Acta*, ed. Colgan, p. 497; *Early Sources*, trans. Anderson, I, 441-42).

[185] *Annals of Ulster*, s.a. 951 [=952].2 (ed. and trans. Mac Airt and Mac Niocaill, pp. 396-97).

[186] *ASC.D*, ed. Cubbin, p. 45; E in *Two of the Saxon Chronicles*, ed. Plummer, I, 113.

[187] *Annals of Ulster*, s.a. 970 [=971].1 (ed. and trans. Mac Airt and Mac Niocaill, pp. 408-09); *Chronicum Scotorum*, s.a. [969] [=971] (ed. and trans. Hennessy, pp. 218-19); 'The Scottish Chronicle', ed. and trans. Hudson, pp. 151, 160. According to *Chronicum Scottorum*, Culén died in a house which was set alight by his enemies.

[188] 'The Scottish Chronicle', ed. and trans. Hudson, pp. 151, 161.

[189] Thornton, 'Edgar', pp. 51-55.

[190] *Ibid.*, pp. 58-61.

[191] See above, pp. 48-49, and below pp. 192-94.

A further link with viking affairs is suggested by the fact that in 1000, Æthelred, king of England, ravaged Strathclyde and Man.[192] The record indicates some association between the kingdom of the Isles and Strathclyde. Æthelred may have sought to exert greater control over this region in order to secure the border between England and Alba. Both countries competed for control of Strathclyde in the tenth and eleventh centuries. Ultimately its territory was divided between the two rivals.[193] The last known king of Strathclyde, Owain, died in the early eleventh century.[194] Despite the termination of Strathclyde as an independent polity at some point after this date and before 1092, awareness of the region's distinct political origins and identity persisted until the late twelfth century.[195]

It has been tempting for historians to see the ninth- and tenth-century history of Strathclyde as part of an inevitable journey towards 'Scottish' domination over the region. Nevertheless, archaeological and place-name evidence points to the influence of vikings on the kingdom's politics and culture. Initially settlement focused on the Cumbrian coastal plain, Dumfrieshire and the Eden Valley.[196] The subsequent penetration of Norse names to more marginal areas has been noted by Nick Higham.[197] Place-names indicate that viking groups came into the area at various times from the Hebrides, Ireland and England.[198]

There are also significant collections of carved stones dating from the tenth century which show Scandinavian influence: the most impressive of these are at Govan and Penrith. At Govan, four monumental crosses and

---

[192] *ASC.C*, ed. O'Keeffe, p. 88; *ASC.D*, ed. Cubbin, p. 50; E in *Two of the Saxon Chronicles*, ed. Plummer, I, 133.

[193] Macquarrie, 'The Kings', pp. 16-17.

[194] *Annales Cambriae, s.a.* [1015] (ed. Williams, p. 22); Duncan, 'The Battle of Carham'. *Annales Cambriae* challenge the date of 1018 assigned to the battle of Carham because of a later statement that Owain fought there. Nevertheless Broun has argued that there may have been two Owains: 'The Welsh Identity', p. 128, n. 66.

[195] Driscoll, 'Church Archaeology', pp. 107, 111-12.

[196] Nicolaisen, *Scottish Place-Names*, pp. 98-108; Higham, 'The Scandinavians', pp. 43-48.

[197] Ekwall, *Scandinavians*, pp. 95, 103; Jackson, 'Angles', p. 72; Graham-Campbell, 'The Irish Sea', p. 74; Graham-Campbell, 'The Early Viking Age', pp. 112, 115; Phythian-Adams, *Land*, p. 123; Higham, 'The Scandinavians', p. 49.

[198] Smyth, *Scandinavian York*, I, 80-88; Fellows-Jensen, 'Scandinavian Settlement in Cumbria', pp. 72-75; Fellows-Jensen, 'Scandinavian Settlement in the Isle of Man', p. 46; See above pp. 84-85.

twenty-six grave-markers have survived, including five hogback-memorials and a high-status sarcophagus.[199] Penrith has a rather smaller collection comprising four hogbacks, two crosses, and the nearby 'Giant's Thumb'.[200] Collingwood suggested that Penrith's significance can be explained by its location on a major route into Strathclyde, and Phythian-Adams has argued that the site received royal patronage.[201] Govan's greater significance suggests that it was a major political centre. Driscoll has asserted that it was the capital of Strathclyde after the demise of Dumbarton.[202] He has also noted that a Scandinavian thing-mound stood at Govan in the tenth century, which has led him to conclude that 'the post ninth century kingdom sought to redefine itself in Norse terms'.[203]

As the level of Scandinavian influence at Govan, and hence in Strathclyde, is re-evaluated, some caution may be necessary. Doomster Hill, which Driscoll has identified as a thing-mound, may not be a Scandinavian feature. Certainly, eighteenth- and nineteenth-century written records and maps demonstrate the existence of a flat-topped steep-sided hill (this has since been destroyed).[204] The hill's origins could however relate to Insular legal practice as much as to Scandinavian influence, as Driscoll has demonstrated.[205] An example of such use is provided in 'The Chronicle of the Kings of Alba' for the year 906: 'Constantinus rex et Cellachus episcopus leges disciplinasque fidei ... in Colle Credulitatis prope regali ciuitati Scoan deuouerunt custodire' ('King Causantín and Bishop Cellach vowed to protect the laws and disciplines of the faith, on the Hill of Belief near the royal *ciuitas* of Scone').[206] Doomster Hill may have pre-dated Scandinavian involvement in Strathclyde. Thomas Clancy has argued that the name Govan is Brittonic *guo-bann*, meaning 'little hill', coined in reference to this feature.[207] He has further suggested that Govan may be the

[199] *Govan*, ed. Ritchie.
[200] Bailey, *Viking Age Sculpture*, p. 264.
[201] Collingwood, 'The Giant's Thumb', p. 60; Phythian-Adams, *Land*, pp. 120-21.
[202] Driscoll, 'Church Archaeology', p. 105.
[203] *Ibid.*, p. 112.
[204] Davidson-Kelly, 'The Govan Collection', pp. 1-3.
[205] Driscoll, 'Church Archaeology', p. 102.
[206] 'The Scottish Chronicle', ed. and trans. Hudson, pp. 150 and 156, and p. 156, n. 35. The meaning of *ciuitas* has been discussed by Swift, 'Forts', pp. 112-14.
[207] Clancy, 'Govan', p. 8. Cf. Breeze, 'Simeon', p. 135; Forsyth and Koch, 'Evidence', pp. 29-30; Macquarrie, 'The Name Govan'.

Ouania named in *Historia Regum Anglorum*, Part I, under the year 756.[208] If this account preserves a contemporary record of the name, it could suggest that Doomster Hill was a pre-Viking-Age monument, albeit one which would also be acceptable within a Scandinavian cultural milieu.[209]

It seems to me that the archaeological evidence at Govan bears testimony to a hybrid culture, rather than merely a consciously Scandinavian one. The hogback-monuments bear the influence of Scandinavian, Pictish, English and Gaelic art.[210] This impression is reinforced by the written evidence which shows the contacts between Strathclyde and the surrounding polities. The kings of Strathclyde did not adopt Norse names, even though some tenth-century kings of Alba did.[211] Nevertheless, intermarriage between the royal lineage of Strathclyde and the families of viking leaders may have occurred. Driscoll has posited such a relationship with Man and the Isles in the tenth century on the basis of that kingdom's geographical proximity and the Scandinavian character of the finds at Govan.[212] Such an alliance could explain why the English king Æthelred chose to attack both Strathclyde and Man in 1000.

Much of the history of Strathclyde is shrouded in obscurity, although it can be seen to play an important part in Irish-Sea politics in the Viking Age. As with Alba, our initial records point to hostility between the rulers of Strathclyde and the dynasty of Ívarr. By the earlier tenth century the ambition of English kings may have brought these previously warring parties together. The fortunes of Strathclyde seem to have been linked with the dynasty of Ívarr. As viking power declined in the eleventh century, the kingdom fell victim to the expansion of its two powerful neighbours, Alba and England.

Galloway

The coasts of Galloway adjoin the North Channel of the Irish Sea. It was therefore of great geographical significance to the viking rulers of Man and

---

[208] *Historia Regum Anglorum*, Part I, *s.a.* 756 (ed. Arnold, *Symeonis Monachi Opera*, II, 40; trans. Stevenson, *The Church Historians*, IV, pt. 2, p. 34); Breeze, 'Simeon'; Clancy, 'Govan', p. 10.

[209] Forsyth and Koch, 'Evidence'. The suggestion that Doomster Hill may be a Norman motte should also be noted: Macquarrie, 'The Name Govan', p. 2.

[210] Davies, 'Ecclesiastical Centres', p. 99.

[211] Crawford, 'The "Norse Background"', p. 110.

[212] Driscoll, 'Kingdom'.

the Isles, whose power was premised on regular contact along this route.[213] Written sources for the political history of Galloway are lacking from the 830s until the earlier eleventh century.[214] For the year 1034, 'The Annals of Ulster' record the death of Suibne mac Cinaeda, *rí Gallgaidhel* ('king of Galloway').[215] This suggests that the area was ruled independently. A close connection with Man and the Isles is also witnessed during the eleventh century. Echmarcach son of Rögnvaldr is recorded as king of the Rhinns of Galloway at his death in 1064.[216] He was a member of the dynasty of Ívarr who ruled Dublin and the Isles intermittently until 1061.[217] Benjamin Hudson has identified Echmarcach as one of the three kings from North Britain who submitted to Knútr, king of England in 1031.[218] This suggests a long-lived Echmarcach's wider involvement in the politics of North Britain; he may have already had a foothold in the Rhinns and been a rival to Suibne mac Cinaeda.[219]

[213] Jackson suggested that Galloway had a greater proportion of Islesmen among its viking migrants and that Cumbria might have had more from Ireland: 'Angles', p. 72. Cf. Ekwall, *Scandinavians*, pp. 102-03; Smyth, *Scandinavian York*, I, 80-81; Fellows-Jensen, 'Scandinavian Settlement in Cumbria', pp. 72, 75; Dumville, *The Churches*, p. 32, n. 93; Bailey, *Viking Age Sculpture*, p. 228.

[214] Dumville, 'Textual Archaeology', pp. 49-51. Gaelic influence prior to the vikings' arrival may be suggested by *sliabh-* ('moor', 'mountain') names in the Rhinns peninsula, and *cill-* ('church') names which are common in Wigtownshire: Fellows-Jensen, 'Scandinavians in Dumfriesshire', p. 78. In an excellent article, Simon Taylor has demonstrated that *-sliabh* names are more widely distributed in Scotland than hitherto realised. This invalidates the long-held view that these names were coined before A.D. 700 during an early phase of Gaelic settlement in North Britain. Many examples could be later: Taylor, 'The Element'. Fellows-Jensen has also held *Baile-* ('settlement') names to be indicative of early medieval Gaelic settlement. These occur frequently west of the River Nith in Galloway and Dumfriesshire. However, these names seem to post-date the tenth century in Ireland: Doherty, 'The Vikings', pp. 315-17. Cf. Brooke, 'Gall-Gaidhil', p. 106. In the late seventh or early eighth century, the Northumbrians conquered the region around Whithorn: Bede, *Historia Ecclesiastica Gentis Anglorum*, V.23 (*Bede's Ecclesiastical History*, ed. and trans. Colgrave and Mynors, pp. 558-61).

[215] *Annals of Ulster*, s.a. 1034.10 (ed. and trans. Mac Airt and Mac Niocaill, pp. 472-73).

[216] Marianus Scottus, *Chronicon*, s.a. [1065] (ed. Waitz, p. 559); Byrne, 'Onomastica'.

[217] Duffy, 'Irishmen', pp. 96-99; Etchingham, 'North Wales', pp. 157-61.

[218] E in *Two of the Saxon Chronicles*, ed. Plummer, I, 157, 159; Hudson, 'Cnut and the Scottish Kings'.

[219] Etchingham, 'North Wales', pp. 160-61; Forte *et al.*, *Viking Empires*, p. 230.

The borders of Galloway are not clear for the period under discussion.[220] References in Irish texts might hint that Galloway included lands to the north and some of the Inner Hebrides.[221] Nevertheless there is uncertainty as to whether places said to be within the lands of the *Gall-goídil* refer to the general culture of an area rather or mark the boundaries of a specific polity. The name Galloway is derivative of the Gaelic term *Gall-goídel* ('Foreigner-Gael').[222] The form of the name can be best explained by the term *Gall-goídel* having first passed through the mouths of Brittonic-speakers (perhaps from within the region of Galloway or Strathclyde) who might render it *Gallwyddel*.[223] This was later anglicised to Galloway.[224] The label *Gall-goídel* indicates that the inhabitants of Galloway were at one point identified as being of mixed Gaelic and Scandinavian culture or ethnicity.

The early activities of vikings in Galloway may be witnessed by the archaeological evidence. The excavations at Whithorn, directed by Peter Hill, indicate that the church was destroyed by fire in the 840s.[225] Some ecclesiastical buildings were restored in the late ninth century, but these were demolished in the following century.[226] Within this context it is relevant to note the deposition of a mixed hoard at Talnotrie in Kirkudbrightshire around 875. Some of its content would appear to have passed through viking hands, including two fragments of Kufic coins and a

---

[220] Jackson, 'Angles', p. 72. Political boundaries do not always follow linguistic ones.

[221] *The Martyrology of Tallaght*, ed. Best and Lawlor, p. 62; Dumville, *The Churches*, p. 28. The date of this text is debated: Dumville, '*Félire*', pp. 21-22, 37-40.

[222] This theory was advanced by William Skene in the later nineteenth century: *Celtic Scotland*, I, 311-13. It was challenged by Daphne Brooke in 1991, who argued that the name was related to Latin *Caledonia*; 'Gall-Gaidhil', pp. 104-05, 110-11. Dispute concerns the location of *Coit Celidon* (Modern Welsh *Coed Celyddon*) and the theory that *Gall-goídel* is a misinterpretation of an earlier Cumbric name whose literal meaning had no bearing on Irish usage. Thomas Clancy, ('Review'), has argued that Brooke's argument is 'linguistically impossible'. It seems unnecessary to discard the conventional interpretation, which is evidenced by both Irish and Norse sources: *The Book of Leinster*, ed. Best *et al.*, VI, 1688; Dumville, *The Churches*, p. 29, n. 81; *Orkneyinga saga*, §23 (ed. Finnbogi Guðmundsson, p. 59; trans. Pálsson and Edwards, p. 61). Daphne Brooke herself pointed out that *Gall-goídel* can be linked etymologically and geographically to Galloway: 'Gall-Gaidhil', p. 104.

[223] Watson, *The History*, p. 174.

[224] Brooke, 'Gall-Gaidhil', pp. 102-03.

[225] Hill, 'Whithorn', p. 33.

[226] Hill, *Whithorn and St Ninian*, p. 48.

fragment of a Frankish denier.[227] There are also non-silver objects which make the hoard unusual.[228] Graham-Campbell has concluded that the hoard belonged to a Northumbrian or Galwegian metal-worker.[229] Nevertheless, it is possible that vikings were responsible for its deposition. The hoard's date corresponds with the North-British campaigns of Hálfdan, brother of Ívarr.[230]

The date of the Talnotrie hoard also corresponds with the supposed time of arrival of the relics of St Cuthbert in Whithorn. This assertion is found in the early twelfth-century *Historia Dunelmensis Ecclesiae*.[231] According to the *Historia*, the keepers of Cuthbert's body were directed by the vision of one Hunred.[232] The evidence has been used to suggest a date for the continuity or restoration of the church at Whithorn.[233] However, the story is late and untrustworthy.[234] It could have been invented at the cathedral at Durham to claim authority over Whithorn through its physical association with their patron saint. The archaeological evidence alone may provide more accurate guidance as to when the church at Whithorn fell into disuse.

A few archaeological discoveries in Galloway can be linked with vikings and witness some involvement in the region from the ninth century. These include possible viking burials at Kirkcudbright and Crossmichael (Kirkcudbrightshire).[235] Viking immigration into Galloway seems to have

---

[227] Graham-Campbell, *The Viking-Age Gold*, p. 4; Graham-Campbell and Batey, *Vikings in Scotland*, p. 109; Pirie, 'Finds', p. 69.

[228] Graham-Campbell, 'The Viking-Age Silver'.

[229] Graham-Campbell and Batey, *Vikings in Scotland*, p. 109; Graham-Campbell, *The Viking-Age Gold*, p. 4.

[230] *ASC.A*, ed. Bately, p. 50; *ASC.B*, ed. Taylor, p. 37; *ASC.C*, ed. O'Keeffe, p. 61; *ASC.D*, ed. Cubbin, p. 27; E in *Two of the Saxon Chronicles*, ed. Plummer, I, 75.

[231] This text was composed in 1104-1107×1115, with the title *Libellus de exordio atque procursu istius hoc est Dunelmensis ecclesie*. The two earliest surviving manuscripts of this work are more or less contemporary with its composition: *Libellus*, ed. and trans. Rollason, pp. xlii-xliv.

[232] *Libellus*, II.12 (ed. and trans. Rollason, pp. 118-19).

[233] Cowan, 'The Vikings', p. 65; Hill, *Whithorn and St Ninian*, pp. 21-22.

[234] *Ibid.*; Dumville, 'Textual Archaeology', pp. 45-48.

[235] Graham-Campbell and Batey, *Vikings in Scotland*, pp. 108-09. Viking-inspired designs can also be seen on the possibly tenth-century cross-slab at Kilmorie (Wigtownshire): Graham-Campbell and Batey, *Vikings in Scotland*, pp. 251-52. Derek Craig has argued that there is no discernible viking influence on other pre-Norman sculptures in Galloway: 'Pre-Norman Sculpture', p. 51. Nevertheless sculptural styles did evolve in Galloway through

been small-scale but of high status.[236] The excavations at Whithorn have
yielded evidence of a flourishing trading settlement in the early eleventh
century.[237] Structural evidence from this site bears close comparison with
house-plans found at Dublin and Waterford, and this suggests links with
territories ruled by the descendants of Ívarr.[238]

The creation of a new political entity with the name *Gall-goídil* –
proclaiming a mixed Scandinavian and Gaelic identity – indicates that
viking settlers of the region had a level of political power which was
disproportionate to their numbers.[239] This hybrid identity may have been
consciously developed to distinguish the political elite of this area from
their Scottish and Brittonic neighbours. If so, this process of ethnogenesis
may have been aided by the fact that the region was already a melting pot of
different cultures before the vikings arrived. Place-names reveal the
existence of British, Gaelic and English settlements in the early Middle
Ages.[240] Richard Oram has convincingly argued that later lords of Galloway
inherited a mixed Gaelic and Scandinavian polity whose leading dynasty
maintained links with Argyll, the Isles and Norway until the thirteenth
century.[241]

It can be concluded that Galloway was born as a result of viking
migrations around the Irish Sea. Vikings from the kingdom of the Isles may

contact with viking communities in Man and Cumbria: Bailey, *Viking Age Sculpture*, pp.
223-29.

[236] Hill, 'Whithorn', p. 38; Oram, 'Fergus', p. 121.

[237] Hill, 'Whithorn', p. 34; Hill, *Whithorn and St Ninian*, pp. 49-55.

[238] Hill, 'Whithorn', pp. 34-35; Hill, *Whithorn and St Ninian*, p. 55. Dagfinn Skre has
recently pointed out that viking houses in Dublin and Waterford resemble those at Kaupang
which date from the early ninth century. Furthermore, he has suggested that this type of
wattle-building was introduced to Ireland from Norway. This contradicts Patrick Wallace's
earlier theory that Dublin's Viking-Age houses were an indigenous adaptation of
Scandinavian designs. Wallace has since expressed agreement with Skre. Wallace, *The Viking
Age*, I, 66-74, 93-95; Skre, 'Investigating Kaupang: Some Central Issues in the Study of
Viking Urbanism', public lecture delivered at the National Museum of Ireland, 22 October,
2002, with comments by Patrick Wallace. If this construction-style was as conservative as
Skre has suggested, it seems more likely that the housing style at Whithorn was introduced
from Ireland, rather than being a local stylistic adaptation, which was another possibility put
forward by Hill.

[239] Oram, 'Fergus', p. 121; Oram, 'Scandinavian Settlement', p. 140.

[240] Hill, 'Whithorn', p. 38. Anglian names are mainly found in the river-valleys of Galloway,
and British place-names in the lands between.

[241] Oram, 'Fergus', pp. 117, 124-26.

have seized control of the Rhinns peninsula in the late tenth or early eleventh century. This is a time when political opportunities in Ireland had lessened through the actions of Brian Bóruma and when economic links with Chester were also in decline. The area north of the Solway may have offered new economic opportunities at this date. Although a relatively small number of viking settlers came to Galloway, they seem to have had a large impact. The area retained a distinct political and cultural identity, linked to viking colonies around the Irish Sea after 1014. Ultimately the region became incorporated into the kingdom of Scotland.

The Viking Age in North Britain was characterised by the creation of new political identities, either proclaiming Scandinavian influence (as in Galloway, Strathclyde and the Isles) or perhaps reacting against it (in the case of Alba). The success of kings of Alba in fighting off viking invasions in the late ninth century set the scene for the territorial gains of their successors in the tenth and eleventh centuries. The kings of Alba extended their borders as viking power declined in Britain. Strathclyde fell victim to this trend, and later on Galloway did too. The Hebrides were to remain a bastion of Scandinavian influence in the Insular viking zone until they were formally incorporated into Scotland in 1266.

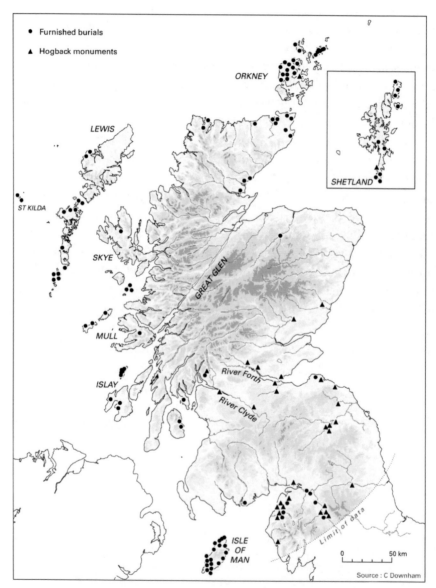

- ● Furnished burials
- ▲ Hogback monuments

ORKNEY

LEWIS

ST KILDA

SKYE

GREAT GLEN

SHETLAND

MULL

ISLAY

River Forth

River Clyde

Limit of data

ISLE
OF
MAN

0   50 km

Source : C Downham

Figure 13: Hogback Monuments and Furnished Burials in North Britain

6

The Kingdom of the Isles

IN the Viking Age mariners travelling from Norway to the Irish Sea would have marked the stages of their journey from their knowledge of the islands which they passed en route. The Hebrides served as stopping-off points for shelter and supplies and their kings drew status from the strategic location of these islands which enabled them to dominate the western seaways. Donnchadh Ó Corráin has argued that in the early ninth century, and again in the early tenth century, the Hebrides were the main base of the dynasty of Ívarr.[1] Nevertheless, these early events must be deduced from archaeology, place-names and historical inference alone. It is not until the tenth century that the kingdom of the Isles begins to appear in the written sources. In this chapter I shall discuss the history of the kingdom as it emerges in association with the dynasty of Ívarr.

What was the Kingdom of the Isles?

The earliest reliable evidence for a unified 'kingdom of the Isles' dates from the second quarter of the tenth century.[2] Later legends relate that this polity, which comprised the Hebrides and Man, began a century earlier. However, the accounts seem propagandist rather than historical. In the Gaelic pseudohistory, the creation of the kingdom of the Isles was associated with Cinaed mac Ailpín, and in Scandinavian sagas it was associated with Haraldr hárfagri.[3] The kingdom's association with these national heroes may represent the competing claims of Scotland and

---

[1] Ó Corráin, 'The Vikings in Scotland'. See above, pp. 28, 30.
[2] *Annals of the Four Masters, s.a.* 939 [=941] (ed. and trans. O'Donovan, II, 640-41); *Chronicum Scotorum, s.a.* [940] [=941] (ed. and trans. Hennessy, pp. 202-05).
[3] *Annals of the Four Masters, s.aa.* 835 [=836], 851 [=853] (ed. and trans. O'Donovan, I, 452-53, 486-87); *Heimskringla, Haralds saga Hárfagri* §22 (*Snorri*, ed. Finnur Jónsson, p. 55; *Heimskringla*, trans. Hollander, pp. 77-78); *Orkneyinga Saga*, §4 (ed. Finnbogi Guðmundsson, pp. 7-8; trans. Pálsson and Edwards, p. 26); *Early Sources*, trans. Anderson, I, 305-45; Woolf, 'The Origins'.

Norway over the Isles, witnessed in the twelfth and thirteenth centuries. Thus doubt may be cast on the reliability of these legends.[4]

It seems likely that 'the kingdom of the Isles', as it emerges in tenth-century sources, took some years to develop after the first viking settlers arrived. Archaeological evidence suggests that different islands were colonised at different times. Place-name and dialectal evidence indicates that 'Scandinavianisation was achieved in varying degrees' in different parts of the Hebrides and western Scotland.[5] This impression of diversity suggests that localised power-structures predominated as this territory was conquered island by island, by viking fleets under the command of various chieftains. The kingdom of the Isles may therefore have been created through the amalgamation of several pre-existing units. Man seems to have been the jewel in the crown of this Insular kingdom in terms of its economic and political power. This is illustrated by the richness of Viking-Age finds on Man, which are distributed more densely than any comparable area of the British Isles.[6] This is also witnessed in contemporary sources which refer to events in Man more than in other parts of the Isles.

Kings who ruled Man and the Isles bore the title *rí Innsi Gall* ('the king of the islands of the Foreigners') in Irish or *plurimarum rex insularum* in Latin (with variants). Scandinavian sources called the Hebrides the 'Southern Isles' (*Suðr-eyjar*), which was later anglicised as 'Sudrey(s)' and 'Sodor'.[7] Later sources refer to 'Man and the Isles', as if they were separate entities.[8] This distinction may result from the political fragmentation of this unit, witnessed from the twelfth century onwards.[9] During the late tenth

---

[4] Hudson, *Kings*, pp. 40-42; Roberts, *Lost Kingdoms*, pp. 90-91; Sawyer, 'Harold Fairhair'; Woolf, 'The Origins'.

[5] Dumville, *The Churches*, pp. 15-16.

[6] Graham-Campbell and Batey, *Vikings in Scotland*, p. 111.

[7] Dumville, *The Churches*, p. 16.

[8] Moore, *A History*, I, 167, 178-79.

[9] Man is referred to several times in tenth- and eleventh-century written sources: e.g. *Annals of Ulster, s.a.* 503 [=504].2, 576 [=577].5, 577 [=578].2, 581 [=582].1 (ed. and trans. Mac Airt and Mac Niocaill, pp. 60-61, 88-91); *Annales Cambriae, s.a.* 584, 684 (ed. Phillimore, pp. 155-56, 159). In Welsh it is referred to as *Manaw* (perhaps risking confusion with *Manaw Gododdin*?) in Irish *Manann*, and *Eubonia*, *Eumania* in Latin (with slight variations). As Colmán Etchingham ('North Wales', p. 168) has argued, commentators have perhaps exaggerated the degree to which Man may be confused with Anglesey (*Mon* in Welsh texts, *Monia* and *Mona* in Latin, *Mon Chonain*, 'Môn of Cynan', in Irish sources). *ByT* (Pen. 20), trans. Jones, p. 145, n. 9.31. Forms found in Irish chronicles are: 'i mMaen

and early eleventh centuries *Innsi Gall* appears to describe Man and some or all of the Hebrides. It is not certain that all of the Hebridean islands were included in this polity throughout the period under discussion. For example, more northerly Isles may, at different times, have fallen within the sphere of influence of the earls of Orkney or, as occurred later, distinct polities might emerge within particular island-groups. The geographically fragmented nature of the region might have encouraged kings to delegate power to local lawmen. The Thing-mound which survives in Man demonstrates the importation of Scandinavian methods of government and law-enforcement into the kingdom.[10]

When was Man taken over by Vikings?

There has long been debate over the circumstances in which Man was seized by vikings. Two issues seem particularly relevant, namely, who occupied the island before the vikings arrived, and when exactly the new rulers moved in. The prevailing assumption has been that Man was Gaelic in culture prior to viking colonisation. Thus the hybridisation of Gaelic and Scandinavian culture represented in Manx sculpture and place-names has been seen to reflect the peaceful integration of viking colonists.[11] However, it has recently been stressed that vikings came to the island as secondary migrants from the Gaelic world. They would have assimilated elements of Gaelic culture before their arrival.[12] During the early Middle Ages, Man was

Chonain', *Annals of Ulster*, s.a. 864 [=865].4 (ed. and trans. Mac Airt and Mac Niocaill, pp. 320-21); 'co Moin Conáinn', *Annals of the Four Masters*, s.a. 960 [=962] (ed. and trans. O'Donovan, II, 682-83). The first element has been interpreted as *maen*, 'fortress', or *móin*, 'bog'. *Leabhar Breathnach*, ed. and trans. Todd and Herbert, p. 190, n. x. However, it may be Welsh *Mon* borrowed into Irish with variation in spelling and flexion. Etchingham is probably correct in identifying a reference to the Irish of *Mon* in *Armes Prydein* as Anglesey: *ibid.*, pp. 185-86.

[10] There is debate as to whether the system of ouncelands and pennylands found in the Isles dates back to the Viking Age, see Easson, 'Ouncelands'. Per Sveaas Andersen has suggested that they originated in the late twelfth or early thirteenth century: 'When was Regular Annual Taxation introduced?'

[11] Megaw, 'Norseman and Native'; Gelling, 'Celtic Continuity'.

[12] Dumville, *The Churches*, pp. 23-24.

at various times under Brittonic or Gaelic suzerainty.[13] In political terms it can be argued that Man was in Brittonic hands when the vikings arrived.[14]

It can be argued that Man was ruled by the royal dynasty of Gwynedd during the ninth century. A fourteenth-century version of *Brenhinedd y Saesson* refers to Hywel, king of Man, at his death in 826, although this is not reliable evidence.[15] Another king of Man may have been Gwriad, son of Elidir. The name 'Guriat' is inscribed on the stone at Port y Vullen. This has been dated to the early ninth century.[16] Gwriad's son Merfyn ruled Gwynedd until his death in 844. He is linked with Man in the early tenth-century poem *Cyfoesi Myrddin a Gwenddydd ei Chwaer*.[17] A poem added to 'The Annals of Ulster' associates Merfyn's son Rhodri Mawr with Man, although it is not known at what date the poem was composed.[18] There is no corresponding evidence to support the theory that Man was affiliated with the Gaelic world immediately before the viking conquest.[19] Nevertheless, any Brittonic elements in the island's culture were eclipsed. This challenges theories of peaceful settlement of vikings on the island and raises questions concerning the events leading to its colonisation.

There is no reliable record of viking activity in Man until the tenth century. 'The Annals of Ulster' report an attack on *Inis Phátraic* in 798, but this has been convincingly identified with Holmpatrick near Dublin, not Holme Patrick on Man, as was previously supposed.[20] Another record thought to relate to Man is in 'The Fragmentary Annals of Ireland'. This records the death of Jarl Tomrar at *Port Manann* in 866. However as a number of locations in Ireland bore the name *Manann* they may fit better with other records of Tomrar's career.[21] It is possible that the Isle of Man is referred to in the 'Old-English Orosius' in an account of a Scandinavian traveller Óttar, given at the court of King Alfred around 890. Reference is

---

[13] *Annals of Ulster, s.aa.* 503 [=504].2, 576 [=577].5, 577 [=578].2, 582 [=582].1 (ed. and trans. Mac Airt and Mac Niocaill, pp. 60-61, 88-91); *ByS, s.aa.* 816, 826 (ed. and trans. Jones, pp. 12-15); Jackson, *Language*, pp. 153-54.

[14] Dumville, *The Churches*, p. 23.

[15] *ByS, s.a.* 826 (ed. and trans. Jones, pp. 14-15).

[16] Jones, 'Gwriad's Heritage'.

[17] *The Poetry*, ed. Evans, col. 578.40; Sims-Williams, 'Historical Need', p. 11.

[18] *Annals of Ulster, s.a.* 877 [=878].3 (ed. and trans. Mac Airt and Mac Niocaill, pp. 332-33).

[19] Charles-Edwards, *Early Christian Ireland*, p. 589.

[20] Moore, *A History*, I, 85; Graham-Campbell and Batey, *Vikings in Scotland*, p. 110.

[21] Downham, 'Tomrar's Death'.

made to the islands lying between Ireland and England, but it is not certain that Man is intended as one of these.[22]

The first indisputable report of vikings' association with Man is in 914.[23] In that year a sea-battle took place off Man between Barðr Óttarsson and Rögnvaldr grandson of Ívarr. Barðr was defeated and killed in the engagement. The event coincided with the re-establishment of viking power in Ireland. It suggests that rival viking groups were seeking to control Man at this date, and the surrounding sea-lanes. In the years 914-18, the dynasty of Ívarr led a number of raids around the Irish Sea. Man was probably victim to such attacks and it possible that the island served as a base for viking ships in these years.

Evidence for permanent viking settlement on the Isle of Man appears rather late in the archaeological record. James Graham-Campbell has recently discussed the range of evidence with emphasis on dating the magnificent heathen graves found on Man. These appear to mark the first generation of incomers. He has concluded that settlement began after 900 and possibly as late as the 930s.[24] Some features of the early viking graves suggest the arrival of a warrior-elite on the island and less-than-peaceful integration with the native population. At Balladoole, recent Christian burials were desecrated to make way for a high-status ship-burial, and at Ballateare human-sacrifice is witnessed by the skeleton of a female with a slashed skull, which accompanied other prestigious grave-goods in the burial of a viking.[25]

Written evidence may help to provide a context for these archaeological findings. After 918, the power of Ívarr's grandsons was fully re-established in Ireland, and their relations with kings of Gwynedd were at a low point.[26]

---

[22] 'igland þe synd betux Iralande 7 þissum lande'; *The Old English Orosius*, I.i (ed. Bately, p. 16).

[23] *Annals of Ulster, s.a.* 913 [=914].4 (ed. and trans. Mac Airt and Mac Niocaill, pp. 362-63).

[24] Graham-Campbell, 'The Irish Sea', pp. 75-78; Graham-Campbell, 'The Early Viking Age', pp. 116-20; cf. Fanning, 'The Hiberno-Norse Pins', pp. 32-33. Fanning suggested that the polyhedral ring-pins found in the heathen burials at Balladoole, Ballateare and Cronk Moar are datable after A.D. 900 through comparison with Irish examples. Bersu and Wilson suggested a date-range from 850 to 950 for the heathen graves: *Three Viking Graves*, p. 87.

[25] Richards, *English Heritage*, pp. 104-07; Bersu and Wilson, *Three Viking Graves*.

[26] *Annals of Clonmacnoise, s.a.* 917 (ed. Murphy, p. 146); *Annals of Ulster, s.a.* 916 [=917].4 (ed. and trans. Mac Airt and Mac Niocaill, pp. 366-67); *Chronicum Scotorum, s.a.* [916] (ed. and trans. Hennessy, pp. 188-89).

The submission given by Idwal, king of Gwynedd, to English kings in 918×939 would have made him a natural enemy to the dynasty of Ívarr because of their involvement in Northumbria. This enmity is indicated by the Dubliners' assault on Anglesey in 918.[27] It may be within this time-frame that Man was seized from Brittonic control. This may correspond with other migrations, including the settlement of Gaelic-speaking vikings in Cumberland, where the remains of high-status viking burials similar to those in Man have been found.[28]

Immigrants may have arrived in Man from viking Northumbria as well as from Gaelic-speaking areas.[29] Artefactual evidence, such as the beads and knife found in the grave of the 'Pagan Lady' at Peel, shows early links with the Danelaw.[30] Gillian Fellows-Jensen has also argued that some of the viking colonisers came from northern England, on the basis of -bý place-names on Man.[31] Kristin Bornholdt-Collins has proposed that the beginning of hoarding on Man was prompted by a new influx of refugees to the island following the collapse of viking York.[32] The wealth attested in the Manx hoards of the 960s and 970s suggests that the island rapidly assumed a position of economic and political eminence in the years immediately after the fall of viking Northumbria.[33] A significant increase in wealth in Man and the Hebrides is also indicated by the creation of a new form of currency, the so-called 'Scoto-Norse' ring-money, which circulated from about 950 to about 1050. A share of York's trade and political links may have been redirected westwards to the Hebrides and Man, under the aegis of a branch of the dynasty of Ívarr.

An economic boom along the seaways between Britain and Ireland at this time may also be attested by the increasing number of coin-hoards deposited in Ireland, Wales, Cheshire and the west of Scotland from about

---

[27] *ASC.A*, ed. Bately, pp. 68-69; *ByS*, *s.a.* 919 (ed. and trans. Jones, pp. 28-29); *ByT* (RBH), *s.a.* 918 (ed. and trans. Jones, pp. 10-11); Loyn, 'Wales and England', pp. 291-95.

[28] Higham, 'The Scandinavians', p. 49.

[29] Graham-Campbell, 'The Early Viking Age', p. 120.

[30] Graham-Campbell, 'The Irish Sea', pp. 75-78.

[31] Fellows-Jensen, 'Scandinavian Place-names', p. 36.

[32] Graham-Campbell, 'The Early Viking Age', p. 118; Bornholdt-Collins, 'Viking Age Coin Finds', I, 149-50.

[33] Blackburn and Pagan, 'A Revised Checklist', nos 143, 155, 159, 165. Bornholdt-Collins ('Viking Age Coin Finds', I, 191) has identified seven hoards deposited in Man *circa* 955-995.

965 to 980.[34] Nevertheless, it is noteworthy that non-numismatic hoards in Ireland rapidly decreased at this time.[35] This could indicate that some wealth was being channelled to the Isle of Man as an economic partner or rival of the viking ports of Ireland.

The Isles and the Descendants of Ívarr

Irish chronicles start to mention *Innsi Gall*, or 'the Islands of the Foreigners' from the 940s.[36] The growing interest in events there could relate to the conquest of Man and its incorporation within a kingdom of the Isles. In 941, Muirchertach son of Niall (overking of the Northern Uí Néill) raided *Innsi Gall*, seizing much booty.[37] In the same year, Óláfr Guðrøðsson, king of York and Dublin, died. It is in some measure quite tempting to link these events. Muirchertach was an implacable enemy of Óláfr Guðrøðsson. He may have used the opportunity of Óláfr's death to make his strike on the Isles.[38] In the early twelfth century John of Worcester identified Óláfr Guðrøðsson as 'King of the Isles'.[39] Although this text should be treated with caution, there is tangible evidence to suggest that Óláfr had a position of influence in Irish-Sea affairs. Welsh chronicles commemorated his death, and his sons seem to have been based in the Hebrides during the 960s, as Colmán Etchingham has noted.[40] On less trustworthy grounds, 'The Annals of Clonmacnoise' identify Gebeachan (Middle Irish Gebechán) as a king of the Isles who fought at *Brunanburh*.[41] Etchingham has suggested that he was a Hebridean leader subordinate to Óláfr Guðrøðsson, if he

---

[34] Blackburn and Pagan, 'A Revised Checklist', nos 144, 150, 152-54, 156-58, 160-64, 166-72, 174, 177.

[35] Sheehan, 'Viking-Age Hoards', p. 323.

[36] An earlier and literary reference to *Innsi Gall*, perhaps dating from the late ninth century, is found in the Irish saga *Cath Maige Tuired* : Ó Corráin, 'Vikings in Scotland', p. 15.

[37] *Annals of the Four Masters*, s.a. 939 [=941] (ed. and trans. O'Donovan, II, 640-41); *Chronicum Scotorum*, s.a. [940] (ed. and trans. Hennessy, pp. 204-05).

[38] *Annals of the Four Masters*, s.a. 939 [=941] (ed. and trans. O'Donovan, II, 640-41).

[39] John of Worcester, *Chronicle*, s.a. 937 (ed. and trans. Darlington *et al.*, II, 392-93); Etchingham, 'North Wales', p. 167.

[40] *Annales Cambriae* (A), s.a. [941] (ed. Dumville, p. 16); *ByS*, s.a. 941 (ed. and trans. Jones, pp. 30-31); *ByT* (RBH), s.a. 941 (ed. and trans. Jones, pp. 12-13); Etchingham, 'North Wales', p. 169.

[41] *Annals of Clonmacnoise*, s.a. 931 [=937].2 (ed. Murphy, p. 151); *The Battle*, ed. Campbell, pp. 56-57; Smyth, *Scandinavian York*, II, 39.

existed.[42] A case can therefore be put that the Isles were linked with the dynasty of Ívarr in late 930s and 940s.

During the 960s, the Isles may have been home to sons of Óláfr Guðrøðsson.[43] A prolonged struggle for Dublin followed Óláfr's death in 941 which resulted in his descendants being excluded from the kingship.[44] However, they may have attempted a come-back. 'The Annals of Ulster' report that in 960 Cammán son of Óláfr Guðrøðsson fought a battle in Ireland at *Dub*.[45] The location of this battle and the identity of Cammán's opponents are uncertain, but it is clear that he failed in his endeavour.[46] As Etchingham has suggested, 'Cammán' may be a diminutive form of the epithet *Camm* ('crooked') possessed by Sigtryggr Cam, who plundered Uí Cholgain (who occupied an area around Lusk, Co. Dublin) from the sea in 962 and who was defeated in battle by Óláfr Sigtryggsson.[47] In 962 the sons of Óláfr Guðrøðsson raided the Irish coasts north of Dublin.[48] These raids may have been intended as a challenge to the authority of Óláfr Sigtryggsson, by relatives who felt excluded from power.

The sons of Óláfr then travelled south and raided an area around Waterford and Cork. 'The Annals of the Four Masters' state that this attack took place to avenge their brother *Oin*, but the circumstances of this earlier insult are not given. This chronicle adds that the Óláfssons were accompanied by *lagmainn* or 'lawmen' in this expedition, but eventually they were defeated in battle in the territory of Uí Liatháin (Co. Cork).[49]

---

[42] Etchingham, 'North Wales', p. 167.

[43] *Ibid.*

[44] *Annals of Clonmacnoise, s.aa.* 933 [=940], 937 [=945] (ed. Murphy, pp. 151-52, 154); *Annals of the Four Masters, s.aa.* 938 [=940], 943 [=945], 945 [=947], 946 [=948] (ed. and trans. O'Donovan II, 640-41, 654-55, 658-59); *Annals of Inisfallen, s.a.* [947] [=948] (ed. and trans. Mac Airt, pp. 152-53); *Annals of Ulster, s.aa.* 944 [=945].6, 946 [=947].1, 947 [=948].1 (ed. and trans. Mac Airt and Mac Niocaill, pp. 392-93); *Chronicum Scotorum, s.a.* [947] [=948] (ed. and trans. Hennessy, pp. 208-09).

[45] Etchingham, 'North Wales', p. 170.

[46] Hogan identified *Dub* as Black River, bar. Rosclougher, Co. Leitrim: *Onomasticon*, p. 370. However, there is a large number of *Dub*-compound place-names (including Dublin!) and another site may be intended. Ó Murchadha has suggested that *Dub* might be equated with the River Blackwater: 'Lagmainn', p. 136, n. 1.

[47] *Annals of the Four Masters, s.a.* 960 [=962] (ed. and trans. O'Donovan, II, 682-83); Etchingham, 'North Wales', p. 170.

[48] *Annals of the Four Masters, s.a.* 960 [=962] (ed. and trans. O'Donovan, II, 680-83).

[49] *Ibid., s.a.* 960 [=962] (ed. and trans. O'Donovan, II, 680-83); Hogan, *Onomasticon*, p. 673.

From this evidence Diarmuid Ó Murchadha has concluded that this campaign was a legally sanctioned act of retribution for Oin's death.[50] Lawmen seem to have been an integral part of the mediaeval Scandinavian legal system. They are recorded in some of the viking colonies – for example, the Danelaw and Iceland; there they were elected by yeomen to preside over assemblies and act as consultants on legal matters.[51] In general, they seem to have enjoyed high social status and were recruited from the most powerful families. One might surmise from the description of the raids on Ireland that lawmen could also act as local military leaders, perhaps with personal armed retinues. Perhaps they assumed functions of the *aire échta* ('lord of blood vengeance') found in Irish law, whose job was to avenge wrongs committed by people outside his territory.[52] A fusion of aspects of Scandinavian and Gaelic law may have occurred in areas of mixed Gaelic-Scandinavian culture. Ó Murchadha's suggestion that the lawmen provided some means of legitimising this raid is therefore worth considering.

It has long been noted that references to *Lagmainn* in Irish chronicles tend to be linked to the Hebrides.[53] This connection is difficult to explain. It is unlikely that lawmen were absent from viking colonies in Ireland or that they were unique to the Isles, although they may have been more prominent there.[54] The presence of *Lagmainn* has been used as evidence that the sons of Óláfr had contacts in the Isles. Their attacks on Ireland certainly seem to have been directed from a base in or around the Irish Sea. The sons of Óláfr also campaigned in North Wales, raiding Llyn and Holyhead in 961, and Anglesey again in the following year.[55]

By the 970s there seems to have been a change in leadership and the Isles were ruled by Maccus and Guðrøðr sons of Haraldr. Their reigns seem

---

[50] Ó Murchadha, 'Lagmainn', p. 137.

[51] Foote and Wilson, *The Viking Achievement*, pp. 91-92.

[52] Kelly, *A Guide*, p. 302; *Críth Gablach*, ed. Binchy, pp. 13-15, 70-72; Latvio, 'Status', pp. 75-76.

[53] *Annals of the Four Masters*, ed. and trans. O'Donovan, II, 698, note w; Hogan, *Onomasticon*, p. 473; Ó Murchadha, 'Lagmainn', pp. 136-38; Etchingham, 'North Wales', pp. 169, 172.

[54] In geographically fragmented kingdoms, lawmen may have enjoyed a higher degree of local autonomy and thus been more prominent members of society.

[55] *ByS*, *s.a.* 961 (ed. and trans. Jones, pp. 36-37); *ByT* (Pen. 20) *s.a.* 961 (ed. Jones, p. 9; trans. Jones, p. 8); *ByT* (RBH) *s.a.* 961 (ed. and trans. Jones, pp. 14-15).

to mark a political high point in the history of the Isles. Until the publication of Benjamin Hudson's book *Viking Pirates and Christian Princes* in 2005, the prevailing view (since the seventeenth century) was that Maccus (and therefore his brother Guðrøðr) was a member of the dynasty of Ívarr.[56] More specifically, these men may be identified as sons of Haraldr, great-grandson of Ívarr, a king of Limerick, who died in 940.[57] Hudson has put forward an alternative view that they were sons of 'Harold of Bayeaux', a leader from Denmark who was active in northern Francia during the 940s and 950s.

Hudson's argument is based on four main points and objections can be raised to each of them.[58] First, there is the evidence of names – Hudson has made the point that Harold of Bayeux would have been a contemporary of the Haraldr whose sons ruled Man. Nevertheless, Haraldr of Limerick was also a contemporary (he was king in 940).[59] The paternity of Maccus and Guðrøðr cannot be proved. However the weight of evidence points to their connection with Ireland.

The descendants of Haraldr on Man bore names which suggest a link with Gaelic-speaking areas. The name Maccus is a good example. Hudson has not referred to the argument put forward by David Thornton in 1997 concerning the form of the name Maccus which is thoroughly grounded in medieval sources.[60] Hudson has instead confused the name with Magnus, as did modern Irish writers.[61] This obscures the point that Maccus is a name derived from Gaelic *macc* ('son') and it originated in areas of mixed Scandinavian and Gaelic culture. It is not therefore a likely name for a ruler from Denmark active in northern France to give to his son. One could try to explain this away. Perhaps Harold of Bayeux married a Hebridean and raised Maccus after he had taken over the Isles? However, it could simply reflect the cultural ancestry of Maccus, and no further explanation is necessary.

---

[56] *Leabhar Mór*, ed. Ó Muraíle, III, 776.2; Hudson, *Viking Pirates*, pp. 68-70.
[57] *Annals of Inisfallen*, s.a. 940 (ed. and trans. Mac Airt, pp. 152-53); *Cogadh*, ed. and trans. Todd, pp. 271-76.
[58] Alex Woolf has stated that Hudson's case 'lacks plausibility', but there was not space in his review to give a more detailed explanation ('Review', p. 516).
[59] *Annals of the Four Masters*, s.aa. 935 [=937], 938 [=940] (ed. and trans. O'Donovan, II, 632-33, 639-41); *Annals of Inisfallen*, s.a. [940] (ed. and trans. Mac Airt, pp. 152-53).
[60] Thornton, 'Hey Macc!'; Woolf, 'Review', p. 516.
[61] *Annals of the Four Masters*, s.a. 972 [=974] (ed. and trans. O'Donovan, II, 698-99).

The names of subsequent rulers of Man and the Isles follow the pattern of name-giving found across all branches of the dynasty of Ívarr, with recurrences of Guðrøðr, Óláfr and Rögnvaldr. These are common enough names; if an alien dynasty planted itself in Man, it made little effort to distinguish itself from the ruling dynasty of its viking neighbours. Other names in the Manx royal dynasty indicate Gaelic influence, including Lagmann (*fl.* 1012), a name which is found in Gaelic-speaking areas settled by vikings, and Echmarchach (*ob.* 1064) although these might be explained away as rapid assimilation of the ruling dynasty to the cultural milieu of the islands. Nevertheless, the similarity of the Manx royal names with other branches of the dynasty of Ívarr requires consideration.

The second point in Hudson's argument is the evidence of economic links between northern France and the Hebrides in the late tenth and early eleventh centuries. Coins from France are found in a wide area and not exclusively in territory under the control of the sons of Haraldr.[62] It is clear that a trade route ran from Northern France into the Irish Sea. However, such links are to be expected at this time for they existed both before and after the Viking Age.[63] These commercial links do not have to be explained by the rulers of the Hebrides having come from France.

Economic links also existed between Limerick and Man and the Isles. One notable example of this is a hoard deposited at Mungret, Co. Limerick, about 955, whose contents suggest that it was assembled on the Isle of Man.[64] This mixed hoard of coins and ingots is comparable with other Irish-Sea finds. However, a striking feature of the Mungret hoard is the presence of three cut halfpennies and one fragment of a cut halfpenny. This is very characteristic of Manx numismatic finds of the period.[65] Later links between Limerick and the kingdom of the Isles are also hinted at by the hoard of three Scoto-Norse currency-rings found at the River

---

[62] Hudson has chosen the coin-distribution in two phases to support his argument. There is the distribution of Continental coins in 965-986 which includes Lough Lerne (Co. Westmeath) and Derrykeighan (Co. Antrim) and the distribution of deniers in 986-1000 which includes Knockmaon (Co. Waterford), Tarbat (Ross, Scotland) and Burray (Orkneys): Hudson, *Viking Pirates*, p. 68.

[63] O'Brien, 'Commercial Relations'; Thomas, 'Imported Pottery'.

[64] Blackburn and Pagan, 'A Revised Checklist', no. 135.

[65] Bornholdt-Collins, 'Viking-Age Coin Finds', I, 286-93.

Shannon.[66] There is no reason to see the economic associations between the Hebrides and Northern France as being more politically significant than ties with southern Ireland.

The third part of Hudson's argument is the evidence for Danish or French cultural influence in the Isle of Man. He referred to the evidence of a rune-stone at Maughold on the Isle of Man whose inscriptions bear the influence of East Norse orthography.[67] R.I. Page has dated these inscriptions to about A.D. 1000, as the dotted 'e' which is featured on the stone first appears in Denmark about that time.[68] However, this provides a *terminus post quem*; the runes of Maughold IV could be much later, and therefore rather too late to suggest a link with Harold of Bayeux. The use of the weak verb *rista*, found in the inscriptions, is witnessed in Denmark from about 1050, which favours a later dating than about 1000 for the runic text at Maughold.[69]

The Danish features in the inscription could result from the presence of Scandinavian war-fleets in Insular waters from the late 980s. Alternatively, the use of the dotted 'e' in the inscriptions may have been an innovation introduced to rune-cutters on Man via England before of during the reign of Knútr. As such it may provide evidence of direct contact with England rather than Denmark.[70] In support of this alternative view it should be noted that the cable moulding ornament on this stone, which is thought to be contemporary with the inscriptions, appears to be English in its inspiration.[71] The inscriptions on the stone at Maughold can therefore be understood in ways other than the theory put forward by Hudson. The cultural character of Viking-Age finds in Man and the Isles is overridingly one of mixed Gaelic and Scandinavian ancestry, and the Maughold IV stone is unusual.[72] However, Man and the Isles were not isolated in the Viking Age and one can see a range of cultural influences in the Isles which does not require a theory of conquest to justify their presence.

---

[66] Sheehan, 'Viking Age Hoards from Munster', p. 154; Graham-Campbell, *Viking-Age Gold*, p. 58.

[67] Maughold IV (Manx Museum no. 142): Kermode, *Manx Crosses*, Appendix C, pp. 24-28.

[68] Page, 'The Manx', p. 137.

[69] *ibid.*

[70] Hudson, *Viking Pirates*, p. 70.

[71] Kermode, *Manx Crosses*, Appendix C, p. 26.

[72] Bailey, 'Irish Sea'.

Hudson has also pointed to the similarities of a 'spiral hip' motif found on Romanesque sculptural reliefs at Evrecy in Normandy and on a cross at Kirk Michael on the Isle of Man.[73] This motif was current in Scandinavian and Orcadian art. It is not clear that transmission was from France to Man as Hudson has implied. Rather, the Irish Sea may have been the conduit for this design to spread from Scandinavia to the Continent. The transmission of this motif may be viewed in the context of commercial links between areas of Scandinavian settlement. It does not present a strong case for the conquest of Man by vikings from Normandy.

The remaining point in Hudson's argument was the evidence for political contacts of the Isles with Normandy and Denmark. He has cited a verse from the late tenth century *Saltair na Rann* referring to the presence of 'Danes from Denmark' in the Irish Sea.[74] There are also references in Irish chronicles to the actions of Danish fleets in Insular waters for the years 986, 987 and 990. The activities of Scandinavian fleets are well attested in English sources at this time.[75] Their activities ultimately led to the conquest of England by Swein Forkbeard in 1013. These references to Danish activity need not be linked to a posited (but unattested) seizure of the kingdom of the Isles by a Danish leader from northern France. The activities of these Scandinavian fleets also postdate by over a decade the establishment of Maccus and Guðrøðr as kings of Man.

As for the French connection, Hudson's assertion that warriors from Francia fought at Clontarf is unfootnoted. This is either speculative or based on late and unreliable texts.[76] He has noted that Lagmann, king of Man, fought for Duke Richard of Normandy in the early eleventh century.[77] However, Harold of Bayeux, whom Hudson has identified as the grandfather of Lagmann, was an implacable enemy of the ducal line. It does not follow that his alleged grandson would be one of their supporters.[78] This event may be interpreted within a broader political context. Lagmann appears on the scene as an opportunist seeking to reap political advantages

---

[73] Hudson, *Viking Pirates*, p. 68; Baylé, 'Reminiscences', p. 36.

[74] Hudson, *Viking Pirates*, pp. 66-70.

[75] Downham, 'England', pp. 59-60.

[76] *Annals of Loch Cé, s.a.* 1014 (ed. and trans. Hennessy, pp. 4-5). For the development of legends surrounding this battle see Downham, 'The Battle'. See above, p. 134.

[77] Cf. Downham, 'England', pp. 60-61.

[78] Hudson, *Viking Pirates*, p. 66.

from the upheavals wrought by Scandinavian fleets in English and Norman politics.[79] In the early eleventh century the Hebrideans seem to have already developed a military reputation which made them desirable as allies or mercenaries to foreign rulers; a reputation that would continue for centuries.[80]

Political links between the Hebrides and Ireland in the tenth and eleventh centuries favour the view that the kings of Man and the Isles were linked to the dynasty of Ívarr.

More specifically, the sons of Haraldr may be linked to the king of Limerick who died in 940. In the 960s and 970s Limerick was ruled by an Ívarr (his patronym is not given in the chronicles).[81] It is possible that he excluded the sons of Haraldr from power, forcing them to seek a new power-base in the Hebrides. In 974, a great fleet led by Maccus and the lawmen of the Isles travelled to Limerick. The fleet plundered Scattery Island and seized Ívarr from the church of St Senán.[82] Maccus may have hoped to win control of the town which his father had ruled.

The Islesmen next appear in Irish politics in 980 as participants in the battle of Tara.[83] In this engagement they allied with Óláfr *Cuarán* against Mael Sechlainn overking of the Southern Uí Néill. After his defeat, Óláfr went on pilgrimage to the Hebridean church of Iona where he died in the same year. From the mid-ninth century, religious life on Iona had been curtailed by viking settlement in the Isles.[84] Abbots of the church are still recorded, but several of these may have been absentee leaders.[85] In the late tenth century, Iona perhaps literally rose from the ashes under the patronage of viking converts.[86] Edel Bhreathnach has shown how Óláfr

---

[79] Downham, 'England', p. 61.

[80] *ByS*, *s.a.* 1014 (ed. and trans. Jones, pp. 50-51); *ByT* (Pen. 20), *s.a.* 1014 (ed. Jones, p. 14; trans. Jones, p. 10); *ByT* (RBH), *s.a.* 1014 (ed. and trans. Jones, pp. 20-21).

[81] *Annals of Inisfallen*, *s.aa.* [969], [977] (ed. and trans. Mac Airt, pp. 158-59, 162-63).

[82] *Annals of the Four Masters*, *s.a.* 972 [=974] (ed. and trans. O'Donovan, II, 698-99); *Annals of Inisfallen*, *s.a.* [974] (ed. and trans. Mac Airt, pp. 160-61).

[83] *Annals of the Four Masters*, *s.a.* 978 [=980] (ed. and trans. O'Donovan, II, 708-09); *Annals of Ulster*, *s.a.* 979 [=980].1 (ed. and trans. Mac Airt and Mac Niocaill, pp. 414-15).

[84] Herbert, *Iona*, p. 72.

[85] *Ibid.*, pp. 73-74. Abbots of Iona died outside the island in 854 and 865. A later abbot, Mael Brigte, held Iona jointly with Armagh 891-927, and he was probably not resident on the island.

[86] *Annals of Ulster*, *s.aa.* 853 [=854].3, 877 [=878].9 (ed. and trans. Mac Airt and Mac Niocaill, pp. 312-23, 334-35). It is possible that the shrine of St Columba came to Ireland

Cuarán promoted the cult of Columba and may have been the founder of the church dedicated to this saint at Skreen (Co. Meath).[87] These ecclesiastical ties between Dublin and the Isles in the late-tenth century may have helped to cement the political alliance evidenced at Tara.

After Óláfr's death, the friendship between leaders of Dublin and the Isles collapsed. This may have resulted from a shift in the balance of power in Ireland after the battle of Tara. Óláfr *Cuarán*'s son and successor, Glúniarann, became allied with his father's enemy, Mael Sechlainn, overking of the Southern Uí Néill.[88] In 983, Glúniarann and Mael Sechlainn won a battle against the Leinstermen and Ívarr of Waterford.[89] This change in political alliances may help to explain why in 984 the sons of Haraldr exchanged hostages with Mael Sechlainn's rival, Brian Bóruma at Waterford and promised to support an attack on Dublin.[90] The combined forces do not seem to have reached Dublin that year, although the Islesmen may have been among the *Gaill* who supported Brian's attack on southern Leinster and the Osraige. The sons of Haraldr were deeply embroiled in Irish politics and their deeds can be attributed to their dynastic connection with the dynasty of Ívarr. In sum, Hudson's argument has less evidence to recommend it than does the received view of their ancestry.

---

from Dunkeld, not Iona, in 878. The *Annals of Roscrea*, §282 (ed. Gleeson and Mac Airt, p. 170), report the death of Fothud, bishop of *Innsi Alban* in 963. This could indicate the renewal of ecclesiastical organisation in the Hebrides: Dumville, *The Churches*, pp. 21-22.

[87] Bhreathnach, 'The Documentary Evidence'. This patronage was not consistent. For example, Óláfr *Cuarán* had plundered Kells in 970: *Annals of Ulster, s.a.* 969 [=970].1 (ed. and trans. Mac Airt and Mac Niocaill, pp. 408-09). During the late tenth century successive Dublin kings had sacked the Columban church at Kells: Herbert, *Iona*, p. 81. This was because Kells was situated in enemy-territory. It had also superseded Iona as head of the Columban Church.

[88] *Annals of Tigernach, s.a.* [983] (ed. and trans. Stokes, II, 235); 'The Ban-Shenchus', ed. Dobbs, pp. 314, 188, 227. Cf. *Annals of the Four Masters, s.a.* 982 [=984] (ed. and trans. O'Donovan, II, 714-15).

[89] *Annals of Boyle*, §274 ('The Annals', ed. Freeman, p. 327); *Annals of Clonmacnoise, s.a.* 977 [=983] (ed. Murphy, p. 159); *Annals of the Four Masters, s.a.* 982 [=984] (ed. and trans. O'Donovan, II, 714-15); *Annals of Tigernach, s.a.* [983] (ed. and trans. Stokes, II, 235); *Annals of Ulster, s.a.* 982 [=983].2 (ed. and trans. Mac Airt and Mac Niocaill, pp. 418-19); *Chronicum Scotorum, s.a.* [981] [=983] (ed. and trans. Hennessy, pp. 228-29).

[90] *Annals of Inisfallen, s.a.* [984] (ed. and trans. Mac Airt, pp. 164-65).

Relationships discussed in this section

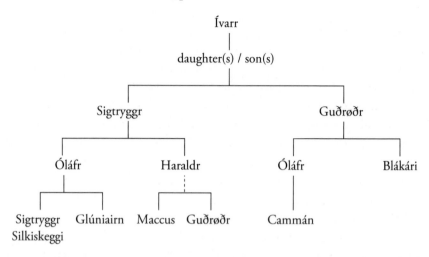

Maccus and Guðrøðr were also active in English and Welsh politics. They raided Anglesey in 971 and 972.[91] Their attacks may have been timed to take advantage of dynastic infighting in Gwynedd following the death of Rhodri ab Idwal in 968.[92]

The campaigns of the sons of Haraldr in North Wales may have brought them to the special attention of Edgar, king of England.[93] In 973, Edgar travelled to Chester, and a group of Insular rulers swore oaths of allegiance to him.[94] According to the twelfth-century historians John of

---

[91] *ByS*, *s.aa.* 971, 972 (ed. and trans. Jones, pp. 38-41); *ByT* (Pen. 20) *s.aa.* 971, 972 (ed. Jones, p. 10; trans. Jones, p. 8); *ByT* (RBH) *s.aa.* 971, 972 (ed. and trans. Jones, pp. 14-15).

[92] Maund, *The Welsh Kings*, p. 56. It is uncertain how long the sons of Óláfr Guðrøðsson were active after 962. The death of Guðrøðr Óláfsson is reported in 963: *Annals of Clonmacnoise*, *s.a.* 957 [=965] (ed. Murphy, p. 157); *Annals of Ulster*, *s.a.* 962 [=963].5 (ed. and trans. Mac Airt and Mac Niocaill, pp. 404-05); *Chronicum Scotorum*, *s.a.* [961] [=963] (ed. and trans. Hennessy, pp. 214-15). He was perhaps a son of Óláfr Guðrøðsson, and possibly (but not certainly) a brother of Sigtryggr Óláfsson, *tigherna Gall*: *Annals of the Four Masters*, *s.a.* 967 [=969] (ed. and trans. O'Donovan, II, 692-93).

[93] Two charters witnessed by Maccus appear to be forgeries: Sawyer, *Anglo-Saxon Charters*, nos 783, 808. Benjamin Hudson (*Kings*, p. 100 and *Viking Pirates*, pp. 47-48) has however urged the authenticity of no. 783 (A.D. 971).

[94] *ASC.D*, ed. Cubbin, p. 46; E in *Two of the Saxon Chronicles*, ed. Plummer, I, 119; *Ælfric*, ed. Needham, p. 80; *English Historical Documents*, trans. Whitelock, no. 239(G). See above, pp. 124-27.

Figure 14: The Royal Dynasty of Man and the Isles, 940-1014

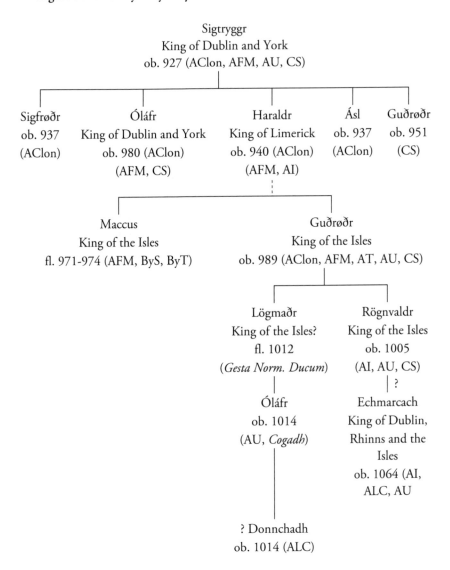

Sigtryggr
King of Dublin and York
ob. 927 (AClon, AFM, AU, CS)

Sigfrøðr
ob. 937
(AClon)

Óláfr
King of Dublin and York
ob. 980 (AClon)
(AFM, CS)

Haraldr
King of Limerick
ob. 940 (AClon)
(AFM, AI)

Ásl
ob. 937
(AClon)

Guðrøðr
ob. 951
(CS)

Maccus
King of the Isles
fl. 971-974 (AFM, ByS, ByT)

Guðrøðr
King of the Isles
ob. 989 (AClon, AFM, AT, AU, CS)

Lögmaðr
King of the Isles?
fl. 1012
(*Gesta Norm. Ducum*)

Rögnvaldr
King of the Isles
ob. 1005
(AI, AU, CS)

Óláfr
ob. 1014
(AU, *Cogadh*)

? Echmarcach
King of Dublin,
Rhinns and the
Isles
ob. 1064 (AI,
ALC, AU

? Donnchadh
ob. 1014 (ALC)

Worcester and William of Malmesbury, Maccus, 'king of many islands', was present at this event along with Cinaed of Alba, Mael Colaim of Strathclyde and three Brittonic kings.[95]

Edgar may have summoned this convention in response to the activities of Maccus Haraldsson in the Irish Sea. His naval power threatened to impinge on Edgar's sphere of influence in Wales and destabilise the northwestern frontiers of his kingdom. Edgar may also have been keen to ensure good trade-relations with the Isles. The early 970s mark a high point of hoarding activity in the Isles, which is indicative of their economic strength.[96] Colmán Etchingham has drawn attention to the fact that coins imitating Edgar's circulated in the Irish-Sea region. He has suggested that these were minted on Man.[97] This would reflect the voluminous trade between the two regions. However, rather than being evidence of good relations, as Etchingham has suggested, the production of imitative coin may have won Edgar's disapproval, and he may have sought to curtail such activity.

Edgar's concern about Irish-Sea affairs could have been combined with worries about the northern borders of his kingdom. Cinaed, king of Alba, had led campaigns against England and Strathclyde since his accession in 971.[98] As the royal family of Alba and the dynasty of Ívarr were closely connected during much of the tenth century, Edgar may have feared collusion between his enemies.[99] The meeting at Chester may therefore have offered a solution to an array of complex but interrelated issues.

It may be in consequence of their oath at Chester that the sons of Haraldr temporarily halted their activity in Wales and turned towards Ireland. Maccus, as mentioned above, attacked Limerick in 974.[100] However, it was not until 977 that his rival Ívarr, king of Limerick, was finally defeated. Ívarr was killed with his two sons at the behest of Brian

---

[95] John of Worcester, *Chronicle*, *s.a.* 973 (ed. and trans. Darlington *et al.*, II, 422-25); William of Malmesbury, *Gesta Regum Anglorum*, II.148 (ed. and trans. Mynors *et al.*, I, 238-41, and II, 132-33).

[96] Blackburn and Pagan, 'A Revised Checklist', nos 155, 159, 162, 165, 168, 169, 171, 186.

[97] Etchingham, 'North Wales', p. 180.

[98] 'The Scottish Chronicle', ed. and trans. Hudson, pp. 151, 161.

[99] See above, p. 126.

[100] See above, p. 54.

Bóruma while they took sanctuary in the church of St Senán on Scattery Island.[101] From this time Limerick seems to have been ruled by Brian.

Soon after an alliance is recorded between Brian Bóruma and the sons of Haraldr in 984, we get the first reports of fleets of *Danair*, 'Danes', in the Irish Sea. Barbara Crawford has suggested that these *Danair* were fleets of Sigurðr of Orkney.[102] As these records immediately pre-date Scandinavian attacks on England, it seems likely that *Danair* refers to the large fleets which attacked England during the 990s, although men from Orkney may have participated in these raids.[103] In 986, *Danair* raided Iona. Here they killed fifteen elders of the monastery and took Abbot Mael Ciaráin to Dublin where he was martyred.[104] This violence may have been entirely indiscriminate. However, the sequence of reported events raises the possibility that *Danair* had allied with the men of Dublin. Their attack on the Isles might be interpreted as revenge for the Islesmen's recent alliance with Brian Bóruma. Nevertheless, in 987 some *Danair* became allied with the Islesmen and they won a victory at Man with a son of Haraldr against an unnamed enemy.[105]

After Edgar's death Guðrøðr Haraldsson renewed his attacks on Wales. Primarily these seem focused on regaining control of Anglesey. Guðrøðr waged war first against Hywel ab Ieuaf and then against Maredudd ab Owain in which he was largely successful. In 987, the Welsh chronicles state, he captured two thousand of Maredudd's men from Anglesey.[106] Two years later, Maredudd paid tribute of a penny for each person to 'Dark

---

[101] *Annals of Clonmacnoise, s.a.* 970 [=977] (ed. Murphy, p. 158); *Annals of the Four Masters, s.a.* 975 [=977] (ed. and trans. O'Donovan, II, 704-05); *Annals of Inisfallen, s.a.* [977] (ed. and trans. Mac Airt, pp. 162-63); *Annals of Tigernach, s.a.* [977] (ed. and trans. Stokes, II, 231); *Chronicum Scotorum, s.a.* [975] [=977] (ed. and trans. Hennessy, pp. 224-25).

[102] Crawford, *Scandinavian Scotland*, p. 66.

[103] Etchingham, 'North Wales', p. 177.

[104] *Annals of Clonmacnoise, s.a.* 980 [=986] (ed. Murphy, p. 160); *Annals of the Four Masters, s.aa.* 985 [=986], 985 [=986] (ed. and trans. O'Donovan, II, 718-19); *Annals of Inisfallen, s.a.* [986] (ed. and trans. Mac Airt, pp. 166-67); *Annals of Roscrea,* §291 (ed. Gleeson and Mac Airt, p. 172); *Annals of Ulster, s.a.* 985 [=986].3 (ed. and trans. Mac Airt and Mac Niocaill, pp. 420-21); *Chronicum Scotorum, s.a.* [984] [=986] (ed. and trans. Hennessy, pp. 230-31).

[105] *Annals of Ulster, s.a.* 986 [=987].1 (ed. and trans. Mac Airt and Mac Niocaill, pp. 420-21).

[106] *ByS, s.a.* 987 (ed. and trans. Jones, pp. 44-45); *ByT* (Pen. 20), *s.a.* 987 (ed. Jones, p. 11; trans. Jones, pp. 7-8); *ByT* (RBH), *s.a.* 987 (ed. and trans. Jones, pp. 16-17).

Foreigners'. It is not certain whether Guðrøðr reaped the benefits of this payment. He was killed in 989 in Dál Riata in northeastern Ireland. As three ships of *Danair* had also been defeated there in 986, the incident may be evidence of political friction over control of the North Channel between Britain and Ireland at this time.[107]

Literary references to Guðrøðr's career are found in thirteenth-century Icelandic sagas. Although these may have little historical value, they show the significance assigned to him long after his death. According to *Njáls saga* and *Eyrbyggja saga*, Sigurðr of Orkney plundered Man during the reign of Guðrøðr Haraldsson, and he took tribute from the northern Hebrides which were ruled by a jarl called Gilli.[108] *Orkneyinga saga* makes no reference to Gilli but does refer to Sigurðr's raids in the Irish Sea.[109] Sigurðr's well attested participation at Clontarf in 1014 suggests that he may have been flexing his muscles in the Irish Sea during these years.[110] It is possible that before his death in 989 Guðrøðr had contact with Sigurðr. Icelandic sagas indicate that the Northern Isles had a significant part to play in the history of the Hebrides. This was probably so, but contemporary written sources give little insight into this dimension of affairs as they are focused on events in Ireland and England.

The careers of Maccus and Guðrøðr seem to mark a political high point in the history of the Hebrides and Man. Following their reigns the Isles suffered a political decline. It may be relevant that coin-hoarding in Man slackened from about 995 to about 1030. Nevertheless, hoarding continued elsewhere in the Isles and on the nearby mainland, as witnessed by significant finds from Stornoway (Isle of Lewis), Inchkenneth (Mull) and Kilmartin (Argyll).[111] This could signify the decentralisation of power in the

---

[107] Both events are reported in *Annals of Ulster, s.aa.* 985 [=986].2, 988 [=989].4 (ed. and trans. Mac Airt and Mac Niocaill, pp. 418-21).

[108] *Njáls saga*, §§85, 89, 154 (ed. Einar Ól. Sveinsson, pp. 205, 224, 440; trans. Magnusson and Pálsson, pp. 182, 196, 341-42); *Eyrbyggja saga*, §29 (ed. Einar Ól. Sveinsson and Matthías Þorðarson, p. 76; trans. Pálsson and Edwards, p. 80).

[109] *Orkneyinga saga*, §11 (ed. Finnbogi Guðmundsson, p. 24; trans. Pálsson and Edwards, p. 36); Etchingham, 'North Wales', pp. 173-74.

[110] *Annals of Boyle*, §281 ('The Annals', ed. Freeman, p. 328); *Annals of the Four Masters, s.a.* 1013 [=1014] (ed. and trans. O'Donovan, II, 776-77); *Annals of Ulster, s.a.* 1014.2 (ed. and trans. Mac Airt and Mac Niocaill, pp. 446-47); *Chronicum Scotorum, s.a.* [1012] [=1014] (ed. and trans. Hennessy, pp. 252-53).

[111] Blackburn and Pagan, 'A Revised Checklist', nos 182a, 191, 194. The dates of deposition are *c.* 990- *c.* 1040, *c.* 1000 and *c.* 1000, respectively.

Isles and a corresponding political crisis as external powers vied for control over the region. In 995, Welsh chronicles report, the Danish king Sveinn Haraldsson ravaged Man.[112] In 1000, Æthelred, king of England, also led a campaign against Man, presumably to offset Scandinavian influence.[113] The next reported king of the Isles, Rögnvaldr son of Guðrøðr Haraldsson, died outside his kingdom, in Munster in 1005.[114] He seems to have been significant enough on the Irish political scene to warrant record, but the circumstances of his death are uncertain. This raises the question whether he was attempting to regain control of Limerick or had he become an ally of Brian Bóruma?[115]

It is not certain who ruled the Isles at the time of the battle of Clontarf. However, king Lagmann, who had been active in northern France, is a strong candidate.[116] This link is suggested by the subsequently reported death of Óláfr son of Lagmann at the battle of Clontarf.[117] William of Jumièges stated that Lagmann worked as a mercenary in England and Normandy shortly before the battle of Clontarf, so he may have been a king living in exile. It is possible that, after the death of Rögnvaldr Guðrøðsson in Munster in 1005, Brian Bóruma expelled Lagmann in an attempt to bring the kingdom of Man and the Isles fully under his own control.[118]

At Clontarf the Islesmen fought alongside the troops of Dublin. According to *Njáls saga*, Bróðir was the leader of a fleet met by Sigtryggr Silkiskeggi off the west coast of Man.[119] The saga states that Sigtryggr promised his mother and his kingdom for Bróðir's support. This may be an exaggeration. Perhaps more reliably, *Brut y Tywysogyon* and *Brenhinedd y*

---

[112] *ByS, s.a.* 995 (ed. and trans. Jones, pp. 48-49); *ByT* (Pen. 20), *s.a.* 995 (ed. Jones, p. 13; trans. Jones, p. 11); *ByT* (RBH), *s.a.* 995 (ed. and trans. Jones, pp. 18-19).

[113] *ASC.C*, ed. O'Keeffe, p. 88; *ASC.D*, ed. Cubbin, p. 50; E in *Two of the Saxon Chronicles*, ed. Plummer, I, 133.

[114] *Annals of Inisfallen, s.a.* [1004] (ed. and trans. Mac Airt, pp. 176-77); *Annals of Ulster, s.a.* 1004 [=1005].1 (ed. and trans. Mac Airt and Mac Niocaill, pp. 434-35); *Chronicum Scotorum, s.a.* [1003] [=1005] (ed. and trans. Hennessy, pp. 242-43).

[115] Etchingham, 'North Wales', p. 180.

[116] *Gesta Normannorum Ducum*, V.8, 11-12 (ed. and trans. van Houts, II, 18-21, 24-27); des Gautries, *Les Noms*, p. 69, n. 12. See above, pp. 133-34.

[117] *Cogadh*, ed. and trans. Todd, p. 271.

[118] *Cogadh*, §78 (ed. and trans. Todd, pp. 136-37); Hudson, *Kings*, p. 113.

[119] *Njáls saga*, §155 (ed. Einar Ól. Sveinsson, p. 445; trans. Magnusson and Pálsson, p. 344).

Saesson state that Sigtryggr hired Bróðir and his followers to fight for him.[120] 'The Annals of Ulster' identify Bróðir as chief (*toísech*) of the fleet of *Lochlann*, which might refer to a broad area of Scandinavian settlement including Norway and the Scottish islands.[121] Óláfr son of Lagmann is named as one of his companions.[122]

After Clontarf, close political links are attested between Dublin and the Isles.[123] Numismatic evidence suggests that the Isles benefited from this association during the reign of Echmarcach Røgnvaldsson, who ruled Dublin and the Isles intermittently from 1030 to 1065.[124] In the eleventh century, Echmarcach attempted to win power in Galloway.[125] This suggests that control of the sea-lanes of the Irish Sea remained significant to Ívarr's descendants after 1014, no doubt because a substantial portion of their revenue depended on external contacts.

The written evidence highlights the involvement of the dynasty of Ívarr in the Hebrides and Man. The kingdom emerges as a significant entity in the historical sources from the mid-tenth century. It may have become a base for viking leaders exiled from York in 954. In the 960s and 970s kings of the Isles influenced affairs of Ireland, Wales and England. The Isles also accrued much wealth through trade and political alliances during these years, as shown by the distribution of coin-hoards. However, during the 990s the political fortunes of the Isles suffered decline. This may be partly

---

[120] *ByS*, *s.a.* 1014 (ed. and trans. Jones, pp. 50-51); *ByT* (Pen. 20), *s.a.* 1014 (ed. Jones, p. 14; trans. Jones, p. 10); *ByT* (RBH), *s.a.* 1014 (ed. and trans. Jones, pp. 20-21).

[121] Less reliably, 'The Annals of Clonmacnoise' identify Bróðir as earl of Orkney (*s.a.* 996 [=1002×1014].1, ed. Murphy, p. 166) and 'The Annals of Loch Cé' state that he was earl of York: *s.a.* 1014 (ed. and trans. Hennessy, I, 4-5); Ó Corráin, 'The Vikings in Scotland', pp. 306-10. On *Lochlann*, see above, pp. xvi, 15-16.

[122] *Annals of Ulster*, *s.a.* 1014.2 (ed. and trans. Mac Airt and Mac Niocaill, pp. 446-49).

[123] Duffy, 'Irishmen', pp. 93-110; Etchingham, 'North Wales', pp. 180-82.

[124] Blackburn and Pagan, 'A Revised Checklist', nos 219, 228, 230, 231, 248, 278, 283; Bornholdt, 'Myth or Mint?'

[125] *Mariani Scoti Chronicon*, ed. Waitz, p. 559; *Historia Gruffud*, §4 (*A Mediaeval Prince*, ed. and trans. Evans, pp. 24, 54); Hill, *Whithorn*, pp. 48-60, 195-97, 335-36, 344-45, 369-70, 621-23; Duffy, 'Irishmen', p. 99; Etchingham, 'North Wales', pp. 157-60. Etchingham has supported the historicity of the statements in *Historia Gruffudd* concerning the power of Óláfr Sigtryggsson (*ob.* 1034). However, the statement that he ruled Galloway may be contradicted by reports of the death of Suibne son of Cinaed, king of Galloway, in 1034: *Annals of Tigernach*, *s.a.* [1034] (ed. and trans. Stokes, II, 266); *Annals of Ulster*, *s.a.* 1034.10 (ed. and trans. Mac Airt and Mac Niocaill, pp. 472-73).

due to the rise of Brian Bóruma in Ireland, at the expense of vikings. Brian seems to have manipulated the potential for dissension between different branches of the dynasty of Ívarr, thus positioning the Isles against Dublin in 984. The decline may also result from political instability in the Irish-Sea region, which followed the arrival of large Scandinavian fleets from the late 980s. Initially the Islesmen seem to have allied with some of the new arrivals, but in the ensuing struggle for power in and around the Irish Sea, Man was attacked by both Danish and English fleets. It is not until after the battle of Clontarf that there is evidence of economic recovery: a new phase in the history of the kingdom of the Isles began through close links with Dublin.[126]

[126] Duffy, 'Irishmen'; Downham, 'Living on the Edge'.

7

Wales

THROUGHOUT the late ninth and tenth centuries the dynasty of Ívarr competed with English rulers to bring Wales within their sphere of influence. Much of this rivalry focused on the north-western territory of Wales, Gwynedd. This was the most powerful of the Welsh kingdoms in the ninth century. Gwynedd was naturally defended against its inland neighbours by the mountains of Snowdonia yet it boasted the agricultural wealth of Anglesey (dubbed 'the Mother of Wales' due to its cornage) and the Llyn peninsula. Anglesey, then as now, was well located for sea-traffic from Ireland, and the north coast of Gwynedd overlooked the main sea-routes to Chester. Chester was a gateway to a Roman road-network which led from the Irish Sea to York and it became a major port in the tenth century as a result of viking activity. In the late tenth century, campaigns were also led against South Wales by the descendants of Ívarr and by fleets from Scandinavia. This shift in operations can be linked with Scandinavian campaigns in southern England and the economic development of Bristol on the River Severn. The location of Wales gave it a strategic significance to vikings based in Ireland. The dynasty of Ívarr had an enduring interest in Welsh affairs which lasted beyond 1014.

As Welsh chronicles are the main sources for this topic, it seems necessary to begin with some remarks on their date and character. They can be broadly grouped into Latin and Welsh texts. *Annales Cambriae* survive in three main versions, each represented by a single manuscript. All versions were apparently based on a Latin chronicle which was kept originally at St Davids (Pembrokeshire). The earliest is the 'A-text' in London, British Library, MS Harley 3859. This version seems to have been compiled between 954 (its last record) and 977. It survives in a manuscript written about 1100.[1] The later 'B' and 'C' texts are more closely related to each other than to 'A'. As they stand they date from the late thirteenth century.[2]

---

[1] Hughes, *Celtic Britain*, p. 67.
[2] *ByT* (Pen. 20), trans. Jones, p. xl.

The ultimate common ancestor of 'B' and 'C' seems to have remained at St Davids until at least 1202.[3]

The Welsh chronicles, published as *Brut y Tywysogyon* (in two versions) and *Brenhinedd y Saesson*, contain closely related records of Welsh events for the period in question.[4] The antecedent text of this group seems to have been compiled in the late thirteenth century, as a translation of a text related to *Annales Cambriae*.[5] The surviving Welsh chronicles thus seem largely dependent on a Latin text which was kept at St Davids during our period of study. It is interesting therefore that, despite the southern orientation of the Welsh record, most viking events in the ninth and early tenth centuries are linked to North Wales.[6] Probably more events took place in North Wales than the records allow us to see, and this impression is confirmed by comparison with English and Irish chronicles for the period. The evident focus of viking attacks on North Wales can be explained by its geographical proximity to Dublin and by the involvement of Dubliners in northern England.

Vikings from Ireland became a force to be reckoned with in Wales from the mid-ninth century. A Welsh leader, Cyngen, was slain by vikings in 850.[7] Three years later, Anglesey was ravaged by 'Dark Foreigners'. In 855 the Wrekin district of Shropshire, near the border with Wales, was also raided.[8] The first Welsh victory against vikings is reported in 856 when Rhodri Mawr, king of Gwynedd, killed a chieftain of the 'Dark Foreigners' named Ormr.[9] According to the eleventh-century saga-element in 'The

---

[3] Hughes, *Celtic Britain*, p. 74; *Annales Cambriae*, ed. and trans. Dumville, p. xiii.

[4] *ByS*, ed. and trans. Jones, p. xiv. For more recent discussion, see *Brenhinoedd*, ed. and trans. Dumville.

[5] *ByT* (Pen. 20), trans. Jones, p. xxxiv.

[6] David Dumville has shown that a North Welsh chronicle was used directly or indirectly as a source in *Annales Cambriae* to 858, and perhaps later: *Annales Cambriae*, ed. and trans. Dumville, pp. ix-x.

[7] *Annales Cambriae* (AB), ed. Dumville, pp. 10-11; *ByS*, ed. and trans. Jones, pp. 18-19; *ByT* (Pen. 20), ed. Jones, p. 5; *ByT* (Pen. 20), trans. Jones, p. 4; *ByT* (RBH), ed. and trans. Jones, pp. 8-9; Maund, *The Welsh Kings*, p. 37.

[8] *Annales Cambriae* (ABC), ed. and trans. Dumville, pp. 12-13; *ByS*, ed. and trans. Jones, pp. 18-19; *ByT* (Pen. 20), ed. Jones, p. 5; *ByT* (Pen. 20), trans. Jones, p. 4; *ByT* (RBH), ed. and trans. Jones, pp. 8-9; Sawyer, *Anglo-Saxon Charters*, no. 206; *English Historical Documents*, trans. Whitelock, no. 90.

[9] *Annals of Ulster*, s.a. 855 [=856].6 (ed. and trans. Mac Airt and Mac Niocaill, pp. 314-15); *Chronicum Scotorum*, s.a. [856] (ed. and trans. Hennessy, pp. 154-55).

Fragmentary Annals of Ireland', Ormr was in Ireland in 852 and around 855.[10] If this account holds any truth, it suggests that campaigns were being led across the Irish Sea. Rhodri's victory seems to have brought some respite from vikings, as no further attacks are reported in Wales for the next decade.

Rhodri Mawr ruled Gwynedd (844-78). During his reign, Rhodri seems to have extended his authority over the central Welsh kingdoms of Powys (after 855) and Ceredigion (872), following the death of native kings.[11] Kari Maund has argued that Rhodri benefited from the political weakness of England caused by viking attacks from the 850s.[12] Nevertheless, Wales also had vikings to contend with and the English invaded Wales in 865. 'The Annals of Ulster' report that an English force drove the Welsh from their land and placed [them] in bondage in *Maen Chonain* (Anglesey).[13] The event corresponds chronologically with Welsh records of a raid led by the English ealdorman Duda on Glywysing (the land between the Tawe and the Usk in South Wales).[14] The inhabitants of this region were also said to have been driven into exile, highlighting the devastating nature of the campaign. Thus it appears that English rulers initially maintained an aggressive stance towards Wales despite viking depredations.

From 865, vikings were making great inroads into British territories. The fall of York in 867 is mentioned in the Welsh chronicles, as is the fall of Dumbarton in 870.[15] The records thus demonstrate interest, and perhaps apprehension, concerning the achievements of viking armies elsewhere in Britain. In 873, Mercia fell into viking hands and viking armies may have extended their campaigns across the Mercian border.[16] Battles are recorded in Anglesey in 874 and 877, which some commentators have associated

[10] *Fragmentary Annals*, §§235, 251, 254 (ed. and trans. Radner, pp. 92-93, 98-101).

[11] Dumville, 'The "Six" Sons', p. 15; Maund, *The Welsh Kings*, pp. 41-44. Ystrad Tywi may also have been brought within Rhodri's dominion, but again this deduction is dependent on negative evidence.

[12] *Ibid.*, p. 50.

[13] *Annals of Ulster, s.a.* 864 [=865].4 (ed. and trans. Mac Airt and Mac Niocaill, pp. 320-21); *Fragmentary Annals*, §315 (ed. and trans. Radner, pp. 116-17).

[14] *ByT* (Pen. 20), trans. Jones, p. 136, n. 4.27.

[15] *Annales Cambriae, s.a.* [867], [871] (ed. and trans. Dumville, pp. 12-13); *ByS, s.a.* 866 [=867], 870 [=871] (ed. and trans. Jones, pp. 20-23); *ByT* (Pen. 20), *s.a.* 866 [=867], 870 [=871] (ed. Jones, p. 5; trans. Jones, pp. 4-5); *ByT* (RBH), *s.a.* [867] [=871] (ed. and trans. Jones, pp. 8-9).

[16] *Fragmentary Annals*, §410 (ed. and trans. Radner, pp. 148-49).

with vikings.[17] The 'Sunday Battle', fought on Anglesey in 877, could be linked with the departure of Rhodri Mawr for Ireland that year, 'in flight from the Foreigners'.[18]

According to 'The Anglo-Saxon Chronicle', vikings were also active in South Wales. A brother of Ívarr and Hálfdan over-wintered in Dyfed in 877, before leading twenty-three ships against Wessex.[19] The king of Dyfed at this date was Hyfaidd ab Bleddri. He was an ally of King Alfred by 885. However it is unclear whether they were already cooperating by 877 and we cannot deduce whether Ívarr's brother was deliberately seeking to subdue Hyfaidd as a precursor to campaigning against Alfred.[20] Nevertheless the movements of Ívarr's brother seem to have been part of a bigger strategy. His subsequent attack on Devon coincided with another campaign against Wessex by another viking army from Chippenham. This looks like a two-pronged attack on the West-Saxon kingdom.

The Sons of Rhodri Mawr

In 878, Rhodri Mawr, king of Gwynedd, and his kinsman Gwriad were killed by the English.[21] It has been suggested that Ceolwulf II, king of the Mercians led the attack under viking orders.[22] Three years later in a battle fought at Conwy between unnamed enemies, the Welsh chronicles agree, 'Rhodri was avenged'.[23] The avengers may have been the sons of Rhodri. Three of them can be clearly identified in Welsh chronicles.[24] Merfyn was killed in 903, Cadell died in 909 and Anarawd in 916 (another son, Gwriad, is also mentioned, but his career is shadowy). Over the next decade

---

[17] Charles, *Old Norse Relations*, p. 6; Collingwood and Powell, *Scandinavian Britain*, p. 189.

[18] *Annals of Ulster*, s.a. 876 [=877].3 (ed. and trans. Mac Airt and Mac Niocaill, pp. 332-33).

[19] *ASC.A*, ed. Bately, p. 50; *ASC.B*, ed. Taylor, p. 37; *ASC.C*, ed. O'Keeffe, p. 61; *ASC.D*, ed. Cubbin, p. 27; E in *Two of the Saxon Chronicles*, ed. Plummer, I, 75.

[20] *De Rebus Gestis Ælfredi*, §80 (*Asser's Life*, ed. Stevenson, pp. 66-67; *Alfred*, trans. Keynes and Lapidge, p. 96).

[21] *Annales Cambriae* (ABC), s.a. [878] (ed. and trans. Dumville, pp. 12-13); *ByS*, s.a. 877 [=878] (ed. and trans. Jones, pp. 24-25); *ByT* (Pen. 20), s.a. 877 [=878] (ed. Jones, p. 6; trans. Jones, p. 5); *ByT* (RBH), s.a. [878] (ed. and trans. Jones, pp. 8-9).

[22] Charles-Edwards, 'Wales and Mercia', p. 101.

[23] *Annales Cambriae* (ABC), s.a. [881] (ed. and trans. Dumville, pp. 12-13); *ByS*, s.a. 880 [=881] (ed. and trans. Jones, pp. 24-25); *ByT* (Pen. 20), s.a. 880 [=881] (ed. Jones, p. 6; trans. Jones, p. 5); *ByT* (RBH), s.a. [881] (ed. and trans. Jones, pp. 8-9).

[24] Dumville, 'The "Six" Sons', p. 8.

these brothers made common cause with enemies of the English. They were also progenitors of a dynasty which was to dominate Welsh politics for the remainder of the Viking Age.

Within the period 878×893, sons of Rhodri were allied with the vikings of Northumbria.[25] Nevertheless, the kings of South Wales (Hyfaidd of Dyfed, Hywel of Glywysing, and Brochfael and Ffernfael of Gwent) submitted to King Alfred by 885. According to Asser, the Welsh biographer of King Alfred, they submitted through fear of Æthelred, Alfred's son-in-law who ruled Mercia, and of the sons of Rhodri. Anarawd son of Rhodri was won over to Alfred's side by 893. According to Asser, Alfred received him honourably and accorded him equal status to his own son-in-law. These generous terms may indicate Alfred's eagerness to draw Anarawd's support away from the family of Ívarr.[26]

The vikings seem to have responded to Anarawd's political realignment by attacking his territory. In 890 (or perhaps 892 – there is a two-year dislocation in the chronology of *Brut y Tywysogyon* and *Brenhinedd y Saesson* at some point in the 890s), vikings harried either in Gwynedd or in Powys 'for the second time'.[27] It is uncertain when the first raid occurred. Then in 893 a viking army from Benfleet (Essex) collected supporters from Northumbria and East Anglia and arrived at the borders of Wales. It travelled to Buttington (Montgomeryshire) where the vikings were besieged and then heavily defeated by a combined force of English and Welsh troops.[28] The survivors fled to Essex.[29] It may have been in the same year that English troops allied with Anarawd to ravage other Welsh territories, perhaps as a reward for his allegiance.[30] It appears that Anarawd was able to turn English anxiety about vikings to his advantage. In 893, the viking

[25] *De Rebus Gestis Ælfredi*, §80 (*Asser's Life*, ed. Stevenson, pp. 66-67; *Alfred*, trans. Keynes and Lapidge, p. 96).

[26] Anarawd seems to have had his base in Anglesey at this date: Dumville, 'The "Six" Sons', p. 17.

[27] *ByT* (Pen. 20), trans. Jones, p. 138, n. 5.28. These vikings are identified as 'Black Northmen'.

[28] Redknap, *Vikings in Wales*, p. 32.

[29] *ASC.A*, ed. Bately, pp. 55-58; *ASC.B*, ed. Taylor, pp. 41-43; *ASC.C*, ed. O'Keeffe, pp. 66-68; *ASC.D*, ed. Cubbin, pp. 31-33.

[30] *Annales Cambriae* (ABC), *s.a.* [893] (ed. and trans. Dumville, pp. 14-15); *ByS*, *s.a.* 893 [=895] (ed. and trans. Jones, pp. 26-27); *ByT* (Pen. 20), *s.a.* 893 [=895] (ed. Jones, p. 6; trans. Jones, p. 5); *ByT* (RBH), *s.a.* [895] (ed. and trans. Jones, pp. 10-11).

army in Essex gathered reinforcements from Northumbria and East Anglia and travelled to the strategically significant site of Chester. Here they used the remaining Roman fortifications for defence.[31]

According to 'The Anglo-Saxon Chronicle', the viking army from Chester raided Wales in 894.[32] This could correspond with the record in *Brut y Tywysogyon*, *Brenhinedd y Saesson* and *Annales Cambriae* (A) of viking attacks on England, Brycheiniog, Morgannwg, Gwent, Buellt and Gwynllwg in south Wales, providing further details of this campaign.[33] The correctness of the chronology of the Welsh chronicles at this point is suggested by their report that there was a famine in Ireland the following year, which agrees with the record of 'The Annals of Ulster' for 895.[34] The areas of Wales which were attacked from Chester all seem to have been outside the control of the sons of Rhodri. It is possible that the vikings deliberately avoided their lands through fear of another confrontation.

By 896, the threat of the main viking force in England seems to have receded, although in the late tenth century Æthelweard suggested that there was some disturbance in the year of Alfred's death.[35] The next viking incursions in Wales are reported soon after the expulsion of the viking leaders from Dublin by the combined forces of Brega and the Laigin in 902.[36] The eleventh-century 'Osraige Chronicle' embodied in 'The Fragmentary Annals of Ireland' provides an account of the arrival of Ingimundr in Wales, following his expulsion from Ireland.[37] His arrival is recorded in the Welsh chronicles, which report his seizure of *Maes Osfeilion*.[38] John O'Donovan identified the location as Penros near

---

[31] *ASC.A*, ed. Bately, pp. 55-58; *ASC.B*, ed. Taylor, pp. 41-43; *ASC.C*, ed. O'Keeffe, pp. 66-68; *ASC.D*, ed. Cubbin, pp. 31-33.

[32] *ASC.A*, ed. Bately, pp. 58-59; *ASC.B*, ed. Taylor, p. 43; *ASC.C*, ed. O'Keeffe, p. 69; *ASC.D*, ed. Cubbin, p. 33.

[33] *Annales Cambriae* (A), *s.a.* [894] (ed. and trans. Dumville, p. 14); *ByS*, *s.a.* 894 [=896] (ed. and trans. Jones, pp. 26-27); *ByT* (Pen. 20), *s.a.* 894 [=896] (ed. Jones, p. 6; trans. Jones, p. 5); *ByT* (RBH), *s.a.* [896] (ed. and trans. Jones, pp. 10-11).

[34] Thomas Jones dated these events two years later. The surrounding annals are one year behind.

[35] Æthelweard, *Chronicon*, IV.3 (ed. and trans. Campbell, p. 51).

[36] *Annals of Ulster*, *s.a.* 901 [=902].2 (ed. and trans. Mac Airt and Mac Niocaill, pp. 352-53).

[37] *Fragmentary Annals*, §429 (ed. and trans. Radner, pp. 168-69).

[38] *Annales Cambriae*, *s.a.* [902] (ed. and trans. Dumville, pp. 14-15); *ByS*, *s.a.* 900 [=903] (ed. and trans. Jones, pp. 26-27); *ByT* (Pen. 20), *s.a.* 900 [=903] (ed. Jones, pp. 6-7; trans. Jones, p. 6); *ByT* (RBH), *s.a.* [903] (ed. and trans. Jones, pp. 10-11).

Holyhead and was followed by B.G. Charles.[39] However, more recent commentators (Wendy Davies, David Griffiths and Mark Redknap) have argued that Maes Rosmelion in eastern Anglesey is more likely because of the similarity of the name.[40]

Ingimundr's invasion is perhaps the most famous record of a viking attack on Wales. Historians have seized upon it as one of the few recorded events which addresses the question of what happened to the exiled vikings of Dublin after 902. According to 'The Fragmentary Annals of Ireland', Ingimundr was soon driven away from Anglesey.[41] Nevertheless some vikings from Dublin may have settled, as archaeological evidence shows viking influence on the island in the tenth century. At Glyn, Llanbedrgoch, a pre-Viking-Age settlement was taken over (or heavily influenced) by vikings in the early tenth century.[42] Three houses in Hiberno-Scandinavian style have been excavated at the site, and there is considerable evidence of craft- and mercantile activity which shows involvement in trade between York, Dublin and other Scandinavian colonies.[43] Near to Llanbedrgoch, a furnished burial was recovered at Benllech; and about 905, five Hiberno-Scandinavian armlets were deposited about at Dinorben quarry in Red Wharf Bay.[44] Elsewhere on Angelesey, at an unrecorded location, a small hoard of Anglo-Saxon and Anglo-Scandinavian coins was deposited about 915.[45] Further evidence of viking influence clusters around the Menai Straits (between Anglesey and the mainland) which includes two tenth-

---

[39] *Annals of Ireland: Three Fragments*, ed. and trans. O'Donovan, p. 226, note n; Charles, *Old Norse Relations*, p. 17.

[40] Davies, *Patterns*, p. 56; Griffiths, 'The North-West Frontier', p. 179; Redknap, *Vikings in Wales*, p. 45.

[41] *Fragmentary Annals*, §429 (ed. and trans. Radner, pp. 168-69).

[42] The excavation-director, Mark Redknap, has suggested that vikings may have taken over the site in the early tenth century. Colmán Etchingham has argued that vikings were responsible for the refortification of this site in the late ninth century. Redknap, *Vikings in Wales*, pp. 69-74; Etchingham, 'North Wales', p. 163.

[43] Redknap, *Vikings in Wales*, pp. 65-80.

[44] Edwards, 'A Possible Viking Grave'; Redknap, *Vikings in Wales*, p. 96.

[45] Davies, *Patterns*, pp. 52-53; Blackburn and Pagan, 'A Revised Checklist', no. 98. Single coins have also been found at Llanbedrgoch (Louis the Pious, 814-40, and Charles the Bald, 840-77), Holyhead (Edward the Martyr, 975-78/79) and Caernarfon (Pepin of Aquitaine, 814-52). Other finds from the island include part of a tenth-century copper-alloy ring-pin from Llanfairpwllgwyngyll: Early Medieval Corpus, nos 1991:0116, 1991:0118, 1976:0006, 1991:0117; Redknap, *Vikings in Wales*, p. 98.

century silver-hoards from Bangor. The designs of two tenth-century crosses at Penmon also show evidence of contact with viking colonies on the Cumbrian coastal plain.[46] The activities of Ingimundr can be seen to mark a new era in the history of north Wales when the area was drawn more tightly within the trading network of viking settlements around the Irish Sea.

According to 'The Fragmentary Annals of Ireland' Ingimundr was expelled from Anglesey by a son of Cadell son of Rhodri.[47] Ingimundr then travelled to Mercia and was granted lands near Chester by Æthelflæd of Mercia.[48] This grant is not witnessed in other sources, although there is ample evidence of Scandinavian settlement around the Dee-estuary and in Chester itself.[49] If the account were true, Æthelflæd would not have been the first ruler in Europe to yield strategic lands at a river-estuary to vikings.[50] Such a policy was used to defend coastal areas from further incursions, by using a group of 'friendly' vikings to fend off others. According to 'The Fragmentary Annals of Ireland' this policy backfired, although Æthelflæd successfully defended Chester from the ensuing attack. 'The Mercian Register' (found in versions B, C and D of 'The Anglo-Saxon Chronicle') reports that Æthelflæd restored the city in 907.[51] This action seems to have been a success. Chester remained in English hands, and the tenth-century development of the city brought considerable revenues to English rulers. Chester's significance for Irish-Sea trade no doubt influenced some of the later policies of both Ívarr's descendants and English rulers towards North Wales.

The continued links between Chester and Dublin are witnessed by finds along the north-east coast of Wales.[52] There are carved stones at Dyserth, Maen Achwyfan and Meliden which can be associated with the Cheshire-

---

[46] *Ibid.*, p. 18; Blackburn and Pagan, 'A Revised Checklist', nos 56a, 98, 106, 150; Bu'Lock, 'Pre-Norman Crosses', pp. 3-4; Edwards, 'Viking-influenced Sculpture', p. 96.

[47] *Fragmentary Annals*, §429 (ed. and trans. Radner, pp. 168-69). The saga-account cannot be regarded as trustworthy on this point.

[48] *Ibid.*

[49] Fellows-Jensen, 'Scandinavian Place-names', pp. 39-40; Smart, 'Scandinavians', p. 182; Jesch, 'Scandinavian Wirral', p. 3.

[50] Nelson, 'The Frankish Empire', p. 41.

[51] *ASC.B*, ed. Taylor, p. 49; *ASC.C*, ed. O'Keeffe, p. 75. This item is not in 'D'.

[52] Davies, *Patterns*, p. 54. Cf. Loyn, *The Vikings in Wales*.

group of Anglo-Scandinavian sculpture.[53] A male viking burial has been excavated at Talacre in Flintshire and a few Scandinavian place-names in the area are also recorded in 'Domesday Book'.[54] The development of a cult of Brigit at Dyserth may point to links with viking colonies in Ireland.[55]

In the year after Ingimundr's adventures in Wales, Merfyn son of Rhodri was slain. *Brut y Tywysogyon* and *Brenhinedd y Saesson* state that he was killed by his own men, but the C-text of *Annales Cambriae* reports that vikings were responsible.[56] Thomas Jones argued that there may have been confusion in the Latin antecedents of these chronicles, between *gentibus* (intended as 'men') and *gentilibus* ('heathens', i.e., vikings), which caused this disparity.[57] He favoured the report of *Annales Cambriae* (C) attributing the deed to vikings. However, this is far from certain.

In seeking to gain a foothold in Britain, two grandsons of Ívarr were fighting in Pictland in 904, accompanied by *Catol*.[58] It has been argued that he was a viking leader named Ketill.[59] However, the names *Catel(l)* in Old Welsh (Modern Welsh Cadell) and Old Norse Ketill are indistinguishable in Irish records, and *Catol* could therefore represent either name.[60] No viking leader named Ketill is otherwise referred to in the Irish chronicles

---

[53] Bu'Lock, 'Pre-Norman Crosses', pp. 7-8; Edwards, 'Viking-Influenced Sculpture', pp. 96, 98.

[54] Smith, 'Talacre'; Davies, *Patterns*, p. 54, n. 8; Redknap, *Vikings in Wales*, p. 19; Edwards, 'Viking-influenced Sculpture', p. 96.

[55] Edwards, 'Viking-influenced Sculpture', pp. 7, 14. The coastal route between Chester and Anglesey is linked by finds which could indicate the activity of viking traders, such as the discovery of a pseudo-penannular brooch at Llys Awel near Abergele (Denbighshire) and finds of tenth-century Chester-ware at Rhuddlan. Most Chester-ware has been found in the borders, which can be explained by its use among the English. It was also exported from Chester to Dublin. It has been found at Llanbedrgoch: see Redknap, *Vikings in Wales*, p. 64.

[56] *Annales Cambriae* (C), s.a. [903] (ed. and trans. Dumville, pp. 14-15); *ByS*, s.a. 901 [=904] (ed. and trans. Jones, pp. 26-27); *ByT* (Pen. 20), s.a. 901 [=904] (ed. Jones, p. 7; trans. Jones, p. 6); *ByT* (RBH), s.a. [904] (ed. and trans. Jones, pp. 10-11).

[57] *ByT* (Pen. 20), trans. Jones, p. 140, n. 6.10.

[58] *Chronicum Scotorum*, s.a. [904] (ed. and trans. Hennessy, pp. 178-81).

[59] *Early Sources*, trans. Anderson, I, 398, n. 9.

[60] The forms *Caittil* and *Cathal* for Ketill are found respectively in: *Annals of Ulster*, s.a. 856 [=857].1 (ed. and trans. Mac Airt and Mac Niocaill, pp. 314-25); *Chronicum Scotorum*, s.a. [857] (ed. and trans. Hennessy, pp. 154-55). The forms *Caittell*, *Caitill*, and *Cathal* for Cadell are found in: *Chronicum Scotorum*, s.a. [908] (ed. and trans. Hennessy, pp. 184-85); *Fragmentary Annals*, §§426, 429 (ed. and trans. Radner, pp. 166-69); *Three Irish Glossaries*, ed. Stokes, p. 8; *Sanas Chormaic*, trans. O'Donovan and Stokes, p. 29.

around this time.[61] However, Cadell ap Rhodri is mentioned in *Chronicum Scotorum*, 'The Fragmentary Annals of Ireland' and 'The Annals of Clonmacnoise' on his death in 909.[62] The possibility that *Catol* might be Cadell is worthy of consideration.

Cadell seems to have developed a power-base in Dyfed following the death of its last native king, Llywarch, in 904.[63] His achievements led to rivalry between the progeny of Cadell based in South Wales and that of his brother Awarawd based in Gwynedd. For a decade after 904, the descendants of Ívarr seem to have ceased hostilities against Wales, as no events are recorded. This is a time when their political power in both Ireland and England was at a low ebb. The presence of vikings in the Irish Sea can however be demonstrated for 913 when a naval battle was fought between vikings and the people of Ulster off the coast of England.[64] In the same year, a Welsh pilgrim was ransomed in Ireland after he had been shipwrecked, and 'The Fragmentary Annals of Ireland' state that he narrowly escaped capture by vikings before falling into the hands of some Munster nobles.[65]

In 914, vikings made a dramatic return to Irish-Sea politics. A great naval force under the command of Óttarr and Hróaldr travelled from Brittany to the River Severn where it proceeded to ravage the adjoining districts of Wales.[66] The army then captured Bishop Cyfeilliog in Archenfield, indicating that the vikings travelled inland along the River Wye. The bishop's ransom was paid by King Edward.[67] Kari Maund has

---

[61] The sole possible incidence of the name 'Ketill' in Welsh chronicles (*s.a.* 844) is distinguished by the use of a front rather than a back vowel in the first syllable, giving the forms *Citil* and *Cetil(l)*. *Annales Cambriae*, ed. and trans. Dumville, pp. 10-11.

[62] *Annals of Clonmacnoise*, *s.a.* 901 [=909] (ed. Murphy, p. 144); *Chronicum Scotorum*, *s.a.* [908] [=909] (ed. and trans. Hennessy, pp. 184-85); *Fragmentary Annals*, §426 (ed. and trans. Radner, pp. 166-67).

[63] Dumville, 'The "Six" Sons', p. 17.

[64] *Annals of Ulster*, *s.a.* 912 [=913].5 (ed. and trans. Mac Airt and Mac Niocaill, pp. 360-61).

[65] *Annals of Ulster*, *s.a.* 912 [=913].8 (ed. and trans. Mac Airt and Mac Niocaill, pp. 360-61); *Fragmentary Annals*, §449 (ed. and trans. Radner, pp. 178-79).

[66] The same fleet was probably responsible for the sack of the monastery of St Winwaloi in Landévennec in 913, where they plundered the tombs, including some where the occupants were still partially decomposed. The church was abandoned for some time after the attack. Chédeville and Guillotel, *La Bretagne*, p. 375; Bardel and Perennec, 'Les Vikings'.

[67] *ASC.A*, ed. Bately, p. 65; *ASC.B*, ed. Taylor, p. 48; *ASC.C*, ed. O'Keeffe, p. 74; *ASC.D*, ed. Cubbin, p. 39.

suggested that the English king's generosity, 'probably brought him into contact with the shadowy kings of Gwent and Glywysing'.[68] The ransom may be evidence of good relations or of Edward's desire to bring the south-east borderlands of Wales more closely within his sphere of influence.[69] In the record of the battle against vikings which followed, there is no reference to an alliance between English and Welsh forces. The invading army was defeated by English levies, and the survivors agreed to leave Edward's lands. They sheltered at Steepholme in the Severn-estuary, before being driven by hunger to Dyfed, they arrived at Waterford in the autumn.[70] This sequence of events raises the question whether the people of Dyfed chose to ally with vikings in the early years of the tenth century.

The Revival of the Dynasty of Ívarr

The renewal of viking power in Ireland after 914 seems to have affected English royal policy in Mercia and towards Wales. It may have prompted Æthelflæd to commission fortified burghs to protect the western borders of Mercia. Those built at Eddisbury and Runcorn in 914 and 915 guarded the Dee and Mersey from viking attack.[71] Another burgh was built at Chirbury in 915.[72] This lay two miles east of Offa's Dyke and a short distance south of the Roman road between Forden Gaer and Wroxeter. It thus dominated an important point on the Welsh frontier. In 916 Æthelflæd attacked Llangorse in Brycheiniog, capturing the king's wife and thirty-three others.[73] This may indicate her determination to keep Mercia as a major player in Welsh politics. When Edward seized Æthelflæd's territories after her death in 918, he continued his sister's policy of defending the north-west borders of Mercia and seeking to subdue Wales. Both tactics may been

---

[68] Maund, *The Welsh Kings*, p. 47.

[69] Thomas Charles-Edwards has suggested that the rulers of South-east Wales may have already recognised Edward's supremacy: 'Wales and Mercia', p. 104.

[70] *ASC.A*, ed. Bately, p. 65; *ASC.B*, ed. Taylor, p. 48; *ASC.C*, ed. O'Keeffe, p. 74; *ASC.D*, ed. Cubbin, p. 39; *Annals of Ulster, s.a.* 913 [=914].5 (ed. and trans. Mac Airt and Mac Niocaill, pp. 362-63). The hypothetical alliance between Cadell and the family of Ívarr in 904 invites the suggestion that vikings sheltered in Dyfed with his assent in 914.

[71] *ASC.B*, ed. Taylor, p. 50; *ASC.C*, ed. O'Keeffe, pp. 73-74; *ASC.D*, ed. Cubbin, pp. 39-40.

[72] *Ibid.*

[73] *ASC.B*, ed. Taylor, p. 50; *ASC.C*, ed. O'Keeffe, p. 76; *ASC.D*, ed. Cubbin, p. 40; Sims-Williams, 'The Provenance', p. 60.

intended to prevent Welsh leaders and the grandsons of Ívarr from undertaking a joint campaign against England.

A key to Edward's policies after 918 may indeed have been his concerns about the influence of the dynasty of Ívarr in Britain. In 918, Edward called Hywel and Clydog, sons of Cadell ap Rhodri (kings of Seisyllwg and Dyfed) and Idwal son of Anarawd ap Rhodri (king of Gwynedd and Powys) to Tamworth. 'The Anglo-Saxon Chronicle' states that they submitted to Edward.[74] In the following year, Edward occupied Manchester in Northumbria and ordered its fortifications to be repaired.[75] The city lay on the Roman road between Chester and York. Its seizure may have been intended to prevent a re-run of the events of 893, whereby a hostile army active in Wales and Mercia could easily enter viking-held Northumbria and withdraw safely across Britain. The construction of the burgh at Rhuddlan at the mouth of the Clwyd, which followed in 921, also secured an important point on the route between North Wales and Chester. It may have been built to inhibit viking-fleet operations in that area.

The strategy of Edward did not proceed without objection. In 918, the men of Dublin attacked Anglesey, perhaps in retaliation for Idwal's submission to the English in that year.[76] Then, around 920, Sigtryggr grandson of Ívarr led a raid against Davenport in Cheshire.[77] This appears as an act of defiance against Edward. However, no more viking activities are recorded in Wales until 954, despite the Welsh kings' cooperation with the kings of England for much of this period. The decrease in activity may be explained during the 920s by the submission of kings of York to Edward in 920 and to Æthelstan in 926. Later on, events in Ireland and York may have made the dynasty of Ívarr unwilling to begin hostilities in Wales.

The continuity of commerce between vikings and the people of Gwynedd is suggested by different types of evidence. Most strikingly this is witnessed by the contents of the silver-hoard deposited at Bangor around 925 and by the archaeological finds already mentioned from

---

[74] *ASC.A*, ed. Bately, pp. 68-69.

[75] *Ibid.*, p. 69.

[76] *ByS, s.a.* 914 [=918] (ed. and trans. Jones, pp. 28-29); *ByT* (Pen. 20), *s.a.* [918] (ed. Jones, p. 7; trans. Jones, p. 6); *ByT* (RBH), *s.a.* [918] (ed. and trans. Jones, pp. 10-11).

[77] *Historia Regum Anglorum*, Part I (*Symeonis Monachi Opera*, ed. Arnold, II, 93; *The Church Historians*, trans. Stevenson, III, pt 2, p. 68). Cf. Collingwood and Powell, *Scandinavian Britain*, p. 189.

Llanbedrgoch.[78] According to William of Malmesbury in the early twelfth century, the Welsh encouraged the people of Chester to rebel against Edward in 924.[79] If the account were true, this would be an interesting comment on the relationship between the people of Gwynedd and the people of Chester, who were partners in trade.

English rulers sought to increase their authority in Wales during the 920s as a counter-weight to vikings. When Æthelstan seized control of Northumbria in 927, he called a royal meeting at Eamont at which Causantín of Alba, Ealdred of Bamburgh, Owain (of Strathclyde?) and Hywel Dda ap Cadell promised to keep the peace.[80] With this agreement any major threat to English power in Britain seems to have been removed, and Welsh rulers may have had little practical choice but to accept Æthelstan's authority. William of Malmesbury described a meeting at Hereford between the Welsh and the English which took place about 927. William claimed that the Welsh agreed to pay a huge tribute each year, namely, twenty pounds of gold, three hundred pounds of silver and twenty-five thousand oxen with other gifts.[81] The amount seems implausibly large. *Armes Prydein Vawr* does mention Welsh tribute being paid to stewards from Cirencester and mentions the impoverishment of the Welsh.[82] So it is possible that William provided an exaggerated account of a real meeting.[83]

From 928 to 937 English royal charters demonstrate the presence of Hywel son of Cadell, Idwal son of Anarawd and lesser Welsh kings at the English court.[84] Hywel was always given precedence over other Welsh kings, which may be in recognition of his consistent loyalty to the English king as well as his significance in Wales.[85]

---

[78] Blackburn and Pagan, 'A Revised Checklist', no. 106; see above, p. 207.

[79] William of Malmesbury, *Gesta Regum Anglorum*, II.133 (ed. and trans. Mynors *et al.*, I, 210-11).

[80] *ASC.D*, ed. Cubbin, p. 41; see above, p. 100.

[81] William of Malmesbury, *Gesta Regum Anglorum*, II.134 (ed. and trans. Mynors *et al.*, I, 214-17).

[82] *Armes Prydein*, lines 69-73 (ed. and trans. Williams and Bromwich, pp. 6-7).

[83] For discussion of William of Malmesbury's sources for the reign of Æthelstan, see Lapidge, 'Some Latin Poems'; Simpson, 'The King Alfred/St Cuthbert episode', p. 403; Wood, 'The Making', pp. 265-66.

[84] Tewdwr ab Elisedd of Brycheiniog, an unidentified Gwriad, Morgan ab Owain of Morgannwg, *Cadmo* who may be identified as Cadwgan, brother of Morgan, or more likely, as an unidentified ruler Cadfan. Loyn, 'Wales and England', pp. 291-92.

[85] Kirby, 'Hywel'.

The association of other Welsh kings with Æthelstan may have been strained in the 930s as an alliance developed between Alba and Dublin against Æthelstan. Only Hywel seems to be found as a witness to Æthelstan's charters after 935.[86] It is possible that other Welsh rulers had withdrawn their support from Æthelstan at this time.[87] There is no conclusive evidence for Welsh participation in the battle of *Brunanburh*. Nevertheless, the dynasty of Ívarr may have attempted to woo the support of Welsh kings during the 930s. The support of Idwal of Gwynedd would have been particularly desirable if the identification of *Brunanburh* with Bromborough on the Wirral is correct.[88] For navigational reasons, viking ships travelling to the Wirral would probably have sailed along the North Welsh coast.

After Æthelstan's death in 939, Idwal of Gywnedd seems to have opposed his successor as he was killed by the English in 942.[89] As Alfred Smyth has pointed out, Idwal may have chosen to make war against Edmund while the English king was preoccupied with fighting Óláfr Sigtryggsson.[90] A somewhat confused account in *Egils saga* also claims that Aðils (Idwal) fought against the English at *Brunanburh*.[91] This source cannot be regarded as reliable. Andrew Breeze has interpreted a reference to *cattybrudawt* in the tenth century Welsh poem *Glaswawd Taliesin* as an allusion to the battle *Brunanburh*. If this interpretation is correct it could support the idea that Idwal was involved in the battle.[92] Some of the other Welsh rulers may have adopted a position of neutrality at the time of the *Brunanburh*-campaign, that is, withdrawing from the English court for some years, but not going so far as to ally with vikings. Morgan, king of

---

[86] Sawyer, *Anglo-Saxon Charters*, no. 433. The authenticity of this charter is in doubt.

[87] Cf. above, p. 103.

[88] Dodgson, 'The Background'; Griffiths, 'Anglo-Saxon England', p. 30; Higham, *The Kingdom*, p. 193; Hudson, *Kings*, p. 80; Crawford, 'The Norse Background', p. 110, n. 2.

[89] *Annales Cambriae*, s.a. [942] (ed. and trans. Dumville, pp. 16-17); *ByS, s.a.* 941 [942] (ed. and trans. Jones, pp. 32-33); *ByT* (Pen. 20), *s.a.* [942] (ed. Jones, p. 8; trans. Jones, p. 7); *ByT* (RBH), *s.a.* [942] (ed. and trans. Jones, pp. 12-13).

[90] Smyth, *Scandinavian York*, II, 113.

[91] *Egils saga*, §§51-3, 55 (ed. Nordal, pp. 129-30, 136-38, 142; trans. Scudder, pp. 81-82, 85-87).

[92] Breeze, 'The Battle'. I prefer to take *coch cad* as 'the redness of battle (i.e., bloodshed)', rather than 'the red one of the battle' identifying a warrior who fought there. Thus Idwal's increase of *coch cad* could indicate that he participated in the bloodshed. I am grateful to Oliver Padel who has pointed out to me some of the difficulties in interpreting this passage.

Morgannwg, may be an example: his realignment with the victors of *Brunanburh* is indicated by his reappearance as a witness on English royal diplomas during the 940s.[93]

Hywel's constant fidelity to the kings of England, in contrast to the actions of Idwal, is suggested by the royal diplomas which he witnessed in 946 and 949.[94] Kirby has portrayed Hywel's attitude towards England as pragmatic rather than affectionate.[95] The southern king may have benefited from consistently backing the right horse. By 934, he had gained control of Brycheiniog and by 944 he appears to have gained control over the lands of Idwal, probably with English consent.[96] Christopher Blunt showed how the status assigned to Hywel in English diplomas grew over time. Before 937 he was generally styled *subregulus*, from 946 to 949 he was generally named *regulus*, and in 949 he was called *rex*.[97] A coin minted at Chester in 946×950 bears Hywel's name and also accords him the honourable title of *rex*.[98] How many such coins were produced is unknown, and the motive behind its production is uncertain. It is however further evidence of co-operation between Hywel and the English king, Eadred.

Despite the political profits which Hywel may have reaped from this strategy, some of his subjects may have resented his policies and preferred enmity towards England. This is suggested by *Armes Prydein Vawr*, a prophetic poem which makes an impassioned call on the Welsh to ally with the peoples of North Britain, Brittany, Ireland and Dublin to drive the English out of Britain. It appears to have been written in south-west Wales, during Hywel's reign.[99]

---

[93] Sawyer, *Anglo-Saxon Charters*, no. 520.

[94] *Ibid.*, nos 520, 550.

[95] Kirby, 'Hywel'.

[96] Maund, *The Welsh Kings*, p. 49.

[97] Blunt, 'The Cabinet', p. 120.

[98] *Ibid.*

[99] *Armes Prydein*, ed. and trans. Williams and Bromwich, p. xx; Smyth, *Scandinavian York*, II, 65-72; Dumville, 'Brittany', pp. 150, 152; Breeze, '*Armes Prydein*', pp. 215-16; Fulton, 'Tenth Century Wales', pp. 14-16; Etchingham, 'North Wales', pp. 185-86. I find myself persuaded by Andrew Breeze's suggestion that the prophecy was written about 941. This is based on an internal reference in the text to 404 years of English oppression, after which the Britons will wreak their revenge. Breeze has suggested that the author counted his years from 537, that is when Arthur is alleged to have died according to *Annales Cambriae s.a.* [537] (ed. Phillimore, p. 154). Version A of *Annales Cambriae* was written in Dyfed, which is where *Armes Prydein Vawr* is thought to have originated

Figure 15: Vikings in Wales

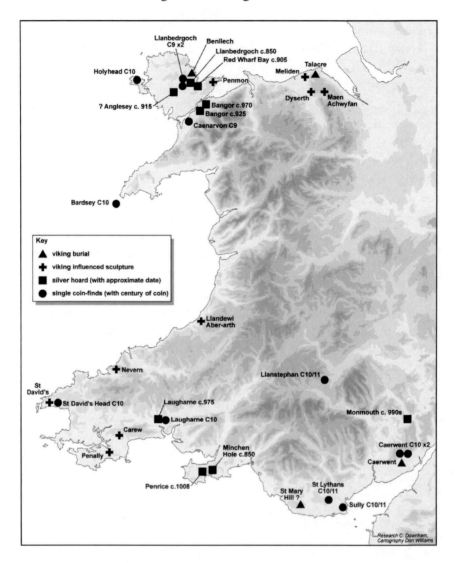

Key

▲ viking burial

✚ viking influenced sculpture

■ silver hoard (with approximate date)

● single coin-finds (with century of coin)

Llanbedrgoch C9 x2
Benllech
Llanbedrgoch c.850
Red Wharf Bay c.905
Talacre
Meliden
Holyhead C10
Penmon
Dyserth
Maen Achwyfan
? Anglesey c. 915
Bangor c.970
Bangor c.925
Caenarvon C9

Bardsey C10

Llandewi Aber-arth

Nevern

St David's
St David's Head C10
Laugharne c.975
Laugharne C10
Carew
Penally
Minchen Hole c.850
Penrice c.1008
Llanstephan C10/11
Monmouth c. 990s
Caerwent C10 x2
Caerwent
St Mary Hill ?
St Lythans C10/11
Sully C10/11

Research C. Downham, Cartography Don Williams

Figure 16: The Descendants of Rhodri Mawr

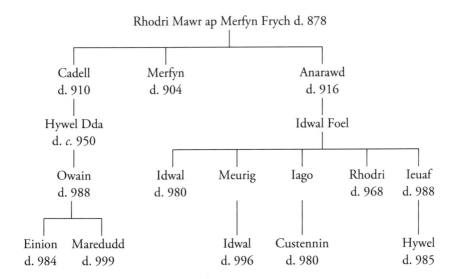

Rhodri Mawr ap Merfyn Frych d. 878

Cadell d. 910 — Merfyn d. 904 — Anarawd d. 916

Hywel Dda d. *c.* 950 — Idwal Foel

Owain d. 988 — Idwal d. 980 — Meurig — Iago — Rhodri d. 968 — Ieuaf d. 988

Einion d. 984 — Maredudd d. 999 — Idwal d. 996 — Custennin d. 980 — Hywel d. 985

Wales after 954

The collapse of viking York was followed by a series of viking campaigns against north Wales. Descendants of Ívarr may have hoped to bring the area under their control as an alternative power-base. Certainly their interests seem to have been focused on maintaining control in the Irish Sea during these years. Man seems to have risen dramatically in importance at this time and some of the raids on Wales were directed from this island. There is evidence that Man was in Brittonic hands before the vikings arrived.[100] If the dynasty of Ívarr seized Man from members of Rhodri's family in the early tenth century, this could explain the pattern of warfare against north Wales.[101] The first recorded victims of the new wave of attacks were Hirfawr and Anarawd, sons of Gwriad.[102] In 957, another son of Gwriad,

---

[100] *Annals of Ulster*, *s.a.* 877 [=878].3 (ed. and trans. Mac Airt and Mac Niocaill, pp. 332-33).

[101] See above, pp. 179-82.

[102] *ByS*, *s.a.* 952 [=954] (ed. and trans. Jones, pp. 34-35); *ByT* (Pen. 20), *s.a.* 952 [=954] (ed. Jones, p. 9; trans. Jones, p. 7); *ByT* (RBH), *s.a.* [954] (ed. and trans. Jones, pp. 12-13).

Gwgon, was slain, although the perpetrator is not named.[103] This raises the question as to who Gwriad was. Some (but not all) versions of *Brut y Tywysogyon* and *Brenhinedd y Saesson* identify him as a son of Rhodri Mawr.[104] Gwriad was a common name within the royal dynasty of Gwynedd, and some link with Rhodri Mawr seems likely.[105] A leader named Gwriad witnessed an English charter in 928 and he may have been the father of Hirfawr and Anarawd.[106] The obscurity of Gwriad and the sudden appearance of his sons on the political scene is hard to explain. It is tempting to link these men with a branch of the dynasty of Rhodri which had continued to rule on Man, for this could explain their persecution by vikings.[107]

A charter of Eadred which is dated 955 could provide an important clue to viking relations with Wales in this difficult period. On the witness-list between the king's nephews and two English *duces* are named 'Morcant regulus 7 Owen, Syferð 7 Iacob'.[108] Three of the witnesses can be identified, namely Morgan of Glywysing, Owain ap Hywel Dda of Deheubarth and Iago ab Idwal of Gwynedd. The other name, *Syferð*, may be Old Norse Sigfrøðr.[109] His place in the witness-list suggests some association with Wales, and perhaps more specifically, north Wales.[110] According to 'The Anglo-Saxon Chronicle' a king by this name committed suicide in 962 and was buried at Wimborne.[111] Another king called *Siferth* is mentioned in John of Worcester's account of the royal meeting on the Dee in 973, although this may be a mistake (William of Malmesbury rendered the name

---

[103] *ByS*, *s.a.* 955 [=957] (ed. and trans. Jones, pp. 34-35); *ByT* (Pen. 20), *s.a.* 955 [=957] (ed. Jones, p. 9; trans. Jones, p. 7); *ByT* (RBH), *s.a.* [957] (ed. and trans. Jones, pp. 14-15).

[104] This assertion is made in 'The Red Book of Hergest' version of *Brut y Tywysogyon*, and three sixteenth-century manuscripts of the version found in Peniarth 20 (but not including Peniarth 20). This link is also made in 'The Black Book of Basingwerk' version of *Brenhinedd y Saesson*.

[105] The Gwriad who fell with Rhodri in 878 was probably his brother.

[106] Sawyer, *Anglo-Saxon Charters*, no. 400.

[107] Gwriad's name may have deliberately echoed that of Gwriad, an earlier ruler of Man who is commemorated on the stone at Port y Vullen. See p. 180, above.

[108] *Ibid.*, no. 566.

[109] Thornton, 'Edgar', p. 71.

[110] Davies, *Patterns*, p. 59

[111] *ASC. A*, ed. Bately, p. 75; see above, p. 123.

Giferth).[112] It therefore seems reasonable to link the Sigfrøðr named in 955 with the king who died in 962.[113] In 'The Anglo-Saxon Chronicle' he is accorded royal status, and he was buried at a church which was closely associated with the royal dynasty of Wessex.[114] There are too many possible ways of interpreting this record, who *Siferð* might have been, where he ruled, the reasons for his suicide, and why he was linked with Wimborne, but it is an interesting mystery.

Siferð may have had some involvement with the 'sons of Óláfr' who appeared in Anglesey in 961 and 962. As Colmán Etchingham has suggested, they were probably sons of Óláfr Guðrøðsson whose death is recorded in Welsh chronicles in 941, and they may have been based on Man.[115] In 961 the brothers raided Holyhead and Llŷn.[116] In the following year Guðrøðr Óláfsson led a plundering expedition from Ireland's Eye to Anglesey.[117] Ireland's Eye was part of Dublin's hinterland and probably in the hands of the dynasty of Ívarr at this date.[118] 'The Annals of the Four Masters' show that the attack was part of a wider campaign: the sons of Óláfr had previously plundered the hinterland of Dundalk Bay, and Howth, before they reached Ireland's Eye. They then travelled south to attack the estuaries of the Rivers Suir, Blackwater and Lee in the south of Ireland.[119] The entry in 'The Annals of the Four Masters' has the formula '*crech la* [name] *a* [or *do*] [place] *co* [place]' to describe Guðrøðr's

---

[112] John of Worcester, *Chronicle*, s.a. 973 (ed. and trans. Darlington *et al.*, II, 422-24); William of Malmesbury, *Gesta Regum Anglorum*, II.148 (ed. and trans. Mynors *et al.*, I, 238-40, II, 132-33). *Siferth* is also named in Roger of Wendover, *Flores Historiarum*, s.a. 974 (ed. Coxe, I, 415; *Roger*, trans. Giles, I, 263); Thornton, 'Edgar', p. 73; see above, p. 125.

[113] Collingwood and Powell, *Scandinavian Britain*, p. 185.

[114] Clegg, *A History*, pp. 19-26.

[115] Etchingham, 'North Wales', pp. 167-71.

[116] *ByS*, s.a. 959 [=961] (ed. and trans. Jones, pp. 36-37); *ByT* (Pen. 20), s.a. 959 [=961] (ed. Jones, p. 9; trans. Jones, p. 8); *ByT* (RBH), s.a. [961] (ed. and trans. Jones, pp. 14-15). It is interesting that a district of Llŷn was Afloegion, allegedly named after Afloeg, a legendary son of Cunedda. The name appears to be a Welsh version of Óláfr, although it may be a substitute rather than a derivative of the name: *Annales Cambriae* (A), s.a. 941 (ed. and trans. Dumville, p. 16); Maund, *The Welsh Kings*, p. 27; Grabowski and Dumville, *Chronicles*, pp. 212, 213, 223, 235; Hughes, *Celtic Britain*, p. 88, n. 23.

[117] *Annals of the Four Masters*, s.a. 960 [=962].14 (ed. and trans. O'Donovan, II, 682-83).

[118] Some of the vikings expelled in 902 were besieged on the island according to 'The Annals of the Four Masters: *Annals of Ulster*, s.a. 901 [=902].2 (ed. and trans. Mac Airt and Mac Niocaill, pp. 352-53).

[119] *Annals of the Four Masters*, s.a. 960 [=962].14 (ed. and trans. O'Donovan, II, 682-83).

expedition, which seems to indicate a raid rather than the transfer of booty as John O'Donovan's translation suggested.[120] The entry may not therefore be used as evidence that Anglesey was under viking control at this date.

Both the English and vikings targeted Gwynedd in the following years. The coastal site of Towyn was ravaged by 'pagans' in 963.[121] The high-status church of St Cadfan at Towyn may have borne the brunt of this attack.[122] At around the same time, two or three Anglo-Saxon coins were deposited near the church of St Deiniol in Bangor, which may be indicative of viking activity.[123] At Bardsey Island, off the tip of the Llyn peninsular, a male burial has been discovered with a silver penny datable 959×972 in his mouth.[124] Contemporary evidence of this practice has been found on the Isle of Man.[125] The burial may be linked with viking raids recorded from Man.[126] In 967, Ælfhere, ealdorman of Mercia ravaged North Wales.[127] His attack may have been intended to keep the kings of Gwynedd in check and to deter them from alliance with vikings. Gwynedd was subject to further attack in the following year, when the royal seat of Gwynedd at Aberffraw in Anglesey was raided and Rhodri ab Idwal was killed, but the perpetrators are not named.[128]

---

[120] *Annals of the Four Masters*, s.a. 960 [=962].15 (ed. and trans. O'Donovan, II, 682-83): *Creach la Sittriucc Cam do mhuir co h-Uibh c-Colgan*, 'a plundering expedition by Sigtryggr Cam from the sea to Uí Cholgain'.

[121] *ByS*, s.a. 961 [=963] (ed. and trans. Jones, pp. 38-39); *ByT* (Pen. 20), s.a. 961 [=963] (ed. Jones, p. 9; trans. Jones, p. 8); *ByT* (RBH), s.a. [963] (ed. and trans. Jones, pp. 14-15).

[122] Lloyd, *A History of Wales*, I, 251-52.

[123] Blackburn and Pagan, 'A Revised Checklist', no. 106.

[124] *Ibid.*, p. 97; Early Medieval Corpus, no. 1998:2120.

[125] Redknap, *Vikings in Wales*, pp. 97-98.

[126] *ByS*, s.a. 959 [=961] (ed. and trans. Jones, pp. 36-37); *ByT* (Pen. 20), s.a. 959 [=961] (ed. Jones, p. 9; trans. Jones, p. 8); *ByT* (RBH), s.a. [961] (ed. and trans. Jones, pp. 14-15).

[127] *Annales Cambriae* (BC), ed. Williams, p. 19; *ByS*, s.a. 965 [=967] (ed. and trans. Jones, pp. 38-39); *ByT* (Pen. 20), s.a. 965 [=967] (ed. Jones, p. 10; trans. Jones, p. 8); *ByT* (RBH), s.a. [967] (ed. and trans. Jones, pp. 14-15); Williams, '*Princeps*', pp. 156-62.

[128] *Annales Cambriae* (BC), ed. Williams, p. 19; *ByS*, s.a. 966 [=968] (ed. and trans. Jones, pp. 38-39); *ByT* (Pen. 20), s.a. 966 [=968] (ed. Jones, p. 10; trans. Jones, p. 8); *ByT* (RBH), s.a. [968] (ed. and trans. Jones, pp. 14-15).

The death of Rhodri seems to have triggered a civil war in Gwynedd as Welsh dynasts contended for power. [129] The political difficulties continued until the end of the century. The descendants of Ívarr were poised, vulture-like, to reap political benefits from Gwynedd's weakness. Two years later, Maccus Haraldsson attacked the important church of St Seiriol at Penmon in southeastern Anglesey.[130] Maccus and his brother represented a segment of Ívarr's dynasty which had taken power in the Hebrides and Man. In the following year, Guðrøðr Haraldsson raided Anglesey again. There is some confusion in the chronicle-record as to what happened next.[131]

Brut y Tywysogyon reports that Guðrøðr subdued Anglesey with great treasure.[132] However, *Brenhinedd y Saesson* in contrast claims that he overran the island and drew tribute. These entries appear to be variant translations of the same Latin record. Thomas Jones generally considered *Brenhinedd y Saesson* to be less accurate than other Welsh chronicles, as it demonstrably contains several errors in its translation, but this may not always be the case.[133] There is no record of the event in *Annales Cambriae* which can be studied for comparison.

Historians have interpreted this record in different ways. B.G. Charles and Wendy Davies have suggested that Guðrøðr took control of Anglesey at this date.[134] Indeed, Davies has gone so far as to argue that vikings from Ireland were ruling much of Gwynedd from 960 (when the raids of Óláfr's sons began) until about 1025 (when a large viking coin-hoard was

---

[129] *Annales Cambriae* (BC), ed. Williams, p. 19; *ByS, s.a.* 967 [=969] (ed. and trans. Jones, pp. 38-39); *ByT* (Pen. 20), *s.a.* 967 [=969] (ed. Jones, p. 10; trans. Jones, p. 8); *ByT* (RBH), *s.a.* [969] (ed. and trans. Jones, pp. 14-15).

[130] *Annales Cambriae* (B), ed. Williams, p. 19; *ByS, s.a.* 969 [=971] (ed. and trans. Jones, pp. 38-39); *ByT* (Pen. 20), *s.a.* 969 [=971] (ed. Jones, p. 10; trans. Jones, p. 8); *ByT* (RBH), *s.a.* [971] (ed. and trans. Jones, pp. 14-15).

[131] *ByS, s.a.* 970 [=972] (ed. and trans. Jones, pp. 40-41); *ByT* (Pen. 20), *s.a.* 970 [=972] (ed. Jones, p. 10; trans. Jones, p. 8); *ByT* (RBH), *s.a.* 970 [=972] (ed. and trans. Jones, pp. 14-15).

[132] So reads the Peniarth 20 version of the text. The corresponding entry in 'The Red Book of Hergest' reports that Guðrøðr plundered the island 'with great sense'. Jones attributed this to a confusion in the Latin original between *census* and *sensus*. In his note, Jones argued that the Peniarth 20 version is more accurate: *ByT* (Pen. 20), ed. and trans. Jones, p. 143, n. 8.21-2.

[133] *ByS*, ed. and trans. Jones, p. xxxix.

[134] Charles, *Old Norse Relations*, p. 32; Davies, *Patterns*, pp. 57-58.

deposited by vikings at Bryn Maelgwn near Llandudno).[135] In contrast, Kari Maund has argued that the record of 972 merely witnessed the collection of tribute by Guðrøðr, and that he may not have exercised any control over the territory.[136] Thus the evidence can be manipulated to support opposing views regarding the involvement of vikings in north Wales at this time.

It can be argued that Guðrøðr successfully brought Anglesey under his control in 972, but that his power there was of a temporary nature. He surely did not have control of the island when he attacked it in 980.[137] Maund has pointed out that Anglesey and Gwynedd are mentioned as if they represented two separate entities under Welsh leaders in the late 970s and 980s.[138] She has credited this to the division of Gwynedd's territories among native rulers. However, it could be due to the temporary seizure of Anglesey by vikings at this date. Furthermore, it should be noted that from 972 to 980 the flood of viking attacks against Anglesey abated. This may be an indication that the sons of Haraldr had fulfilled their ambitions there. The economic development of Man in these years could have prompted Guðrøðr to seek Anglesey as a strategic base in the Irish Sea from which he could control the sea-lanes between Britain and Ireland and between Man and the southern coasts of Ireland and Wales.

King Edgar's intervention in North Welsh affairs in 973 may also have helped to reduce the number of viking attacks on Gwynedd. He called a royal meeting at Chester 973 with the sons of Haraldr, and Hywel and Iago, kings of North Wales, and the kings of Strathclyde and Alba.[139] Edgar's convention may have met to deal with concerns about political instability in North Wales and the growing power of the sons of Haraldr in the Irish Sea. If Guðrøðr had conquered Anglesey, this would have given him nearly unrivalled control over maritime trade-routes into Chester, whose economic importance at this date was second only to that of

---

[135] *Ibid.*, p. 59.

[136] Maund, 'Dynastic Segmentation', p. 159.

[137] *ByS*, s.a. 979 [=980] (ed. and trans. Jones, pp. 42-43); *ByT* (Pen. 20), s.a. 979 [=980] (ed. Jones, p. 11; trans. Jones, p. 9); *ByT* (RBH), s.a. [980] (ed. and trans. Jones, pp. 16-17); Etchingham, 'North Wales', p. 175.

[138] Maund, 'Dynastic Segmentation', p. 159, n. 19. In relation to 993, Gwynedd and Anglesey are also mentioned separately. *ByS*, s.a. 992 [=993] (ed. and trans. Jones, pp. 46-47); *ByT* (RBH), s.a. [993] (ed. and trans. Jones, pp. 18-19).

[139] Thornton, 'Edgar'. See above, pp. 125, 218.

London.[140] Edgar's meeting may have prompted the sons of Haraldr to redirect their attentions to Ireland, where they campaigned in 974.[141]

The meeting did not, however, bring peace to Gwynedd. In 974, Hywel ab Ieuaf expelled his uncle Iago ab Idwal.[142] Hywel failed to hold power in Gwynedd, and in 978 he ravaged Llyn and the church of Clynnog Fawr (Caernarfonshire) with English help.[143] In the same year an unidentified leader, *Gwrmid*, raided Llyn 'for the second time'.[144] Then Hywel arranged for his rival Iago to be captured by a viking force.[145] Although Hywel won the support of the English and possibly some vikings, his actions were strenuously resisted by Guðrøðr Haraldsson. Guðrøðr allied with Custennin, a son of Iago, to attack Anglesey and Llyn in 980 and Hywel killed Custennin in the same year.[146]

Given Hywel's alliance with the English, it is possible that Guðrøðr Haraldsson had a hand in the viking attacks on England in the early 980s, as Simon Keynes has suggested.[147] As Hywel was allied with Ælfhere of Mercia, it is certainly tempting to link Guðrøðr with the attack on Cheshire in 980. Guðrøðr may have had some support from Ireland. He was allied with Dublin at the battle of Tara in 980; and as the fortunes of the dynasty of Ívarr waned in Ireland after the battle, some viking leaders from Ireland may have sought to win wealth and fame in England.[148] In 981 and 982, further attacks were mounted, but this time on the south-west of England; these may have been an extension of Guðrøðr's attacks on South Wales.[149]

---

[140] Griffiths, 'Anglo-Saxon England', pp. 136-40; Thornton, 'Edgar', pp. 74-75.

[141] *Annals of the Four Masters*, s.a. 972 [=974] (ed. and trans. O'Donovan, II, 698-99); *Annals of Inisfallen*, s.a. 974 (ed. and trans. Mac Airt, pp. 160-61).

[142] *Annales Cambriae* (BC), ed. Williams, p. 19; *ByS*, s.a. 972 [=974] (ed. and trans. Jones, pp. 40-41); *ByT* (Pen. 20), s.a. 972 [=974] (ed. Jones, p. 10; trans. Jones, p. 8); *ByT* (RBH), s.a. [974] (ed. and trans. Jones, pp. 14-15).

[143] *ByS*, s.a. 977 [=978] (ed. and trans. Jones, pp. 42-43); *ByT* (Pen. 20), s.a. 977 [=978] (ed. Jones, p. 10; trans. Jones, p. 9); *ByT* (RBH), s.a. [978] (ed. and trans. Jones, pp. 14-15).

[144] *ByT* (Pen. 20), s.a. 977 [=978] (ed. Jones, p. 10; trans. Jones, p. 9).

[145] *Annales Cambriae* (BC), ed. Williams, p. 20.

[146] *ByS*, s.a. 979 [=980] (ed. and trans. Jones, pp. 42-43); *ByT* (Pen. 20), s.a. 979 [=980] (ed. Jones, p. 11; trans. Jones, p. 9); *ByT* (RBH), s.a. [980] (ed. and trans. Jones, pp. 16-17).

[147] Keynes, 'The Historical Context', pp. 85-86.

[148] *Annals of Ulster*, s.a. 979 [=980].1 (ed. and trans. Mac Airt and Mac Niocaill, pp. 414-15). However, the economic crisis which the campaign in 980 brought to Chester would prove detrimental to trading interests in Guðrøðr's kingdom: Dolley and Pirie, 'The Repercussions'.

[149] *ASC.C*, ed. O'Keeffe, pp. 84-85.

In 982, he led a force against Dyfed and targeted the church of St Davids.[150] Curiously, his political enemy, Hywel, attacked South Wales the following year, allied with the English.[151] Each side may have sought to bring the South within their sphere of influence to strengthen its position in the war for Gwynedd.

Perhaps in consequence of these attacks, the next king of Deheubarth, Maredudd ab Owain, engaged in war both with the royal dynasty of Gwynedd and with Guðrøðr Haraldsson of Man. In 985 Hywel ab Ieuaf was 'treacherously' killed by the English, and his brother Cadwallon succeeded to the throne of Gwynedd. [152] Then Cadwallon was slain by Maredudd.[153] Guðrøðr opposed Maredudd's seizure of Gwynedd and attacked Anglesey in 987. He is credited with taking two thousand people from the island as well as devastating much of the land. This caused Maredudd to flee with the remainder of his troops back to South Wales.[154]

From 986 large fleets of vikings from Scandinavia (identified in Irish chronicles as *Danair*) are reported in the Irish Sea, and they may have affected events in Wales.[155] In 987 *Danair* allied with Guðrøðr, and he may have used his new allies to attack Anglesey in the same year.[156] In 988 Scandinavian fleets raided Devon and probably led the attacks against

[150] *Annales Cambriae* (BC), ed. Williams, p. 20; *ByS*, s.a. 981 [=982] (ed. and trans. Jones, pp. 44-45); *ByT* (Pen. 20), s.a. 981 [=982] (ed. Jones, p. 11; trans. Jones, p. 9); *ByT* (RBH), s.a. 980 [=982] (ed. and trans. Jones, pp. 16-17).

[151] *Annales Cambriae* (BC), ed. Williams, p. 20; *ByS*, s.a. 982 [=983] (ed. and trans. Jones, pp. 44-45); *ByT* (Pen. 20), s.a. 982 [=983] (ed. Jones, p. 11; trans. Jones, p. 9); *ByT* (RBH), s.a. [983] (ed. and trans. Jones, pp. 16-17).

[152] *Annales Cambriae* (BC), ed. Williams, p. 20; *ByS*, s.a. 984 [=985] (ed. and trans. Jones, pp. 44-45); *ByT* (Pen. 20), s.a. 984 [=985] (ed. Jones, p. 11; trans. Jones, p. 9); *ByT* (RBH), s.a. [985] (ed. and trans. Jones, pp. 16-17). Ælfhere of Mercia had died in 983. Kari Maund has suggested that his political enemies in England were responsible for Hywel's death: 'Dynastic Segmentation', p. 162.

[153] *Annales Cambriae* (BC), ed. Williams, p. 20; *ByS*, s.a. 985 [=986] (ed. and trans. Jones, pp. 44-45); *ByT* (Pen. 20), s.a. 985 [=986] (ed. Jones, p. 11; trans. Jones, p. 9); *ByT* (RBH), s.a. [986] (ed. and trans. Jones, pp. 16-17).

[154] Jones speculated that the Latin exemplar of this entry read *reliquas* ('relics') rather than *reliquos* ('remainders'), but I do not think this emendation necessary, *ByT* (Pen. 20), trans. Jones, pp. 145-46, n. 10.1-2; Maund, 'Dynastic Segmentation', p. 163.

[155] *Annals of Ulster*, s.a. 985 [=986].2, 985 [=986].3 (ed. and trans. Mac Airt and Mac Niocaill, pp. 418-21).

[156] *Annals of Ulster*, s.a. 986 [=987].1 (ed. and trans. Mac Airt and Mac Niocaill, pp. 420-21).

churches in South Wales that year.[157] The casualties named in the Welsh chronicles are St Davids and St Dogmaels in Pembrokeshire, Llanbadarn Fawr in Cardiganshire, and Llanilltud Fawr and Llancarfan in Glamorganshire.[158] All were important sites near the coast, and they would have offered relatively rich pickings for the invaders. The Scandinavian fleets brought a new element of instability into the political affairs of Wales.[159]

In relation to the arrival of Scandinavian fleets, Colmán Etchingham has noted a brief revival in the terminology 'Dark Foreigners' in Welsh chronicles in the 980s.[160] This colour-terminology was otherwise used in contemporary Irish and Welsh chronicles in the mid- to late ninth century and early tenth century.[161] The term has no corresponding revival in Ireland in the late tenth century. Etchingham has argued that its re-introduction in Welsh chronicles was because *Dubgaill* meant Danes, and thus the term was used to describe the Scandinavian fleets which had recently arrived in the Irish Sea, to distinguish them from vikings settled in the Gaelic world. Nevertheless, David Dumville has recently challenged the ethnocentric interpretation of this colour-terminology.[162] In the ninth century and early tenth century, the family of Ívarr and its followers were identified as 'Dark Foreigners'.[163] The description is only found twice in relation to the 980s, once for the vikings who attacked Anglesey with Guðrøðr Haraldsson (a member of the dynasty of Ívarr who allied with the Scandinavian fleets in 986) and then to describe the army which came to Anglesey in 989 to

---

[157] *ASC.C*, ed. O'Keeffe, p. 86; *ASC.D*, ed. Cubbin, p. 48; E in *Two of the Saxon Chronicles*, ed. Plummer, I, 125.

[158] *Annales Cambriae* (B), ed. Williams, p. 21; *ByS, s.a.* 987 [=988] (ed. and trans. Jones, pp. 46-47); *ByT* (Pen. 20), *s.a.* 987 [=988] (ed. Jones, p. 12; trans. Jones, p. 10); *ByT* (RBH), *s.a.* [988] (ed. and trans. Jones, pp. 16-17).

[159] The legend of Pálnatóki seems to have been based on the viking raids in Wales during this period. *Jómsvíkinga saga*, ed. and trans. Blake.

[160] Etchingham, 'North Wales', pp. 175-76.

[161] The terminology appears first in Irish records, and it may have been borrowed into Welsh. *Annals of Ulster*, *s.a.* 850 [=851].3 (ed. and trans. Mac Airt and Mac Niocaill, pp. 310-11).

[162] Dumville, 'Old Dubliners'.

[163] It may be relevant that the term *y Normanyeid duon*, 'the black Northmen' in *Brut y Tywysogion* for the year 892. An early modern glossator wrote *Dani* in the margin of this entry in MS. Peniarth 20, which indicates a later interpretation of this term.

---

demand money from Maredudd.[164] In 989, Maredudd paid a tribute of a penny for each of his men to the 'black army' in Anglesey. This may have been a ransom for the men whom Guðrøðr seized in 987. It seems likely that the two events were connected.[165] Curiously, the payment coincides with a record that the men of Dublin were obliged to pay large sums of money to Mael Sechlainn, overking of the Southern Uí Néill.[166] The Dubliners may have sought to offset their costs by taking money from Maredudd. In either case, it seems probable that Welsh chroniclers still recognised 'Dark Foreigners' as vikings under the leadership of the dynasty of Ívarr.

During the 990s, Maredudd waged war against Glamorgan and against the sons of Meurig ab Idwal who had a claim to the throne of Gwynedd. In both struggles vikings played a part. Maredudd hired vikings to raid Glamorgan in 992, and he seems to have paid the mercenaries with the booty gathered there.[167] In the following year the sons of Meurig campaigned against Maredudd in Gwynedd. They may have been allied with the vikings who attacked Anglesey on Ascension Thursday in the same year.[168] According to *Brenhinedd y Saesson*, the vikings destroyed all the corn on the island, leading to famine in the territory of Maredudd in 994. In the same year as the famine, Meurig's sons defeated Maredudd in battle.[169]

---

[164] *Annales Cambriae* (BC), ed. Williams, pp. 20-21; *ByS, s.a.* 986 [=987], 987 [=989] (ed. and trans. Jones, pp. 44-47); *ByT* (Pen. 20), *s.a.* 986 [=987], 987 [=989] (ed. Jones, pp. 11-12; trans. Jones, pp. 9-10); *ByT* (RBH), *s.a.* [987], [989] (ed. and trans. Jones, pp. 16-17).

[165] *Annals of Ulster, s.a.* 988 [=989].4 (ed. and trans. Mac Airt and Mac Niocaill, pp. 420-21); Thornton, 'Maredudd', pp. 578-79. Guðrøðr died in 989.

[166] *Annals of Clonmacnoise, s.a.* 982 [=989] (ed. Murphy, pp. 160-61); *Annals of the Four Masters, s.a.* 988 [=989] (ed. and trans. O'Donovan, II, 722-25); *Annals of Tigernach, s.a.* [999] (ed. and trans. Stokes, II, 238). See above, p. 57. It is probable that Mael Sechlainn did exact tribute from the Dubliners in this year, although the amount may have been exaggerated.

[167] *ByS, s.a.* 991 [=992] (ed. and trans. Jones, pp. 46-47); *ByT* (Pen. 20), *s.a.* 991 [=992], (ed. Jones, p. 12; trans. Jones, p. 10); *ByT* (RBH), *s.a.* 990 [=992] (ed. and trans. Jones, pp. 18-19).

[168] *Annales Cambriae* (BC), ed. Williams, p. 21; *ByS, s.a.* 992 [=993] (ed. and trans. Jones, pp. 46-47); *ByT* (Pen. 20), *s.a.* 992 [=993], (ed. Jones, pp. 12-13; trans. Jones, p. 10); *ByT* (RBH), *s.a.* [993] (ed. and trans. Jones, pp. 18-19).

[169] *Annales Cambriae* (BC), ed. Williams, p. 21; *ByS, s.a.* 993 [=994] (ed. and trans. Jones, pp. 48-49); *ByT* (Pen. 20), *s.a.* 993 [=994], (ed. Jones, p. 13; trans. Jones, p. 10); *ByT* (RBH), *s.a.* [994] (ed. and trans. Jones, pp. 18-19).

However, the campaign of the sons of Meurig apparently collapsed in 996 when one of their number, Idwal, died.[170]

At the end of the 990s, South Wales, rather than the North, became the focus of attacks. Nevertheless, viking fleets were active throughout the Irish Sea.[171] In 997, a Scandinavian army attacked Cornwall, Devon and Wales.[172] In 999 vikings harried St Davids and killed the bishop, Morgenau.[173] Dyfed was ravaged again in 1001.[174] The raids on south-west Wales which are reported in the historical record from 988 can be seen as an extension of the Scandinavian campaigns against Wessex in the 980s and 990s. These attacks may also have been influenced by the growth of Bristol, whose importance is attested in eleventh-century records.[175] Vikings may have sought to control the sea-lanes to this port. Three hoards of Anglo-Saxon coins have been found in South Wales, which date from the late tenth and early eleventh centuries. These could be linked with the Scandinavian campaigns in the Severn-estuary.[176] That at Laugharne was deposited about 978, another at Monmouth about 995. The coins from Penrice on the Gower peninsula were deposited in a wooden box about 1008.[177] While these discoveries need not be connected with vikings from Ireland, they do indicate the growing wealth of this area.[178]

[170] *Annales Cambriae* (BC), ed. Williams, p. 21; *ByS, s.a.* 995 [=996] (ed. and trans. Jones, pp. 48-49); *ByT* (Pen. 20), *s.a.* 995 [=996], (ed. Jones, p. 13; trans. Jones, p. 10); *ByT* (RBH), *s.a.* [996] (ed. and trans. Jones, pp. 18-19); Thornton, 'Maredudd', p. 587.

[171] *Annales Cambriae* (B), ed. Williams, p. 21; *ByS, s.a.* 994 [=995] (ed. and trans. Jones, pp. 48-49); *ByT* (Pen. 20), *s.a.* 994 [=995], (ed. Jones, p. 13; trans. Jones, p. 10); *ByT* (RBH), *s.a.* [995] (ed. and trans. Jones, pp. 18-19); *ASC.C*, ed. O'Keeffe, p. 88; *ASC.D*, ed. Cubbin, p. 50; E in *Two of the Saxon Chronicles*, ed. Plummer, I, 131.

[172] *ASC.C*, ed. O'Keeffe, p. 88; *ASC.D*, ed. Cubbin, pp. 49-50; E in *Two of the Saxon Chronicles*, ed. Plummer, I, 131.

[173] *Annales Cambriae* (BC), ed. Williams, p. 22; *ByS, s.a.* 998 [=999] (ed. and trans. Jones, pp. 48-49); *ByT* (Pen. 20), *s.a.* 998 [=999], (ed. Jones, p. 13; trans. Jones, p. 10); *ByT* (RBH), *s.a.* [999] (ed. and trans. Jones, pp. 18-19).

[174] *Annales Cambriae* (B), ed. Williams, p. 22; *ByS, s.a.* 1000 [=1001] (ed. and trans. Jones, pp. 48-49); *ByT* (Pen. 20), *s.a.* 1000 [=1001] (ed. Jones, p. 13; trans. Jones, p. 11); *ByT* (RBH), *s.a.* [1001] (ed. and trans. Jones, pp. 18-19).

[175] Gwynn, 'Medieval Bristol'.

[176] Blackburn and Pagan, 'A Revised Checklist', nos 172, 187c, 203.

[177] Besly, 'Recent Coin Hoards', pp. 84-85.

[178] The development of Dublin's trading links with Bristol from the late tenth century has been discussed by Wallace, 'Archaeology', p. 156. This may have brought artistic influences to South Wales, seen in late eleventh-century sculpture at St Davids: Edwards, 'Monuments', pp. 67-68.

The 980s and 990s appear to have been a particularly brutal period in the history of viking activity in Wales. Vikings from the Hebrides and Man also seem to have pursued specific agenda in seeking to bring Anglesey within their sphere of influence.

Other fleets of vikings from around the Irish Sea and from Scandinavia were also campaigning in Wales. As well as engaging in hit-and-run raiding against coastal churches, different groups of vikings took advantage of the political struggles within Wales, sometimes allying with one Welsh leader against another, or offering their services as mercenaries to whoever might hire them. This could have dire consequences not only for Welsh lay and clerical leaders, but also for the general populace whose voice is rarely heard in the historical record. The record of famine aggravated by war, the seizure of captives and the payment of tribute during these years do suggest the localised sufferings of Welsh people in consequence of viking campaigns.

The turbulence at the close of the tenth century contrasts with the record of viking activity in Wales from 1001 until after the battle of Clontarf. This silence may be because Scandinavian fleets were focusing their attention on England. Nevertheless, Welsh kings were not outside the field of action. Eadric Streona, ealdorman of Mercia, attacked St Davids in 1012.[179] It is possible that vikings were sheltering there in 1012 just as Dyfed had previously been used a base for viking ships in 877 and 914. The tacit cooperation of the local king, or his failure to fight vikings, could have provoked Eadric's attack.[180] Ireland, like Wales, has many fewer reports of viking warfare in the years from 1001 to 1013. This may be both because (as in the case of Wales) viking activity was focused on England and because of the influence which Brian Bóruma wielded over the viking towns of Ireland.

The Welsh chronicles show significant interest in the battle of Clontarf, and Welsh observers may have felt that the outcome would influence their

[179] *ByS*, *s.a.* 1011 [=1012] (ed. and trans. Jones, pp. 48-49); *ByT* (Pen. 20), *s.a.* [=1012] (ed. Jones, p. 14; trans. Jones, p. 11); *ByT* (RBH), *s.a.* [1012] (ed. and trans. Jones, pp. 18-19).
[180] As royal succession in South Wales is uncertain at this date, it is also possible that Eadric led an expedition to exploit political weaknesses there for his own gain, as Kari Maund has suggested: *The Welsh Kings*, p. 59 and p. 151, n. 23. Russell Poole has argued that, five years after this attack, Welsh troops assisted in the defence of London against Knútr (Cnut). This is based on the evidence of *Liðsmannaflokkr*: Poole, 'Skaldic Verse', pp. 292-98.

own affairs.[181] Etchingham has drawn attention to the record of Brian as *ardrí Gaídhel Érenn ocus Gall ocus Bretan* ('over-king of the Gaels of Ireland, and of the Foreigners and of the Britons') in 'The Annals of Ulster' in 1014.[182] He has argued that Guðrøðr Haraldsson's successors in the Isles maintained a claim to Anglesey and recognised the supremacy of Brian Bóruma, which is why Brian's title included an assertion of power in Wales. The idea is interesting, particularly Etchingham's suggestion that Brian may have cultivated relations in the Isles as a counterweight to the growing influence of Sigurðr of Orkney. However, Brian's claim to rule Wales probably represents wishful thinking rather than any kind of political reality. After 1014, it has been argued by Seán Duffy that, 'Irishmen were sucked into the politics of the Irish Sea as a result of their assertion of authority over the Ostmen'.[183] The studies of Irish-Sea politics undertaken by Maund and Duffy show that Wales continued to figure significantly in the history of the viking towns of Ireland.[184]

Around the coasts of Wales there is a scatter of Norse place-names and finds. These demonstrate the presence of viking ships on raiding and trading expeditions. Viking settlement may have occurred in coastal areas of Gwynedd before 1014.[185] Commercial links between vikings and inhabitants

[181] *ByS, s.a.* 1013 [=1014] (ed. and trans. Jones, pp. 50-51); *ByT* (Pen. 20), *s.a.* [1014] (ed. Jones, p. 14; trans. Jones, p. 11); *ByT* (RBH), *s.a.* [1014] (ed. and trans. Jones, pp. 20-21).

[182] *Annals of Ulster, s.a.* 1013 [=1014].2 (ed. and trans. Mac Airt and Mac Niocaill, pp. 446-49); Etchingham, 'North Wales', p. 180.

[183] Duffy, 'Islesmen', p. 100.

[184] References to Wales in Icelandic sagas of the twelfth and thirteenth centuries, suggests that contact continued between Scandinavia and Wales. Charles, *Old Norse Relations*, pp. 89-123; Hines, *Old-Norse Sources*.

[185] Possible written evidence for viking camps in Wales may be indicated by the term *llongborth* (the Welsh equivalent of Irish *longphort*) found in *The Black Book of Carmarthen*, ed. and trans. Pennar, pp. 105-09; Gruffydd, 'A Poem', p. 206. The term may have been paralleled in Welsh with the same later and more general meaning which evolved in Ireland: 'military encampment'. Farther south, there is evidence of viking influence in Cardigan Bay. Llanddewi Aberarth boasts the only clearly identified hogback-monument in Wales. This dates from the late tenth century or later, and demonstrates Northumbrian-Scandinavian influence: Redknap, *Vikings in Wales*, p. 99. This could be taken as evidence of viking contact in this area rather than permanent settlement. A little further south, Cardigan Island sported the Norse name Hastaholm, although this has now fallen out of use. The name is found in an extent of Cardigan dated 1268 (Longleat MS. 624). I am indebted to Gerald Morgan for this reference. In Pembrokeshire, there is a dense scatter of Scandinavian names. With the exception of Fishguard, they are focused in the south and west of the peninsula; there are habitative names as well as those which describe coastal features: Charles, *Old Norse*

of the southern coasts of Wales are attested by archaeological evidence.[186] The sustained nature of viking activity along the Severn-estuary is suggested, for example, by coin-finds and the discovery of a furnished male burial at Caerwent in Monmouthshire.[187] The sea-routes from Ireland to Wales were economically significant, but above all they were strategically important to the viking towns of Ireland during the ninth and tenth centuries.

The dynasty of Ívarr loomed large in Welsh politics during the period under discussion. At times they appear to have cultivated alliances with Welsh rulers in opposition to English kings, at other times they sought to hinder the ambitions of Wales's most powerful rulers, including Anawawd ap Rhodri, Hywel Dda and Maredudd ap Owain. Through their involvement in Wales, vikings aggravated segmentary conflict between the descendants of Rhodri. Thus it may be argued, as in relation to Ireland, that vikings were a force which acted against the possibility of the unification of the country under one king. In the tenth century the descendants of Ívarr sought to develop a power-base in Anglesey, and around the millennium, a branch of the family based in Man made common cause with Scandinavian fleets to harry the southern coasts of Wales. These activities provide further evidence of the breadth of the political involvements of the dynasty of Ívarr outside Ireland.

Relations, pp. 138-47. In contrast, no silver-hoards or viking burials have been recovered from the area, although a coin of Edmund or Eadred (939×955) has been found at St Davids: Early Medieval Corpus, no. 1985:0055. The names probably reflect secondary migration from England. There is also a cluster of late Norse-influenced names around Cardiff: Charles, *Old Norse Relations*, p. 153.

[186] Blackburn and Pagan, 'A Revised Checklist', nos 55, 172, 187c, 203; Early Medieval Corpus, no. 1976:0003, 1993:0218, 1989:0083; Lane, 'The Vikings in Glamorgan?', p. 355-56; Knight, 'Glamorgan', pp. 350, 355; Redknap, 'The Limits', p. 13; Charles, *Old Norse Relations*, pp. 149-52; Redknap, *Vikings in Wales*, p. 20. Collingwood and Powell regarded a carved stone at Llanrhidian on the Gower as part of a hogback-monument: *Scandinavian Britain*, p. 187; Nash-Williams, *The Early Christian Monuments*, no. 218. However, Nancy Edwards has suggested, in conversation, that this is unlikely.

[187] A ring-pin and two single coins, of Edmund I (939-46) and Æthelred (978/79×1016) have also been recovered from the town: Redknap, *Vikings in Wales*, pp. 97-98; Early Medieval Corpus, nos. 1976:0004, 1976:0007.

8

Conclusion

THIS book is intended to provide a political analysis of the deeds of Ívarr's family from their first appearance in Insular records down to the year 1014. In this conclusion I shall provide a brief overview of their endeavours and make some general comments about their impact on the history of Britain and Ireland.

From the mid-ninth century Ívarr and his associates dominated the major viking settlements of Ireland. Their power was based in Dublin, and from there they challenged the authority of the most powerful kings of the Northern and Southern Uí Néill. Soon they extended their ambitions to Britain. During the 860s and 870s, Ívarr and his associates participated in the viking conquest of Northumbria, East Anglia and Mercia. These conquests paved the way for a larger-scale settlement of areas of eastern England by people from Scandinavia. Ívarr, his brother Hálfdan, and Óláfr also led campaigns against Pictland and Strathclyde with significant effect, notably the fall of Dumbarton. Following the deaths of these three kings, and the major defeat of viking forces in England at the end of the 870s, viking conquests in southern Britain were halted for some years. At this date some viking troops may have turned to Ireland, where an increase in viking activity is suggested in the chronicle-records.

The 880s and 890s witnessed fewer attacks from Ireland on Britain, although a feud between rival groups in Dublin in 893 seems to have caused some activity in Wales, Mercia, and perhaps in Pictland. A more significant burst of activity is recorded in 903 and 904 after the dynasty of Ívarr was expelled from Dublin, a development aided by continuing divisions within the viking elite. One of the main bases of the dynasty of Ívarr during this period of exile may have been the Hebrides. Their presence there could be linked with the migrations of people to northern England from the Hebrides in the early tenth century. From 914, the dynasty of Ívarr began to re-establish itself in Ireland. This marked a renewal of the pan-Insular empire created by Ívarr and ruled by his descendants.

The strength of this revival was threatened by the increasing power of kings of Wessex. From the end of the ninth century they made a series of territorial gains in England at the expense of vikings. In 927 Æthelstan seized control of York. This corresponded with a conflict in Ireland between the rulers of Limerick and Dublin which was not resolved until 937 and which limited the campaigns of the dynasty of Ívarr outside Ireland. The increasing efforts of West-Saxon kings of England to dominate affairs in the North may have pushed Strathclyde and Alba into the arms of the dynasty of Ívarr who were former enemies. These three parties made common cause against the English in the battle of *Brunanburh* in 937.

During the 930s, Welsh leaders expressed differing opinions: some supported the kings of England and others favoured the vikings of Dublin. This conflict is represented in the poem *Armes Prydein Vawr*, written in Deheubarth, probably during the reign of King Hywel Dda, who was one of the most loyal Welsh supporters of the English cause. The poem called for the Welsh to support the dynasty of Ívarr and kings in North Britain against the English. A few Welsh kings seem to have abstained from visiting the English court for a decade from the mid-930s and they may have adopted a position of neutrality, awaiting the outcome of events. The killing of Idwal, king of Gwynedd, by the English in 942 suggests that at least one king had cast off association with England.

The alliance of Strathclyde, Alba and the dynasty of Ívarr, which had posed such a threat to England in 937, was sundered in 945. After the viking leaders were expelled from York in 944, the English attacked Strathclyde and granted it to Mael Colaim of Alba in exchange for his allegiance. The struggle for control of York dragged on until 954 when the last viking king of the city was slain. It could not be apparent to contemporaries that the dynasty of Ívarr would never rule there again. Nevertheless, from the 940s vikings from Ireland enjoyed less political success. They were less able to lead campaigns to the east of England, and their relations with other Insular kings were ambiguous.

After 954, the power-base of the dynasty of Ívarr in Britain shifted towards the Irish Sea. As viking power weakened in Ireland, members of the dynasty who were based on the Isle of Man now posed the greatest threat to English power in Britain. The rulers of Man and the Isles during the late tenth century represented branches of the dynasty of Ívarr which were excluded from power elsewhere. In the early 960s the sons of Óláfr

Guðrøðsson, a king of York and Dublin who had died in 941, seem to have been based in the Isles. They represented a segment of the dynasty of Ívarr which was rival to Óláfr Sigtryggsson. Then during the 970s and 980s the Isles were ruled by Maccus and Guðrøðr, who may be identifiable as sons of Haraldr, king of Limerick and therefore grandsons of Sigtryggr, king of York and Dublin. These viking rulers may have seen themselves as heirs to the viking kingdom of Northumbria. They certainly held ambitions to win control of parts of western Britain: Maccus and Guðrøðr campaigned in North Wales and may have held Anglesey in the 970s. Their ambitions in North Wales were curbed by Edgar in 973, who orchestrated the famous meeting of kings on the River Dee. Nevertheless, after Edgar's death the Islesmen were soon campaigning in Wales, benefiting from rivalries between various Welsh kings. They may also have gained a foothold in Galloway around this time. During the 980s and 990s, vikings from Dublin and the Isles allied with some of the Scandinavian fleets which came to attack England. Thus it seems that the dynasty of Ívarr may have had some hand in the great campaigns which culminated in the conquests of England by Sveinn in 1013 and Knútr (Cnut) in 1016.

The battle of Clontarf in 1014, which marks the end-point of this study, is significant in demonstrating the range of political contacts which the dynasty of Ívarr had in Ireland, Britain and beyond. News of the event spread through northern Europe, and it is commemorated in famous literary works, notably *Njáls saga* and *Cogad Gaedel re Gallaib*.[1] The battle also represents divisions within the dynasty of Ívarr, as Waterford and Limerick had allied with the Irish overking Brian Bóruma, while Dublin and the Islesmen fought against him. During the eleventh and twelfth centuries, the descendants of Ívarr fell increasingly under the control of neighbouring kings. The battle of Clontarf may be regarded as a major

---

[1] These compositions and others were discussed by Goedheer, *Irish and Norse Traditions*. It has been debated whether the poem *Darraðarljóð*, in *Njáls saga*, was written to commemorate Clontarf or an earlier battle, fought by Sigtryggr Caech in 919. *Anglo-Saxon and Norse Poems*, ed. and trans. Kershaw, p. 117; Poole, *Viking Poems*, pp. 121-5; Hines, *Old Norse Sources*, pp. 4-6. I agree with Hines's recent argument that *Darraðarljóð* was indeed about Clontarf, not only on stylistic grounds but also because contingents from Scandinavia and Orkney are attested at this battle, which cannot be said of the battle at Dublin in 919. This poem about norns weaving a web of human guts, symbolising the battle, is one of the most memorable literary references to this conflict.

effort (and failed endeavour) of vikings in Dublin and the kingdom of the Isles to reverse this trend.

Overall, how does one sum up the impact of the dynasty of Ívarr on British and Irish politics? Their actions can be seen as part of a broader pattern of viking activity which stimulated long-distance trade and military campaigns. The descendants of Ívarr were involved in the foundation of viking settlements. This activity contributed to the development of distinct hybrid identities in Dublin, the Danelaw, Galloway, Strathclyde and the Hebrides. It is also possible to argue that vikings contributed to the development of national identities in England, Alba and Ireland through their impact on political structures and political rhetoric, as archetypal foreigners whom national heroes defeated.[2] During the Viking Age, England and Alba each underwent a process of political unification and expansion, under the leadership of the descendants of Alfred and the dynasty of Cinaed after they had vigorously fought against Ívarr's family in the late ninth century. Wales and Ireland had similar potential, but for various reasons the dynasty of Rhodri Mawr and the overkings of Uí Néill failed in the tenth century to subdue the descendants of Ívarr. As a result, these vikings became embroiled in local rivalries which in time made it harder for a monarchy to emerge. The descendants of Ívarr were therefore involved in formative processes of political development in Britain and Ireland. They can be seen to have had a long-term impact which outlived their own political effectiveness.

The regional and national identities of Britain and Ireland were transformed during the Viking Age. Along with these developments we see the dynasty of Ívarr acting as cross cultural brokers as they established a network of contacts along the seaways of the Insular world. The development of towns in Ireland and urban expansion in Viking England was promoted by their policies. This book has focused on political rather than economic issues (which is another large topic). Nevertheless, the towns ruled by this family (most notably Dublin and York) served as centres of political power as well as hubs of international trade. As military and economic entrepreneurs the dynasty of Ívarr fostered closer connections

---

[2] Ó Corráin, 'Nationality'; Foot, 'The Making'; 'The Scottish Chronicle', ed. and trans. Hudson.

between Insular kings and their Continental neighbours. This was to have long-term consequences.

The court of these Insular viking kings represented a meeting place for different cultures; Scandinavian, Gaelic, Brittonic, and English. The identity of the dynasty of Ívarr was coloured by their pan-cultural allegiances, but remained rooted within concepts of royal descent. The family proved to be a resilient institution for brokering power (as it was throughout medieval Europe). Nevertheless inter-dynastic conflict and the division of resources between different branches of the dynasty took their toll. Furthermore the territorially fragmented nature of their maritime kingdoms left the dynasty vulnerable to incursions by their land based rivals. Piece by piece, the wealthy but disjointed territories of the descendants of Ívarr were taken under the control of neighbouring kings. Even so, the dynasty remained a power to be reckoned with far beyond the period covered in this book.

I hope that this study has demonstrated that the influence of the dynasty of Ívarr was greater – chronologically, geographically, and politically – than has often been allowed.[3] This raises a question as to why the history of this dynasty has been sidelined. The old adage that 'history is written by the victors' may be relevant. The pan-Insular sea-kingdoms of Ívarr and his descendants ceased many centuries ago. No modern state is their heir. Another factor may be that historical research tends to proceed within the confines of modern national boundaries. The activities of the dynasty of Ívarr did not observe such boundaries. It is only by absorbing ourselves in the history of various political units that we can obtain a bigger picture of their achievements. There has been a growing number of studies on historical links across the Irish Sea since the 1990s.[4] This approach may help to cast light on some unjustly neglected areas of Insular history, of which the dynasty of Ívarr is a remarkable example.

---

[3] Several scholars who have worked on Irish history during the Viking Age, including Charles Haliday, J.H. Todd, Alfred Smyth and David Dumville, have recognised their significance. This book builds upon their analyses.

[4] For example, Griffiths, 'Anglo-Saxon England' (1991); Maund, *Ireland* (1991), and Duffy, 'Ireland' (1993).

Prosopography of Viking leaders named in Irish Chronicles to A.D. 1014

This prosopography is limited to information found in Irish chronicles. I have restricted discussion to the chronicle-entries in which individual viking leaders are named (for example, if someone is a king of Dublin I do not provide general discussion on the activity of Dublin-vikings during his reign). The names are given in alphabetical order (and secondly by order of appearance in the Irish-chronicle record). I have used Middle-Irish orthography. Where possible, equivalents of first names are given in Old Norse, in brackets.[1] Additional information on some of the characters named below may be found by consulting the index.

Accolb (?ON. Hególfr)

AFM 919 [=921]; AU 920 [=921]

He led a fleet of 32 ships to Lough Foyle. Fergal son of Domnall, overking of the Northern Uí Néill, killed the crew of one ship and took its booty.

AFM 928 [=930]

Jarl Accolb was killed along with many vikings by Uí Cheinnselaig.

Agonn (ON. Hákon)

AU 846 [=847]; CS [847]

In 847 he was defeated in battle by Cerball son of Dúngal, overking of the Osraige, in which 1200 men are said to have fallen. AFM 845 [=847] does not name Agonn but identifies the location of the battle as *Carn Brammit* and reports that it was the vikings of Dublin who were defeated.

[1] Old-Norse forms are based on information provided by Cleasby and Vigfusson, *An Icelandic-English Dictionary*; Marstander, *Bidrag*; Ó Corráin, 'Vikings in Scotland'; Ó Cuív, 'Personal Names'; *Fragmentary Annals*, ed. and trans. Radner, pp. 211-27; Smyth, *Scandinavian York*. I am grateful to Martin Syrett for his advice on many of the names.

airlabraid Átha Cliath = spokesman (law-speaker?) of Dublin

AClon 974 [=980]; AFM 978 [=980]; AT [980]; AU 979 [=980]; CS 978 [=980]
He was a civic official who fell at the battle of Tara in 980, in which Mael Sechlainn son of Domnall defeated vikings of Dublin and the Hebrides.

Albann (ON. Hálfdan)

AU 874 [=875]
He deceitfully killed Oistin son of Amlaíb.

AFM 874 [=877]; AU 876 [=877]; CS [877]
Lord of the 'Dark Foreigners'. He was killed in a battle on Strangford Lough between 'Fair Foreigners' and 'Dark Foreigners'. 'The Anglo-Saxon Chronicle' enables him to be identified as a brother of Ímar (d. 873).

Albdann mac Gofrith (ON. Hálfdan)

AU 925 [=926]
He led a fleet from Strangford Lough to Linns (Co. Louth) on 4 September.

AClon 921 [=926]; AFM 924 [=926]; ALL (lines 3128-29); CS [925] [=926]
King of the Foreigners. Albdann was killed in battle alongside Aufer and Roilt in 926. Eight hundred are said to have fallen in the engagement in which Muirchertach son of Niall, overking of the Northern Uí Néill, and the army of Ulster were the victors. According to AFM the battle took place on 28 December. He may be identifiable as a son of Gofraid (d. 934).

Amlaíb (ON. Óláfr)

AFM 851 [=853]; AU 852 [=853]; CS [853]; FAISS 239, 259
Son of the king of *Laithlinn*. In 853 he came to Ireland: the vikings of Ireland submitted to him, and he took tribute from the Gaels.

AU 856 [=857]; CS [857]
In 857 he was allied with Ímar and they defeated Cathal Finn and the Foreigner-Gaels in Munster.

AFM 857 [=859]; AU 858 [=859]; FAI §268

In 859 he was allied with Ímar and Cerball son of Dúngal, overking of Osraige, in an attack on Meath.[2]

FAI §279

According to the saga embedded in FAI, in 860 Amlaíb allied with the Northern Uí Néill overking, Aed Finnliath, against the Southern Uí Néill overking, Mael Sechlainn.

AFM 860 [=862]; AU 861 [=862]; FAI §292

Amlaíb raided Meath with Aed Finnliath in 862. According to the saga embedded in FAI, Amlaíb was married to Aed's daughter.

AFM 861 [=863]; AU 862 [=863]

Amlaíb, Ímar, and Auisle are identified as three kings of the Foreigners. In alliance with Lorcán son of Cathal, overking of Meath, they invaded the lands of Flann son of Conaing, overking of North Brega. During the raid they plundered a series of underground chambers including that at Knowth (Co. Meath).

AClon 862 [=864]; AFM 862 [=864]; AU 863 [=864]; CS [864]; FAI §317

In 864 he drowned Conchobar son of Donnchad, one of two kings (or 'half-king') of Meath, at Clonard (Co. Meath).

AClon 864 [=866]; AU 865 [=866]

Amlaíb and Auisle went with vikings from Ireland and Britain to invade Pictland where they took hostages.

FAI §347

According to the saga embedded in FAI, Amlaíb slew his brother, or kinsman, Auisle in 867. The act was said to have been aggravated by the fact that Auisle wanted to take Amlaíb's wife who is there identified as a daughter of Cinaed (perhaps Cinaed son of Alpin, or Cinaed son of Conaing).

---

[2] Middle Irish *Mide*, the medieval province of Meath, not modern County Meath.

AI [867]

Amlaíb committed an act of treachery against the church of Lismore (Co. Waterford) and held the abbot Martán, who was liberated from him.

AClon 865 [=867] and cf. AClon 897; AFM 865 [=867]; AU 866 [=867]; FAI §349

In 867 Cennétig son of Gaethíne, overking of the Loígis, and Mael Ciaráin son of Rónán attacked Amlaíb's camp at Clondalkin. They are said to have killed one hundred viking leaders.

AClon 867 [=869]; AFM 867 [=869]; AU 868 [=869]; CS [869]; FAI §374

In 869 Amlaíb plundered Armagh where 1000 people were said to have been killed.

AU 869 [=870]

In 870 there was a four-month siege of Dumbarton Rock by Amlaíb and Ímar, 'two kings of the Northmen', after which they plundered and destroyed the fortress.

AU 870 [=871]; CS [871]; FAI §393

In 871 Amlaíb and Ímar returned to Dublin from North Britain with two hundred ships and a great booty of people, of English and Britons and Picts.

FAI §400

According to the saga embedded in FAI, Amlaíb went to *Lochlann* at the behest of his father Gofraid. We know from 'The Chronicle of the Kings of Alba' that Amlaíb was killed in North Britain in 874. There is no contemporary evidence to support the statement that his father was called Gofraid.

Amlaíb may have been the father of Oistin (d. 875) and Carlus (d. 868).

Amlaíb Cenncairech (ON. Óláfr)

AFM 931 [=933]

Amlaíb Cenncairech of Limerick won a victory against Uí Maine.

AClon 930 [=936]; AFM 934 [=936]

He travelled from Lough Erne to Lough Ree and remained seven months on the River Shannon from where he plundered the borders of Connaught.

AFM 935 [=937]

His ships were destroyed on Lough Ree by Amlaíb son of Gofraid (d. 941), and he was taken captive with his men.

Amlaíb Cuarán mac Sitric (ON. Óláfr)

AClon 933 [=940]; AFM 938 [=940]

Amlaíb Cuarán went to York and Blácaire son of Gofraid took control of Dublin.

AClon 937[=945]; AFM 943 [=945]; AU 944 [=945]

Blácaire was expelled from Dublin and Amlaíb succeeded him.

AU 944 [=945]

A band of followers of Ruaidrí ua Canannáin were killed by Congalach son of Maelmithig and Amlaíb Cuarán in Conaille.

AFM 944 [=946]

Amlaíb Cuarán and his men plundered Kilcullen (Co. Kildare).

AU 946 [=947]; AFM 945 [=947]

Ruaidrí ua Canannáin defeated Amlaíb Cuarán and Congalach son of Maelmithig in battle at Slane (Co. Meath).

AClon 946 [=951]

Amlaíb was king of York for another year.

AFM 954 [=956]

Amlaíb son of Gofraid (d. 941) is confused with Amlaíb Cuarán in an account of how the Dubliners ambushed Congalach son of Maelmithig and killed him.

AFM 960 [=962]
Amlaíb led a force of vikings and Leinstermen to oppose the invasion of Uí Cholgain by Sitriuc Cam. Sitriuc was defeated, but escaped, and Amlaíb was wounded in the thigh by an arrow.

CS 962 [=964]
Amlaíb son of Sitriuc led an attack on Kildare.

AFM 962 [=964]
Amlaíb son of Sitriuc was defeated by the Osraige in battle at Inistogue (Co. Kilkenny), where many vikings were killed.

AFM 965 [=967]
Lord of the Foreigners
   Amlaíb and Cerball, son of Lorcán, killed Muiredach, son of Faelán, Abbot of Kildare.

AFM 976 [=970/8]; AU 969 [=970]
The battle of Kilmona (Co. Westmeath) was won by Amlaíb and Domnall son of Congalach against Domnall ua Néill. The list of fallen includes Ardgar son of Matudán, overking of Ulster; Donnacán son of Mael Muire, overking of the Airgialla and Cinaed son of Cróngall, overking of the Conaille.

AFM 968 [=970]; AU 969 [=970]; CS [968] [=970]
Amlaíb Cuarán plundered Kells (Co. Meath) with vikings and Leinstermen.

AB §272; AFM 975 [=977]; AU 976 [=977]; AT [977]
Amlaíb son of Sitriuc killed Muirchertach son of Domnall ua Néill and Congalach son of Domnall.

AClon 974 [=980]; AFM 978, 979 [=980]; AT [980]; CS [978] [=980]
Ardrí of the Foreigners of Dublin,
   After the battle of Tara, Amlaíb went on pilgrimage to Iona and died there.

He can be identified as the father of Rögnvaldr (d. 980), Glúniarann (d. 989), Sigtryggr (d. 1042), Haraldr (d. 999), Dubgall (d. 1014) and Mael Muire (d. 1021).

Amlaíb 'ffroit' (ON. Óláfr)

AClon 931 [=937]
He is listed among the dead at the battle of *Brunanburh*. The origin of this list in AClon is uncertain.

Amlaíb mac Gofrith (ON. Óláfr)

AClon 923 [=928]; AFM 926 [=928]; CS [927] [=928]
The son of Gofraid attacked Kildare from Waterford.

AClon 928 [=933]; AFM 931 [=933]; CS [932] [=933]
Amlaíb son of Gofraid plundered Armagh from Strangford Lough on the feast of St Martin. In alliance with Matudán, son of Aed, overking of Ulster, he ravaged as far as Slieve Beagh, but Muirchertach, son of Niall, overtook them, and they lost men (AClon: 1200) (AFM, CS: 240) and booty as a result.

AU 934 [=935]
Amlaíb ua Ímair attacked Lagore crannog (Co. Meath). The burial chamber at Knowth (Co. Meath) was sacked in the same week.

AFM 935 [=937]
Lord of the Foreigners
Amlaíb son of Gofraid came from Dublin to Lough Ree where he destroyed the ships of Amlaíb Cenncairech and captured him.

AClon 931 [=937], AU 936 [=937]
Amlaíb son of Gofraid departed from Dublin and fought a battle [at *Brunanburh*] against the English. (AU: Amlaíb escaped with a few followers.)

AFM 938 [=937/940]

AFM contains a brief record of *Brunanburh*, apparently drawn from an English source. It has been mistakenly inserted under the year 938 [=940] and Amlaíb son of Gofraid is confused with Amlaíb son of Sitriuc.

AFM 936 [=938]; AU 937 [=938]

Amlaíb son of Gofraid returned to Dublin.

AClon 932 [=938]; AFM 936 [=938]; AU 937 [=938]; CS [937] [=938]

Amlaíb, son of Gofraid ua Ímair, plundered Kilcullen (Co. Kildare) and is said to have taken 1000 captives.

AClon 934 [=941]; CS [940] [=941]

Amlaíb son of Gofraid (AClon, 'king of Danes'; CS, 'The king of the Fair Foreigners and the Dark Foreigners') died.

He can be identified as a son of Gofraid (d. 934) and a brother of Albdann (d. 926).

He was the father of Sitriuc Cam (*fl.* 962).

Amlaíb mac Ímair (ON. Óláfr)

AClon 970 [=977]; AFM 975 [=977]; AI [977]; AT [977]; CS [975] [=977]

Brian Bóruma killed Ímar of Limerick and his two sons, Amlaíb and Dubcenn, on Scattery Island (Co. Clare).

Amlaíb mac Lagmainn (ON. Óláfr)

ALC 1014; AU 1014

He was killed at the battle of Clontarf, in which the army of Brian Bóruma defeated the forces of Dublin and Leinster.

Amlaíb mac Sitric (ON. Óláfr)

AFM 1012 [=1013]; AI [1013]; AU 1012 [=1013]; CS [1011] [=1013]

Son of the king of the Foreigners

He participated in an attack on Munster by vikings from Dublin and was treacherously slain, with Mathgamain mac Dubgaill, by Cathal mac Domnaill.

He can be identified as a son of Sitriuc mac Amlaíb (d. 1042) and he may have been a brother of Artalach (d. 999).

Amlaíb ua Ímair (ON. Óláfr)

AFM 891 [=896]; AU 895 [=896]; CS [896]

He was killed in battle in 896 along with Glúntradna mac Glúniarainn against the Conaille and Aiteid son of Láigne. Eight hundred are said to have fallen in the engagement.

He was a grandson of Ímar.

Amlaide (ON. Haflidi)

AFM 904 [=909], 917 [=919]; FAI §424

According to a poem of uncertain origin within AFM and FAI, a viking called Amlaide killed Niall Glúndub in 919.

Aralt mac Amlaíb (ON. Haraldr)

AClon 992 [=999]; AFM 998 [=999]; AT [999]; CS [997] [=999]

One of the nobles of Dublin

He was killed in the battle of Glen Máma, in which Mael Sechlainn son of Domnall and Brian Bóruma defeated the vikings of Dublin.

He can be identified as a son of Amlaíb mac Sitric (d. 980) and as a brother of Ragnall (d. 980), Glúniarann (d. 989) and Sitriuc (d. 1042).

Aralt mac Sitric (ON. Haraldr)

AClon 933 [=940]; AFM 938 [=940]; AI [940]; CS [939] [=940]

King of Limerick

Aralt, son of Sitriuc ua Ímair, was killed in Connaught.

Aric mac Báirith (ON. Eirikr or Hárekr)

AClon 931 [=937]

Murphy's edition of AClon (based on Dublin, Trinity College, MS. 673 [F.3.19]) reads 'abbot of Arick mᶜ Brith', but London, British Library, MS. Add. 4817 reads 'about Arick mᶜ Brith' and this may be taken as the more reliable witness (*The Battle*, ed. and trans. Campbell, p. 159).

Aric is listed among the dead at the battle of *Brunanburh*. The origin of this list in AClon is uncertain.

He may have been a son of Bárid (d. 881) or Bárid (d. 914).

He may have been the same as mac Báirith (*fl.* 937).

Artalach mac Sitric

AT [999]

He was killed in the battle of Glen Máma in 999, in which Mael Sechlainn son of Domnall and Brian Bóruma defeated the vikings of Dublin.

He may have been a son of Sitriuc mac Amlaíb (d. 1042) and a brother of Amlaíb (d. 1013).

Aufer (?ON. Ávarr)

AClon 921 [=926]; AFM 924 [=926]; CS [925] [=926]

He was killed in battle alongside Roilt and Albdann son of Gofraid in 926. Eight hundred are said to have fallen in the engagement in which Muirchertach son of Niall, overking of the Northern Uí Néill, and the army of Ulster were the victors. According to AFM the battle took place on 28 December.

Auisle (?ON. Ásl or Auðgísl)

AFM 861 [=863]; AU 862 [=863]

Auisle, Ímar, and Amlaíb are identified as 'three kings of the Foreigners'. In alliance with Lorcán son of Cathal, overking of Mide, they invaded the lands of Flann son of Conaing, overking of North Brega. During the raid they plundered a series of underground chambers including that at Knowth (Co. Meath).

AClon 864 [=866]; AU 865 [=866]

Auisle and Amlaíb went with vikings from Ireland and Britain to invade Pictland where they took hostages.

AClon 865 [=867]; AU 866 [=867]

Auisle is identified as one of the 'three kings of the Foreigners'. He was deceitfully killed in 867 by his kinsmen / brothers.

FAI §347

According to the saga embedded in FAI, Auisle was the younger brother of Amlaíb and Ímar and he was killed by Amlaíb.

He may be identifiable as the father of 'mac Ausli' who was killed in 883.

Auisle mac Sitric Gáile (ON. Ásl or Auðgísl)

AClon 931 [=937]
Auisle is listed among the dead at the battle of *Brunanburh*. The origin of this list in AClon is uncertain.

He can be identified as a son of Sitriuc (d. 927).

Bárid (ON. Bárðr)

FAI §350
According to the saga-element of FAI, he was a jarl from *Lochlann* who was ambushed with Háimar about 867 by the men of Connaught. Nevertheless, he survived the encounter.

FAI §408
According to the saga embedded in FAI, Bárid was the fosterfather of a son of Aed Finnliath, overking of the Northern Uí Néill.

He is said to have plundered the islands of Lough Ree and Moylurg (Co. Roscommon) about 872.

AI [873]
Bárid led a naval expedition from Dublin to Ciarraige Luachra (Co. Kerry) where he raided the caves.

AFM 878 [=881]; AU 880 [=881]; CS [881]
Bárid was killed and burnt in Dublin after leading an attack on Duleek (Co. Meath). His death is attributed to a miracle of Saint Cianán.

CS [881]
He is identified as a son of Ímar and 'the head of the Northmen'.

He may be identifiable as the father of Eloir (d. 891) and the grandfather of the son of Uathmarán son of Bárid (*fl.* 921).

It is uncertain whether he was the father of Colla (*fl.* 924) and of mac Bárid (d. 937), as it can be argued that these two men were descended from Bárid mac Otir (d. 914).

Bárid mac Oitir (ON. Bárðr)

AU 913 [=914]

He was killed in a naval battle off the Isle of Man against Ragnall grandson of Ímar. Nearly all his followers perished in the engagement.

He may have been a son of Otir son of Iercne (*fl.* 883) and/or Jarl Otir (d. 918).

Batbarr mac Nirae (ON. Bøðvarr)

AFM 962 [=964]

The Osraige won a battle against Amlaíb Cuarán at Inistogue (Co. Kilkenny) where many vikings were slain including Batbarr, son of Nira.

Blácaire mac Gofrith (ON. Blákári)

AClon 933 [=940]

'Awley Cwaran came to Yorck, and Blackare m^c Godfrey arrived in Dublin to govern the Danes.'

AClon 935 [=942]; AFM 940 [=942]; CS [941] [=942]

Blácaire mac Gofrith led the vikings of Dublin in an attack on Clonmacnoise (Co. Offaly).

AFM 941 [=943]; AU 942 [=943]

King of the Foreigners

Blácaire's men killed Muirchertach son of Niall, overking of the Northern Uí Néill, at Ardee (Co. Louth). The same men plundered Armagh on the following day.

AClon 937 [=945]; AFM 943 [=945]; AU 944 [=945]

Blacaire was expelled from Dublin and Amlaíb Cuarán succeeded him.

AClon 943 [=948]; AFM 946 [=948]; AI [947 [=948]; AU 947 [=948]; CS [947] [=948]

King of the Northmen/Foreigners, ua Ímair

Blácaire was killed in the battle of Dublin against Congalach mac Maelmithig, overking of the Southern Uí Néill, where 1000 or more are said to have fallen.

He can be identified as a son of Gofraid (d. 934).

Bruatur (ON. Bróðir)

AB §281; AClon 1007 [=1014]; AFM 1013 [=1014]; ALC 1014; AU 1014; CS [1012] [=1014]

AB, AFM, CS: Lord of the Danes
ALC, AU: Lord of the fleet of Lochlainn
AClon: jarl of Orkney
ALC: jarl of York

He was killed at the battle of Clontarf, in which the army of Brian Bóruma defeated the forces of Dublin and Leinster.

Búitíne

AI [857]

In 857 his fleet came to Ireland.

Cammán mac Amlaíb

AU 959 [=960]

Cammán son of Amlaíb son of Gofraid was defeated at a place called Dub.

He can be identified as a son of Óláfr (d. 941). He may have been one of the meic Amlaíb active in 962, and in particular he may have been the same figure as Sitriuc Cam.

Carlus son of Amlaíb

AFM 866 [=868]

Son of the lord of the Foreigners (= Amlaíb d. 874)

He was killed in battle at Killineer (Co. Louth) fighting alongside the men of Brega and Leinster against Aed Finnliath, overking of the Northern Uí Néill.

Cathal Finn

AU 856 [=857]; CS [857]

In 857 Cathal Finn and the Foreigner-Gaels in Munster were defeated by Amlaíb and Ímar.

Catol

CS [904]

In 904 he won a battle along with two sons of Ímar against a Pictish king, Ead, and five hundred men are said to have fallen.

Colla mac/ua Báirid (?ON. Kolli)

AFM 922 [=924]; CS 923 [=924]

King of Limerick

Colla, son of Bárid, brought a fleet to Lough Ree and they killed Echtigern, son of Flannchad, overking of Bregmaine.

CS [931] [=932]

Colla, grandson of Barid, king of Limerick, died.

Colla may have been a son of Bárid (d. 914) or grandson of Bárid (d. 881).

Conamal

AClon 974 [=980]; AFM 978 [=980]; AT [980]; AU 979 [=980]; CS 978 [=980]

Conamal is listed among the fallen in the battle of Tara which was won by Mael Sechlainn son of Domnall against vikings of Dublin and the Hebrides. AU identifies Conamal as the son of a viceroy (*airrí*). There seems to be confusion between *airrí Gall* and *Gille Airre* (a personal name, which I have not yet found attested elsewhere). He is identified as a son of Gille Airre in the other accounts.

Cuilén son of Étigén

AClon 992 [=999]; AFM 998 [=999]; AT [999]; CS [997] [=999]

One of the nobles of Dublin

He was killed in the battle of Glen Máma in 999, in which Mael Sechlainn son of Domnall and Brian Bóruma defeated the vikings of Dublin.

Donnchad ua Eruilb

ALC 1014; AU 1014

He was killed at the battle of Clontarf, in which the army of Brian Bóruma defeated the forces of Dublin and Leinster.

Donnduban mac Ímair

AFM 995 [=996]; AT [996]; CS [994] [=996]

Donnduban killed Diarmait mac Domnaill, overking of Uí Cheinnselaig, in treachery in the year 996. He also killed Gilla Pátraic son of Donnchad, overking of the Osraige in the same year. Donnduban was killed shortly after by Leinstermen.

He can be identified as a son of Ímar of Waterford.

Dubcenn mac Ímair

AClon 970 [=977]; AFM 975 [=977]; AI [977]; AT [977]; CS [975] [=977]

Brian Bóruma killed Ímar of Limerick and his two sons, Amlaíb and Dubcenn, on Scattery Island (Co. Clare).

Dubgall mac Amlaíb

AB §281; AFM 1013 [=1014]; ALC 1014; AU 1014; CS [1012] [=1014]

rígdamna (king-material) of the Foreigners

He was killed at the battle of Clontarf, in which the army of Brian Bóruma defeated the forces of Dublin and Leinster.

He can be identified as son of Amlaíb mac Sitriuc (d. 1013) and the father of Mathgamain (d. 1013).

Eloir mac Báirid (?ON. Heløri)

AFM 887 and 888 [=891]; CS [891]

Killed in a battle between vikings and Uí Amalgada, in which many vikings were killed.

He may have been a son of Bárid (d. 881).

Eloir mac Iargni (?ON. Heløri)

AFM 885 [=886]; AU 885 [=886]; CS [886]

In 886 he killed Éremón son of Aed, overking of Ulster.

He may have been a son of Iercne (d. 852).

Gebechán

AClon 931 [=937]

'King of the Islands'

Gebechán is listed among the dead at the battle of *Brunanburh*. The origin of this list in AClon is uncertain.

Gilla Ciaráin mac Glúniarann

AB §281; AFM 1013 [=1014]; ALC 1014; AU 1014; CS [1012] [=1014]

rígdamna (king-material) of the Foreigners

He was killed at the battle of Clontarf, in which the army of Brian Bóruma defeated the forces of Dublin and Leinster.

He may be identified as a son of Glúniarann (d. 989)

Gilla Pátraic mac Ímair

AB §274; AClon 974 [=983]; AFM 982[=983]; AT [983]; AU 982 [=983]; CS [981] [=983]

A battle was won by Glúniarann son of Amlaíb and Mael Sechlainn son of Domnall against Domnall Claen, overking of Leinster, and Ímar of Waterford, in which many fell including Gilla Pátraic mac Ímair. In what seem to be later additions to the original chronicle-entry, Glúniarann is mistakenly identified as a son of Amlaíb.

He may be identified as a son of Ímar of Waterford (d. 1000).

Glúniarann (ON. Járnkné)

AFM 890 [=895]; AU 894 [=895]

In 895 he plundered Armagh with an army from Dublin. He is said to have taken seven hundred and ten captives in this attack.

He may have been the father of Glúntradna (d. 896)

Glúniarann mac Amlaíb (ON. Járnkné)

AB §274; AClon 974 [=983]; AFM 982[=983]; AT [983]; AU 982 [=983]; CS [981] [=983]

A battle was won by Glúniarann son of Amlaíb and Maelsechlainn son of Domnall against Domnall Claen, overking of Leinster, and Ímar of Waterford, in which many fell including Gilla Pátraic mac Ímair.

AClon 982 [=989]; AFM 988 [=989]; AI [989]; AT [989]; AU [988] [=989]; CS[987] [=989]

King of the Foreigners

Glúniarann son of Amlaíb was killed when drunk by his slave called Colbain.

Glúniarann can be identified as a son of Amlaíb mac Sitric (d. 980) and as a brother of Ragnall (d. 980), Haraldr (d. 999) and Sitriuc (d. 1042).

Glúntradna mac Glúniarainn

AFM 891 [=896]; CS [896]

He was killed in 896, with Amlaíb grandson of Ívarr, in battle against the Conaille and Aietid son of Láigne. Eight hundred are said to have fallen in the engagement.

He may have been the son of Glúniarann (*fl.* 895).

Gnímbéolu

AFM 865 [=867]; FAI §342

Leader of the Foreigners of Cork

He was killed by the Déisi.

Gofraid (ON. Guðrøðr)

FAI §§ 400, 401, 409

According to the saga embedded in FAI, Gofraid was a king of *Lochlann* and the father of Amlaíb and Ímar. Amlaíb is said to have travelled from Ireland about 871 to help him against warring subjects. He is said to have died in 873 of a hideous disease. None of these details can be relied upon.

Gofraid mac Amlaíb (ON. Guðrøðr)

AClon 957 [=963]; AU 962 [=963]; CS [961] [=963]

Gofraid mac Amlaíb died.

He may have been a son of Amlaíb mac Gofraid (d. 941) or Amlaíb mac Sitric (d. 980).

Gofraid mac Arailt (ON. Guðrøðr)

AI [984]

A great naval expedition by the sons of Aralt to Waterford. They exchanged hostages with the sons of Cennétig to confirm an alliance against Dublin.

AU 986 [=987]

A son of Aralt (Gofraid or Maccus?) won a battle at Man in alliance with the *Danair*.

AClon 982 [=989]; AFM 988 [=989]; AT [989]; AU 988 [=989]; CS [987] [=989]

King of the Hebrides

Gofraid, son of Aralt, was killed in Dál Riata.

He was the father of Ragnall (d. 1005), a brother of Maccus (*fl.* 974), and perhaps a son of Aralt (d. 940).

Gofraid mac Fergusa (ON. Guðrøðr)

AFM 851 [=853]

Lord of the Hebrides

He is said to have died in 853. There has been much doubt over the historicity of this character: see Woolf, 'The Origins'.

Gofraid mac Sitriuc (ON. Guðrøðr)

AClon 945 [=950]; AFM 948 [=950]; CS [949] [=950]

He escaped from a battle in Brega between Ruaidrí ua Canannáin and the men of Dublin, where 6,000 are said to have fallen.

AClon 946 [=951]; AFM 949 [=951]; AU950 [=951]; CS 950 [=951]

He took possession of Dublin, and plundered Kells (Co. Meath). From there he attacked Donaghpatrick, Ardbrackan, Dulane, Castlekieran, and Kilskyre. It is said that 3,000 people were captured and a great quantity of gold and silver. Gofraid died soon after. This was attributed to divine vengeance.

He may have been a son of Sitriuc (d. 927) and a brother of Amlaíb (d. 980) and Aralt (d. 940).

Gofraid ua Ímair (ON. Guðrøðr)

AU 917 [=918]

Grandson of Ívarr

He led a battalion at the battle of Corbridge in support of Ragnall ua Ímair.

AClon 917 [=921]; AFM 919 [=921]; AU 920 [=921]; CS [920] [=921]

In 921 he took control of Dublin and then raided Armagh. According to AFM and AU he spared the prayer-houses, with their culdees and the sick.

AI [924]; AU 923 [=924]

In 924 he led an expedition by sea from Dublin. AI report that he took the hostages of southern Ireland to Roscarbery (Co. Cork). AU report that he took his fleet to Limerick where many of his men were killed in battle against the son of Ailchi.

AFM 924 [=926]; AU 925 [=926]

King of the Foreigners

He sent a relief-force to assist vikings from Loch Cuan who were besieged for a week at Athcrathin (Co. Down) after they were defeated in battle by the overking of the Northern Uí Néill, Muirchertach son of Niall.

AFM 925 [=927]; AU 926 [=927]

Gofraid left Dublin but returned after six months. In the same year, there was a departure of vikings from Dublin and Linns (Co. Louth) from Ireland, presumably to support Gofraid.

AClon 922 [=927]

A son of Ailchi and the sons of Sitriuc temporarily seized Dublin from Gofraid in 927.

AFM 927 [=929]

Gofraid plundered Kildare in 929.

AFM 928 [=930]; AU 929 [=930]

In 930 he plundered Dunmore Cave (Co. Kilkenny).

AFM and CS [929] [=930] report that 1000 people were killed in the attack.

AClon 926 [=931]; AFM 929 [=931]

In 931 Gofraid went into the territory of the Osraige to expel a grandson of Ímar from *Mag Raigne* (Co.Kilkenny).

AClon 929 [=934]; AFM 932 [=934]; AU 933 [=934]; CS [933] [=934]

He died of a sickness in 934.

He can be identified as the father of Amlaíb (d. 941) and Albdann (d. 926).

Graggabai (?ON. Krákubeinn)

AU 917 [=918]

He was a jarl who accompanied Ragnall (d. 921) from Waterford to North Britain. He died in the battle of Corbridge in 918.

Greisiam

ALC 1014

The historicity of this character is in doubt. He is listed among the fallen at the battle of Clontarf.

Grísíne (ON. Gríss + Gaelic diminutive ending)

ALC 1014; AU 1014

He was killed at the battle of Clontarf, in which the army of Brian Bóruma defeated the forces of Dublin and Leinster.

Háimar (? ON. Ævarr or Heimarr)

FAI §350

According to the saga-element of FAI he was a noble from *Lochlann* who was killed about 867 in an ambush by the men of Connaught.

Hingamund (ON. Ingimundr)

FAI §429

According to the saga embedded in FAI Hingamund is said to have left Ireland in 902. He was defeated in Wales by a son of Cadell son of Rhodri, and he then went to Æthelflæd, who granted him lands near Chester. His followers later seized Chester, but the city was retaken when the Irish among them were drawn to Æthelflæd's side.

Hona (ON. Auni)

FAI §278

According to the saga-element in FAI, Hona was a noble leader from *Lochlann* and a druid. He is said to have been killed about 860 by the men of Munster while travelling from Limerick to Waterford with Tomrir Torra.

Horm (ON. Ormr)

AU 855 [=856]; CS [856]; FAI§ 254

Lord of the 'Dark Foreigners'

He was killed in 856 by Rhodri son of Merfyn, king of Gwynedd.

FAI §§235, 251, 254, 260

The eleventh-century saga embedded in FAI asserts that Horm was the victor of the battle at Carlingford Lough in 852 in which Stain and Iercne were defeated. The saga adds that Horm became an ally of Cerball son of Dúngal, overking of the Osraige, and that together they defeated an army of *Lochlannaig* at Cruachan (Co. Tipperary) in 856.[3] After Horm's departure from Ireland some of his followers are said to have remained with Cerball.

Iercne/Iargni (ON. Járnkné)

AU 851 [=852]; CS [852]; FAI §235

One of two lords of 'Fair Foreigners'

In 852 he was defeated in battle by 'Dark Foreigners' at Carlingford Lough where he was beheaded. AFM 850 [=852] records the battle but does not mention him. He may have been the father of Otir (*fl.* 883) and/or Eloir (*fl.* 886).

Iloa Deck

AClon 931 [=937]

In London, British Library, MS. Add. 4817 there is a comma after Iloa, so these may be two separate names.

Iloa Deck is listed among the dead at the battle of *Brunanburh*. The origin of this list in AClon is uncertain.

?Ímar (ON. Ívarr)

AClon 915 [=919]; AFM 917 [=919]; CS 918 [=919]

Ímar is said to fight alongside Sitriuc in the battle of Dublin (AClon, 'Himer and Sitrick'; AFM, *ria n-Iomhar agus ria Sitriug Gále*). CS states *ría nGalloibh .i. ria nImar .i. Sitriuc Gaile* ('by the Foreigners, i.e. by Ívarr, i.e. by Sitriuc'). It is just possible that the original record read *ria h.*

---

[3] For the dating of saga-entries in FAI, see Downham, 'The Career', p. 18.

nImair .i. Sitriuc ('by the grandson of Ímar, namely Sitriuc'). Alternatively, this may be a reference to Ímar (d. 937).

Ímar (ON. Ívarr)

FAI §239
The saga embedded in FAI identifies Ímar as a younger brother of Amlaíb (*fl.* 853-74). He is said to follow Amlaíb in exacting tribute from the Irish in 853.

AU 856 [=857]; CS [857]
In 857 he was allied with Amlaíb; they defeated Cathal Finn and the Foreigner-Gaels in Munster.

AFM 856 [=858]; CS [858]
Ímar and Cerball son of Dúngal, overking of the Osraige, defeated Cenél Fiachach and the Foreigner-Gaels of Leth Cuinn, in the territory of Ara Tíre (Co. Tipperary). They are said to have led 6,400 men in the engagement.

AFM 857 [=859]; AU 858 [=859]; FAI §268
In 859 he was allied with Amlaíb and Cerball son of Dúngal in an attack on Meath.

AFM 861 [=863]; AU 862 [=863]
Ímar, Amlaíb, and Auisle are identified as three kings of the Foreigners. In alliance with Lorcán son of Cathal, overking of Meath, they invaded the lands of Flann son of Conaing, overking of North Brega. During the raid they plundered a series of underground chambers including that at Knowth (Co. Meath).

FAI §347
According to the saga embedded in FAI, Ímar was a brother of Amlaíb and Auisle. Ímar is said to have been involved in the plot to kill Auisle in 867.

AU 869 [=870]

In 870 there was a four-month siege of Dumbarton Rock by Ímar and Amlaíb, 'two kings of the Northmen', after which they plundered and destroyed the fortress.

AU 870 [=871]; CS [871]; FAI §393

In 871 Ímar and Amlaíb returned to Dublin from North Britain with two hundred ships and a great booty of people, of English and Britons and Picts.

FAI §401

The saga-element of FAI gives a genealogy of Ímar (son of Gofraid, son of Ragnall, son of Gofraid Conung, son of Gofraid) which cannot be relied upon.

    Ímar is said to have plundered Ireland in alliance with a son of Amlaíb about 871.

FAI §429

He may be the Ímar Conung who is mentioned in the saga embedded in FAI. It is said that in his youth he brought three large troops to plunder North Britain. His arrival is said to have caused the laity and clergy to embark on prayers, fasting and acts of charity, and to adopt the Crozier of Colum Cille as their battle-standard.

AB §256; AFM 871 [=873]; AU 872 [=873]; CS [873]

In 873 Ímar, 'king of the Northmen of all Ireland and Britain', died.

    He can be identified as the father of Bárid (d. 881), Sichfrith (d. 888), and Sitriuc (d. 896).

Ímar (ON. Ívarr)

AClon 931 [=937]

A son of the king (i.e., Amlaíb?)

    Ímar is listed among the dead at the battle of *Brunanburh*. The origin of this list in AClon is uncertain.

Ímar (ON. Ívarr)

AFM 948 [=950]

Tánaise (second in command / heir designate) of the Foreigners[4]

He was killed in a battle between Ruaidrí ua Canannáin and the men of Dublin in 950, where 6,000 are said to have fallen.

Ímar (ON. Ívarr)

AI [969]

Ímar of Limerick

He killed Béolan Lítil and his son.

AFM 972 [=974]; AI [974]

AFM: Lord of the Foreigners of Limerick

He was seized from Scattery Island (Co. Clare) by Maccus son of Aralt and the lawmen of the Isles.

AI [975]

Ímar escaped overseas and King's Island (Co. Limerick) was captured.

AClon 970 [=977]; AFM 975 [=977]; AI [977]; AT [977]; CS [975] [=977]

AI: King of the Foreigners

Ímar and his two sons, Amlaíb and Dubcenn, were killed by Brian Bóruma on Scattery Island (Co. Clare).

He was father of Amlaíb and Dubcenn (d. 977).

Ímar (ON. Ívarr)

AFM 967 [=969]

Ímar of Waterford

He allied with Mathgamain, overking of Dál Cais, to defend the Osraige against an attack by Murchad son of Finn, overking of Leinster.

AFM 981 [=982]; AT [982]; AU 981 [=982]; CS [980] [=982]

Ímar of Waterford plundered Kildare.

---

[4] McGowan, 'Royal Succession'.

AB §274; AClon 977 [=983]; AFM 982 [=983]; AT [983]; AU 982 [=983]; CS [981] [=983]

A battle was won by Mael Sechlainn, overking of the Southern Uí Néill, and Glún Iarainn son of Amlaíb against Domnall Claen, overking of Leinster, and Ímar of Waterford, where many fell, including Gilla Pátraic, son of Ímar.

AFM 992[=993], AI [993]

Ímar was expelled from Dublin by Amlaíb's son.

AClon 988 [=995]; AFM 994 [=995]; AT [995]

Ímar reigned in Dublin after Sitriuc son of Amlaíb.

AClon 988 [=995]

Ímar was put to flight and Sitriuc replaced him as king of Dublin.

AFM 997 [=998]

Ímar led a raid into Uí Cheinnselaig. There the viking army lost most of their horses and some of their men.

AClon 993 [=1000]; AFM 999 [=1000]; AT [1000]; AU 999 [=1000]; CS [998] [=1000]

Ímar of Waterford died.

He may be identifiable as the father of Gilla Pátraic (d. 983) and Donndubán (d. 996).

Ímar ua Ímair (ON. Ívarr)

AU 903 [=904]

He was killed in battle by the men of Fortriu.

CS [904]

He may have been one of the two sons of Ímar who killed a Pictish king, Ead, in 904.

FAI §429

An Ímar Conung who as a youth brought three large troops to plunder North Britain is mentioned in the saga embedded in FAI. However this is a retrospective account and I think it more likely that it refers to Ímar (d. 873).

'King of Danes'

AClon 937 [=945]

He was killed by the English at York

This could be Ragnall mac Gofraid (Rögnvaldr Guðrøðsson) who is mentioned in ASC. He may have been a son of Gofraid (d. 934).

?Laraic

AFM 951 [=953]

St Mullins (Co. Carlow) was plundered from *Laraic* by sea.

O'Donovan (AFM, II.698) assumed that Laraic was a viking leader, but it is probably a place-name, perhaps to be equated with Waterford (Port Lairge).

Lommíne

ALC 1014; AU 1014

He was killed at the battle of Clontarf, in which the army of Brian Bóruma defeated the forces of Dublin and Leinster.

mac Acuind

AFM 937 [=939]

He led a troop from Waterford in alliance with Cellachán, overking of Munster, against Meath. Together they attacked Clonenagh (Co. Laois) and Killeigh (Co. Offaly) and captured the abbots. Their forces were defeated in battle by Aimergin, overking of Uí Fhailge.

On chronological grounds it seems unlikely that he was the son of Hákon (*fl.* 847).

mac Ailchi

AI [924]; AU 923 [=924]

A son of Ailchi defeated the fleet of Gofraid (d. 934) which attacked Limerick in 924.

AClon 922 [=927]

A son of Ailchi and the sons of Sitriuc temporarily seized Dublin from Gofraid in 927.

AU 927 [=928]

Ailche's son went on Lough Neagh with a fleet of vikings, and he ravaged the islands of the lake and the territories bordering it.

He may be the same as Tomrair mac Ailchi.

mac/meic Amlaíb

AFM 960 [=962]

The fleet of the sons of Amlaíb and the lawmen came to Ireland, and they plundered Conaille and Howth as far as Ireland's Eye. The lawmen then went to Munster to avenge their brother, Oin, and they ravaged Little Island (Co. Waterford) and Uí Liatháin, and burnt Lismore (Co. Waterford) and Cork. They were defeated in a skirmish in the territory of Uí Liáthain, where 365 are said to have been killed. A raid was led by the son of Amlaíb from Ireland's Eye to Anglesey and Britain.

mac Auisli

AU 882 [=883]; CS [883]

He was killed by Otir son of Iercne and Muirgel daughter of Mael Sechlainn (overking of the Southern Uí Néill).

He may be identifiable as a son of Auisle (d. 867).

mac Báirith

AFM 935 [=937]

Cill Clethi (Kilclief, Co. Down?) was plundered by the son of Bárid.

He may have been a son of Bárid (d. 881) or Bárid (d. 914).

He may have been the same as Aric mac Báirith (d. 937).

Maccus mac Arailt

AFM 972 [=974]; AI [974]

Maccus son of Aralt and the lawmen of the islands plundered Scattery Island (Co. Clare) and seized Ímar, lord of the Foreigners of Limerick, from there.

AI [984]

A great naval expedition by the sons of Aralt to Waterford. They exchanged hostages with the sons of Cennétig to confirm an alliance against Dublin.

He was the brother of Gofraid (d. 989) and perhaps a son of Aralt (d. 940).

AU 986 [=987]

A son of Aralt (Gofraid or Maccus?) won a battle at Man in alliance with the *Danair*.

mac /meic Gillamáire

AI [1013]

The sons of Gilla Máire participated in an attack on Munster with vikings from Dublin. They were slain in Munster on the same occasion as Mathgamain mac Dubgaill.

mac Ímair

AU 892 [=893], 893 [=894]

Following a disagreement between the people of Dublin, a contingent left the port with the son of Ímar. He returned in 894. He may be the same person as Sitriuc mac Ímair.

mac Ímair

AI 990

The son of Ímar left Waterford.

He may be identified as a son of Ímar of Waterford (d. 1000).

mac Ragnall

AClon 935 [=942]; AFM 940 [=942]; AU 941 [=942]; CS [941] [=942]

AFM call him a jarl, AU refer to him as a king.

He plundered Downpatrick (Co. Down) and was killed within a week by Matudán, overking of Ulster. AFM mentions that he had a base on an island.

He may have been a son of Ragnall (d. 921).

mac Uathmaráin meic Báirid

AFM 919 [=921]; AU 920 [=921]

He brought a fleet of twenty ships to Kinnaweer (Co. Donegal) in 921, but no depredations are recorded.

He may have been the same person as Sichfrith mac Uathmaráin (*fl.* 932), and a grandson of Bárid (d. 881).

Mael Ísu

AClon 931 [=937]

Mael Ísu is listed among the dead at the battle of *Brunanburh*. The origin of this list in AClon is uncertain.

Mael Muire

AClon 931 [=937]

'sonn of Cosse Warce'

Mael Muire is listed among the dead at the battle of *Brunanburh*. The origin of this list in AClon is uncertain.

Mathgamain mac Dubgaill meic Amlaíb

AFM 1012 [=1013]; AI [1013]; AU 1012 [=1013]; CS [1011] [=1013]

He participated in an attack on Munster by vikings from Dublin and was treacherously slain, with Amlaíb mac Sitric, by Cathal mac Domnaill.

He can be identified as a son of Dubgall (d. 1014).

Odolb Micle (ON. Auðólfr)

AFM 865 [=867]; FAI §362

He was defeated along with the vikings of Dublin in battle against Cennétig son of Gaethíne, overking of the Loígis, in 867. Odolb was slain in the engagement.

Oin (?ON. Ónn or Jón)

AFM 960 [=962]

The fleet of the sons of Amlaíb and the lawmen came to Ireland, and they plundered Conaille and Howth as far as Ireland's Eye. The lawmen then went to Munster to avenge their brother, Oin, and they ravaged Little Island (Co. Waterford) and Uí Liatháin, and burnt Lismore (Co.

Waterford) and Cork. They were defeated in a skirmish in the lands of Uí Liáthain, where 365 are said to have been killed.

Oistin mac Amlaíb (ON. Eysteinn)

AU 874 [=875]

Son of Amlaíb, king of the Northmen (= Amlaíb d. 874),
  He was deceitfully killed by Albann.

Otir (ON. Óttarr)

AU 917 [=918]; FAI §459

He was a jarl who accompanied Ragnall (d. 921) from Waterford to North Britain. He died in the battle of Corbridge in 918.

  Joan Radner (*Fragmentary Annals*, p. 207) has suggested that he was identical with Otir mac Iargni (*fl.* 883), but this is uncertain.

  He may have been the father of Bárid (d. 914).

Otir Dub (ON. Óttarr)

ALC 1014; AU 1014

He was killed at the battle of Clontarf, in which the army of Brian Bóruma defeated the forces of Dublin and Leinster.

Otir mac Iargni (ON. Óttarr)

AU 882 [=883]; CS [883]

He killed a son of Auisle in alliance with Muirgel daughter of Mael Sechlainn (overking of the Southern Uí Néill).

FAI §§429, 459

According to the saga embedded in FAI he was a king killed in battle in North Britain, an event which might be datable to the first decade of the tenth century.

  Joan Radner (*Fragmentary Annals*, p. 207) has identified this leader with the jarl Otir who fell in the battle of Corbridge (918), but it is by no means certain that he is the same person.

  Otir may have been a son of Iercne (d. 852).

Ragnall mac Albdain (ON. Rögnvaldr Hálfdanarson)

FAI §330

In a fanciful account Ragnall is identified as son of a king of *Lochlann*. He is said to have travelled with his three sons to Orkney. Ragnall's two eldest sons then sailed to Spain and Africa and they brought a number of African captives to Ireland. These events are said to have occurred about 866/7. For commentary see Ó Corráin, 'Viking Ireland', p. 447.

Ragnall mac Amlaíb (ON. Rögnvaldr)

AB §273; AFM 978 [=980]; AI [980]; AT [980]; AU 979 [=980]; CS 978 [=980]

AU: the son of the king of the Foreigners

AFM, AT, CS: *rígdamna* (king-material) of the Foreigners

AI: mac Ímair (this may result from h. Ímair being confused with m. Ímair)

Mael Sechlainn son of Domnall won the battle of Tara against the vikings of Dublin and the Hebrides. Ragnall son of Amlaíb fell on the viking side along with Conamal, and the Orator (*airlabraid*) of Dublin, and many others.

Ragnall can be identified as a son of Amlaíb mac Sitric (d. 980) and as a brother of Glúniarann (d. 989), Haraldr (d. 999) and Sitriuc (d. 1042).

Ragnall mac Gofraid meic Arailt (ON. Rögnvaldr)

AI 1004 [=1005]; AU 1004 [=1005]; CS [1003] [=1005]

King of the Islands

He died in Munster.

He can be identified as the son of Gofraid mac Arailt (d. 989).

Ragnall mac / ua Ímair (ON. Rögnvaldr)

AFM 994 [=995]; AI [995]; AT [995]; AU 994 [=995]

AI grandson/descendant of Ímar, king of the Foreigners

AU son of Ímar

Ragnall was killed by Leinstermen.

Ragnall ua Ímair (ON. Rögnvaldr)

AU 913 [=914]

He defeated Bárid mac Oitir in a naval battle off the Isle of Man.

AFM 915 [=917]; AU 916 [=917]

In 917 Ragnall went with a fleet to Waterford, and Sitriuc, grandson of Ímair, went with a fleet to Cenn Fuait, in the east of Leinster. Ragnall brought reinforcements to support Sitriuc in a battle in Mag Femen (Co. Tipperary) against Niall son of Aed, overking of the Northern Uí Néill. He may have participated in the battle of Cenn Fuait against Ugaire son of Ailill, overking of Leinster.

AU 917 [=918]

In 918 Ragnall, identified as 'the King of the Dark Foreigners', led the troops of Waterford with two jarls, Otir and Graggabai, to North Britain. He fought a battle against the men of Alba on the banks of the River Tyne (the battle of Corbridge) in which neither side had a clear victory.

AU 920 [=921]

Ragnall ua hÍmair 'the King of the Fair Foreigners and the Dark Foreigners' died.

He was a grandson of Ímar. He may have been the father of mac Ragnaill (d. 942).

Rodolb (ON. Rauðúlfr)

AFM 860 [=862]; FAI §§ 249, 281, 308

There is some doubt about the historicity of this character. He appears in the eleventh-century saga embedded in FAI, from which information was included in AFM.

He is said to have been defeated in battle three times by Cerball son of Dúngal, overking of the Osraige.

Roilt (ON. Hróaldr or Haraldr)

AClon 921 [=926]; AFM 924 [=926]; CS [925] [=926]

He was killed in battle alongside Aufer and Albdann son of Gofraid in 926. Eight hundred are said to have fallen in the engagement in which Muirchertach son of Niall, overking of the Northern Uí Néill, and the army of Ulster were the victors. According to AFM the battle took place on 28 December.

Saxolb (ON. Saxólfr)

AClon 834 [=837]; AFM 836 [=837]; AU 836 [=837]; CS [837]
Lord of the Foreigners
> He was killed by the Cianachta in 837.

Sichfrith (ON. Sigfrøðr)

AU 892 [=893]
He is identified as a jarl.
> In 893 there was a great disturbance among the Foreigners of Dublin: 'They dispersed, one of their divisions went with the son of Ívarr, and the other division with Sigfrøðr the jarl'.
> There is record of a Sichfrith son of Uathmarán (*fl.* 933), but there is no reason to suppose that the two characters are the same. He may be identifiable with a leader of the same name who was active in England.

Sichfrith mac Ímair (ON. Sigfrøðr)

AClon 888; AU 887 [=888]; CS [888]
King of Northmen
> He was deceitfully killed in 888 by his kinsman / brother.

AI [883]
> A son of Ímar burned Lismore (Co. Waterford) in 883, and this may have been Sichfrith (or Sitriuc, d. 896).
> He was a son of Ímar and may have been a brother of Bárid (d. 881) and Sitriuc (d. 896).

Sichfrith mac Sitric Gáile (ON. Sigfrøðr)

AClon 931 [=937]
Sichfrith is listed among the dead at the battle of *Brunanburh*. The origin of this list in AClon is uncertain.
> He can be identified as a son of Sitriuc (d. 927).

Sichfrith mac Uathmaráin (ON. Sigfrøðr)

AFM 931 [=933]; AU 932 [=933]; CS [932] [=933]
Son of the daughter of Domnall mac Aeda
> He won a victory with Fergal, son of Domnall, against Muirchertach son of Niall, near Athlone (Co. Westmeath).

?Sitriuc (ON. Sigtryggr)

AFM 939 [=941]

Lord of Dublin

Sitriuc was taken hostage by Muirchertach son of Niall. The historical accuracy of this report has been challenged by Ó Corráin, 'Muirchertach', pp. 240, 247.

Sitriuc Cam

AFM 960 [=962]

He attacked Uí Cholgain from the sea, but he was overtaken by a force of Dubliners and Leinstermen. He escaped to his ships, after the slaughter of his people.

He may have been the same person as Cammán mac Amlaíb, and he may be identifiable as one of the sons of Amlaíb who attacked an area north of Dublin in the same year.

Sitriuc mac Amlaíb (ON. Sigtryggr)

AFM 967 [=969]

Son of Amlaíb, Lord of the Foreigners

He plundered Kells (Co. Meath) with Murchad son of Finn, overking of Leinster, but they were overtaken and defeated by Domnall, overking of the Northern Uí Néill.

AFM 992 [=993]; AI [993]

Ímar was expelled from Dublin by Amlaíb's son.

AFM 993 [=995]; AU 994 [=995]

Sitruic son of Amlaíb was expelled from Dublin.

AClon 988 [=995]; AFM 994 [=995]; AT [995]

Ímar reigned in Dublin after Sitriuc son of Amlaíb.

AClon 988 [=995]

Ímar was put to flight and Sitriuc was king of Dublin in his place.

AClon 992 [=999]; AFM 998 [=999]; AT [999]; AU 999 [=999]; CS [997] [=999]

AU: king of the Foreigners.

Sitruic son of Amlaíb imprisoned Donnchad son of Domnall, overking of Leinster.

AClon 992 [=999]; AFM 998 [=999]; AT [999]; CS [997] [=999]

Sitruic son of Amlaíb was expelled from Dublin by Brian Bóruma following the defeat of Sitriuc's men at the battle Glen Máma by Brian Bóruma and Mael Sechlainn, overking of the Southern Uí Néill.

AFM 1001 [=1002]; AT [1002]

Sitruic son of Amlaíb led a fleet to attack Ulster. He plundered Kilclief (Co. Down) and Inch (Co. Down) and took many captives from both.

AFM 1012 [=1013]; AI [1013]; AU 1012 [=1013]; CS [1011] [=1013]

King of the Foreigners

Sitriuc's son Amlaíb and his grandson Mathgamain were treacherously killed by Cathal son of Dubdabairenn.

AFM 1012 [=1013]; CS [1011] [=1013]

Mael Sechlainn attacked the territory of the Foreigners, and he burned the country as far as Howth; but Sitriuc and Mael Mórda killed two hundred of his men, including Flann, son of Mael Sechlainn.

AClon 1011 [=1018]; AFM 1017 [=1018]; AI [1018]; ALC [1018]; AU 1018; CS [1016] [=1018]

Braen son of Mael Mórda, overking of Leinster, was blinded in Dublin, by Sitriuc son of Amlaíb.

AClon 1012 [=1019]; AFM 1017 [=1018]; AT [1019]; CS [1017] [=1019]

Sitriuc son of Amlaíb attacked Kells (Co. Meath) where many people were slaughtered in the church and others were taken captive.

AFM 1021; ALC1021; ALL [1021]; AT [1021]; AU 1021

Ugaire son of Dúnlang, overking of Leinster, defeated Sitruic son of Amlaíb, king of Dublin, at Delgany (Co. Wicklow).

AClon 1027; AFM 1027; AT [1027]; CS [1025] [=1027]
Sitriuc son of Amlaíb, and Donnchad overking of Brega, led an army into Meath.

Raen ua Mael Sechlainn, met them in battle and was killed alongside Donnchad overking of Brega and many others.

AFM 1028; AI [1028]; ALC 1028; AT [1028]; AU 1028; CS [1026] [=1028]
Sitriuc son of Amlaíb, king of the Foreigners, and Flannacán ua Cellaig, king of Brega, went to Rome.

AT [1028]
Sitriuc son of Amlaíb came back from Rome.

AFM 1030; AT [1030]; CS [1028]
Gormfhlaith, daughter of Murchad, son of Finn, mother of the king of the Foreigners, i.e. of Sitriuc son of Amlaíb, died.

AFM 1032; ALC 1032; AU 1032
A battle was won by Sitriuc son of Amlaíb at the Boyne-estuary, against the Conaille, Uí Dortháin and Uí Meith, and many of their men were killed.

AFM 1035; ALC 1035; AU 1035
Sitriuc son of Amlaíb killed Ragnall ua Ímair, king of Waterford, in Dublin.

AClon 1155; AFM 1035; ALC 1035; AU 1035
Sitriuc son of Amlaíb plundered Ardbrackan (Co. Meath).

AT [1036]
Sitriuc left his kingdom and went overseas. Echmarcach ruled in his place.

AFM 1042; AI [1042]; AT 1042
AI: king of Dublin
Sitriuc mac Amlaíb and his daughter Caillech Finnén died in the same month.

He can be identified as a son of Amlaíb Cuarán (d. 980) and as the father of Amlaíb (d. 1013).

Sitriuc mac Ímair (ON. Sigtryggr)

AFM 891[=896]; AU 895 [=896]

In 896 Sitriuc mac Ímair was killed by other Northmen.

AI [883]

A son of Ímar burned Lismore (Co. Waterford) in 883, and this may have been Sitriuc (or Sichfrith, d. 888).

AU 892 [=893], 893 [=894]

Sitriuc may have been the son of Ívarr who left Dublin following a great disturbance among the inhabitants in 893, and who returned in 894.

He was a son of Ímar and may have been a brother of Bárid (d. 881) and Sichfrith (d. 888).

Sitriuc ua Ímair (ON. Sigtryggr)

AFM 915 [=917]; AU 916 [=917]

In 917 Sitriuc, grandson of Ímair, went with a fleet to Cenn Fuait, in the east of Leinster. Ragnall went with a fleet to Waterford. Sitriuc then fought in a battle in Mag Femen (Co. Tipperary) against Niall son of Aed, overking of the Northern Uí Néill, in which the viking side was saved from destruction by reinforcements brought by Ragnall. In the same year Sitriuc won the battle of Cenn Fuait against Ugaire son of Ailill, overking of Leinster. After the battle Sitriuc seized control of Dublin.

FAI §459

FAI date the battle of Corbridge after the installation of Sitriuc as king.

AU 917 [=918]

AU report warfare between Niall son of Aed, overking of the Northern Uí Néill, and Sitriuc grandson of Ímar.

AClon 915 [=919]; AFM 917 [=919]; AI [919]; CS [918] [=919]

In 919 Sitriuc won a battle at Dublin against an Irish coalition led by Niall son of Aed, overking of the Northern Uí Néill. Niall fell in the engagement along with Aed son of Eochucán, overking of Ulster, Mael Mithig son of Flannacán, overking of Brega, and many others.

Sitriuc is given the nicknames *Gále* and *Caech*.

AU 919 [=920]
Sitriuc departed from Dublin 'through the power of God'.

AFM 925 [=927]; AU 926 [=927]; CS [926] [=927]
Sitriuc grandson of Ímar, 'the King of the Fair Foreigners and the Dark Foreigners', died.

AU add 'at an immature age'; AClon 922 [=927] call him 'prince of the new and old Danes'.

AClon 922 [=927]
Two sons of Sitriuc seized control of Dublin with a son of Ailchi.

AClon 931 [=937]
Auisle and Sichfrith, two sons of Sitriuc Gále, are said to have fallen at the battle of *Brunanburh*. The origins of this report are not clear.

Sitriuc can be identified as the father of Aralt (d. 940) and Amlaíb (d. 980). He may have been the father of Gofraid (d. 951).

Siucraid mac Loduir (ON. Sigurðr Hlǫðvisson)
AB §281; AFM 1013 [=1014]; ALC 1014; AU 1014; CS [1012] [=1014]
Earl of Orkney

He was killed at the battle of Clontarf, in which the army of Brian Bóruma defeated the forces of Dublin and Leinster.

Stain / Zain (ON. Steinn)
AU 851 [=852]; CS [852]; FAI §235
One of two lords of 'Fair Foreigners'

In 852 he was defeated in battle by 'Dark Foreigners' at Carlingford Lough from which he escaped. The saga-account embedded in FAI gives a lengthier narrative of the conflict, stating that Stain was an ally of Matudán, overking of Ulster but this cannot be relied upon as accurate. AFM 850 [=852] record the battle at Carlingford Lough but does not mention Stain.

Suartgair (ON. Svartgeirr)
ALC 1014; AU 1014
He was killed at the battle of Clontarf, in which the army of Brian Bóruma defeated the forces of Dublin and Leinster.

Tomrair (ON. Þórir)

AFM 846 [=848]; AI [848]; AU 847 [=848]; CS [848]
Jarl and deputy of the king of *Laithlinn*
    In 848 he was defeated and killed in battle by Ólchobur, overking of
Munster, and Lorcán son of Cellach at Skeanagun (Co. Kildare) where
1200 men are said to have fallen.

Tomrair mac Ailchi (ON. Þórir)

AI [922]; AU 921 [=922]
A jarl
    Tomrair led the fleet of Limerick in a raid on Muckinish (Co. Clare),
Holy Island in Lough Derg (Co. Clare), Clonmacnoise (Co. Offaly), the
islands of Lough Ree, and Meath.

AI [924]; AU 923 [=924]
A son of Ailchi defeated the fleet of Gofraid (d. 934) which attacked
Limerick in 924.

AClon 922 [=927]
A son of Ailchi and the sons of Sitriuc temporarily seized Dublin from
Gofraid in 927.

AClon 922 [=927]
'Tomair mcAlchi king of Denmarck (is reported to goe to hell with his
pains) as he deserved.' This entry may be misplaced, or there may have
been more than one son of Ailche who was active in these years.

AU 927 [=928]
Ailche's son went on Lough Neagh with a fleet of vikings, and he ravaged
the islands of the lake and the territories bordering it.

Tomrair Torra (ON. Þórir)

FAI §278
According to the saga embedded in FAI, Tomrair was a noble leader from
Lochlann. He is said to have been killed about 860 by the men of
Munster while travelling from Limerick to Waterford with Hona.

Tomrar (ON. Þórarr)

AI 866; FAI §340

He plundered Clonfert (Co. Galway) in 866 and died at his camp soon afterwards. His death was attributed to the vengeance of St Brénainn, patron of Clonfert.

Tomrar mac Tomralt (ON. Þórarr)

AFM 923 [=925]

He was killed by the Conmaicne Mara.

Torolb (?ON. Þórhrólfr)

AClon 925 [=930]; AFM 928 [=930]; CS [929] [=930]

Torolb established a base at *Ruba mena* on Lough Neagh.

AFM 930 [=932]; AU 931 [=932]

A jarl

Torolb was killed by Muirchertach son of Niall, overking of the Northern Uí Néill, and Dál nAraide.

Turges (ON. Þórgísl)

AB §251; AClon 842 [=845]; AFM 843 [=845]; ALL (lines 3110-11); ARC §243; AU 844 [=845]; CS [845]

In 845 he organised an encampment of vikings on Lough Ree from where Connaught and Meath were raided (including the churches of Clonmacnoise, Co. Offaly; Clonfert, Co. Galway; Terryglass and Lorrha, Co. Tipperary). He was captured by Mael Sechlainn son of Mael Ruanaid, overking of the Southern Uí Néill, and drowned in Lough Owel.

ua Ímair / Ímar (ON. Ívarr)

AClon 926 [=931]; AFM 929 [=931]

He was banished from Ossory by Gofraid (d. 934).

AClon: 'Himar' may be a mistake for *h. Ímair* or may be a reference to Ímar (d. 937)

AFM: *Ua nIomhair* (= 'the descendant [or grandson] of Ívarr').

Ulb (ON. Úlfr)

AClon 901 [=909]; AFM 904 [=909], 917 [=919]; FAI §424

According to a poem of uncertain origin within AFM and FAI, a viking called Ulb killed Cerball son of Muirecán, overking of Leinster.

Ulf (ON. Úlfr)

AClon 868 [=870]; AU 869 [=870]; CS [870]

In 870 Mael Sechlainn son of Niall, one of two kings (or the 'half-king') of southern Brega, was deceitfully killed by Ulf, a 'Dark Foreigner'.

Bibliography

ABRAMS, Lesley, *Anglo-Saxon Glastonbury: Church and Endowment*, Studies in Anglo-Saxon History 8 (Woodbridge, 1996)

ABRAMS, Lesley, 'Edward the Elder's Danelaw', in *Edward the Elder, 899-924*, edited by N.J. Higham and D.H. Hill (London, 2001), pp. 128-43

ABRAMS, Lesley, 'England, Normandy and Scandinavia', in *A Companion to the Anglo-Norman World*, edited by C. Harper-Bill and E. van Houts (Woodbridge, 2003), pp. 43-62

ABRAMS, Lesley, 'The Anglo-Saxons and the Christianization of Scandinavia', *Anglo-Saxon England*, 24 (1995), 213-50

ABRAMS, Lesley, 'The Conversion of the Danelaw', in *Vikings and the Danelaw: Select Papers from the Proceedings of the Thirteenth Viking Congress*, edited by James Graham-Campbell *et al.* (Oxford, 2001), pp. 31-44

ABRAMS, Lesley, 'The Conversion of the Scandinavians of Dublin', *Anglo-Norman Studies*, 20 (1997), 1-29

AHLQVIST, Anders, *'Is acher in gaíth ... úa Lothlind'*, *CSANA Yearbook* 3-4 (2005), 19-27

AMORY, Patrick, 'The Meaning and Purpose of Ethnic Terminology in the Burgundian Laws', *Early Medieval Europe*, 2 (1993), 1-28

ANDERSEN, Per Sveaas, 'Norse Settlement in the Hebrides: what happened to the Natives and what happened to the Immigrants?', in *People and Places in Northern Europe, 500-1600. Essays in Honour of Peter Hayes Sawyer*, edited by Ian Wood and Niels Lund (Woodbridge, 1991), pp. 131-47

ANDERSEN, Per Sveaas, 'When was Regular Annual Taxation Introduced in the Norse Islands of Britain? A Comparative Study of Assessment Systems in North-Western Europe', *Scandinavian Journal of History*, 16 (1991), 73-83

ANDERSON, Alan Orr, trans., *Early Sources of Scottish History, A.D. 500 to 1286*, 2 vols (Edinburgh, 1922; revised impression, Stamford, 1990)

ANDERSON, Marjorie Ogilvie, *Kings and Kingship in Early Scotland*, second edition (Edinburgh, 1980)

ANDERSSON, Theodore M., 'The Viking Policy of Ethelred the Unready in Anglo-Saxon England', in *Anglo-Scandinavian England: Norse-English Relations in the Period before the Conquest*, edited by John D. Niles and Mark Amodio, Old English Colloquium Series 4 (Lanham, MD, 1989), pp. 1-11

ANGUS, W. S., 'Christianity as a Political Force in Northumbria in the Danish and Norse Periods', in *The Fourth Viking Congress, York, August 1961*, edited by Alan Small (Edinburgh, 1965), pp. 142-64

ANGUS, W. S., 'The Annals for the Tenth Century in Symeon of Durham's Historia Regum', *Durham University Journal*, 32 (1940), 213-29

ANGUS, W. S., 'The Chronology of the Reign of Edward the Elder', *English Historical Review*, 53 (1938), 194-210

ARMSTRONG, Simon, 'Carolingian Coin Hoards and the Impact of Viking Raids in the Ninth Century', *Numismatic Chronicle*, 158 (1997), 131-64

ARNOLD, Thomas, ed., *Memorials of St Edmund's Abbey*, Rerum Britannicarum Medii Aevi Scriptores 96, 3 vols (London, 1890-96)

ARNOLD, Thomas, ed., *Symeonis Monachi Opera Omnia*, Rerum Britannicarum Medii Aevi Scriptores 75, 2 vols (London, 1882-85)

AUSTIN, T., 'Viking-Period Chester: An Alternative Perspective', *Journal of the Chester Archaeological Society*, 74 (1996-97), 63-87

BAGGE, Sverre, 'Law and Justice in Norway in the Middle Ages: A Case Study', in *Medieval Spirituality in Scandinavia and Europe: A Collection of Essays in Honour of Tore Nyberg*, edited by Lars Bisgaard *et al.* (Odense, 2001), pp. 73-85

BAILEY, Richard N., 'Aspects of Viking-Age Sculpture in Cumbria', in *The Scandinavians in Cumbria*, edited by John R. Baldwin and Ian D. Whyte, Scottish Society for Northern Studies Publications 3 (Edinburgh, 1985), pp. 53-63

BAILEY, Richard N., 'Irish Sea Contacts in the Viking Period – The Sculptural Evidence', *Tvaerfaglige Vikingesymposium*, 3 (1984), 7-36

BAILEY, Richard N., *Viking Age Sculpture in Northern England* (London, 1980)

BAKER, Peter S., ed., *The Anglo-Saxon Chronicle. A Collaborative Edition, Volume 8, MS F* (Cambridge, 2000)

BANNERMAN, John, '*Comarba Coluim Chille* and the Relics of Columba', *Innes Review*, 44 (1993), 14-47

BARDEL, Annie, and Ronan PERENNEC, 'Les Vikings à Landavennec: les traces du "passage" des Normands en 913', *Chronique de Landévennec*, 85 (1996), 32-40

BARROW, G.W.S., *The Kingdom of the Scots: Government, Church and Society from the Eleventh to the Fourteenth Century* (London, 1973)

BARROW, Julia, 'Chester's Earliest Regatta? Edgar's Dee-Rowing revisited', *Early Medieval Europe*, 10 (2001), 81-93

BARROW, Julia, 'English Cathedral Communities and Reform in the Late Tenth and the Eleventh Centuries', in *Anglo-Norman Durham, 1093-1193*, edited by David Rollason *et al.* (Woodbridge, 1994), pp. 25-39

BARTLETT, Robert, *The Making of Europe: Conquest, Colonization and Cultural Change 950-1350* (London, 1993)

BASSETT, Steven, 'Lincoln and the Anglo-Saxon See of Lindsey', *Anglo-Saxon England*, 18 (1989), 1-32

BATELY, Janet, ed., *The Anglo-Saxon Chronicle. A Collaborative Edition, Volume 3, MS A* (Cambridge, 1986)

BATELY, Janet, ed., *The Old English Orosius*, Early English Text Society (Woodbridge, 1980)

BATES, David, *Normandy Before 1066* (London, 1982)

BAYLÉ, Maylis, 'Reminiscences Anglo-Scandinaves dans la sculpture romaine de Normandie', *Anglo-Norman Studies*, 13 (1990), 35-48

BEAVEN, Murray L.R., 'King Edmund I and the Danes of York', *English Historical Review*, 33 (1918), 1-9

BEAVEN, Murray L.R., 'The Beginning of the Year in the Alfredian Chronicle (866-87)', *English Historical Review*, 33 (1918), 328-42

BELL, Alexander, ed., *L'Estoire des Engleis by Geoffrei Gaimar*, Anglo-Norman Texts 14-16 (Oxford, 1966)

BENEDIKTSSON, Jakob, '*Landnámabók*', *Saga-book of the Viking Society*, 17 (1966-69), 275-92

BERSU, Gerhard and David M. WILSON, *Three Viking Graves in the Isle of Man*, Society for Medieval Archaeology Monograph Series 1 (London, 1966)

BESLY, Edward, 'Recent Coin Hoards from Wales, 1985-1992', *British Numismatic Journal*, 63 (1993), 84-90

BEST, Richard Irvine, and H.J. LAWLOR, ed., *The Martyrology of Tallaght from the Book of Leinster and MS 5100-4 in the Royal Library, Brussels*, Henry Bradshaw Society 68 (London, 1931)

BEST, R.I., *et al.*, ed., *The Book of Leinster, formerly Lebar na Núachongbála*, 6 vols (Dublin, 1954-83)

BEST, R.I., and O. BERGIN, ed., 'Do Fhlaithesaib Hérend iar Creitim' in *The Book of Leinster, formerly Lebar na Núachongbála*, edited by R.I. Best *et al.*, 6 vols (Dublin, 1954-83), I.94-99

BHREATHNACH, Edel, 'Columban Churches in Brega and Leinster: Relations with the Norse and the Anglo-Normans', *Journal of the Royal Society of Antiquaries of Ireland*, 129 (1999), 5-18

BHREATHNACH, Edel, 'The Documentary Evidence for Pre-Norman Skreen, County Midhe', *Ríocht na Midhe*, 9, no. 2 (1996), 37-45

BIDDLE, M., and B. KJØLBYE-BIDDLE, 'Repton and the "Great Heathen Army", 873-4', in *Vikings and the Danelaw: Select Papers from the Proceedings of the Thirteenth Viking Congress*, edited by James Graham-Campbell *et al.* (Oxford, 2001), pp. 45-96

BINCHY, D.A., ed., *Críth Gablach*, Medieval and Modern Irish Series 11 (Dublin, 1941)

BINNS, Alan, 'The York Vikings: Relations between Old English and Old Norse Culture', in *The Fourth Viking Congress, York, August 1961*, edited by Alan Small (Edinburgh, 1965), pp. 179-89

BLACKBURN, Mark, 'Expansion and Control: Aspects of Anglo-Scandinavian Minting South of the Humber', in *Vikings and the Danelaw: Select Papers from the Proceedings of the Thirteenth Viking Congress*, edited by James Graham-Campbell *et al.* (Oxford, 2001), pp. 125-42

BLACKBURN, Mark, 'The Coinage of Scandinavian York' in *Aspects of Scandinavian York*, edited by R.A. Hall *et al.* (York, 2005), pp. 325-49

BLACKBURN, Mark, and Hugh PAGAN, 'A Revised Checklist of Coin Hoards from the British Isles, c. 500-1100', in *Anglo-Saxon Monetary History: Essays in Memory of Michael Dolley*, edited by M.A.S. Blackburn (Leicester, 1986), pp. 291-313

BLAIR, John, 'Wimborne', in *The Blackwell Encyclopaedia of Anglo-Saxon England*, edited by Michael Lapidge *et al.* (Oxford, 1999), p. 480

BLAKE, E.O., ed., *Liber Eliensis*, Camden Third Series 92 (London, 1962)

BLAKE, Norman J., ed. and trans., *Jómsvíkinga saga: The Saga of the Jomsvikings*, Nelson's Icelandic Texts (Edinburgh, 1962)

BLUNT, C.E., 'The Cabinet of the Marquess of Ailesbury and the Penny of Hywel Dda', *British Numismatic Journal*, 52 (1982), 117-22

BLUNT, C.E., *et al.*, *Coinage in Tenth-Century England from Edward the Elder to Edgar's Reform* (Oxford, 1989)

BORNHOLDT, K., 'Myth or Mint? The Evidence for a Viking-Age Coinage from the Isle of Man', in *Recent Archaeological Research on the Isle of Man*, edited by P.J. Davey, B.A.R. British Series 278 (Oxford, 1999), pp. 199-213

BORNHOLDT-COLLINS, Kristin A., 'Viking-Age Coin Finds from the Isle of Man: A Study of Coin Circulation, Production and Concepts of Wealth', 2 vols (unpublished Ph.D. Dissertation, University of Cambridge, 2003)

BOSWORTH, Joseph, and T. Northcote TOLLER, *An Anglo-Saxon Dictionary* (Oxford, 1898)

BOUET, Pierre, 'Les chroniqueurs francs et normands face aux invasions vikings', in *L'Héritage Maritime des Vikings en Europe de l'ouest*, edited by E. Ridel (Caen, 2002), pp. 57-73

BOURGAIN, P., *et al.*, ed., *Ademari Cabannensis Chronicon*, Corpus Christianorum, Continuatio Mediaevalis 129 (Turnhout, 1999)

BRADLEY, John, 'The Interpretation of Scandinavian Settlement in Ireland', in *Settlement and Society in Medieval Ireland: Studies presented to F.X. Martin, O.S.A.*, edited by John Bradley, Studies in Irish Archaeology and History (Kilkenny, 1988), pp. 49-78

BREESE, Lauren Wood, 'The Persistence of Scandinavian Connections in Normandy in the Tenth and Eleventh Centuries', *Viator*, 8 (1977), 47-61

BREEZE, Andrew, '*Armes Prydein*, Hywel Dda, and the Reign of Edmund of Wessex', *Études celtiques*, 33 (1997), 209-22

BREEZE, Andrew, 'The *Anglo-Saxon Chronicle* for 949 and Olaf Cuaran', *Notes and Queries*, new series, 44 (1997), 160-61

BREEZE, Andrew, 'Edgar at Chester in 973: a Breton link?' *Northern History*, 44 (2007), 153-57

BREEZE, Andrew, 'The Battle of Brunanburh and Welsh Tradition', *Neophilologus* 83 (1999), 479-82

BREEZE, Andrew, 'The Irish Nickname of Sitric Caoch (d. 927) of York', *Saga-book of the Viking Society*, 25 (1998-2001), 86-87

BREEZE, Andrew, 'Simeon of Durham's Annal for 756 and Govan, Scotland', *Nomina*, 22 (1999), 133-37

BREMNER, Robert Locke, *The Norsemen in Alban* (Glasgow, 1923)

BRODERICK, George, 'Irish and Welsh Strands in the Genealogy of Godred Crovan', *Journal of the Manx Museum*, 8 (1980), 32-38

BROOKE, Daphne, 'Gall-Gaidhil and Galloway', in *Galloway: Land and Lordship*, edited by Richard D. Oram and Geoffrey P. Stell (Edinburgh, 1991), pp. 97-116

BROOKE, Daphne, *Wild Men and Holy Places: St Ninian, Whithorn, and the Medieval Realm of Galloway* (Edinburgh, 1994)

BROOKS, N.P., 'England in the Ninth Century: The Crucible of Defeat', *Transactions of the Royal Historical Society*, fifth series, 29 (1979), 1-20

BROUN, Dauvit, 'Dunkeld and the Origins of Scottish Identity', *Innes Review*, 48 (1997), 112-24

BROUN, Dauvit, 'Pictish Kings, 761-839: Integration with Dál Riata or Separate Development?', in *The Saint Andrews Sarcophagus: A Pictish Masterpiece and its International Connections*, edited by Sally Foster (Dublin, 1998), pp. 71-83

BROUN, Dauvit, *The Irish Identity of the Kingdom of the Scots in the Twelfth and Thirteenth Centuries*, Studies in Celtic History 18 (Woodbridge, 1999)

BROUN, Dauvit, 'The Welsh Identity of the Kingdom of Strathclyde, ca 900-ca 1200', *Innes Review*, 55 (2004), 111-80

BROWN, Phyllis R., 'The Viking Policy of Ethelred: A Response', in *Anglo-Scandinavian England: Norse-English Relations in the Period before the Conquest*, edited by John D. Niles and Mark Amodio, Old English Colloquium Series 4 (Lanham, MD, 1989), pp. 13-15

BUGGE, Alexander, ed. and trans., *Caithreim Cellachain Caisil: The Victorious Career of Cellachan of Cashel, or the Wars between the Irish and the Norsemen in the Middle of the Tenth Century*, Det Norske historiske Kildeskriftfonds Skrifter (Oslo, 1905)

BUGGE, Alexander, 'Contributions to the History of the Norsemen in Ireland', I-III, *Videnskabsselskabets Skrifter, II, Historisk-filosofisk Klasse* (1900), nos. 4-6

BU'LOCK, J.D., 'Pre-Norman Crosses of West Cheshire and the Norse Settlements around the Irish Sea', *Transactions of the Lancashire and Cheshire Antiquarian Society*, 68 (1958), 1-11

BYOCK, Jesse, *Viking Age Iceland* (London, 2001)

BYRNE, F.J., 'Heads of Churches to *c.* 1200', in *A New History of Ireland*, IX, *Maps, Genealogies, Lists*, edited by T. W. Moody *et al.* (Oxford, 1984), pp. 237-63

BYRNE, Francis John, *Irish Kings and High-Kings*, second edition (Dublin, 2001)

BYRNE, Francis John, 'Onomastica 2: Na Renna', *Peritia*, 1 (1982), 267

BYRNE, Paul, 'The Community of Clonard from the Sixth to the Twelfth Centuries', *Peritia*, 4 (1985), 157-73

CAMPBELL, Alistair, ed. and trans., *Chronicon Æthelweardi: The Chronicle of Æthelweard*, Nelson's Medieval Texts (Edinburgh, 1962)

CAMPBELL, Alistair, ed. and trans., *Encomium Emmae Reginae*, second edition, with new introduction by Simon Keynes (Cambridge, 1998)

CAMPBELL, Alistair, *Skaldic Verse and Anglo-Saxon History*, Dorothea Coke Memorial Lecture 1970 (London, 1971)

CAMPBELL, Alistair, ed. and trans., *The Battle of Brunanburh* (London, 1938)

CAMPBELL, A. 'Two Notes on the Norse Kingdom in Northumbria', *English Historical Review*, 57 (1942), 85-97

CHARLES, B. G., *Old Norse Relations with Wales* (Cardiff, 1934)

CHARLES-EDWARDS, T.M., *Early Christian Ireland* (Cambridge, 2000)

CHARLES-EDWARDS, T.M., 'Irish Warfare before 1100', in *A Military History of Ireland*, edited by Thomas Bartlett and Keith Jeffery (Cambridge, 1996), pp. 26-51, 463-65

CHARLES-EDWARDS, T.M., 'Wales and Mercia, 613-918', in *Mercia: An Anglo-Saxon Kingdom in Europe*, edited by Michelle P. Brown and Carol A. Farr, Studies in the Early History of Europe (London, 2001), pp. 89-105

CHÉDEVILLE, André, and Hubert GUILLOTEL, *La Bretagne des saints et des rois, V^e-Xe siècle*, Histoire de la Bretagne 4 (Rennes, 1984)

CHRISTIANSEN, Eric, trans., *Dudo of St Quentin, History of the Normans* (Woodbridge, 1998)

CHRISTIANSEN, Eric, *The Norsemen in the Viking Age* (Oxford, 2002)

CHRISTIANSEN, Reidar Th., 'The People of the North', *Lochlann*, 2 (1961), 137-64

CLANCY, Thomas, 'Govan, the Name, again', *Annual Report, Society of Friends of Govan Old*, 8 (1998), 8-13

CLANCY, Thomas Owen, 'Review: Daphne Brooke, *Wild Men and Holy Places: St Ninian, Whithorn and the Medieval Realm of Galloway*', *Innes Review*, 48 (1997), 88-89

CLANCY, Thomas Owen, and Barbara E. CRAWFORD, 'The Formation of the Scottish Kingdom', in *The New Penguin History of Scotland, from the Earliest Times to the Present Day*, edited by R.A. Houston and W.W.J. Knox (London, 2001), pp. 28-95

CLARK, Cecily, 'The Narrative Mode of *The Anglo-Saxon Chronicle* before the Conquest', in *England before the Conquest: Studies in Primary Sources presented to Dorothy Whitelock*, edited by Peter Clemoes and Kathleen Hughes (Cambridge, 1971), pp. 215-35

CLARKE, Howard B., 'Proto-Towns and Towns in Ireland and Britain in the Ninth and Tenth Centuries', in *Ireland and Scandinavia in the Early Viking Age*, edited by Howard B. Clarke *et al.* (Dublin, 1998), pp. 331-80

CLARKE, Howard B., 'The Topographical Development of Early Medieval Dublin', *Journal of the Royal Society of Antiquaries of Ireland*, 107 (1977), 29-51

CLEASBY, Richard, and Gudbrand VIGFUSSON, *An Icelandic-English Dictionary* (Oxford, 1874)

CLEGG, Lindsay, *A History of Wimborne Minster and District* (Bournemouth, 1960)

CLUNIES ROSS, Margaret, 'The Art of Poetry and the Figure of the Poet in Egils saga', *Parergon*, 22 (1978), 3-12

COCKBURN, J.H., *The Battle of Brunanburh and its Period elucidated by Place-Names* (London, 1931)

COHEN, Marc, 'From Throndheim to Waltham to Chester: Viking- and Post-Viking-Age attitudes in the Survival Legends of Óláfr Tryggvason and Harold Godwinson', in *The Middle Ages in the North-West*, edited by Tom Scott and Pat Starkey (Oxford, 1995), pp. 143-54

COLGAN, John, ed., *Acta Sanctorum Hiberniae: Acta Sanctorum Veteris et Maioris Scotiae seu Hiberniae Sanctorum Insulae* (Leuven, 1645); second edition, with introduction by B. Jennings, Irish Manuscripts Commission Reflex Facsimiles 5 (Dublin, 1948)

COLGRAVE, Bertram, and R.A.B. MYNORS, ed. and trans., *Bede's Ecclesiastical History of the English People*, Oxford Medieval Texts (Oxford, 1969; revised impression, 1991)

COLLINGWOOD, W. G., 'King Eirík of York', *Saga-book of the Viking Club*, 2 (1898-1901), 313-27

COLLINGWOOD, W. G., 'The Battle of Stainmoor in Legend and History', *Transactions of the Cumberland and Westmorland Antiquarian and Archaeological Society*, new series, 2 (1902), 231-41

COLLINGWOOD, W. G., 'The Giant's Thumb', *Transactions of the Cumberland and Westmorland Antiquarian and Archaeological Society*, new series, 20 (1920), 53-65

COLLINGWOOD, W.G., 'The Vikings in Lakeland: Their Place Names, Remains and History', *Saga-book of the Viking Club*, 1 (1895-97), 182-96

COLLINGWOOD, W. G., and F. York POWELL, *Scandinavian Britain*, Early Britain (London, 1908)

CONNON, Anne, 'Sitriuc Silkenbeard', in *Medieval Ireland: An Encyclopedia*, edited by Seán Duffy (New York, 2006), pp. 429-30

CONNON, Anne, 'The *Banshenchas* and the Uí Néill Queens of Tara' in *Seanchas: Studies in Early Medieval Irish Archaeology, History and Literature in Honour of Francis J. Byrne*, edited by Alfred P. Smyth (Dublin, 2000), pp. 98-108

CORLETT, Chris, 'A Castledermot Hogback', *Archaeology Ireland*, 13, no. 4 (1999), 11

CORMACK, Margaret, '*Egils saga*, Heimskringla, and the Daughter of Eiríkr Blóðøx', *Alvíssmál*, 10 (2000), 61-68

COUPLAND, Simon, 'The Rod of God's Wrath or the People of God's Wrath? The Carolingian Theology of the Viking Invasions', *Journal of Ecclesiastical History*, 42 (1991), 535-54

COWAN, Edward J., 'The Vikings in Galloway: A Review of the Evidence', in *Galloway: Land and Lordship*, edited by Richard D. Oram and Geoffrey P. Stell, Scottish Society for Northern Studies Publications 5 (Edinburgh, 1991), pp. 62-75

COXE, Henry O., ed., *Rogeri de Wendover Chronica, sive Flores Historiarum*, 5 vols, English Historical Society (London, 1841-44)

CRAIG, Derek, 'Pre-Norman Sculpture in Galloway: Some Territorial Implications', in *Galloway: Land and Lordship*, edited by Richard D. Oram and Geoffrey P. Stell, Scottish Society for Northern Studies Publications 5 (Edinburgh, 1991), pp. 45-61

CRASTER, Edmund, 'The Patrimony of St. Cuthbert', *English Historical Review*, 69 (1954), 177-99

CRAWFORD, Barbara E., *Earl and Mormaer: Norse-Pictish Relations in Northern Scotland*, Groam House Lecture Series 6 (Rosemarkie, 1995)

CRAWFORD, Barbara E., *Scandinavian Scotland*, Studies in the Early History of Britain (Leicester, 1987)

CRAWFORD, Barbara E., 'The "Norse Background" to the Govan Hogbacks', in *Govan and its Early Medieval Sculpture*, edited by Anna Ritchie (Stroud, 1994), pp. 103-12

CRAWFORD, Barbara E., 'The Pawning of Orkney and Shetland: A Reconsideration of the Events of 1460-9', *Scottish Historical Review*, 48 (1969), 35-53

CUBBIN, G.P., ed., *The Anglo-Saxon Chronicle: A Collaborative Edition, Volume 6, MS D* (Cambridge, 1996)

DARLINGTON, R.R., *et al.*, ed. and trans., *The Chronicle of John of Worcester*, Oxford Medieval Texts, 3 vols (Oxford, 1995-)

DAVIDSON, H.R. Ellis, 'Thor's Hammer', *Folklore*, 76 (1965), 1-15

DAVIDSON, Hilda Ellis and Peter FISHER, trans., *Saxo Grammaticus: The History of the Danes, Books I-IX* (Cambridge, 1998)

DAVIDSON, Michael, 'The (non) Submission of the Northern Kings in 920', in *Edward the Elder, 899-924,* edited by N.J. Higham and D.H. Hill (London, 2001), pp. 200-11

DAVIDSON-KELLY, T.A., 'The Govan Collection in the Context of Local History', in *Govan and its Early Medieval Sculpture,* edited by Anna Ritchie (Stroud, 1994), pp. 1-19

DAVIES, Wendy, 'Ecclesiastical Centres and Secular Society in the Brittonic World in the Tenth and Eleventh Centuries', in *Govan and its Early Medieval Sculpture,* ed. Anna Ritchie (Stroud, 1994), pp. 92-101

DAVIES, Wendy, *Patterns of Power in Early Wales,* O'Donnell Lectures 1983 (Oxford, 1990)

DAVIS, R.H.C., 'Alfred and Guthrum's Frontier', *English Historical Review,* 97 (1982), 803-10

DAVIÐSDÓTTIR, Sigrún, 'Old Norse Court Poetry: Some Notes on its Purpose, Transmission and Historical Value', *Gripla,* 3 (1979), 186-203

DE BHALDRAITHE, Eoin, 'Adult Baptism in the Early Church', *Anabaptism Today,* 15 (June, 1997), 10-15

DE PAOR, Liam, 'The Viking Towns in Ireland', in *Proceedings of the Seventh Viking Congress, Dublin, 15-21 August 1973,* edited by Bo Almqvist and David Greene (Dublin, 1976), pp. 29-38

DE PAOR, Liam, 'Viking Dublin', *Dublin Historical Record,* 31 (1978), 142-45

DES GAUTRIES, J. Adigard, *Les Noms de personnes scandinaves en Normandie de 911 à 1066,* Nomina Germanica 11 (Lund, 1954)

DILLON, Myles, ed. and trans., *Lebor na Cert: The Book of Rights,* Irish Texts Society 46 (London, 1962)

DOBBIE, Elliott van Kirk, ed., *The Anglo-Saxon Minor Poems,* The Anglo-Saxon Poetic Records 6 (New York, 1942)

DOBBS, Margaret E., ed., 'The Ban-Shenchus', *Revue celtique,* 47 (1930), 283-339; 48 (1931), 163-234; 49 (1932), 437-89

DODGSON, J. McN., 'The Background of *Brunanburh*', *Saga-book of the Viking Society,* 14 (1953-57), 303-16

DOHERTY, Charles, 'Cluain Dolcáin: a Brief Note', in *Seanchas: Studies in Early Medieval Irish Archaeology, History and Literature in Honour of Francis J. Byrne,* edited by Alfred P. Smyth (Dublin, 2000), pp. 182-88

DOHERTY, Charles, 'Exchange and Trade in Early Medieval Ireland', *Journal of the Royal Society of Antiquaries of Ireland,* 110 (1980), 67-89

DOHERTY, Charles, 'Some Aspects of Hagiography as a Source for Irish Economic History', *Peritia*, 1 (1982), 300-28

DOHERTY, Charles, 'The Vikings in Ireland: A Review', in *Ireland and Scandinavia in the Early Viking Age*, edited by Howard B. Clarke *et al.* (Dublin, 1998), pp. 288-330

DOLLEY, Michael, 'Some Irish Evidence for the Date of the Crux Coins of Aethelred II', *Anglo-Saxon England*, 2 (1973), 145-54

DOLLEY, R.H.M., *The Hiberno-Norse Coins in the British Museum*, Sylloge of Coins of the British Isles 8 (London, 1966)

DOLLEY, R.H.M., 'The "Lost" Hoard of Tenth-Century Anglo-Saxon Silver Coins from Dalkey', *Journal of the Royal Society of Antiquaries of Ireland*, 91 (1961), 1-18

DOLLEY, Michael, 'The Palimpsest of Viking Settlement on Man', in *Proceedings of the Eighth Viking Congress, Aarhus, 24-31 August 1977*, edited by Hans Bekker-Nielsen *et al.*, Mediaeval Scandinavia Supplements 2 (Odense, 1981), pp. 173-81

DOLLEY, R.H.M., and J. INGOLD, 'Viking Age Coin-Hoards from Ireland and their Relevance to Anglo-Saxon Studies', in *Anglo-Saxon Coins: Studies presented to F.M. Stenton on the Occasion of his 80th Birthday, 17 May 1960*, ed. R.H.M. Dolley (London, 1961), pp. 241-65

DOLLEY, R.H.M., and D.M. METCALF, 'The Reform of the English Coinage under Edgar', in *Anglo-Saxon Coins: Studies presented to F.M. Stenton on the Occasion of his 80th Birthday, 17 May 1960*, ed. R.H.M. Dolley (London, 1961), pp. 136-68

DOLLEY, R.H.M., and E. PIRIE, 'The Repercussions on Chester's Prosperity of the Viking Descent on Cheshire in 980', *British Numismatic Journal*, 33 (1964), 39-44

DOUGLAS, David C., *Time and the Hour: Some Collected Papers* (London, 1977)

DOWNHAM, Clare, 'An Imaginary Viking Raid on Skye in 795?', *Scottish Gaelic Studies*, 20 (2000), 192-96

DOWNHAM, Clare, 'England and the Irish Sea Zone in the Eleventh Century', *Anglo-Norman Studies*, 26 (2003), 55-73

DOWNHAM, Clare, 'Eric Bloodaxe – axed? The Mystery of the Last Viking King of York', *Mediaeval Scandinavia*, 14 (2004), 51-77

DOWNHAM, Clare, 'Irish Chronicles as a Source for Inter-Viking Rivalry A.D. 795-1014', *Northern Scotland*, 26 (2006), 51-63

DOWNHAM, Clare, 'Living on the Edge: Scandinavian Dublin in the Twelfth Century' in *West Over Sea. Studies in Scandinavian Seaborne Expansion and Settlement before 1300*, edited by Beverley Ballin-Smith *et al.* (Leiden, 2007), pp. 33-52

DOWNHAM, Clare, 'Non-Urban Settlements of Vikings in Ireland before1014', in *Proceedings of the Conference on Irish-Norse Relations 800-1200, held in Oslo on 5 November 2005*, edited by Timothy Bolton (Leiden, forthcoming)

DOWNHAM, Clare, 'St Bega – Myth, Maiden, or Bracelet? An Insular Cult and its Origins', *Journal of Medieval History*, 33 (2007), 33-42

DOWNHAM, Clare, 'The Battle of Clontarf in Irish History and Legend', *History Ireland*, 13, no. 5 (2005), 19-23

DOWNHAM, Clare, 'The Career of Cearbhall of Osraighe', *Ossory, Laois and Leinster*, 1 (2004), 1-18

DOWNHAM, Clare, 'The Chronology of the Last Scandinavian Kings of York', *Northern History*, 40 (2003), 25-51

DOWNHAM, Clare, 'The Good, the Bad and the Ugly: Portrayals of Vikings in "The Fragmentary Annals of Ireland"', *The Medieval Chronicle*, 3 (2005), 28-40

DOWNHAM, Clare, 'The Historical Importance of Viking-Age Waterford', *Journal of Celtic Studies*, 4 (2005), 71-96

DOWNHAM, Clare, 'The Loígis: a Population-Group in Mediaeval Leinster, A.D. 600-1170', (unpublished M.Phil. Dissertation, University of Cambridge, 1999)

DOWNHAM, Clare, '"Hiberno-Norwegians" and "Anglo-Danes": Anachronistic Ethnicities in Viking Age England', *Mediaeval Scandinavia*, 19 (2009), 139–69

DOWNHAM, Clare, 'The Vikings in Southern Uí Néill to 1014', *Peritia*, 17 (2003-2004), 233-55

DOWNHAM, Clare, 'Tomrar's death at Port Manann and a Possible *Longphort* Site in Ireland', *Ainm* (forthcoming)

DOYLE, Ian W., 'The Early Medieval Activity at Dalkey Island, Co. Dublin: A Re-Assessment', *Journal of Irish Archaeology*, 9 (1998), 89-103

DRISCOLL, M.J., ed. and trans., *Ágrip af Nóregskonungasögum: A Twelfth Century Synoptic History of the Kings of Norway* (London, 1995)

DRISCOLL, Stephen T., 'Church Archaeology in Glasgow and the Kingdom of Strathclyde', *Innes Review*, 49 (1998), 95-114

DRISCOLL, Stephen T., 'Exploring the Christian Origins of Glasgow: Excavations at Glasgow Cathedral and Govan Old Parish Church', in *Death and Burial in Medieval Europe: Papers from the Brugge 1997 Conference*, Volume II, edited by Guy de Boe and Frans Verhaeghe (Zellik, 1997), pp. 101-09

DRISCOLL, Stephen T., 'Kingdom of Strathclyde's final chapter' *British Archaeology*, 27 (1997) http://www.britarch.ac.uk/BA/ba27/ba27feat.html#driscoll accessed 21/01/07

DUCZKO, Wladyslaw, *Viking Rus: Studies on the Presence of Scandinavians in Eastern Europe* (Leiden, 2004)

DUFFY, Seán, 'Ireland and the Irish Sea Region, 1014-1318' (unpublished Ph.D. Dissertation, University of Dublin, Trinity College, 1993)

DUFFY, Seán, 'Irishmen and Islesmen in the Kingdoms of Dublin and Man, 1052-1171', *Ériu*, 43 (1992), 93-133

DUFFY, Seán, 'Ostmen, Irish and Welsh in the Eleventh Century', *Peritia*, 9 (1995), 378-96

DUMVILLE, David N., 'A Millennium of Gaelic Chronicling', *The Medieval Chronicle*, 1 (1999) 103-15

DUMVILLE, David N., ed. and trans., *Annales Cambriae, A.D. 682-954: Texts A-C in Parallel*, Basic Texts for Brittonic History 1 (Cambridge, 2002)

DUMVILLE, David N., 'A Pictish or Gaelic Ecclesiastic in Mercia', *Scottish Gaelic Studies*, 21 (2003), 1-8

DUMVILLE, David N., 'Brittany and "Armes Prydein Vawr"', *Études celtiques*, 20 (1983), 145-59 (reprinted in his *Britons and Anglo-Saxons in the Early Middle Ages*, Variorum Reprints Collected Studies Series 379, London 1993, essay XVI, with same pagination)

DUMVILLE, David N., '*Félire Óengusso*: Problems of Dating a Monument of Old Irish', *Éigse*, 33 (2002), 19-48

DUMVILLE, David N., 'Images of the Viking in Eleventh-Century Latin Literature', in *Latin Culture in the Eleventh Century. Proceedings of the Third International Conference on Medieval Latin Studies, Cambridge, 9-12 September 1998*, edited by Michael Herren *et al.*, Publications of the Journal of Medieval Latin 5, 2 vols (Turnhout, 2002), I, 250-63

DUMVILLE, David N., 'Ireland and Britain in *Táin Bó Fráich*', *Études celtiques*, 32 (1996), 175-87

DUMVILLE, David N., 'Kingship, Genealogies and Regnal Lists', in *Early Medieval Kingship*, edited by P.H. Sawyer and I.N. Wood (Leeds, 1977), pp. 72-104 (reprinted in his *Histories and Pseudo-Histories of the Insular Middle Ages*, Variorum Reprints Collected Studies Series 316, London 1988, essay XV, with same pagination)

DUMVILLE, David N., 'Old Dubliners and New Dubliners in Ireland and Britain: a Viking-Age Story', *Medieval Dublin*, 6 (2004), 78-93

DUMVILLE, David N., 'St Cathróe of Metz and the Hagiography of Exoticism', in *Studies in Irish Hagiography: Saints and Scholars,* edited by John Carey *et al.* (Dublin, 2001), pp. 172-88

DUMVILLE, David N., 'Some Aspects of Annalistic Writing at Canterbury in the Eleventh and Early Twelfth Centuries', *Peritia*, 2 (1983), 24-57

DUMVILLE, David N., 'Textual Archaeology and Northumbrian History Subsequent to Bede', in *Coinage in Ninth-Century Northumbria*, edited by D.M. Metcalf (Oxford, 1987), pp. 43-55 (reprinted in his *Britons and Anglo-Saxons in the Early Middle Ages*, Variorum Reprints Collected Studies Series 379, London 1993, essay X, with same pagination)

DUMVILLE, David N., 'The Chronicle of the Kings of Alba', in *Kings, Clerics and Chronicles in Scotland 500-1297: Essays in Honour of Marjorie Ogilvie Anderson on the Occasion of her Ninetieth Birthday*, ed. Simon Taylor (Dublin, 2000), pp. 73-86

DUMVILLE, David N., *The Churches of North Britain in the First Viking-Age*, Whithorn Lecture 5 (Whithorn, 1997)

DUMVILLE, David N., 'The "Six" Sons of Rhodri Mawr: A Problem in Asser's *Life of King Alfred*', *Cambridge Medieval Celtic Studies*, 4 (1982), 5-18 (reprinted in his *Britons and Anglo-Saxons in the Early Middle Ages*, Variorum Reprints Collected Studies Series 379, London 1993, essay XV, with same pagination)

DUMVILLE, David N., *Three Men in a Boat: Scribe, Language, and Culture in the Church of Viking-Age Europe* (Cambridge, 1997)

DUMVILLE, David N., 'Vikings in the British Isles: A Question of Sources', in *The Scandinavians from the Vendel Period to the Tenth Century: An Ethnographic Perspective*, edited by Judith Jesch, Studies in Historical Archaeoethnology 5 (San Marino, 2002), pp. 209-50

DUMVILLE, David N., *Wessex and England from Alfred to Edgar: Six Essays on Political, Cultural, and Ecclesiastical Revival*, Studies in Anglo-Saxon History 3 (Woodbridge, 1992)

DUMVILLE, David N., 'What is a Chronicle?', *The Medieval Chronicle*, 2 (2002), 1-27

DUMVILLE, David N., and Peter A. STOKES, ed., *Liber Vitae Dunelmensis: London, British Library MS Cotton Domitian A.vii, Trial Version for Limited Circulation*, 2 parts (Cambridge, 2001)

DUNCAN, A.A.M., 'The Battle of Carham, 1018', *Scottish Historical Review*, 55 (1976), 20-28

DUNCAN, A.A.M., 'The Kingdom of the Scots', in *The Making of Britain: The Dark Ages*, ed. L.M. Smith (Basingstoke, 1984), pp. 131-44

DUNCAN, A.A.M., *Scotland: The Making of the Kingdom* (Edinburgh, 1975; revised impression, 1979)

EASSON, A.R., 'Ouncelands and Pennylands in the West Highlands of Scotland', in *Ouncelands and Pennylands*, edited by L.J. Macgregor and B.E. Crawford, St John's House Papers 3 (St Andrews, 1987), pp. 1-11

ECKEL, Auguste, *Charles le Simple*, Annales de l'histoire de France à l'époque carolingienne, Bibliothèque de l'École des Hautes Études 124 (Paris, 1899)

EDMONDS, Fiona Louise, 'Hiberno-Saxon and Hiberno-Scandinavian Contact in the West of the Northumbrian Kingdom: A Focus on the Church', 2 vols (unpublished D.Phil. Dissertation, University of Oxford, 2005)

EDWARDS, Nancy, 'A Possible Viking Grave from Benllech, Anglesey', *Transactions of the Anglesey Antiquarian Society and Field Club* (1985), 19-24

EDWARDS, Nancy, 'Monuments in a Landscape: the Early Medieval Sculpture of St David's', in *Image and Power in the Archaeology of Early Medieval Britain: Essays in Honour of Rosemary Cramp*, edited by Helena Hamerow and Arthur MacGregor (Oxford, 2001), pp. 53-77

EDWARDS, Nancy, 'New Research on Stone Sculpture in Wales', *Church Archaeology*, 4 (2000), 60-62

EDWARDS, Nancy, 'Viking-Influenced Sculpture in North Wales: Its Ornament and Context', in *Art and Symbolism in Medieval Europe: Papers from the Brugge 1997 Conference*, volume V, edited by Guy de Boe and Frans Verhaeghe (Zellik, 1997), pp. 95-100

EKWALL, Eilert, *English River Names* (Oxford, 1928)

EKWALL, Eilert, *Scandinavians and Celts in the North-West of England* (Lund, 1918)

EKWALL, Eilert, *The Concise Oxford Dictionary of English Place-Names*, fourth edition (Oxford, 1960)

EQUIANO, Olaudah, *Sold as a Slave* (London, 2007)

ETCHINGHAM, Colmán, 'Evidence of Scandinavian Settlement in Wicklow', in *Wicklow – History and Society: Interdisciplinary Essays on the History of an Irish County*, edited by Ken Hannigan and William Nolan, Irish County History Series (Dublin, 1994), pp. 113-38

ETCHINGHAM, Colmán, 'Les Vikings dans les sources documentaires irlandaises: les cas des annales', in *L'Héritage maritime des vikings en Europe de l'ouest*, edited by E. Ridel (Caen, 2002), pp. 35-56

ETCHINGHAM, Colmán, 'North Wales, Ireland and the Isles: the Insular Viking Zone', *Peritia*, 15 (2001), 145-87

ETCHINGHAM, Colmán, 'The Location of Historical *Laithlinn/Lochla(i)nn*: Scotland or Scandinavia?', in *Studia Celtica Upsaliensia*, edited by M. Ó Flaithearta (forthcoming)

ETCHINGHAM, Colmán, *Viking Raids on Irish Church Settlements in the Ninth Century: A Reconsideration of the Annals*, Maynooth Monographs, Series Minor 1 (Maynooth, 1996)

EVANS, D. Simon, ed. and trans., *A Mediaeval Prince of Wales: The Life of Gruffudd ap Cynan* (Felinfach, 1990)

EVANS, J. Gwenogvyryn, ed., *The Poetry in the Red Book of Hergest*, I, Series of Old Welsh Texts 11 (Llanbedrog, 1911)

FANNING, Thomas, 'The Hiberno-Norse Pins from the Isle of Man', in *The Viking Age in the Isle of Man. Select Papers from the Ninth Viking Congress, Isle of Man, 4-14 July 1981*, edited by Christine Fell *et al.* (London, 1983), pp. 27-36

FELL, Christine E., 'Edward King and Martyr and the Anglo-Saxon Hagiographic Tradition', in *Ethelred the Unready: Papers from the Millenary Conference*, edited by David Hill, B.A.R. British Series 59 (Oxford, 1978), pp. 1-13

FELL, Christine E., 'Modern English *Viking*', *Leeds Studies in English*, new series, 18 (1987), 111-22

FELLOWS-JENSEN, Gillian, 'Common Gaelic *áirge*, Old Scandinavian *ærgi* or *erg*?', *Nomina*, 4 (1980), 67-84

FELLOWS-JENSEN, Gillian, 'Place-Names and Settlements: Some Problems of Dating as Exemplified by Place-Names in *-bý* ', *Journal of Medieval History*, 8 (1984), 29-39

FELLOWS-JENSEN, Gillian, 'Scandinavian Influence on the Place-Names of England', in *Language Contact in the British Isles, Proceedings of the Eighth International Symposium on Language Contact in Europe, Douglas, Isle of Man, 1988*, edited by P. Sture Ureland and George Broderick (Tübingen, 1991), pp. 337-54

FELLOWS-JENSEN, Gillian, 'Scandinavian Place-Names of the Irish Sea Province', in *Viking Treasure from the North West: The Cuerdale Hoard in its Context*, edited by James Graham-Campbell (Liverpool, 1992), pp. 31-42

FELLOWS-JENSEN, Gillian, 'Scandinavian Settlement in Cumbria and Dumfriesshire: The Place-Name Evidence', in *The Scandinavians in Cumbria*, edited by John R. Baldwin and Ian D. Whyte, Scottish Society for Northern Studies Publications 3 (Edinburgh, 1985), pp. 65-82

FELLOWS-JENSEN, Gillian, 'Scandinavian Settlement in the Isle of Man and North-West England: The Place-name Evidence', in *The Viking Age in the Isle of Man. Select Papers from the Ninth Viking Congress*, edited by Christine Fell *et al.* (London, 1983), pp. 37-52

FELLOWS-JENSEN, Gillian, 'Scandinavians in Dumfriesshire and Galloway: The Place-Name Evidence', in *Galloway: Land and Lordship*, edited by Richard D. Oram and Geoffrey P. Stell (Edinburgh, 1991), pp. 77-95

FELLOWS-JENSEN, Gillian, 'Scandinavians in Southern Scotland?', *Nomina*, 13 (1989-90), 41-60

FELLOWS-JENSEN, Gillian, 'The Mystery of the *bý*-names in Man', *Nomina*, 24 (2001), 33-46

FLEMING, Robin, 'Monastic Lands and England's Defence in the Viking Age', *English Historical Review*, 100 (1985), 247-65

FLETCHER, Richard, *Bloodfeud: Murder and Revenge in Anglo-Saxon England* (London, 2002)

FOOT, Sarah, 'Remembering, Forgetting and Inventing: Attitudes to the Past in England at the End of the First Viking Age', *Transactions of the Royal Historical Society*, sixth series, 9 (1999), 185-200

FOOT, Sarah, 'The Making of *Angelcynn*: English Identity before the Norman Conquest', *Transactions of the Royal Historical Society*, sixth series, 6 (1996), 25-49

FOOTE, P.G., and R. QUIRK, ed. and trans., *Gunnlaugs Saga Ormstungu: The Saga of Gunnlaug Serpent-Tongue*, Nelson's Icelandic Texts (Edinburgh, 1957)

FOOTE, Peter, and David M. WILSON, *The Viking Achievement: The Society and Culture of Early Medieval Scandinavia* (London, 1970)

FORSYTH, Katherine, and John T. KOCH, 'Evidence of a Lost Pictish Source in the *Historia Regum Anglorum* of Symeon of Durham', in *Kings, Clerics and Chronicles in Scotland 500-1297: Essays in Honour of Marjorie Ogilvie Anderson on the Occasion of her Ninetieth Birthday*, ed. Simon Taylor (Dublin, 2000), pp. 19-34

FORTE, Angelo, *et al.*, *Viking Empires* (Cambridge, 2005)

FRANCE, John, *et al.*, ed., *Rodulfi Glabri Historiarum Libri Quinque; Rodulfus Glaber, The Five Books of the Histories*, Oxford Medieval Texts (Oxford, 1989)

FREEMAN, A.M., ed. and trans., 'The Annals in Cotton MS Titus A xxv', *Revue celtique*, 41 (1924), 301-30; 42 (1925), 283-305; 43 (1926), 358-84; 44 (1927), 336-61

FULTON, Helen, 'Tenth-Century Wales and *Armes Prydein*', *Transactions of the Honourable Society of Cymmrodorion*, new series, 7 (2001), 5-18

GAHAN, Audrey, *et al.*, 'Medieval Pottery', in *Late Viking Age and Medieval Waterford, Excavations 1986-1992*, edited by Maurice Hurley *et al.* (Waterford, 1997), pp. 285-336

GELLING, P.S., 'Celtic Continuity in the Isle of Man', in *Studies in Celtic Survival*, edited by Lloyd Laing, B.A.R. British Series 37 (Oxford, 1977), pp. 77-81

GERRIETS, Marilyn, 'Money among the Irish: Coin Hoards in Viking Age Ireland', *Journal of the Royal Society of Antiquaries of Ireland*, 115 (1985), 121-39

GILES, J.A., trans., *Roger of Wendover's Flowers of History, comprising the History of England from the Descent of the Saxons to A.D. 1235*, 2 vols, Bohn's Antiquarian Library (London, 1849; facsimile reprint Felinfach, 1993)

GILLINGHAM, John, 'Chronicles and Coins as Evidence for Levels of Tribute and Taxation in Late Tenth- and Early Eleventh-Century England', *English Historical Review*, 105 (1990), 939-50

GILLINGHAM, John, '"The Most Precious Jewel in the English Crown": Levels of Danegeld and Heregeld in the Early Eleventh Century', *English Historical Review*, 104 (1989), 373-84

GILLMOR, Carrol, 'Wars on the Rivers: Viking Numbers and Mobility on the Seine and the Loire, 841-86', *Viator*, 19 (1988), 97-110

GLEESON, D., and S. MAC AIRT, ed., 'The Annals of Roscrea', *Proceedings of the Royal Irish Academy*, 59 C (1957-59), 137-80

GOEDHEER, Albertus Johannes, *Irish and Norse Traditions about the Battle of Clontarf* (Haarlem, 1938)

GORDON, E.V., *An Introduction to Old Norse*, second edition, revised by A.R. Taylor (Oxford, 1957)

GOVER, J.E.B., *et al.*, *The Place-Names of Devon*, I, English Place-Names Society 8 (Cambridge, 1931)

GRABOWSKI, Kathryn, and David DUMVILLE, *Chronicles and Annals of Mediaeval Ireland and Wales: The Clonmacnoise-Group Texts*, Studies in Celtic History 4 (Woodbridge, 1984)

GRAHAM-CAMPBELL, James, 'A "Vital" Yorkshire Viking Hoard Revisited', in *In Search of Cult: Archaeological Investigations in Honour of Philip Rahtz*, edited by Martin Carver (Woodbridge, 1993), pp. 79-84

GRAHAM-CAMPBELL, James, ed., *Cultural Atlas of the Viking World* (New York, 1994)

GRAHAM-CAMPBELL, James, 'Some Archaeological Reflections on the Cuerdale Hoard', in *Coinage in Ninth-Century Northumbria. The Tenth Oxford Symposium on Coinage and Monetary History*, edited by D.M. Metcalf, B.A.R. British Series 180 (Oxford, 1987), pp. 329-54

GRAHAM-CAMPBELL, James, 'The Early Viking Age in the Irish Sea Area', in *Ireland and Scandinavia in the Early Viking Age*, edited by Howard B. Clarke *et al.* (Dublin, 1998), pp. 104-30

GRAHAM-CAMPBELL, James, 'The Irish Sea Vikings: Raiders and Settlers', in *The Middle Ages in the North-West*, edited by Tom Scott and Pat Starkey (Oxford, 1995), pp. 59-84

GRAHAM-CAMPBELL, James, 'The Northern Hoards', in *Edward the Elder, 899-924*, edited by N.J. Higham and D.H. Hill (London, 2001), pp. 212-29

GRAHAM-CAMPBELL, James, *et al.*, *The Viking Age Gold and Silver of Scotland (A.D. 850-1100)* (Edinburgh, 1995)

GRAHAM-CAMPBELL, James, 'The Viking-Age Silver and Gold Hoards of Scandinavian Character from Scotland', *Proceedings of the Society of Antiquaries of Scotland*, 107 (1975-76), 114-35

GRAHAM-CAMPBELL, James, and Colleen E. BATEY, *Vikings in Scotland: An Archaeological Survey* (Edinburgh, 1998)

GRANT, Alison, 'A New Approach to the Inversion Compounds of North-West England', *Nomina*, 25 (2002), 65-90

GRAT, Félix, *et al.*, ed., *Annales de Saint-Bertin*, Société de l'histoire de France 470 (Paris, 1964)

GREEN, John Richard, *The Conquest of England*, 2 vols (London, 1899)

GREENWAY, Diana, ed. and trans., *Henry, Archdeacon of Huntingdon, Historia Anglorum, The History of the English People*, Oxford Medieval Texts (Oxford, 1996)

GRIERSON, Philip, and Mark BLACKBURN, *Medieval European Coinage, with a Catalogue of the Coins in the Fitzwilliam Museum, Cambridge*, I, *The Early Middle Ages (Fifth to Tenth Centuries)* (Cambridge, 1986)

GRIFFITHS, David Wyn, 'Anglo-Saxon England and the Irish Sea Region, A.D. 800-1100. An Archaeological Study of the Lower Dee and Mersey as a Border Area' (unpublished Ph.D. Dissertation, University of Durham, 1991)

GRIFFITHS, David, 'The North-West Frontier', in *Edward the Elder, 899-924*, edited by N.J. Higham and D.H. Hill (London, 2001), pp. 167-87

GRUFFYDD, R. Geraint, ed. and trans., 'A Poem in Praise of Cuhelyn Fardd from the Black Book of Carmarthen', *Studia Celtica*, 10/11 (1975-76), 198-209

GUÐMUNDSSON, Finnbogi, ed., *Orkneyinga saga, Legenda de Sancto Magno, Magnúss saga skemmri, Magnúss saga lengri, Helga páttr ok Úlfs*, Íslenzk Fornrit 34 (Reykjavík, 1965)

GWYNN, Aubrey, *Cathal Óg Mac Maghnusa and the Annals of Ulster*, edited by Nollaig Ó Muraíle (Enniskillen, 1998)

GWYNN, Aubrey, 'Medieval Bristol and Dublin', *Irish Historical Studies*, 5 (1946-47), 275-86

GWYNN, Aubrey, 'The First Bishops of Dublin', *Reportorium Novum*, 1 (1955-56), 1-26

GWYNN, Edward J., ed. and trans., *The Metrical Dindshenchas*, 5 vols, Todd Lecture Series 8-12 (Dublin, 1903-35)

HADLEY, Dawn, '"Cockle among the Wheat": The Scandinavian Settlement in England', in *Social Identity in Early Medieval Britain*, edited by William O. Frazer and Andrew Tyrell, Studies in the Early History of Britain (London, 2000), pp. 111-36

HADLEY, Dawn, 'Conquest, Colonisation and the Church: Ecclesiastical Organization in the Danelaw', *Historical Research*, 69 (1996), 109-28

HADLEY, Dawn, *The Vikings in England: Settlement, Society and Culture* (Manchester, 2006)

HADLEY, Dawn, 'Viking and Native: Re-Thinking Identity in the Danelaw', *Early Medieval Europe*, 11 (2002), 45-70

HALIDAY, Charles, *The Scandinavian Kingdom of Dublin*, second edition (Dublin, 1884)

HALL, Richard, 'A Checklist of Viking Age Coin Finds from Ireland', *Ulster Journal of Archaeology*, third series, 36/37 (1973-74), 71-86

HALL, R. A., *Exploring the World of the Vikings* (London, 2007)

HALL, R. A., 'The Five Boroughs of the Danelaw: a Review of Present Knowledge', *Anglo-Saxon England*, 18 (1989), 149-206

HALL, R. A., ed., *Viking Age York and the North*, CBA Research Report 27 (London, 1978)

HANSEN, S.S., 'The Norse Landnam in the Faroe Islands in the Light of Recent Excavations at Toftanes, Leirvík', *Northern Studies*, 25 (1988), 58-84

HARDY, Thomas Duffus, and Charles Trice MARTIN, ed. and trans., *L'Estoire des Engles solum la translacion Maistre Geffrei Gaimar,* Rerum Britannicarum Medii Aevi Scriptores 91, 2 vols (London, 1888-89)

HARRIS, J., 'Saga as a Historical Novel', in *Structure and Meaning in Old Norse Literature: New Approaches to Textual Analysis and Literary Criticism,* edited by John Lindow *et al.* (Odense, 1986), pp. 187-219

HARRISON, Stephen, 'Viking Graves and Grave-goods in Ireland', in *The Vikings in Ireland,* edited by Anne-Christine Larsen (Roskilde, 2001), pp. 61-75

HART, Cyril, 'Byrhtferth's Northumbrian Chronicle', *English Historical Review,* 97 (1982), 558-82

HART, Cyril, *The Danelaw* (London, 1992)

HART, Cyril, *The Early Charters of Northern England and the North Midlands,* Studies in Early English History 6 (Leicester, 1975)

HENNESSY, William M., ed. and trans., *Chronicum Scotorum: A Chronicle of Irish Affairs, from the Earliest Times to A.D. 1135, with a Supplement containing the Events from A.D. 1114 to A.D. 1150,* Rerum Britannicarum Medii Aevi Scriptores 46 (London, 1866)

HENNESSY, William M., ed. and trans., *The Annals of Loch Cé: A Chronicle of Irish Affairs from A.D. 1014 to A.D. 1590,* Rerum Britannicarum Medii Aevi Scriptores 54, 2 vols (London, 1871)

HERBERT, Máire, *Iona, Kells, and Derry: The History and Hagiography of the Monastic* Familia *of Columba* (Oxford, 1988)

HERMANSSON, Halldór, ed. and trans., *The Book of the Icelanders: Íslendingabók by Ari Thorgilsson,* Islandica 20 (Ithaca, NY, 1930)

HIGHAM, Mary C., 'Scandinavian Settlements in North-West England, with a Special Study of *Ireby* Names', in *Scandinavian Settlement in Northern Britain: Thirteen Studies of Place-Names in their Historical Context,* edited by Barbara E. Crawford, Studies in the Early History of Britain (London, 1995), pp. 195-205

HIGHAM, Nick, 'Edward the Elder's Reputation: An Introduction', in *Edward the Elder, 899-924,* edited by N.J. Higham and D.H. Hill (London, 2001), pp. 1-11

HIGHAM, N.J., *The Kingdom of Northumbria, A.D. 350-1100* (Stroud, 1993)

HIGHAM, Nick, 'The Scandinavians in North Cumbria: Raids and Settlements in the Later Ninth to Mid Tenth Centuries', in *The Scandinavians in Cumbria,* edited by John R. Baldwin and Ian D. Whyte, Scottish Society for Northern Studies 3 (Edinburgh, 1985), pp. 37-51

HIGHAM, Nicholas, 'Viking-Age Settlement in the North-Western Countryside: Lifting the Veil?' in *Land, Sea and Home: Proceedings of a Conference on Viking-Period Settlement, at Cardiff, July 2001,* edited by John Hines *et al.* (Leeds, 2004), pp. 297-311

HILL, David, *An Atlas of Anglo-Saxon England* (Oxford, 1981)

HILL, Peter, *et al.*, *Whithorn and St Ninian: The Excavation of a Monastic Town, 1984-91* (Stroud, 1997)

HILL, Peter, 'Whithorn: The Missing Years', in *Galloway: Land and Lordship*, edited by Richard D. Oram and Geoffrey P. Stell (Edinburgh, 1991), pp. 27-44

HINES, John, 'Egill's Höfuðlausn in time and place', *Saga-book of the Viking Society*, 24 (1994-97), 83-104

HINES, John, 'Kingship in Egils Saga', in *Introductory Essays in Egils Saga and Njáls Saga*, edited by John Hines and Desmond Slay (London, 1992), pp. 15-32

HINES, John, *Old Norse Sources for Gaelic History*, Quiggin Pamphlets on the Sources of Mediaeval Gaelic History 5 (Cambridge, 2002)

HINES, John, 'Scandinavian English: A Creole in Context', in *Language Contact in the British Isles. Proceedings of the Eighth International Symposium on Language Contact in Europe, Douglas, Isle of Man, 1988*, edited by P. Sture Ureland and George Broderick (Tübingen, 1991), pp. 403-27

HOFMANN, Dietrich, 'Das Reimwort *giör* in Egill Skallagrímssons Höfuðlausn', *Mediaeval Scandinavia*, 6 (1973), 93-101

HOGAN, Edmund I., *Onomasticon Goedelicum Locorum et Tribuum Hiberniae et Scotiae* (Dublin, 1910)

HOLDER-EGGER, O., ed. 'Vita Sancti Findani', in *Monumenta Germaniae Historica, Scriptores* [in folio], XV, part 1 (Hanover, 1887), pp. 502-06

HOLLANDER, Lee M., trans., *Heimskringla, History of the Kings of Norway, by Snorri Sturluson* (Austin, TX, 1964)

HOLM, Poul, 'Between Apathy and Antipathy: The Vikings in Irish and Scandinavian History', *Peritia*, 8 (1994), 151-69

HOLM, Poul, 'The Slave Trade of Dublin, Ninth to Twelfth Centuries', *Peritia*, 5 (1986), 317-45

HOLM, Poul, 'Viking Dublin and the City-State Concept: Parameters and Significance of the Hiberno-Norse Settlement', in *A Comparative Study of Thirty City-State Cultures: An Investigation conducted by the Copenhagen Polis Centre*, edited by Mogens Herman Hansen, Det Kongelige Danske Videnskabernes Selskab Historiske-filosofiske Skrifter 21 (Copenhagen, 2000), pp. 251-62

HOOKE, Della, *Pre-Conquest Charter-Bounds of Devon and Cornwall* (Woodbridge, 1994)

HORE, Herbert Francis, 'The Scandinavians in Leinster', *Journal of the Kilkenny and South-East of Ireland Archaeological Society*, 1 (1856-57), 430-43

HOWLETT, David, *Caledonian Craftsmanship: The Scottish Latin Tradition* (Dublin, 2000)

HUDSON, Benjamin T., 'Cnut and the Scottish Kings', *English Historical Review*, 107 (1992), 350-60

HUDSON, B.T., '*Elech* and the Scots in Strathclyde', *Scottish Gaelic Studies*, 15 (1988), 145-49

HUDSON, Benjamin T., *Kings of Celtic Scotland*, Contributions to the Study of World History 43 (Westport, CT, 1994)

HUDSON, Benjamin T., ed. and trans., *Prophecy of Berchán: Irish and Scottish High-Kings of the Early Middle Ages*, Contributions to the Study of World History 54 (Westport, CT, 1996)

HUDSON, Benjamin T., 'The Changing Economy of the Irish Sea Province', in *Britain and Ireland, 900-1300: Insular Responses to Medieval European Change*, edited by Brendan Smith (Cambridge, 1999), pp. 39-66

HUDSON, Benjamin T., ed. and trans., 'The Scottish Chronicle', *Scottish Historical Review*, 77 (1998), 129-61

HUDSON, Benjamin, *Viking Pirates and Christian Princes: Dynasty, Religion, and Empire in the North Atlantic* (New York, 2005)

HUGHES, Kathleen, *Celtic Britain in the Early Middle Ages: Studies in Welsh and Scottish Sources*, Studies in Celtic History 2 (Woodbridge, 1980)

HUGHES, Kathleen, *Early Christian Ireland: Introduction to the Sources*, The Sources of History (London, 1972)

HUGHES, Kathleen, *The Church in Early Irish Society* (London, 1966)

HULL, Eleanor, 'The Gael and the Gall: Notes on the Social Condition of Ireland during the Norse Period', *Saga-book of the Viking Society*, 5 (1907-08), 363-92

HUNTER BLAIR, Peter, *An Introduction to Anglo-Saxon England*, second edition (Cambridge, 1977)

HUNTER BLAIR, Peter, 'Olaf the White and the Three Fragments of Irish Annals', *Viking: Tidsskrift for norrøn arkeologi*, 3 (1939), 1-36

HUNTER BLAIR, Peter, 'Some Observations on the *Historia Regum* attributed to Symeon of Durham', in *Celt and Saxon: Studies in the Early British Border*, edited by Nora K. Chadwick (Cambridge, 1963; revised impression, 1964), pp. 63-118

JACKSON, Kenneth, 'Angles and Britons in Northumbria and Cumbria', in *Angles and Britons, O'Donnell Lectures*, edited by Henry Lewis (Cardiff, 1963), pp. 60-84

JACKSON, Kenneth, *Language and History in Early Britain: A Chronological Survey of the Brittonic Languages, 1st to 12th Centuries A.D.* (Edinburgh, 1953)

JASKI, Bart, 'Additional Notes to the Annals of Ulster', *Ériu*, 48 (1997), 103-52

JASKI, Bart, *Early Irish Kingship and Succession* (Dublin, 2000)

JASKI, Bart, 'The Vikings and the Kingship of Tara', *Peritia*, 9 (1995), 310-53

JEFFERIES, Henry A., 'The History and Topography of Viking Cork', *Journal of the Cork Historical and Archaeological Society*, 90 (1985), 14-25

JESCH, Judith, 'Norse Historical Traditions and *Historia Gruffudd vab Kenan*: Magnús berfœttr and Haraldr hárfagri', in *Gruffudd ap Cynan: A Collaborative*

Biography, edited by K.L. Maund, Studies in Celtic History 16 (Woodbridge, 1996), pp. 117-48

JESCH, Judith, 'Scaldic Verse in Scandinavian England', in *Vikings and the Danelaw: Select Papers from the Proceedings of the Thirteenth Viking Congress*, edited by James Graham-Campbell *et al.* (Oxford, 2001), pp. 314-27

JESCH, Judith, 'Scandinavian Wirral', in *Wirral and its Viking Heritage*, edited by Paul Cavill *et al.* (Nottingham, 2000), pp. 1-10

JESCH, Judith, *Ships and Men in the Late Viking Age. The Vocabulary of Runic Inscriptions and Skaldic Verse* (Woodbridge, 2001)

JOHN, Eric, 'War and Society in the Tenth Century: The Maldon Campaign', *Transactions of the Royal Historical Society*, fifth series, 27 (1977), 173-95

JOHNSON, Ruth, 'An Archaeological and Art Historical Investigation into the Supposed Hiatus in Irish Art during the Tenth Century AD, with Particular Reference to Excavations carried out in Dublin City (1962-81) and Ballinderry Crannog No. 1 (1936)', 3 vols (unpublished Ph.D. Dissertation, University of Dublin, Trinity College, 1997)

JOHNSON-SOUTH, Ted, ed. and trans., *Historia de Sancto Cuthberto. A History of Saint Cuthbert and a Record of his Patrimony*, Anglo-Saxon Texts 3 (Cambridge, 2002)

JOHNSON-SOUTH, Theodore, 'The "Historia de Sancto Cuthberto": A New Edition and Translation, with Discussions of the Surviving Manuscripts, the Text, and Northumbrian Estate Structure' (unpublished Ph.D. Dissertation, Cornell University, 1990)

JONES, Barri, and David MATTINGLY, *An Atlas of Roman Britain* (Oxford, 1990)

JONES, Bedwyr Lewis, 'Gwriad's Heritage: Links between Wales and the Isle of Man in the Early Middle Ages', *Transactions of the Honourable Society of Cymmrodorion* (1990), 29-44

JONES, Gwyn, 'Egill Skallagrímsson in England', *Proceedings of the British Academy*, 37 (1952), 127-44

JONES, Thomas, ed. and trans., *Brenhinedd y Saesson or The Kings of the Saxons*, Board of Celtic Studies University of Wales History and Law Series 25 (Cardiff, 1971)

JONES, Thomas, trans., *Brut y Tywysogyon or The Chronicle of the Princes – Peniarth MS 20 Version*, Board of Celtic Studies University of Wales History and Law Series 11 (Cardiff, 1952)

JONES, Thomas, ed. and trans., *Brut y Tywysogyon or The Chronicle of the Princes – Red Book of Hergest Version*, Board of Celtic Studies University of Wales History and Law Series 16 (Cardiff, 1955; 2nd edn, 1973)

JONES, Thomas, ed., *Brut y Tywysogyon – Peniarth MS 20*, Board of Celtic Studies University of Wales History and Law Series 6 (Cardiff, 1941)

JÓNSSON, Finnur, ed., *Den Norsk-Islandske Sjaldedigtning*, 4 vols (Copenhagen, 1912-15)

JÓNSSON, Finnur, *Den Oldnorske og Oldislandske Litteraturs Historie*, second edition, 3 vols (Copenhagen, 1920-24)

JÓNSSON, Finnur, ed., *Fagrskinna: Nóregs Konunga Tal* (Copenhagen, 1902)

JÓNSSON, Finnur, ed., *Snorri Sturluson, Heimskringla: Nóregs Konunga Sögur* (Copenhagen, 1911)

JÓNSSON, Guðni, ed., *Fornaldar Sögur Norðurlanda*, 4 vols (Reykjavik, 1950)

JORANSON, Einar, *The Danegeld in France*, Augustana Library Publications 10 (Rock Island, IL. 1923)

KAPELLE, William E., *The Norman Conquest of the North: The Region and its Transformation, 1000-1135* (Chapel Hill, NC 1979)

KARRAS, Ruth Mazo, 'Haraldr hárfagri', in *Medieval Scandinavia: An Encyclopaedia*, edited by Phillip Pulsiano *et al.* (New York, 1993), pp. 267-68

KELLY, Eamonn P., and Edmond O'DONOVAN, 'A Viking *Longphort* near Athlunkard, Co. Clare', *Archaeology Ireland*, 12, no. 4 (1998), 13-16

KELLY, Eamonn P., and John MAAS, 'Vikings on the Barrow: Dunrally Fort, a Possible Viking *Longphort* in County Laois', *Archaeology Ireland*, 9, no. 3 (1995), 30-32

KELLY, Fergus, *A Guide to Early Irish Law*, Early Irish Law Series 3 (Dublin, 1988)

KELLY, Fergus, *Early Irish Farming*, Early Irish Law Series 4 (Dublin, 1997)

KENNEY, James F., *The Sources for the Early History of Ireland, Ecclesiastical: An Introduction and Guide*, Records of Civilization Sources and Studies 11 (New York, 1929; revised impression, by Ludwig Bieler, 1966)

KENNY, Michael, 'A Find of Anglo-Saxon Pennies from Newtownlow, Co. Westmeath', *Ríocht na Midhe*, 7, no. 3 (1984), 37-43

KEPPIE, Laurence, *Scotland's Roman Remains* (Edinburgh, 1986)

KERMODE, P.M.C., 'Further Discoveries of Cross-Slabs in the Isle of Man', *Proceedings of the Society of Antiquaries of Scotland*, 1 (1915), 50-62 (reprinted in his *Manx Crosses*, Balgavies 1994, Appendix C, pp. 20-28)

KERSHAW, Nora, ed. and trans., *Anglo-Saxon and Norse Poems* (Cambridge, 1922)

KEYNES, Simon, *Anglo-Saxon England: A Bibliographical Handbook for Students of Anglo-Saxon History*, second edition, ASNC Guides, Texts, and Studies 1 (Cambridge, 2001)

KEYNES, Simon, 'Anglo-Saxon Entries in the "Liber Vitae" of Brescia', in *Alfred the Wise: Studies in Honour of Janet Bately on the Occasion of her Sixty-Fifth Birthday*, edited by Jane Roberts *et al.* (Cambridge, 1997), pp. 99-119

KEYNES, Simon, 'Apocalypse then: England A.D. 1000', in *Europe around the Year 1000*, edited by Przemysław Urbańczyk (Warsaw, 2001), pp. 247-70

KEYNES, Simon, 'Cnut's Earls', in *The Reign of Cnut, King of England, Denmark and Norway*, edited by Alexander R. Rumble, Studies in the Early History of Britain (London, 1994), pp. 43-88

KEYNES, Simon, 'Crime and Punishment in the Reign of King Æthelred the Unready', in *People and Places in Northern Europe, 500-1600: Essays in Honour of Peter Hayes Sawyer*, edited by Ian Wood and Niels Lund (Woodbridge, 1991), pp. 67-82

KEYNES, Simon, 'Danegeld', in *The Blackwell Encyclopaedia of Anglo-Saxon England*, edited by Michael Lapidge *et al.* (Oxford, 1999), p. 235

KEYNES, Simon, 'King Alfred and the Mercians', in *Kings, Currency, and Alliances: History and Coinage of Southern England in the Ninth Century*, edited by Mark A.S. Blackburn and David N. Dumville, Studies in Anglo-Saxon History 9 (Woodbridge, 1998), pp. 1-45

KEYNES, Simon, 'The Cult of King Alfred', *Anglo-Saxon England*, 28 (1999), 225-356

KEYNES, Simon, 'The Declining Reputation of King Æthelred the Unready', in *Ethelred the Unready: Papers from the Millenary Conference*, edited by David Hill, B.A.R. British Series 59 (Oxford, 1978), pp. 227-53

KEYNES, Simon, 'The Historical Context of the Battle of Maldon', in *The Battle of Maldon, AD 991*, edited by Donald Scragg (Oxford, 1991), pp. 81-113

KEYNES, Simon, 'The Vikings in England, *c.* 760-1016', in *The Oxford Illustrated History of the Vikings*, edited by Peter Sawyer (Oxford, 1997), pp. 48-82

KEYNES, Simon, 'Wulfstan I', in *The Blackwell Encyclopaedia of Anglo-Saxon England*, edited by Michael LAPIDGE *et al.* (Oxford, 1999), pp. 492-93

KEYNES, Simon, and Michael LAPIDGE, trans., *Alfred the Great: Asser's* Life of King Alfred *and Other Contemporary Sources*, Penguin Classics (Harmondsworth, 1983)

KIRBY, D.P., 'Hywel Dda: Anglophil?', *Welsh History Review*, 8 (1976-77), 1-13

KIRBY, D.P., 'Northumbria in the Ninth Century', in *Coinage in Ninth-Century Northumbria: The Tenth Oxford Symposium on Coinage and Monetary History*, edited by D.M. Metcalf, B.A.R. British Series 180 (Oxford, 1987), pp. 11-25

KIRBY, D.P., 'Strathclyde and Cumbria: A Survey of Historical Developments to 1092', *Transactions of the Cumberland and Westmorland Antiquarian and Archaeological Society*, new series, 62 (1962), 77-94

KNIGHT, Jeremy, 'Glamorgan, A.D. 400-1100: Archaeology and History', in *Glamorgan County History, II: Early Glamorgan Pre-History and Early History*, edited by Hubert N. Savory (Cardiff, 1984), pp. 315-64

KNIRK, James E., 'Runes from Trondheim and a Stanza by Egill Skalla-Grímsson', in *Studien zum Altgermanischen: Festschrift für Heinrich Beck*, edited by Heiko Uecker (Berlin, 1994), pp. 411-21

KUHN, Hans, 'Extended Elements in the Kenning', *Parergon*, 22 (1978), 13-22

KUNZ, Keneva, trans., 'The Saga of the People of Laxardal', in *The Sagas of the Icelanders*, translated by Katrina C. Attwood *et al.*, with preface by Jane Smiley (London, 1997), pp. 270-421

LAIR, Jules, ed., *De Moribus et Actibus Primorum Normanniae Ducum*, Mémoires de la Société des Antiquaires de Normandie 3, vol. 23, pt 2 (Caen, 1865)

LANDES, Richard, 'The Fear of an Apocalyptic Year 1000: Augustinian Historiography, Medieval and Modern', *Speculum*, 75 (2000), 97-145

LANE, Alan M., 'The Vikings in Glamorgan? A Note', in *Glamorgan County History*, II: *Early Glamorgan Pre-History and Early History*, edited by Hubert N. Savory (Cardiff, 1984), pp. 354-56

LANG, J.T., 'The Castledermot Hogback', *Journal of the Royal Society of Antiquaries of Ireland*, 101 (1971), 154-58

LANG, J.T., 'The Hogback: A Viking Colonial Monument', *Anglo-Saxon Studies in Archaeology and History*, 3 (1984), 85-176

LAPIDGE, Michael, 'Byrhtferth of Ramsey and the Early Sections of the *Historia Regum* attributed to Symeon of Durham', *Anglo-Saxon England*, 10 (1982), 97-122 (reprinted in his book *Anglo-Latin Literature, 900-1066*, London 1993, pp. 317-42)

LAPIDGE, Michael, 'Some Latin Poems as Evidence for the Reign of Athelstan', *Anglo-Saxon England*, 9 (1981), 61-98 (reprinted in his book *Anglo-Latin Literature, 900-1066*, London 1993, pp. 49-86)

LAPPENBERG, J.M., *A History of England under the Anglo-Saxon Kings*, translated by Benjamin Thorpe, 2 vols (London, 1845)

LARRINGTON, Carolyne, 'Egill's Longer Poems: *Arinbjarnarkviða* and *Sonatorrek*', in *Introductory Essays in Egils Saga and Njáls Saga*, edited by John Hines and Desmond Slay (London, 1992), pp. 49-63

LATHAM, R.E., *Revised Medieval Latin Word-List from British and Irish Sources* (London, 1965)

LATOUCHE, Robert, ed. and trans., *Richer: Histoire de France (888-995)*, Les classiques de l'histoire de France au moyen âge 12, 2 vols (Paris, 1930-37)

LATVIO, Riita, 'Status and Exchange in Early Irish Laws', *Studia Celtica Fennica*, 2 (2005), 67-96

LAWSON, M.K., 'Danegeld and Heregeld Once More', *English Historical Review*, 105 (1990), 951-61

LAWSON, M.K., 'The Collection of Danegeld and Heregeld in the Reigns of Æthelred II and Cnut', *English Historical Review*, 99 (1984), 721-38

LAWSON, M.K., '"Those Stories Look True": Levels of Taxation in the Reigns of Æthelred II and Cnut', *English Historical Review*, 104 (1989), 385-406

LEECH, Roger H., '*Cogadh Gaedhel re Gallaibh* and The Annals of Inisfallen', *North Munster Antiquarian Journal*, 11 (1968), 13-21

LINDOW, John, 'Íslendingabók and Myth', *Scandinavian Studies*, 69 (1997), 454-64

LITTLE, George A., 'The Thingmote', *Dublin Historical Record*, 41 (1987-88), 123-30

LLOYD, John Edward, *A History of Wales from the Earliest Times to the Edwardian Conquest*, third edition, 2 vols (London, 1939)

LLOYD, John Edward, 'The Welsh Chronicles', *Proceedings of the British Academy*, 14 (1928), 369-91

LOGAN, F. Donald, *The Vikings in History*, second edition (London, 1991)

LOT, Ferdinand, *Recueil des Travaux Historiques,* II, Hautes Études Médiévales et Modernes 9 (Paris, 1970)

LOYN, Henry, *The Vikings in Wales*, The Dorothea Coke Memorial Lecture 1976 (London, 1976), reprinted in his book *Society and Peoples: Studies in the History of England and Wales, c. 600–1200*, Westfield Publications in Medieval Studies 6 (London, 1992), pp. 200-23

LOYN, Henry, 'Wales and England in the Tenth Century: The Context of the Athelstan Charters', *Welsh History Review*, 10 (1980-81), 283-301, reprinted in his book *Society and Peoples: Studies in the History of England and Wales, c. 600–1200*, Westfield Publications in Medieval Studies 6 (London, 1992), pp. 173-99

LUND, Niels, 'Allies of God or Man? The Viking Expansion in a European Perspective', *Viator*, 20 (1989), 45-59

LUND, Niels, 'King Edgar and the Danelaw', *Mediaeval Scandinavia*, 9 (1976), 181-95

LUND, Niels, 'The Armies of Swein Forkbeard and Cnut: *leding* or *lið?*', *Anglo-Saxon England*, 15 (1986), 105-19

LUND, Niels, 'The Settlers: Where do We get Them from – and do We need Them?', in *Proceedings of the Eighth Viking Congress, Aarhus, 24-31 August 1977*, edited by Hans Bekker-Nielsen *et al.*, Mediaeval Scandinavia Supplements 2 (Odense, 1981), pp. 147-69

LYNCH, Joseph H., *Christianizing Kinship: Ritual Sponsorship in Anglo-Saxon England* (Ithaca, NY, 1988)

LYON, Stewart, 'Ninth-Century Northumbrian Chronology', in *Coinage in Ninth-Century Northumbria: The Tenth Oxford Symposium on Coinage and Monetary History*, edited by D.M. Metcalf, B.A.R. British Series 180 (Oxford, 1987), pp. 27-41

MAC AIRT, Séan, ed. and trans., *The Annals of Inisfallen (MS. Rawlinson B 503)* (Dublin, 1951)

MAC AIRT, Séan, and Gearóid MAC NIOCAILL, ed. and trans., *The Annals of Ulster (to A.D. 1131)*, I (Dublin, 1983)

MACALISTER, R.A.S., 'A Runic Inscription at Killaloe Cathedral', *Proceedings of the Royal Irish Academy*, 33 C (1916-17), 493-98

MAC CANA, Proinsias, 'The *Topos* of the Single Sandal in Irish Tradition', *Celtica*, 10 (1973), 160-66

MAC GIOLLA EASPAIG, Dónall, 'L'influence scandinave sur la toponymie irlandaise', in *L'Héritage maritime des vikings en Europe de l'ouest*, edited by Élisabeth Ridel (Caen, 2002), pp. 441-82

MAC MATHÚNA, Liam, 'The Vikings in Ireland: Contemporary Reaction and Cultural Legacy', in *Celts and Vikings. Proceedings of the Fourth Symposium of the Societas Celtologica Nordica*, ed. Folke Josephson (Gothenburg, 1997), pp. 41-65

MACNEILL, Eoin, 'Chapters of Hebridean History – I. The Norse Kingdom of the Hebrides', *The Scottish Review*, new series, 39 (1916), 254-76

MAC NIOCAILL, Gearóid, *The Medieval Irish Annals*, Medieval Irish History Series 3 (Dublin, 1975)

MACQUARRIE, Alan, 'The Kings of Strathclyde, c. 400-1018', in *Medieval Scotland: Crown, Lordship and Community. Essays Presented to G.W.S. Barrow*, edited by Alexander Grant and Keith J. Stringer (Edinburgh, 1993), pp. 1-20

MACQUARRIE, Alan, 'The Name Govan, the Kirk and the Doomster Hill', *Annual Report, Society of the Friends of Govan Old*, 7 (1997), 1-3

MACQUEEN, John, 'Pennyland and Davoch in South-Western Scotland: A Preliminary Note', *Scottish Studies*, 23 (1979), 69-74

MAC SHAMHRÁIN, Ailbhe, 'The Battle of Glen Máma, Dublin and the High-Kingship of Ireland', *Medieval Dublin*, 2 (2000), 53-64

MAC SHAMHRÁIN, Ailbhe, *The Vikings: An Illustrated History* (Dublin, 2002)

MAGNUSSON, Magnus, and Hermann PÁLSSON, trans., *Njal's Saga*, Penguin Classics (Harmondsworth, 1960)

MARSTRANDER, Carl J.S., *Bidrag til det Norske Sprogs Historie i Irland*, Videnskapsselskapets Skrifter II., Hist. Filos. Klasse 5 (Oslo, 1915)

MAUND, K. L., 'Dynastic Segmentation and Gwynedd, c. 950 – c. 1000', *Studia Celtica*, 32 (1998), 155-67

MAUND, K. L., *Ireland, Wales, and England in the Eleventh Century*, Studies in Celtic History 12 (Woodbridge, 1991)

MAUND, Kari, *The Welsh Kings: The Medieval Rulers of Wales* (Stroud, 2000)

MAWER, Allen, 'Ragnar Lothbrók and his Sons', *Saga-book of the Viking Society*, 6 (1908-09), 68-89

MAWER, Allen, 'The Redemption of the Five Boroughs', *English Historical Review*, 38 (1923), 551-57

MAWER, Allen, 'The Scandinavian Kingdom of Northumbria', *Saga-book of the Viking Society*, 7 (1910-11), 38-64

MAWER, Allen, *The Vikings*, The Cambridge Manuals of Science and Literature (Cambridge, 1913)

MCDONOUGH, Christopher J., ed. and trans., *Warner of Rouen, Moriuht: A Norman Latin Poem from the Early Eleventh Century*, Studies and Texts 121 (Toronto, 1995)

MCDOUGALL, David, and Ian MCDOUGALL, trans., *Theodoricus Monachus, Historia de Antiquitate Regum Norwagiensium, An Account of the Ancient History of the Norwegian Kings* (London, 1998)

MCGOWAN, Megan, 'Royal Succession in Earlier Medieval Ireland: the Fiction of Tanistry', *Peritia*, 17-18 (2003-04), 357-81

MCGURK, P., 'Pilgrimage', in *The Blackwell Encyclopaedia of Anglo-Saxon England*, edited by Michael Lapidge *et al.* (Oxford, 1999), pp. 366-67

MCKINNELL, John, 'Eddic Poetry in Anglo-Scandinavian Northern England', in *Vikings and the Danelaw. Select Papers from the Proceedings of the Thirteenth Viking Congress*, edited by James Graham-Campbell *et al.* (Oxford, 2001), pp. 327-44

MCLEOD, Wilson, '*Rí Innsi Gall, Rí Fionnghall, Ceannas nan Gàidheal*: Sovereignty and Rhetoric in the Late Medieval Hebrides', *Cambrian Medieval Celtic Studies*, 43 (2002), 25-48

MCTURK, Rory, 'Ívarr the Boneless and the Amphibious Cow', in *Islanders and Water-Dwellers: Proceedings of the Celtic-Nordic-Baltic Folklore Symposium held at University College Dublin, 16-19 June 1996*, edited by Patricia Lysaght *et al.* (Blackrock, 1999), pp. 189-204

MCTURK, R.W., 'Ragnarr Loðbrók in the Irish Annals?', in *Proceedings of the Seventh Viking Congress, Dublin, 15-21 August 1973*, edited by Bo Almqvist and David Greene (Dublin, 1976), pp. 93-123

MCTURK, R.W., 'Review: Alfred P. Smyth, *Scandinavian York and Dublin*', *Saga-book of the Viking Society*, 19 (1974-77), 471-74

MCTURK, Rory, *Studies in Ragnars Saga Loðbrókar and its Major Scandinavian Analogues*, Medium Ævum Monographs, new series, 15 (Oxford, 1991)

MEEHAN, Bernard, 'The Siege of Durham, the Battle of Carham and the Cession of Lothian', *Scottish Historical Review*, 55 (1976), 1-19

MEGAW, B., 'Norseman and Native in the Kingdom of the Isles: A Re-assessment of the Manx Evidence', *Scottish Studies*, 20 (1976), 1-44

MEGAW, Basil, 'Note on "Pennyland and Davoch in South-Western Scotland"', *Scottish Studies*, 23 (1979), 75-77

MEYER, Kuno, ed. and trans., *Aislinge Meic Conglinne: The Vision of Mac Conglinne. A Middle-Irish Wonder Tale* (London, 1892)

MEYER, Kuno, 'Gäl. Long-phort in Ortsnamen', *Sitzungsberichte der Koeniglich-Preussischen Akademie der Wissenschaften*, 49 (1913), 951-53

MEYER, Kuno, ed., 'Mitteilungen aus irischen Handschriften', *Zeitschrift für celtische Philologie*, 8 (1910-12), 102-20, 195-232, 559-65

MILLER, Molly, 'Amlaíb trahens centum', *Scottish Gaelic Studies*, 19 (1999), 241-45

MILLER, Molly, 'Historicity and The Pedigrees of the Northcountrymen', *Bulletin of the Board of Celtic Studies*, 26 (1974-76), 255-80

MILLER, Sean, 'Edgar', in *The Blackwell Encyclopaedia of Anglo-Saxon England*, edited by Michael Lapidge *et al.* (Oxford, 1999), pp. 158-59

MILLER, Sean, 'Eric Bloodaxe', in *The Blackwell Encyclopaedia of Anglo-Saxon England*, edited by Michael Lapidge *et al.* (Oxford, 1999), p. 174

MOON, Rosamund, 'Viking Runic Inscriptions in Wales', *Archaeologia Cambrensis*, 127 (1978), 124-26

MOORE, A.W., *A History of the Isle of Man*, 2 vols (London, 1900)

MORRIS, Christopher D., 'Raiders, Traders and Settlers: The Early Viking Age in Scotland', in *Ireland and Scandinavia in the Early Viking Age*, edited by Howard B. Clarke *et al.* (Dublin, 1998), pp. 73-103

MORRIS, Christopher D., 'Viking and Native in Northern England: A Case Study', in *Proceedings of the Eighth Viking Congress, Aarhus, 24-31 August 1977*, edited by Hans Bekker-Nielsen *et al.*, Mediaeval Scandinavia Supplements 2 (Odense, 1981), pp. 223-44

MURPHY, Denis, ed., *The Annals of Clonmacnoise, being Annals of Ireland from the Earliest Times to A.D. 1408*, Royal Society of Antiquaries of Ireland, extra volume for 1893-95 (Dublin, 1896; facsimile reprint Felinfach, 1993)

MURRAY, Alexander, *Suicide in the Middle Ages*, I: *The Violent Against Themselves* (Oxford, 1998)

MUSSET, Lucien, *Nordica et Normannica: Receuil d'études sur la Scandinavie ancienne et médiévale, les expéditions des vikings et la fondation de la Normandie* (Paris, 1997)

MYHRE, Bjørn, 'The Archaeology of the Early Viking Age in Norway', in *Ireland and Scandinavia in the Early Viking Age*, edited by Howard B. Clarke *et al.* (Dublin, 1998), pp. 3-36.

MYHRE, Bjørn, 'The Beginning of the Viking Age – Some Current Archaeological Problems', in *Viking Revaluations: Viking Society Centenary Symposium, 14-15 May 1992*, edited by Anthony Faulkes and Richard Perkins (London, 1993), pp. 182-204

MYNORS, R.A.B., *et al.*, ed. and trans., *William of Malmesbury, Gesta Regum Anglorum, The History of the English Kings*, Oxford Medieval Texts, 2 vols (Oxford, 1998-99)

MYTUM, Harold, 'The Vikings and Ireland: Ethnicity, Identity, and Culture Change', in *Contact, Continuity, and Collapse: The Norse Colonisation of the North Atlantic*, edited by James H. Barrett (Turnhout, 2003), pp. 113-37

NASH-WILLIAMS, V.E., *The Early Christian Monuments of Wales* (Cardiff, 1950)

NEEDHAM, G. I., ed., *Ælfric: Lives of Three English Saints*, second edition, Exeter Medieval English Texts (Exeter, 1976)

NELSON, Janet L., *Charles the Bald*, The Medieval World (Harlow, 1992)

NELSON, Janet L., 'Inauguration Rituals', in *Early Medieval Kingship*, edited by Peter Sawyer and I.N. Wood (Leeds, 1977), pp. 50-71, reprinted in her book *Politics and Ritual in Early Medieval Europe* (London, 1986), pp. 283-307

NELSON, Janet L., trans., *The Annals of St-Bertin*, Manchester Medieval Sources (Manchester, 1991)

NELSON, Janet L., 'The Frankish Empire', in *The Oxford Illustrated History of the Vikings*, edited by Peter Sawyer (Oxford, 1997), pp. 19-47

NÍ BHROLCHÁIN, Muireann, 'The Prose Banshenchas' (unpublished Ph.D. dissertation, National University of Ireland, Galway, 1980)

NICOLAISEN, W.F.H., *Scottish Place-Names: Their Study and Significance* (London, 1976; revised impression 1979)

NICOLAISEN, W.F.H., 'The Viking Settlement of Scotland: Evidence of Place-Names', in *The Vikings*, edited by R.T. Farrell (Chichester, 1982), pp. 95-115

NÍ MHAONAIGH, Máire, '*Cogad Gáedhel re Gallaib* and the Annals: A Comparison', *Ériu*, 48 (1996), 101-26

NÍ MHAONAIGH, Máire, '*Cogad Gáedhel re Gallaib*: Some Dating Considerations', *Peritia*, 9 (1995), 354-77

NÍ MHAONAIGH, Máire, 'Friend and Foe: Vikings in Ninth- and Tenth-Century Irish Literature', in *Ireland and Scandinavia in the Early Viking Age*, edited by Howard B. Clarke *et al.* (Dublin, 1998), pp. 381-402

NÍ MHAONAIGH, Máire, 'The Outward Look: Britain and Beyond in Medieval Irish Literature', in *The Medieval World*, edited by Peter Linehan and Janet L. Nelson (London, 2001), pp. 381-97

NORDAL, Sigurður, ed., *Egils saga Skalla-grímssonar*, Íslenzk Fornrit 2 (Rejkjavík, 1933)

O'BRIEN, A., 'Commercial relations between Aquitaine and Ireland, 1000 to 1550', in *Aquitaine and Ireland in the Middle Ages*, edited by Jean-Michel Picard (Dublin, 1995), pp. 31-80

O'BRIEN, A.F., 'The Development of the Privileges, Liberties and Immunities of Medieval Cork and the Growth of an Urban Autonomy, *c.* 1189 to 1500', *Journal of the Cork Historical and Archaeological Society*, 90 (1985), 46-64

Ó CORRÁIN, Donnchadh, '*Caithréim Chellacháin Chaisil*: History or Propaganda?', *Ériu*, 25 (1974), 1-69

Ó CORRÁIN, Donnchadh, 'High-Kings, Vikings and Other Kings', *Irish Historical Studies*, 21 (1978-79), 283-323

Ó CORRÁIN, Donncha, *Ireland before the Normans*, The Gill History of Ireland 2 (Dublin, 1972)

Ó CORRÁIN, Donnchadh, 'Irish Regnal Succession: a Reappraisal', *Studia Hibernica*, 11 (1971), 7-39

Ó CORRÁIN, Donnchadh, 'Ireland, Wales, Man, and the Hebrides', in *The Oxford Illustrated History of the Vikings*, edited by Peter Sawyer (Oxford, 1997), pp. 83-109

Ó CORRÁIN, Donnchadh, 'Muirchertach Mac Lochlainn and the Circuit of Ireland', in *Seanchas: Studies in Early and Medieval Irish Archaeology, History and Literature in Honour of Francis J. Byrne*, edited by Alfred Smyth (Dublin, 2000), pp. 238-50

Ó CORRÁIN, Donnchadh, 'Nationality and Kingship in Pre-Norman Ireland', *Historical Studies* [Irish Conference of Historians], 11 (1975), 1-35

Ó CORRÁIN, Donnchadh, 'Old-Norse Place Names, I-II', *Peritia*, 11 (1997), 52 and 187

Ó CORRÁIN, Donnchadh, 'The Second Viking Age in Ireland', in *Three Studies on Vikings and Christianization*, edited by Magnus Rindal, KULTs skriftserie 28 (Oslo, 1994), pp. 27-35

Ó CORRÁIN, Donnchadh, 'The Vikings in Ireland', in *The Vikings in Ireland*, edited by Anne-Christine Larsen (Roskilde, 2001), pp. 17-27

Ó CORRÁIN, Donnchadh, 'The Vikings in Scotland and Ireland in the Ninth Century', *Peritia*, 12 (1998), 296-339

Ó CORRÁIN, Donnchadh, 'Viking Ireland – Afterthoughts', in *Ireland and Scandinavia in the Early Viking Age*, edited by Howard B. Clarke *et al.* (Dublin, 1998), pp. 421-52

Ó CORRÁIN, D., 'Vikings, I-III', *Peritia*, 10 (1996), 224, 236 and 273

Ó CRÓINÍN, Dáibhí, *Early Medieval Ireland, 400-1200*, Longman History of Ireland 1 (London, 1995)

Ó CUÍV, Brian, 'Personal Names as an Indicator of Relations between Native Irish and Settlers in the Viking Period', in *Settlement and Society in Medieval Ireland. Studies Presented to F.X. Martin, O.S.A.*, edited by John Bradley, Studies in Irish Archaeology and History (Kilkenny, 1988), pp. 79-88

O'DONOVAN, John, ed. and trans., *Annala Rioghachta Eireann. Annals of the Kingdom of Ireland, by the Four Masters, from the Earliest Period to the Year 1616*, second edition, 7 vols (Dublin, 1856)

O'DONOVAN, John, ed. and trans., *Annals of Ireland: Three Fragments copied from Ancient Sources by Dubhaltach Mac Firbisigh*, Publications of the Irish Archæological and Celtic Society 4 (Dublin, 1860)

O'DONOVAN, John, and Whitley STOKES, ed. and trans., *Sanas Chormaic: Cormac's Glossary*, Publications of the Irish Archæological and Celtic Society 6 (Calcutta, 1868)

O'DONOVAN, Mary Anne, 'An Interim Revision of Episcopal Dates for the Province of Canterbury', *Anglo-Saxon England*, 1 (1972), 23-44, and 2 (1973), 91-113

OFTEDAL, Magne, 'Scandinavian Place Names in Ireland', in *Proceedings of the Seventh Viking Congress, Dublin, 15-21 August 1973*, edited by Bo Almqvist and David Greene (Dublin, 1976), pp. 125-33

Ó FLOINN, Raghnall, 'The Archaeology of the Early Viking Age in Ireland', in *Ireland and Scandinavia in the Early Viking Age*, edited by Howard B. Clarke *et al.* (Dublin, 1998), pp. 131-65

Ó HAODHA, Donncha, 'The First Middle Irish Metrical Tract', in *Metrik und Medienwechsel: Metrics and Media*, edited by Hildegard L.C. Tristram, ScriptOralia 35 (Tübingen, 1991), pp. 207-44

Ó HÉAILIDHE, P., 'Early Christian Grave Slabs in the Dublin Region', *Journal of the Royal Society of Antiquaries of Ireland*, 103 (1973), 51-64

O'KEEFFE, Katherine O'Brien, ed., *The Anglo-Saxon Chronicle: A Collaborative Edition, Volume 5, MS C* (Cambridge, 2001)

ÓLASON, Vésteinn, 'Jorvik Revisited – with Egil Skalla-Grimsson', *Northern Studies*, 27 (1990), 64-76

OLRIK, J., *et al.*, ed., *Saxonis Gesta Danorum*, 2 vols (Copenhagen, 1931-57)

Ó MÁILLE, Tomás, *The Language of The Annals of Ulster*, Publications of the University of Manchester, Celtic Series 2 (Manchester, 1910)

OMAND, Christine J., trans., 'The Life of Saint Findan', in *The People of Orkney*, edited by R.J. Berry and H.N. Firth, Aspects of Orkney 4 (Kirkwall, 1986), pp. 284-87

O'MEARA, John J., trans., *Gerald of Wales, The History and Topography of Ireland*, Penguin Classics (Harmondsworth, 1982)

O'MEARA, John J., ed., 'Giraldus Cambrensis in Topographia Hibernie: Text of the First Recension', *Proceedings of the Royal Irish Academy*, 52 C (1948-50), 113-78

Ó MURAÍLE, Nollaig, ed. and trans., *Leabhar Mór na nGenealach, The Great Book of Irish Genealogies, compiled (1645-66) by Dubhaltach Mac Fhirbhisigh*, 5 vols (Dublin, 2003-04)

Ó MURAÍLE, Nollaig, *The Celebrated Antiquary Dubhaltach Mac Fhirbhisigh (c. 1600-1671): His Lineage, Life and Learning*, Maynooth Monographs 6 (Maynooth, 1996)

Ó MURCHADHA, Diarmuid, 'A Reconsideration of Some Place-Names from *Fragmentary Annals of Ireland* ', *Ainm*, 8 (1998-2000), 41-51

Ó MURCHADHA, Diarmuid, 'Lagmainn, Lögmenn', *Ainm*, 2 (1987), 136-40

Ó NÉILL, John, 'A Norse Settlement in Rural County Dublin', *Archaeology Ireland*, 13, no. 4 (1999), 8-10

Ó NÉILL, Pádraig P., 'Irish Observance of the Three Lents and the Date of the St Gall Priscian (MS 904)', *Ériu*, 51 (2000), 159-80

O'RAHILLY, Thomas F., *Early Irish History and Mythology* (Dublin, 1946)

ORAM, R.D., 'Davachs and Pennylands in South-West Scotland: A Review of the Evidence', in *Ouncelands and Pennylands*, edited by L.J. Macgregor and B.E. Crawford, St John's House Papers 3 (St Andrews, 1987), pp. 46-59

ORAM, Richard D., 'Fergus, Galloway and the Scots', in *Galloway: Land and Lordship*, edited by Richard D. Oram and Geoffrey P. Stell, Scottish Society for Northern Studies Publications 5 (Edinburgh, 1991), pp. 117-30

ORAM, Richard D., 'Scandinavian Settlement in South-West Scotland, with a Special Study of Bysbie', in *Scandinavian Settlement in Northern Britain: Thirteen Studies of Place-Names in Their Historical Context*, edited by Barbara E. Crawford, Studies in the Early History of Britain (London, 1995), pp. 127-40

Ó RIAIN, Pádraig, 'Hagiography without Frontiers: Borrowing of Saints across the Irish Sea', in *Scripturus Vitam: Festgabe für Walter Berschin zum 65. Geburtstag*, edited by Dorothea Walz (Heidelberg, 2002), pp. 41-48

O'SULLIVAN, William, 'The Earliest Irish Coinage', *Journal of the Royal Society of Antiquaries of Ireland*, 79 (1949), 190-235

Ó SÚILLEABHÁIN, Pádraig, 'Nótaí ar thrí fhocal ó na hAnnála', *Éigse*, 15 (1973-74), 22-23

PADEL, O.J., '*Talkarn Mackus*', *Nomina*, 20 (1997), 95-98

PAGE, R.I., *'A Most Vile People': Early English Historians on the Vikings*, The Dorothea Coke Memorial Lecture, 1986 (London, 1987)

PAGE, R.I., 'A Tale of Two Cities', *Peritia*, 1 (1982), 335-51

PAGE, R. I., trans., *Chronicles of the Vikings: Records, Memorials and Myths* (London, 1995)

PAGE, R.I., 'The Audience of *Beowulf* and the Vikings', in *The Dating of Beowulf*, edited by Colin Chase (Toronto, 1981), pp. 113-23

PAGE, R.I., 'The Manx Rune Stones', in *The Viking Age in the Isle of Man: Select Papers from the Ninth Viking Congress, Isle of Man, 4-14 July 1981*, edited by Christine Fell *et al.* (London, 1983), pp. 133-46

PÁLSSON, Hermann, 'A Foundation Myth in *Landnámabók*', *Mediaeval Scandinavia*, 12 (1988), 24-28

PÁLSSON, Hermann, and Paul EDWARDS, trans., *Eyrbyggja Saga*, Penguin Classics (Harmondsworth, 1989)

PÁLSSON, Hermann, and Paul EDWARDS, trans., *Orkneyinga Saga. The History of the Earls of Orkney*, Penguin Classics (Harmondsworth, 1981)

PÁLSSON, Hermann, and Paul EDWARDS, trans., *The Book of Settlements. Landnámabók*, University of Manitoba Icelandic Studies 1 (Manitoba, 1972)

PARKES, Peter, 'Celtic Fosterage: Adoptive Kinship and Clientage in Northwest Europe', *Comparative Studies in Society and History*, 48 (2006), 359-95

PENNAR, Meirion, ed. and trans., *The Black Book of Carmarthen* (Felinfach, 1989)

PERTZ, Georg Heinrich, ed., 'Annales Vedastini', in *Monumenta Germaniae Historica, Scriptores* [in folio], I (Hanover, 1826), pp. 516-31.

PETERS, P., 'Skaldic Verse as a Historical Source', *Parergon*, 22 (1978), 29-37

PHILLIMORE, E., ed., The *Annales Cambriæ* and Old-Welsh Genealogies from *Harleian MS, 3859*', *Y Cymmrodor*, 9 (1888), 141-83

PHYTHIAN-ADAMS, Charles, *Land of the Cumbrians. A Study in British Provincial Origins, A.D. 400-1120* (Aldershot, 1996)

PICARD, Jean-Michel, 'Early Contacts between Ireland and Normandy: the Cult of Irish Saints in Normandy before the Conquest', in *Ogma: Essays in Celtic Studies in Honour of Próinséas Ní Chatháin*, edited by Michael Richter and Jean-Michel Picard (Dublin, 2002), pp. 85-93

PIRIE, Elizabeth J.E., 'Finds of "sceattas" and "stycas" of Northumbria', in *Anglo-Saxon Monetary History: Essays in Memory of Michael Dolley*, edited by M.A.S. Blackburn (Leicester, 1986), pp. 67-90

PLUMMER, Charles, ed., *Two of the Saxon Chronicles Parallel, with Supplementary Extracts from the Others*, 2 vols (Oxford, 1892-99; revised impression, by Dorothy Whitelock, 1952)

POOLE, Russell, 'Skaldic Verse and Anglo-Saxon History: Some Aspects of the Period 1009-1016', *Speculum*, 62 (1987), 265-98

POOLE, Russell G., 'Variants and Variability in the Text of Egill's Hofuðlausn', in *The Politics of Editing Medieval Texts: Papers given at the Twenty-Seventh Annual Conference on Editorial Problems, University of Toronto, 1-2 November 1991*, edited by Roberta Frank (New York, 1993), pp. 65-106

POOLE, R. G., *Viking Poems on War and Peace: A Study in Skaldic Narrative*, Toronto Medieval Texts and Translations 8 (Toronto, 1991)

PRICE, Glanville, ed., *Languages in Britain and Ireland* (Oxford, 2000)

PRICE, Neil, 'Ethnic Attitudes, Ethnic Landscapes: Some Thoughts on the Viking Age', in *Etnicitet Eller Cultur*, edited by B. Johnsen and S. Welinder (Östersund, 1998), pp. 37-59

PRICE, Neil S., 'The Vikings in Brittany', *Saga-book of the Viking Society*, 22 (1986-89), 323-440

QUIN, E.G., gen. ed., *Dictionary of the Irish Language based mainly on Old and Middle Irish Materials: Compact Edition* (Dublin, 1983)

RADNER, Joan Newlon, ed. and trans., *Fragmentary Annals of Ireland* (Dublin, 1978)

RANDSBORG, Klavs, 'Offensive Armies and Navies', *Acta Archaeologica*, 69 (1998), 163-74

REDKNAP, Mark, 'The Limits of Viking Influence in Wales', *British Archaeology*, 40 (1998), 12-13

REDKNAP, Mark, *Vikings in Wales: An Archaeological Quest* (Cardiff, 2000)

RENAUD, Jean, *Les Vikings et les Celtes* (Rennes, 1992)

REUTER, Timothy, 'Plunder and Tribute in the Carolingian Empire', *Transactions of the Royal Historical Society*, fifth series, 35 (1985), 75-94

RICHARDS, Julian D., *English Heritage Book of Viking-Age England* (London, 1991)

RICHARDS, Melville, 'Norse Place-Names in Wales', in *The Impact of the Scandinavian Invasions on the Celtic-Speaking Peoples, c. 800-1100 A.D.*, edited by Brian Ó Cuív (Dublin, 1975), pp. 51-60

RILEY, Henry T., trans., *The Annals of Roger de Hoveden, comprising the History of England and of Other Countries of Europe from A.D. 732 to A.D. 1201*, Bohn's Antiquarian Library, 2 vols (London, 1853; reprinted Felinfach, 1994)

RITCHIE, Anna, ed., *Govan and its Early Medieval Sculpture* (Stroud, 1994)

ROBERTS, Brian K., 'Late -*bý* Names in the Eden Valley, Cumberland', *Nomina*, 13 (1989-90), 25-40

ROBERTS, John L., *Lost Kingdoms: Celtic Scotland and the Middle Ages* (Edinburgh, 1997)

ROBERTSON, A.J., ed. and trans., *The Laws of the Kings of England from Edmund to Henry I* (Cambridge, 1925)

ROBINSON, J. Armitage, *The Times of Saint Dunstan*, The Ford Lectures 1922 (Oxford, 1923)

ROESDAHL, Else, *The Vikings* (London, 1991)

ROLLASON, David, ed. and trans., *Libellus de Exordio atque Procursu istius, hoc est Dunhelmensis Ecclesie: Tract on the Origins and Progress of this the Church of Durham*, Oxford Medieval Texts (Oxford, 2000)

ROLLASON, David, 'St Cuth[b]ert and Wessex: The Evidence of Cambridge Corpus Christi College MS 183', in *St Cuthbert, his Cult, and his Community to A.D. 1200*, edited by Gerald Bonner *et al.* (Woodbridge, 1989), pp. 413-24

ROLLASON, D. W., *et al.*, *Sources for York History to A.D. 1100*, The Archaeology of York 1 (York, 1998)

RUKAVISHNIKOV, Alexandr, '*Tale of Bygone Years*: the *Russian Primary Chronicle* as a family chronicle', *Early Medieval Europe*, 12 (2003), 53-74

RUTHERFORD, Anthony, '*Giudi* revisited', *Bulletin of the Board of Celtic Studies*, 26 (1974-76), 440-44

RYAN, John, 'Pre-Norman Dublin', *Journal of the Royal Society of Antiquaries of Ireland*, 79 (1949), 64-83

RYAN, John, 'The Battle of Clontarf', *Journal of the Royal Society of Antiquaries of Ireland*, 68 (1938), 1-50

RYAN, John, 'The Historical Content of the "Caithréim Ceallacháin Chaisil"', *Journal of the Royal Society of Antiquaries of Ireland*, 71 (1941), 89-100

SAWYER, P.H., *Anglo-Saxon Charters: An Annotated List and Bibliography*, Royal Historical Society Guides and Handbooks 8 (London, 1968) [see website-details below]

SAWYER, Peter, *Anglo-Saxon Lincolnshire*, History of Lincolnshire 3 (Lincoln, 1998)

SAWYER, Peter, 'Anglo-Scandinavian Trade in the Viking Age and after', in *Anglo-Saxon Monetary History: Essays in Memory of Michael Dolley*, edited by M.A.S. Blackburn (Leicester, 1986), pp. 185-99

SAWYER, Peter, 'Conquest and Colonisation: Scandinavians in the Danelaw and in Normandy', in *Proceedings of the Eighth Viking Congress, Aarhus, 24-31 August 1977*, edited by Hans Bekker-Nielsen *et al.*, Mediaeval Scandinavia Supplements 2 (Odense, 1981), pp. 123-45

SAWYER, Peter, 'Ethelred II, Olaf Tryggvason and the Conversion of Norway', in *Anglo-Scandinavian England: Norse-English Relations in the Period before the Conquest*, edited by John D. Niles and Mark Amodio, Old English Colloquium Series 4 (Lanham, MD, 1989), pp. 17-24

SAWYER, Peter, 'Harold Fairhair and the British Isles', in *Les Vikings et leur civilisation: problèmes actuels*, edited by Régis Boyer (Paris, 1976), pp. 105-09

SAWYER, Peter, *Kings and Vikings: Scandinavia and Europe, A.D. 700-1100* (London, 1982)

SAWYER, Peter, *Scandinavians and the English in the Viking Age*, H.M. Chadwick Memorial Lectures 5 (Cambridge, 1994)

SAWYER, Peter, 'Some Sources for the History of Viking Northumbria', in *Viking Age York and the North*, edited by R.A. Hall, CBA Research Report 27 (London, 1978), pp. 3-7

SAWYER, P.H., *The Age of the Vikings*, second edition (London, 1971)

SAWYER, Peter, 'The Age of the Vikings, and Before', in *The Oxford Illustrated History of the Vikings*, edited by Peter Sawyer (Oxford, 1997), pp. 1-18

SAWYER, Peter, 'The Charters of Burton Abbey and the Unification of England', *Northern History*, 10 (1975), 28-39

SAWYER, Peter, 'The Last Scandinavian Kings of York', *Northern History*, 31 (1995), 39-44

SAWYER, Peter, 'The Vikings and Ireland', in *Ireland in Early Mediaeval Europe: Studies in Memory of Kathleen Hughes*, edited by Dorothy Whitelock *et al.* (Cambridge, 1982), pp. 345-61

SAYERS, William, 'Poetry and Social Agency in Egils Saga Skalla-Grímssonar', *Scripta Islandica*, 46 (1995), 29-62

SCHLAUCH, Margaret, trans., *The Saga of the Volsungs, the Saga of Ragnar Lothbrok, together with the Lay of Kraka*, Scandinavian Classics 35, second edition (New York, 1949)

SCHMEIDLER, Bernhard, ed., *Magistri Adam Bremensis Gesta Hammaburgensis Ecclesiae Pontificum*, Monumenta Germaniae Historica, Scriptores Rerum Germanicarum in Usum Scholarum (Hanover, 1917)

SCOTT, A.B., and F.X. MARTIN, ed. and trans., *Expugnatio Hibernica, The Conquest of Ireland, by Giraldus Cambrensis*, New History of Ireland Ancillary Publications 3 (Dublin, 1978)

SCRAGG, Donald, ed. and trans., 'The Battle of Maldon', in *The Battle of Maldon, A.D. 991*, edited by Donald Scragg (Oxford, 1991), pp. 1-36

SCUDDER, Bernard, trans., 'Egil's Saga', in *The Sagas of the Icelanders*, translated by Katrina C. Attwood *et al.*, with preface by Jane Smiley (London, 1997), pp. 3-185

SEARLE, Eleanor, 'Frankish Rivalries and Norse Warriors', *Anglo-Norman Studies*, 8 (1985), 198-213

SEARLE, Eleanor, *Predatory Kinship and the Creation of Norman Power, 840-1066* (Berkeley, CA, 1988)

SEARLE, William George, *Anglo-Saxon Bishops, Kings and Nobles* (Cambridge, 1899)

SEARLE, William George, *Onomasticon Anglo-Saxonicum. A List of Anglo-Saxon Proper Names from the Time of Bede to that of King John* (Cambridge, 1897)

SEEBERG, Axel, 'Five Kings', *Saga-book of the Viking Society*, 20 (1978-81), 106-13

SELLAR, W.D.H., 'Warlords, Holy Men and Matrilineal Succession', *Innes Review*, 36 (1985), 29-43

SHEEHAN, John, 'Early Viking-Age Silver Hoards from Ireland and their Scandinavian Elements', in *Ireland and Scandinavia in the Early Viking Age*, edited by Howard B. Clarke *et al.* (Dublin, 1998), pp. 166-202

SHEEHAN, John, 'Ireland's Early Viking-Age Silver Hoards: Components, Structure and Classification', *Acta Archaeologica*, 71 (2000), 49-63

SHEEHAN, John, 'Viking Age Hoards from Munster: A Regional Tradition?', in *Early Medieval Munster: Archaeology, History and Society*, edited by Michael A. Monk and John Sheehan (Cork, 1998), pp. 147-63

SHEEHAN, John, 'Viking-Age Hoards in Scotland and Ireland: Regional Diversities', in *Viking and Norse in the North Atlantic: Select Papers from the Proceedings of the Fourteenth Viking Congress, Tórshaven, 19-30 July 2001*, edited by Andras Mortensen and Símun V. Arge (Tórshaven, 2005), pp. 323-28

SHEEHAN, John, *et al.*, 'A Viking Age Maritime Haven: A Reassessment of the Island Settlement at Beginish, Co. Kerry', *Journal of Irish Archaeology*, 10 (2001), 93-120

SHIPPEY, Thomas A., 'A Missing Army: Some Doubts about the Alfredian Chronicle', *In Geardagum*, 4 (1982), 41-55; revised version in *Anglo-Saxon* 1 (2007)

SIMMS, Anngret, 'Medieval Dublin in a European Context', in *Medieval Dublin: The Making of a Metropolis*, ed. Howard B. Clarke (Dublin, 1990), pp. 37-69

SIMPSON, Linzi, 'Forty Years a-digging: A Preliminary Synthesis of Archaeological Investigations in Medieval Dublin', *Medieval Dublin*, 1 (2000), 11-68

SIMPSON, Linzi, 'Viking Warrior Burials in Dublin: is this the *longphort*?', *Medieval Dublin*, 6 (2004), 11-62

SIMPSON, Luisella, 'The King Alfred/St Cuthbert Episode in the *Historia de Sancto Cuthberto*: its Significance for Mid-Tenth-Century English History', in *St Cuthbert, His Cult, and His Community to A.D. 1200*, edited by Gerald Bonner *et al.* (Woodbridge, 1989), pp. 397-411

SIMS-WILLIAMS, Patrick, 'Historical Need and Literary Narrative: A Caveat from Ninth-Century Wales', *Welsh History Review*, 17 (1994-95), 1-40

SIMS-WILLIAMS, Patrick, 'The Provenance of the Llywarch Hen Poems: A Case for Llan-gors, Brycheiniog', *Cambrian Medieval Celtic Studies*, 26 (1993), 27-63

SKENE, William F., *Celtic Scotland: A History of Ancient Alban*, 3 vols (Edinburgh, 1876-80)

SKOVGAARD-PETERSON, Inge, 'The Historical Context of the First Towns in Northern and Eastern Europe', in *Proceedings of the Eighth Viking Congress, Aarhus, 24-31 August 1977*, edited by Hans Bekker-Nielsen *et al.*, Mediaeval Scandinavia Supplements 2 (Odense, 1981), pp. 9-18

SKYUM-NIELSEN, Niels, 'Nordic Slavery in an International Setting', *Mediaeval Scandinavia*, 11 (1978-79), 126-48

SMART, Veronica, 'Scandinavians, Celts and Germans in Anglo-Saxon England: The Evidence of Moneyers' Names', in *Anglo-Saxon Monetary History: Essays in Memory of Michael Dolley*, edited by M.A.S. Blackburn (Leicester, 1986), pp. 171-84

SMITH, A. H., 'The Sons of Ragnar Lothbrok', *Saga-book of the Viking Society*, 11 (1928-36), 173-91

SMITH, F. Gilbert, 'Talacre and the Viking Grave', *Proceedings of the Llandudno, Colwyn Bay and District Field Club*, 17 (1931-33), 42-56

SMITHERS, G. V., ed., *Havelok* (Oxford, 1987)

SMYTH, Alfred P., *Celtic Leinster: Towards an Historical Geography of Early Irish Civilization, A.D. 500-1600* (Blackrock, 1982)

SMYTH, Alfred P., *Scandinavian Kings in the British Isles, 850-880*, Oxford Historical Monographs (Oxford, 1977)

SMYTH, Alfred P., *Scandinavian York and Dublin: The History and Archaeology of Two Related Viking Kingdoms*, 2 vols (Dublin, 1975-79)

SMYTH, Alfred P., 'The *Black* Foreigners of York and the *White* Foreigners of Dublin', *Saga-book of the Viking Society*, 19 (1974-77), 101-17

SMYTH, Alfred P., 'The Effect of Scandinavian Raiders on the English and Irish Churches: A Preliminary Assessment', in *Britain and Ireland, 900-1300: Insular Responses to Medieval European Change*, edited by Brendan Smith (Cambridge, 1999), pp. 1-38

SMYTH, Alfred P., 'The Solar Eclipse of Wednesday 29 October AD 878: Ninth-Century Historical Records and the Findings of Modern Astronomy', in *Alfred the Wise: Studies in Honour of Janet Bately on the Occasion of her Sixty-Fifth Birthday*, edited by Jane Roberts *et al.* (Cambridge, 1997), pp. 187-210

SMYTH, Alfred P., *Warlords and Holy Men: Scotland, A.D. 80-1000*, The New History of Scotland 1 (London, 1984)

STAFFORD, Pauline, 'Political Women in Mercia, Eighth to Early Tenth Centuries', in *Mercia: An Anglo-Saxon Kingdom in Europe*, edited by Michelle P. Brown and Carol A. Farr, Studies in the Early History of Europe (London, 2001), pp. 35-49

STEFFENSEN, Jón, 'A Fragment of Viking History', *Saga-book of the Viking Society*, 18 (1970-73), 59-78

STENTON, F.M., *Anglo-Saxon England*, third edition (Oxford, 1971)

STENTON, F.M., *Preparatory to 'Anglo-Saxon England'* (Oxford, 1970)

STEVENSON, Joseph, trans., *Simeon of Durham, A History of the Kings of England*, facsimile reprint of *The Church Historians of England*, trans. Joseph Stevenson, III, part 2 (London, 1858; facsimile reprint Felinfach, 1987)

STEVENSON, Joseph, trans., *William of Malmesbury, A History of the Norman Kings (1066-1125)*, facsimile reprint of *The Church Historians of England*, trans. Joseph Stevenson, III, part 1 (London, 1854; facsimile reprint Felinfach, 1989)

STEVENSON, William Henry, ed., *Asser's Life of King Alfred, together with the Annals of Saint Neots erroneously ascribed to Asser* (Oxford, 1904; revised impression, by Dorothy Whitelock, 1959)

STEWART, Ian, 'Cunnetti reconsidered', in *Coinage in Ninth-Century Northumbria: The Tenth Oxford Symposium on Coinage and Monetary History*, edited by D.M. Metcalf, B.A.R. British Series 180 (Oxford, 1987), pp. 345-54

STOKES, Whitley, ed. and trans., *Félire Húi Gormáin: The Martyrology of Gorman*, Henry Bradshaw Society (London, 1895)

STOKES, Whitley, ed. and trans., *Félire Óengusso Céli Dé: The Martyrology of Oengus the Culdee*, Henry Bradshaw Society (London, 1905)

STOKES, Whitley, ed. and trans., *The Annals of Tigernach*, second edition, 2 vols (Felinfach, 1993)

STOKES, Whitley, ed. and trans., *The Tripartite Life of Patrick with Other Documents relating to that Saint*, Rerum Britannicarum Medii Aevi Scriptores 89, 2 vols (London, 1887)

STOKES, Whitley, ed., *Three Irish Glossaries: Cormac's Glossary, O'Davoren's Glossary, and a Glossary to the Calendar of Oingus the Culdee* (London, 1862)

STONES, E.L.G., ed. and trans., *Anglo-Scottish Relations, 1174-1328: Some Selected Documents*, Oxford Medieval Texts (London 1965; revised impression, Oxford, 1970)

STORM, Gustav, ed., *Monumenta Historica Norwegiae latine conscripta: Latinske Kildeskrifter til Norges Historie i Middelalderen*, Det Norske historiske Kildeskriftfonds Skrifter (Oslo, 1888)

STORY, J. E., 'Symeon as an Annalist', in *Symeon of Durham: Historian of Durham and the North*, edited by David Rollason, Studies in North-Eastern History 1 (Stamford, 1998), pp. 202-13

STUBBS, William, ed., *Chronica Magistri Rogeri de Houedene*, Rerum Britannicarum Medii Aevi Scriptores 51, 4 vols (London, 1868-71)

SVEINSSON, Einar Ól., ed., *Brennu-Njáls Saga*, Íslenzk Fornrit 12 (Reykjavík, 1954)

SVEINSSON, Einar Ól., ed., *Laxdæla Saga, Halldórs Þættir Snorrasonar Stúfs Þáttr*, Íslenzk Fornrit 5 (Reykjavík, 1934)

SVEINSSON, Einar Ól., and Matthías ÞORÐARSON, ed., *Eyrbyggja Saga*, Íslenzk Fornrit 4 (Reykjavík, 1935)

SWANTON, Michael, trans., *The Anglo-Saxon Chronicle* (London, 1996)

SWIFT, Catherine, 'Forts and Fields: A Study of "Monastic Towns" in Seventh and Eighth Century Ireland', *Journal of Irish Archaeology*, 9 (1998), 105-25

SYRETT, Martin, *Scandinavian History in the Viking Age: A Select Bibliography*, ASNC Guides, Texts, and Studies 2 (Cambridge, 2002)

SYRETT, Martin, *The Vikings in England: The Evidence of Runic Inscriptions*, ASNC Guides, Texts, and Studies 4 (Cambridge, 2002)

TAYLOR, Simon, ed., *The Anglo-Saxon Chronicle: A Collaborative Edition, Volume 4, MS B* (Cambridge, 1983)

TAYLOR, Simon, 'The Element *sliabh* and the Rhinns of Galloway, or Place-Names and History: a Case Study', *History Scotland*, 2, no. 6 (2002), 49-52

TAYLOR, Simon, 'The Scandinavians in Fife and Kinross: the Onomastic Evidence', in *Scandinavian Settlement in Northern Britain: Thirteen Studies of Place-Names in their Historical Context*, edited by Barbara E. Crawford, Studies in the Early History of Britain (London, 1995), pp. 141-69

THACKER, Alan, 'The Cult of King Harold at Chester', in *The Middle Ages in the North-West*, edited by Tom Scott and Pat Starkey (Oxford, 1995), pp. 155-76

THOMAS, Charles, *Exploration of a Drowned Landscape: Archaeology and History of the Scilly Isles* (London, 1985)

THOMAS, C., 'Imported pottery in Dark-Age Western Britain', *Medieval Archaeology*, 3 (1959), 89-111

THOMSON, Rodney, *William of Malmesbury* (Woodbridge, 1987)

THORNTON, David E., 'Edgar and the Eight Kings, A.D. 973: *Textus et Dramatis Personae*', *Early Medieval Europe*, 10 (2001), 49-79

THORNTON, David E., 'Hey Macc! The Name *Maccus*, Tenth to Fifteenth Centuries', *Nomina*, 20 (1997), 67-94

THORNTON, David E., 'Maredudd ab Owain (d. 999): The Most Famous King of the Welsh', *Welsh History Review*, 18 (1996-97), 567-91

THORNTON, David E., 'The Death of Hywel Dda: A Note', *Welsh History Review*, 20 (2000-01), 743-49

THORNTON, David E., 'The Genealogy of Gruffudd ap Cynan', in *Gruffudd ap Cynan. A Collaborative Biography*, edited by K.L. Maund, Studies in Celtic History 16 (Woodbridge, 1996), pp. 79-108

TIERNEY, J.J., and Ludwig BIELER, ed. and trans., *Dicuili Liber de Mensura Orbis Terrae*, Scriptores Latini Hiberniae 6 (Dublin, 1967)

TODD, James Henthorn, ed. and trans., *Cogadh Gaedhel re Gallaibh: The War of the Gaedhil with the Gaill; or, The Invasions of Ireland by Danes and Other Norsemen*, Rerum Britannicarum Medii Aevi Scriptores 48 (London, 1867)

TODD, James Henthorn, and Algernon HERBERT, ed. and trans., *Leabhar Breathnach annso sis: The Irish Version of the Historia Britonum of Nennius*, Publications of the Irish Archæological Society (Dublin, 1848)

TODD, John M., 'British (Cumbric) Place-Names in the Barony of Gilsland, Cumbria', *Transactions of the Cumberland and Westmorland Antiquarian and Archaeological Society*, third series, 5 (2005), 89-102

TOLOCHKO, O., 'Kievan Rus around the Year 1000', in *Europe around the Year 1000*, edited by Przemysław Urbańczyk (Warsaw, 2001), pp. 123-39

TOWNEND, Matthew, 'Contextualizing the *Knútsdrápur*: Skaldic Praise-Poetry at the Court of Cnut', *Anglo-Saxon England*, 30 (2001), 145-79

TOWNEND, Matthew, 'Whatever happened to York Viking Poetry? Memory, Tradition and the Transmission of Skaldic Verse', *Saga-book of the Viking Society*, 27 (2003), 48-90

TRILLMICH, Werner, and Rudolf BUCHNER, ed. and trans., *Quellen des 9. und 11. Jahrhunderts zur Geschichte der Hamburgischen Kirche und des Reiches* (Darmstadt, 1961)

TSCHAN, Francis J., trans., *Adam of Bremen, History of the Archbishops of Hamburg-Bremen*, Records of Civilization Sources and Studies 53 (New York, 1959)

TURVILLE-PETRE, Joan, 'On Ynglingatal', *Mediaeval Scandinavia*, 11 (1978-79), 48-67

VALANTE, Mary, 'Dublin's Economic Relations with Hinterland and Periphery in the Later Viking Age', *Medieval Dublin*, 1 (2000), 69-83

VALANTE, Mary A., 'Reassessing the Irish "Monastic Town"', *Irish Historical Studies*, 31 (1998-99), 1-18

VALANTE, Mary A., 'Urbanization and Economy in Viking-Age Ireland' (unpublished Ph.D. Dissertation, Pennsylvania State University, 1998)

VAN HOUTS, Elisabeth M.C., ed. and trans., *The Gesta Normannorum Ducum of William of Jumièges, Orderic Vitalis, and Robert of Torigni*, Oxford Medieval Texts, 2 vols (Oxford, 1992-95)

VAN HOUTS, Elisabeth M.C., 'Scandinavian Influence in Norman Literature of the Eleventh Century', *Anglo-Norman Studies*, 6 (1983), 107-21

VIGFUSSON, Gubrand, and F. York POWELL, ed. and trans., *Corpus Poeticum Boreale: The Poetry of the Old Northern Tongue*, 2 vols (Oxford, 1883)

VÍGFUSSON, Guðbrandr, and C.R. UNGER, ed., *Flateyjarbók: En Samlinge af Norske Konge-sagaer*, 3 vols (Oslo, 1860-68)

VON SIMSON, B. ed., *Annales Xantenses et Annales Vedastini*, Monumenta Germaniae Historica, Scriptores Rerum Germanicarum in Usum Scholarum (Hanover, 1909)

VOS, Johanna C., 'The Other Side of Old English *Hæðen*: A Survey of the Semantics and Semantic Development of Old English *Hæðen*' (unpublished M.A. Dissertation, Rijksuniversiteit Groningen, 2006).

WAINWRIGHT, F. T., 'Duald's "Three Fragments"', *Scriptorium*, 2 (1948), 56-59

WAINWRIGHT, F.T., *Scandinavian England: Collected Papers* (Chichester, 1975)

WAINWRIGHT, F.T., 'The Chronology of the "Mercian Register"', *English Historical Review*, 60 (1945), 385-92

WAITZ, Georg, ed., 'Hugonis Liber qui modernorum regum Francorum continet actus', in *Monumenta Germaniae Historica, Scriptores* [in folio], IX (Hanover, 1851), pp. 376-95

WAITZ, Georg, ed., 'Mariani Scotti Chronicon', in *Monumenta Germaniae Historica, Scriptores* [in folio], V (Hanover, 1844), pp. 481-564

WALLACE, Patrick F., 'Archaeology and the Emergence of Dublin as the Principal Town of Ireland', in *Settlement and Society in Medieval Ireland: Studies presented to F.X. Martin, O.S.A.*, edited by John Bradley, Studies in Irish Archaeology and History (Kilkenny, 1988), pp. 123-60

WALLACE, Patrick F., 'Garrda and airbeada: The Plot Thickens in Viking Dublin', in *Seanchas: Studies in Early and Medieval Irish Archaeology, History and Literature in Honour of Francis J. Byrne*, edited by Alfred P. Smyth (Dublin, 2000), pp. 261-74

WALLACE, Patrick F., 'The Economy and Commerce of Viking Age Dublin', in *Untersuchungen zu Handel und Verkehr der vor- und frühgeschichtlichen Zeit in Mittel- und Nordeuropa, Teil IV: Der Handel der Karolinger- und Wikingerzeit*, edited by Klaus Düwel *et al.* (Göttingen, 1987), pp. 200-45

WALLACE, Patrick F., 'The English Presence in Viking Dublin', in *Anglo-Saxon Monetary History: Essays in Memory of Michael Dolley*, edited by M.A.S. Blackburn (Leicester, 1986), pp. 201-21

WALLACE, Patrick F., *The Viking Age Buildings of Dublin*, 2 vols, Medieval Dublin Excavations 1962-81, A.1 (Dublin, 1992)

WALLACE-HADRILL, J.M., *The Vikings in Francia*, The Stenton Lecture, 1974 (Reading, 1975)

WALSH, Claire, 'Dublin's Southern Town Defences, Tenth to Fourteenth Centuries: The Evidence from Ross Road', *Medieval Dublin*, 2 (2000), 88-127

WALSH, Paul, 'The Dating of the Irish Annals', *Irish Historical Studies*, 2 (1940-41), 355-75

WALSH, Paul, *The Four Masters and Their Work* (Dublin, 1944)

WAMERS, Egon, 'Insular Finds in Viking Age Scandinavia and the State Formation of Norway', in *Ireland and Scandinavia in the Early Viking Age*, edited by Howard B. Clarke *et al.* (Dublin, 1998), pp. 37-72

WAMERS, Egon, 'Some Ecclesiastical and Secular Insular Metalwork found in Norwegian Viking Graves', *Peritia*, 2 (1983), 277-306

WARD, Simon, 'Edward the Elder and the Re-establishment of Chester', in *Edward the Elder, 899-924*, edited by N.J. Higham and D.H. Hill (London, 2001), pp. 60-66

WATERHOUSE, Ruth, 'Stylistic Features as a Factor in detecting Change of Source in the Ninth Century Anglo-Saxon Chronicle', *Parergon*, 27 (1980), 3-8

WATSON, William J., *The History of the Celtic Place-Names of Scotland* (Edinburgh, 1926)

WATT, D.E.R., 'Bishops in the Isles before 1203: Bibliography and Biographical Lists', *Innes Review*, 45 (1994), 99-119

WATTS, V. E., 'North-Western Place-Names', *Northern History*, 23 (1987), 229-30

WAUGH, David, *Geography: An Integrated Approach* (Walton-on-Thames, 1990)

WAWN, Andrew, *'Fast er drukkið og fátt lært': Eiríkr Magnússon, Old Northern Philology, and Victorian Cambridge*, H.M. Chadwick Memorial Lectures 11 (Cambridge, 2000)

WAWN, Andrew, 'Hereward, the Danelaw and the Victorians', in *Vikings and the Danelaw: Select Papers from the Proceedings of the Thirteenth Viking Congress*, edited by James Graham-Campbell *et al.* (Oxford, 2001), pp. 357-68

WHITELOCK, Dorothy, trans., *English Historical Documents, c. 500-1042*, second edition (London, 1979)

WHITELOCK, Dorothy, 'Fact and Fiction in the Legend of St. Edmund', *Proceedings of the Suffolk Institute of Archaeology*, 31 (1961), 217-33 (reprinted in her book *From Bede to Alfred: Studies in Early Anglo-Saxon Literature and History*, Variorum Reprints Collected Studies Series 121, London, 1980, essay XI, with same pagination)

WHITELOCK, Dorothy, *et al.*, trans., *The Anglo-Saxon Chronicle* (London, 1961; revised impression, 1965)

WHITELOCK, Dorothy, 'The Dealings of Kings of England with Northumbria in the Tenth and Eleventh Centuries', in *The Anglo-Saxons: Studies in Some Aspects of their History and Culture, presented to Bruce Dickins*, edited by Peter Clemoes (London, 1959), pp. 70-88 (reprinted in her book *History, Law and Literature in 10th-11th Century England*, Variorum Reprints Collected Studies Series 128, London 1981, essay III, with same pagination)

WHITELOCK, Dorothy, 'The Importance of the Battle of Edington', *Report for 1975, 1976 and 1977 of the Society of Friends of the Priory Church of Edington, Wiltshire*, pp. 6-15 (reprinted in her book *From Bede to Alfred: Studies in Early Anglo-Saxon Literature and History*, Variorum Reprints Collected Studies Series 121, London, 1980, essay XIII, with same pagination)

WILLIAMS, Ann, 'An Outing on the Dee: King Edgar at Chester, A.D. 973', *Mediaeval Scandinavia*, 14 (2004), 229-43

WILLIAMS, Ann, *Kingship and Government in Pre-Conquest England, c. 500-1066*, British History in Perspective (Basingstoke, 1999)

WILLIAMS, Ann, '*Princeps Merciorum Gentis*: The Family, Career and Connections of Ælfhere, Ealdorman of Mercia, 956-83', *Anglo-Saxon England*, 10 (1981), 143-72

WILLIAMS, Ann, 'The Battle of Maldon and "The Battle of Maldon": History, Poetry and Propoganda', *Medieval History*, 2, no. 2 (1992), 35-44

WILLIAMS, Gareth, 'Hákon *Aðalsteins fóstri*: Aspects of Anglo-Saxon Kingship in Tenth-Century Norway', in *The North Sea World in the Middle Ages: Studies in the Cultural History of North-Western Europe*, edited by Thomas R. Litzka and Lorna E.M. Walker (Dublin, 2001), pp. 108-26

WILLIAMS, Ifor, and Rachel BROMWICH, ed. and trans., *Armes Prydein, The Prophecy of Britain, from the Book of Taliesin*, Mediaeval and Modern Welsh Series 6 (Dublin, 1972)

WILLIAMS (Ab Ithel), John, ed. *Annales Cambriæ*, Rerum Britannicarum Medii Aevi Scriptores (London, 1860)

WILLIAMS, Henrik, 'Runsvenska namnproblem 2. Det runsvenska mansnamnet Øysl (?) och det fonsvenska Asle', *Studia anthroponymica Scandinavica*, 12 (1994), 5-31

WILSON, P.A., 'On the Use of the Terms "Strathclyde" and "Cumbria"', *Transactions of the Cumberland and Westmorland Antiquarian and Archaeological Society*, new series, 66 (1966), 57-92

WINTERBOTTOM, Michael, ed., *Three Lives of English Saints*, Toronto Medieval Latin Texts 1 (Toronto, 1972)

WOOD, Michael, '*Brunanburh* revisited', *Saga-book of the Viking Society*, 20 (1978-81), 200-44

WOOD, Michael, 'The Making of Aethelstan's Empire: An English Charlemagne?', in *Ideal and Reality in Frankish and Anglo-Saxon Society: Studies presented to J.M. Wallace-Hadrill*, edited by Patrick Wormald *et al.* (Oxford, 1983), pp. 250-72

WOOLF, Alex, 'Amlaíb Cuarán and the Gael, 941-81', *Medieval Dublin*, 3 (2001), 34-43

WOOLF, Alex, 'Dún Nechtain, Fortriu and the Geography of the Picts', *Scottish Historical Review*, 85 (2006), 182-201

WOOLF, Alex, 'Erik Bloodaxe revisited', *Northern History*, 34 (1998), 189-93

WOOLF, Alex, 'Review: *Viking Pirates and Christian Princes: Dynasty, Religion and Empire in the North Atlantic*. By Benjamin Hudson', *Early Medieval Europe*, 14 (2006), 515-17

WOOLF, Alex, 'The "Moray Question" and the Kingship of Alba in the Tenth and Eleventh Centuries', *Scottish Historical Review*, 79 (2000), 145-64

WOOLF, Alex, 'The Origins and Ancestry of Somerled: Gofraid mac Fergusa and "The Annals of the Four Masters"', *Mediaeval Scandinavia*, 15 (2005), 199-213

WORMALD, Patrick, *The Making of English Law: King Alfred to the Twelfth Century*, I: *Legislation and its Limits* (Oxford, 1999)

WORMALD, C. Patrick, 'Viking Studies: whence and whither?', in *The Vikings*, edited by R.T. Farrell (London, 1982), pp. 128-53

WYATT, David, 'Gruffudd ap Cynan and the Hiberno-Norse World', *Welsh History Review*, 19 (1998-99), 595-617

YORKE, Barbara, 'Edward as Ætheling', in *Edward the Elder, 899-924*, edited N.J. Higham and D.H. Hill (London, 2001), pp. 25-39

YORKE, Barbara, 'Guthrum', in *The Blackwell Encyclopaedia of Anglo-Saxon England*, edited by Michael Lapidge *et al.* (Oxford, 1999), p. 223

YORKE, Barbara, *Wessex in the Early Middle Ages*, Studies in the Early History of Britain (London, 1995)

YOUNG, Jean I., 'A Note on the Norse Occupation of Ireland', *History*, new series, 35 (1950), 11-33

Websites

Anglo-Saxon Charters: The New Regesta Regum Anglorum,
   http://www.trin.cam.ac.uk/sdk13/chartwww/NewRegReg.html
Early Medieval Corpus: Single Finds of Coins in the British Isles, 410-1180,
   http://www-cm.fitzmuseum.cam.ac.uk/coins/emc.html
IreAtlas Townland Database, http://www.seanruad.com/cgi-bin/iresrch
The Voyage of Ohthere, ed. and trans. Grant Chevallier and Murray McGillivray
   http://www.ucalgary.ca/UofC/eduweb/engl401/texts/ohthfram.htm

Index

I – J

M